Raciolinguistics

Raciolinguistics

HOW LANGUAGE SHAPES OUR IDEAS ABOUT RACE

EDITED BY H. SAMY ALIM, JOHN R. RICKFORD

and

ARNETHA F. BALL

OXFORD
UNIVERSITY PRESS

Oxford University Press is a department of the University of Oxford. It furthers
the University's objective of excellence in research, scholarship, and education
by publishing worldwide. Oxford is a registered trade mark of Oxford University
Press in the UK and certain other countries.

Published in the United States of America by Oxford University Press
198 Madison Avenue, New York, NY 10016, United States of America.

Library of Congress Cataloging-in-Publication Data
Names: Alim, H. Samy, editor. | Rickford, John R., 1949– editor. | Ball, Arnetha F., 1950– editor.
Title: Raciolinguistics : how language shapes our ideas about race /
edited by H. Samy Alim, John R. Rickford & Arnetha F. Ball.
Description: Oxford ; New York : Oxford University Press, [2016] | Includes index.
Identifiers: LCCN 2016018924| ISBN 9780190625696 (hardcover : alk. paper) |
ISBN 9780190625719 (epub) | ISBN 9780190625726 (online)
Subjects: LCSH: Racism in language. | Critical discourse analysis—
Social aspects. | Sociolingusitics.
Classification: LCC P120.R32 R34 2016 | DDC 306.44089—dc23 LC record
available at https://lccn.loc.gov/2016018924

9 8
Printed by Sheridan Books, Inc., United States of America

The book cover art—"Fight Racism"—was designed by Favianna Rodriguez, an Afro-Peruvian,
transnational, interdisciplinary artist and cultural organizer based in Oakland, CA
(www.favianna.com).

This piece commemorates the International Day for the Elimination of Racism, celebrated on
March 21. On that date in 1960, more than 60 Black demonstrators were killed and about 180
wounded by police in South Africa. This poster was developed in collaboration with a worker's
union in Canada.

Esta obra conmemora el Día Internacional de la Eliminación de la Discriminación Racial, celebrado
el 21 de marzo. En esa fecha en el año 1960, más de 60 manifestantes africanos negros fueron
asesinados y aproximadamente 180 fueron lesionados por la policía en Sudáfrica. Este póster se
realizó en colaboración con un grupo sindical de Canadá.

Contents

Raciolinguistics

Introducing Raciolinguistics

Racing Language and Languaging Race in Hyperracial Times

H. SAMY ALIM

In 2008, the United States elected its first "Black-language-speaking" president, Barack Obama. I, along with many others, was fascinated not only by Obama's language use but also by America's response to it. It quickly became evident that Obama's linguistic production (how he talks) and the metalinguistic commentary that surrounded it (how Americans talked about how Obama talked) revealed much about language and racial politics in the United States. Among those commenting on his language were linguist John McWhorter's playful use of the term "Blaccent," Hip Hop icon Snoop Dogg's observation that Obama had "the right conversation," and independent candidate Ralph Nader's quip that Obama was "talking White." Later, Harry Reid's racialized comments about Barack Obama—that he spoke with "no Negro dialect, unless he wanted to have one"—gave us all pause. What *exactly* did all of this mean? Why was everyone so closely monitoring the first Black president's language?

As Geneva Smitherman and I wrote in *Articulate While Black: Barack Obama, Language, and Race in the U.S.* (Alim and Smitherman 2012), Barack Obama has had to constantly navigate between discriminatory discourses of race, citizenship, religion, and (most critically for this volume) language. President Obama may have been the object of our analysis at the start—why was everyone calling him *articulate* (using the adjective)?—but he was also, importantly, a point of departure for us to consider the social, cultural, linguistic, and educational implications of what it means to *articulate while Black* (using the verb). For us, that was really the deeper, philosophical question underlying our work: What does it mean to speak as a racialized subject in contemporary America? This is a central concern of raciolinguistics.

In using President Obama as a starting point, we sought to *race language* and *language race* (Alim 2009a)—that is, to view race through the lens of language, and vice versa—in order to gain a better understanding of language and the process of racialization. The present volume builds upon our discussion about how Barack Obama *translates* himself as "Black" through his mostly successful (that is, ratified) raciolinguistic performances (for example, vociferous debate surrounded his performance using "Black preacher style" and singing "Amazing Grace" at the eulogy for slain Reverend Clementa Pinckney, who was murdered along with eight others in June 2015 in a racist attack on an African American church in Charleston, South Carolina). As we come into a new understanding that language varieties are not just lists of features that belong to a given "race," even questioning the very notion of a fixed "language variety," we can move toward speaking in terms of the more fluid sense of "linguistic resources" (see García and Wei 2014 on development of the concept *translanguaging*). We can now view linguistic resources as being employed by speakers as they shape and engage in processes and projects of identification. President Barack Obama's use of what has been racialized as "Black Language," for example, is very much a conscious raciolinguistic project.

In the same way that the president selected "Black" on the U.S. Census to mark a racial identity, he also employs particular linguistic resources in the complex project of *becoming Black* (Ibrahim 2003, 2014) or of *racial becoming* more generally. In many ways, Barack Obama's book *Dreams from My Father* chronicles his search for "a Black identity." He writes:

> Away from my mother, away from my grandparents, I was engaged in a fitful interior struggle. I was trying to raise myself to be a black man in America, and beyond the given of my appearance, no one around me seemed to know exactly what that meant. (Obama 2004, 76)

Many Americans who are racialized as "Black," particularly those on the margins of what many view as a normative Black identity, are very familiar with this process. Awad Ibrahim, Sudanese professor of education at the University of Ottawa, described the process in these terms: "To become black is to become an ethnographer who *translates* and searches around in an effort to understand what it means to be black in North America." It is a process of "entering already pronounced regimes of Blackness" (2003, 154). Black feminist and cultural critic Joan Morgan, who identifies as Jamaican, described the process of *becoming Black* in America in these terms: "As a matter of both acclimation and survival, we learn [African American] history. We absorb the culture. Some of us even acquire the *accent*" (Morgan 2009, 63). These authors write about racialization as a process of socialization in and through language, as a continuous project of becoming as opposed to being.

These raciolinguistic projects and processes represent only some of the complexities that authors engage in this book. This current volume represents a critical mass of scholars committed to theorizing language and race together, paying particular attention to how both social processes mediate and mutually constitute each other. Collectively, we forge a new field of *racio-linguistics* that is dedicated to bringing to bear the diverse methods of linguistic analysis to ask and answer critical questions about the relations between language, race, and power across diverse ethnoracial contexts and societies.[1]

Racing Language and Languaging Race in a Hyperracial(izing) America

America's varied and passionate responses to Barack Obama's language—from monitoring to mocking to "marveling" ("he's *soooo* articulate!")—revealed the complex contours of contemporary forms of linguistic racism. These responses also exploded the myth of America as a "postracial" society. Over the last two decades, American society has become more and more segregated since integration, and all of America's major institutions (e.g., educational, religious, and political institutions) remain highly segregated (Orfield and Yun 1999; Orfield and Lee 2007). It is now nearly impossible to ignore social scientific research of all stripes, from social psychology (Eberhardt et al. 2004; Goff et al. 2008; Steele 2010) to linguistics (Purnell et al. 1999; Cross et al. 2001; Baugh 2003; Alim 2004a; Rickford et al. 2015; Rickford in press), which demonstrates that, rather than *postracial*, American society is in fact *hyperracial*, or *hyperracializing*. That is, as demonstrated throughout the chapters in this book, we are constantly orienting to race while at the same time denying the overwhelming evidence that shows the myriad ways that American society is *fundamentally* structured by it. All of this remains so, ironically, at a time when discourses of colorblind-ness ("race is not seen") and postracialism ("race is not relevant") reinforce one another to lead to some rather uncomplicated logic: "I don't see race, therefore race doesn't matter" (Markus and Moya 2010). As political scientist and race theorist Gary Segura has recently argued, quite forcefully, if not humorously, "If you believed American society to be 'post-racial' in 2008, you were, at best, an idealist; if you believe that *now*, you are, at best, an idiot" (see Barreto and Segura 2014, 7). This state of affairs is the contemporary racial context within which raciolinguistics emerges.

To be sure, the relationship between language, race, and culture has long been a topic of interest in linguistic anthropology (e.g., Boas 1940) and sociolinguistics (see Smitherman 1977; 2000). In the introduction to *Race, Language, and Culture*, Boas wrote:

> I believe the present state of our knowledge justifies us in saying that, while individuals differ, biological differences between races are small. There is no reason to believe that one race is by nature so much

more intelligent, endowed with great will power, or emotionally more stable than another that the difference would materially influence its culture.(1940, 13–14)

Nearly two decades before Boas, Sapir wrote poetically: "When it comes to linguistic form, Plato walks with the Macedonian swineherd, Confucius with the head-hunting savage of Assam" (Sapir 1921, 219). Despite being wrapped in somewhat problematic language, given the now obviously outdated discourses of "head-hunting savages," the intellectual case for linguistic and racial equality was made long ago.

Yet, as many would argue, the usual silence, sometimes reluctance, to take issues of race seriously among mainstream linguistics and anthropology was (and is) troubling. This came to a head during the launch of the American Anthropological Association's project "Race: Are We So Different?" (the Race Project). Funded by the Ford Foundation and the National Science Foundation, this project recognized the need for scholarly interventions in the public discourse on race. Looking through the eyes of history, science, and lived experience, the Race Project was designed to explain differences among people and reveal the reality—and unreality—of race (www.understandingrace.org). However, the subtitle "Are We So Different?" received wide critique from scholars of Color as leading the public strongly in the direction of the "unreality" of race and therefore, not unproblematically, the "irrelevance" of race.

At the November 2008 meeting of the Society of Linguistic Anthropology in San Francisco, there was some serious discussion about the need for *language* to be included in the Race Project, and breakout discussions focused on the need to theorize language and race together (after all, the election of Barack Obama just *days* before the meeting brought obvious attention to these issues). These discussions led to a symposium, "Race and Ethnicity in Language, Interaction and Culture," hosted by the Center for Language, Interaction and Culture at the University of California, Los Angeles (UCLA), where the frame of "racing language" and "languaging race" was first introduced. Held on February 27, 2009, the symposium was co-organized by H. Samy Alim and Marjorie H. Goodwin and featured Jane Hill, John Baugh, Ben Rampton, Mary Bucholtz, Elaine Chun, Lanita Jacobs, Lauren Mason Carris, and Adrienne Lo. More recently on May 3–4, 2012, as director of the Center for Race, Ethnicity, and Language (CREAL) at Stanford University, Alim was lead organizer of a gathering of several hundred scholars of language to flesh out these concepts, which have now become a central organizing frame for this current volume.

Despite this long history of considering language and racial equality (Boas, Smitherman, etc.) and these more recent organizing efforts to galvanize the field of raciolinguistics at UCLA and Stanford, when it comes to broad scholarship on race and ethnicity, language is often overlooked as one of the most important cultural means that we have for distinguishing ourselves from others. At the same time, while sociolinguists have often used race as an analytic prime (Labov 1972; Rampton 1995; Rickford 1999; Alim 2004a), and while linguistic anthropologists have produced substantive research examining race and language (Urciuoli 1996; Zentella 1997; Spears 1999; Makoni et al. 2003) and continue to do so (Reyes 2007; Mendoza-Denton 2008; Reyes and Lo 2009; Alim and Reyes 2011; Bucholtz 2011; Dick and Wirtz 2011; Ibrahim 2014; Roth-Gordon 2016; Rosa 2017), it is only recently that there has been a focused, collective effort to theorize race and ethnicity within and across language studies. *Raciolinguistics: How Language Shapes Our Ideas about Race* addresses both the fields of linguistics and race and ethnic studies—as well as the general reader—by foregrounding the role of language in shaping ethnoracial identities. The volume brings together cutting-edge, innovative scholars interested in explicating and complicating the increasingly vexed relationships between race, ethnicity, and language in a rapidly changing world. As raciolinguistics—the interdisciplinary field of "language and race"—continues to take on a growing importance across anthropology, linguistics, education, and other fields, this volume represents our collective effort to focus these fields on both the central role that language plays in racialization and on the enduring relevance of race and racism in the lives of People of Color.

This volume begins by acknowledging that a growing number of language scholars across all subfields of linguistics hold that, rather than fixed and predetermined, racial and ethnic identities are (re)created through continuous and repeated language use. Further, while recent research has begun to focus more critically on race and ethnicity as constructs, with exciting developments in how speakers "do" race and ethnicity in interaction, this volume extends this work by integrating social constructivist theories of race with attempts to theorize the impact of racism on those who experience race as an everyday lived reality. *Raciolinguistics*, then, seeks both to crystallize this perspective by building upon the aforementioned seminal works and to theorize new ways forward. Specifically, the volume seeks to accomplish this by:

(1) Articulating a commitment to analyzing language and race together rather than as discrete and unconnected social processes and employing the diverse methods of linguistics to raise critical questions about the relations between language, race, and power;

(2) Highlighting research that contributes to our understanding of how ethnoracial identities are styled, performed and constructed through minute features of language (variations in phonological and morphosyntactic features, for example) as well as diverse modes of interaction, from embodied, face-to-face conversations to widely circulating media discourses;

(3) Integrating theoretical areas of *style, stance*, and *performance* (among others) in order to look more closely at how these approaches might inform each other and processes of racialization;

(4) Taking intersectional approaches that understand race as always produced in conjunction with class, gender, sexuality, religion, (trans)national, and other axes of social differentiation;

(5) Looking comparatively across diverse ethnoracial and linguistic contexts to better understand the role of language in maintaining and challenging racism as a global system of capitalist oppression;

(6) Emphasizing the linguistic and discursive construction of race and ethnicity while at the same time noting their endurance as social realities for subjugated racial and ethnic minorities, (im)migrants, and other oppressed groups;

(7) Considering the complexities of racialization within the rapidly changing demographic shifts and technological advances of the twenty-first century (particularly in new media forms such as Facebook, YouTube, and Twitter);

(8) Considering the implications of research for social transformation and developing various antiracist strategies to impact public discourses on language, race, and education.

Raciolinguistics breaks new ground by consolidating various perspectives within language studies. By bringing together diverse scholars, this volume deepens the conversation on language and race by providing an interdisciplinary space for interaction between sociolinguistics, linguistic anthropology, and educational linguistics. With a shared vision, the authors in this book work across various contexts and provide in-depth yet accessible essays on the linguistic construction of ethnoracial identities, the role of language in racial and ethnic relations, and the linguistic marginalization of racialized populations across all social domains. Working within and beyond the United States, authors share powerful research that testifies to the critical role that language plays in our lives—including the language use of African American Jews to the struggle over the very term "African American"; racialized language education debates within the increasing number of "majority-minority" immigrant communities as well as indigenous communities of Color in the United States; the dangers of multicultural education in Europe; links between language, race, and ethnicity in Brazilian favelas, South African townships, Korean American "cram schools," and Mexican and Puerto Rican neighborhoods in Chicago.

With rapidly changing demographics in the United States—population resegregation, shifting Asian and Latino patterns of immigration, new African American (im)migration patterns, and so on—and changing global cultural and media trends (e.g., global Hip Hop cultures, transnational Mexican popular and street cultures, and new immigration trends across Africa and Europe), this volume shapes the future of studies on race, ethnicity, and language. By taking a comparative look across a diverse range of language and literacy contexts, the volume seeks not only to set the research agenda in this burgeoning area of study but also to help resolve the often contentious educational and political problems at the intersection of race, ethnicity, and language in the United States and elsewhere.

In This Volume

LANGUAGING RACE

The chapters in this section undertake the project of *languaging race*; that is, the contributors theorize race through the lens of language. These chapters collectively enhance our understanding of the processes of racialization by highlighting language's central role in the construction, maintenance, and transformation of racial and ethnic identities. These processes are examined across the richly diverse contexts of the Brazilian favelas in Rio de Janeiro; the Coloured townships of Cape Town, South Africa; Mexican and Puerto Rican neighborhoods in Chicago; rapidly transforming White and Asian American suburbs of California; and newly emerging transnational U.S. and pan-Latino online spaces—all of which are contexts where language and ethnoracial identities are contested and are seen as part-and-parcel of larger, sociopolitical struggles, demographic shifts and transformations.

The first two chapters, taken together, do the important work of upending "race" as fixed and immutable by theorizing the inextricable yet fluid links between language, race, and phenotype. These chapters call stark attention to how, as Roth-Gordon writes, "the instability of race is negotiated through language" and how race is a social process that is remade daily by speakers "who must reconcile powerful linguistic ideologies with the social interactions that make up the substance of our everyday lives."

In "Who's Afraid of the Transracial Subject?: Raciolinguistics and the Political Project of Transracialization," Alim argues for a new way of thinking about race—*transracialization*. Conceptualizing transracialization as a political project, he analyses Barack Obama's linguistic styleshifting as well as his own raciolinguistic practices (an autoethnographic account of being racialized nine different ways over the span of five days) in order to demonstrate that, rather than stable and predetermined, racial identities can shift across contexts and even within specific interactions (Bailey 2000; Bucholtz 1995). Alim critiques White public discourses of "postracial America" as having remained largely colorblind—arguing that race is irrelevant—as well as "postrace" theorists of Color who

continue to argue for the need to redefine and expand race groups beyond traditionally narrow conceptions. For Alim, both strategies of avoidance and redefinition, however, leave race groups intact. He urges us to develop a transracial
politics as a means to move beyond attempts to demonstrate our loyalty and
belonging to particular racial categories and work toward problematizing the
very process of racial categorization itself.

Similarly, Roth-Gordon brings the concepts of *racial malleability* and the *sensory regime*—drawn from eugenic theories and colonial studies—to bear on the
role of language in the social construction of race and continued oppression of
"Black" bodies. In "From Upstanding Citizen to North American Rapper and
Back Again: The Racial Malleability of Poor Male Brazilian Youth," Roth-Gordon
draws from her ethnographic research on the daily practices of well-known
Brazilian rappers and poor male rap fans living in Rio de Janeiro to illustrate
how individuals "play with the racial malleability of their bodies through aesthetics, consumption, and language, among other social practices." Expanding
on the linguistic notion of styleshifting, she embraces the concept of racial malleability "to explain how cultural and linguistic practices (what people actually
do and how they speak) matter to our everyday assessments of someone's race."
Specifically, Roth-Gordon analyzes how Brazilian youth both shift toward whiteness when dealing with police officers and away from whiteness when they seek
to affiliate with popular cultures such as politically conscious Brazilian Hip Hop.

Both Alim and Roth-Gordon examine the fluid raciolinguistic practices and
performances of People of Color as a response to historic and pervasive White
supremacist ideologies of race and language. As agentive acts of self-positioning,
these practices allow us to imagine the possibilities for destabilizing hegemonic
and oppressive processes of racial categorization. Drawing on Pennycook's
(2007, 55) productive reworking of linguistic theories of translation, Alim's
"transracial subject" is transgressive because crossing borders becomes central
to disrupting the "ontologies" upon which definitions of race rest. For Alim,
transracialization is productively viewed as the transgressive practice of not
only resisting racial categorization but also *employing it—loudly—in struggles for
racial justice* (as in Black queer activists Alicia Garza, Patrisse Cullors, and Opal
Tometi's #BlackLivesMatter network, which affirms the value of Black life in the
midst of widespread police and state violence against Black bodies, for example).

Importantly, and as long as societies are structured racially, the transracial political project necessitates the alternative subversion and maintenance
of racial categorization. Alim argues that the idea that our theorizing should
always be about destabilizing the idea of race—no matter the context—is
naïve, at best, and counterproductive at worst. Building upon Pollock's theorizing in *Colormute* (2005), to *think transracially* requires a heightened level of
sophistication, a recognition that racially discriminatory contexts require the

simultaneous/alternating strategies of transracialization with moments of strategic racialization.

The next three chapters analyze language and racism as they relate to the two fastest-growing populations in the United States—Asian Americans and Latinos. Both Lo and Rosa, through deep ethnographic engagement with communities, argue convincingly that linguistic racialization is central to analyzing the shifting place of Asian Americans and Latinos in the U.S. raciolinguistic landscape. These three chapters (Rosa, Chun, and Lo), when taken together, demonstrate the concrete and consequential ways that ideologies of language, race, and nation work together to produce "Asians" and "Latinos" as foreign, inassimilable, racialized Others in the White American imaginary—and how, at least for Chun and Rosa, marginalized speakers can subvert these hegemonic ideologies through satirical performance and everyday heteroglossic linguistic practice. (We see the subversive potential of performance also in Williams's account, this volume, of multilingual Hip Hop ciphers in Cape Town.)

Lo's research in "'Suddenly Faced with a Chinese Village': The Linguistic Racialization of Asian Americans," describes the increasingly familiar and contested context of the rapidly diversifying, formerly White suburbs of California. Lo argues that White residents in the community of Laurelton strongly racialized Asian Americans through language and interpreted their linguistic production through racializing frames. She shows powerfully how Whites used language in covertly racist ways (through the use of pronouns and seemingly colorblind terms like "oldtimers" and "newcomers") to situate Asian Americans as illegitimate, peripheral members of the community while centering Whites as legitimate residents with entitlement, ownership, and authority over Laurelton's future growth. Through language, White residents "linguistically portrayed Asian Americans as toxic and unwelcome neighbors," as many believed "their" community was becoming "too Asian" (with some White realtors steering White homebuyers away from Laurelton and toward communities where they might feel more "comfortable"). Within this racially discriminatory context, Lo shows how White discourses linked speaking an Asian language with "secrecy" and "deception," and public displays of writing an Asian language as not only "illegible" but "inappropriate."

White anxiety about what many are now calling "the new America"—that is, the rapid ethnic, racial, and linguistic diversification of the United States—plays a similar role in the construction of Latinos as racialized, foreign Others (what Rosa and others refer to as "Hispanophobia," or what I have termed more generally, #demographobia, i.e., the irrational fear of a changing demographic). Through an analysis of minute linguistic forms, Rosa and others in this volume make it possible to understand how macro-processes of racialization are brought into being through everyday interactions. As Rosa explains, ideas about language—both proficiency in English and public displays of Spanish—figure centrally in conservative dialogues (and diatribes) about whether U.S. Latinos will "ever" melt into (White) Americanness or remain "separate and apart from White Americans." Focusing specifically on the raciolinguistic ideologies and practices of Latina/o youth in Chicago, he analyzes "the specific ways that typifications of whiteness and 'Latina/o-ness' are enacted" in everyday, hybrid language use. Through these practices, these youth demonstrated "a shared investment in the ability to speak unmarked or 'unaccented' English, as well as intimate familiarity with and affinity for Puerto Rican and Mexican varieties of Spanish." Through engaged ethnographic fieldwork, Rosa documents how youth were able to use a register that he refers to as *Inverted Spanglish* in order to voice in-group knowledge of English and Spanish, while simultaneously parodying aspirational, assimilationist ideologies that covertly linked appropriateness and professionalism to middle-class whiteness.

These covert linkages between ideologies of appropriateness and whiteness are sometimes made straightforwardly overt, as in the case of Chun's analysis of language and racism in "The Meaning of *Ching-Chong*: Language, Racism, and Response in New Media." The covertly racist depictions of Asian Americans as perpetually foreign and woefully inassimilable (which we witness in Lo's ethnographic investigation of Laurelton as well) are given disturbingly new life in the viral YouTube video made by a White UCLA student—self-described as "a polite, nice American girl"—that mocked "Asians" as foreign, rude, and lacking manners. Chun uses this viral moment in social media as a jumping-off point for analyzing the racist use of *ching-chong* as "the language of racial Others, reminding *us* of *their* difference" in order to help shed light on the "complex contours of ideologies of language and racism in the United States." Chun's chapter offers a refreshing analysis in that she goes beyond describing various *ching-chong* incidents (including Shaquille O'Neal in 2002, Rosie O'Donnell in December 2005, and Rush Limbaugh in 2011, among others) and offers an analysis of the variable success of antiracist strategies that foreground different axes of linguistic meaning in responses to racist speech. Chun not only provides a useful framework for considering the how, when, and where of racist language use but also raises the possibility that certain antiracist strategies, such as satire, have the potential to significantly "shift public consciousness" and "particularly as new media technologies continue to change how we experience words and their meanings." In raising these possibilities, Chun's chapter serves as a pivot of sorts for the final two chapters in this section. As in Alim, Roth-Gordon, and Rosa, these chapters highlight the potential of performance to disrupt hegemonic, racist discourses. The final two chapters in the volume also both consider language use in media and popular culture in transnational and global youth cultural contexts.

Moving in Hip Hop cultural spaces in the "Coloured" townships of Cape Town, South Africa, Williams provides an ethnographic account of race and multilingualism in improvised verbal duels. His chapter, "Ethnicity and Extreme Locality in South Africa's Multilingual Hip Hop Ciphas," demonstrates how, through live performance, youth forge a local variety of Hip Hop Nation Language (Alim 2004b, 2009b) that relies on the strategic and creative use of linguistic resources associated with English, Cape Afrikaans (*Kaaps* or Cape Afrikaans is a variety of Afrikaans spoken widely in the Cape Flats), the local street variety Sabela (an admixture of isiXhosa, Kaaps, Zulu, and nonverbal gang signs), and African American Language. At least three zones of language ideological combat are relevant here. First, the hegemonic dominance of African American Language in some global Hip Hop sites, including Cape Town, is being challenged in favor of more local varieties that privilege locally relevant identities, politics, and epistemologies. Second, in a linguistic context where Cape Afrikaans is stigmatized across nearly all social domains related to power and upward mobility (from education to politics to the job market), "these youth registers challenge the supposed inferiority of this variety; its very use resists long-held stereotypes about Cape Afrikaans—and its speakers, mostly working-class Coloureds—as unintelligent, lazy, and criminal." Third, in a context where the nation-state espouses multilingualism as the law of the land, yet hegemonic language ideologies continue to frame South Africans of Color as "illiterate" and their linguistic behavior as "disorderly" or "threatening," youth are creating an agentive multilingual citizenship through their performances.

As in Roth-Gordon's and Williams's chapters, the globalized culture of Hip Hop and the emphasis on local forms of language play important roles in Mendoza-Denton's analysis of localism and the politics of territory in the constitution of "subaltern California language varieties." In her chapter, "Norteño and Sureño Gangs, Hip Hop, and Ethnicity on YouTube: Localism in California through Spanish Accent Variation," Mendoza-Denton builds upon her long-term ethnographic research among Latino gangs in California to highlight various kinds of Chicano/Mexican identity work through language. As she describes, the language ideological fault lines between Norteños and Sureños positioned the former as mostly speakers of Chicano English from Northern California and the latter as Spanish speakers from either Southern California or possibly of recent immigrant Mexican background. In an interesting interplay with Rosa's chapter on Mexican and Puerto Rican youth language ideologies and practices of Inverted Spanglish, Mendoza-Denton builds upon Hill's (2008) analysis of Mock Spanish and Talmy's (2010) use of "Mock ESL," as a mock register "surrounding the widely stigmatized acquisition of English as a Second Language," to uncover further layers of complexity in U.S. Latino language use in transnational, mass-mediated contexts. Mendoza-Denton adds cyberspace as a potential context where young people become political analysts (and actors) and synthesize their understanding of the larger processes of race (various forms of *Latinidad*), language (multiple regional, ethnic, and mock varieties of both English and Spanish), capital structures, and global power relations.

Each of the contributors in this section brings to bear ethnographic and discourse analytic methods to enhance our theorizing of race and ethnicity in rapidly changing communities. By languaging race across a wide array of contexts—from Southern California to South Africa—this intertextual conversation collectively contributes to our understanding of the workings of racialization by foregrounding the critical role of language ideologies and practices (see Schieffelin et al. 1998; Kroskrity 2000). Further, the contributors exemplify raciolinguistic studies by theorizing language and race together, by viewing language ideologies as inextricable from ideologies of race and vice versa, and by uncovering the ways that our everyday linguistic interactions and performances are both racialized and reproduce/transform racial orders.

RACING LANGUAGE

The chapters in this section continue to highlight the theme of language's central role in ethnoracial identification and struggle. Contributors undertake the project of *racing language*, or theorizing language through the lens of race. Whereas the chapters in the first section used linguistic data to theorize processes of racialization, the chapters in this section are mainly concerned with using race theory to better understand the social and political process of sociolinguistic variation. Contributors in each section of this volume attempt to achieve both goals simultaneously, but there are differences in theoretical emphasis and methodological preferences. While there are considerable overlaps in methodology, authors in this section shift from linguistic anthropological methods (discourse analysis, deep ethnographic engagement, etc.) to sociolinguistic methods (quantitative analyses of linguistic variables, analyses of subtle vowel shifts, etc.) in raciolinguistics. Considering contexts as diverse as the bustling urban centers of London, Los Angeles, and Washington, DC, the rural Southeastern United States, as well as one of the most contested regions of the world, Israel, the chapters in this section collectively aim to make race a central, rather than marginal, analytic category in the study of sociolinguistics.

In response to changing demographics, several authors call for a reconsideration of traditional concepts in sociolinguistic studies and a reevaluation of mainstream sociolinguistics' commitment to, and perhaps complicity in maintaining, hegemonic ideas around race, ethnicity, and language. These ideas not only urge us to move beyond traditional categories of raciolinguistic classification but also provide a critical frame by expanding upon traditional methodological and theoretical perspectives in sociolinguistics.

The chapters herein follow Fought's (2006) productive reading of Anzaldúa (1987) to argue that sociolinguists must describe and learn from people and societies in all their ambiguities: individuals at the margins of categories, multifaceted identities, and multiple, overlapping, or even conflicting communities of practice. In a reflexive critique of sociolinguistics that sets the stage for the analyses to follow, Blake ("Toward Heterogeneity: A Sociolinguistic Perspective on the Classification of Black People in the Twenty-First Century") argues that language scholars need to analyze raciolinguistic data in ways that "go beyond social categories defined in the national imagination and incorporate the nuances of how groups and individuals understand themselves" in ways that are not beholden to dominant national ideologies of race. She highlights how these new perspectives can help us focus on new kinds of ethnoracial identity work and view oft-studied concepts and communities with a new lens. For Blake, she problematizes straightforward definitions of "African American Language" and calls for increased attention to the sociolinguistic behavior of "Black ethnics," or of those that fall outside of hegemonic definitions of what it means to be "Black" in America (sons and daughters of African or Caribbean immigrants, for example).

Benor's analysis of African American Jews takes up these ideas, particularly the need to not only consider those on the periphery of racialized groupings but also reconsider the sociolinguistic notion of "ethnolect." Benor analyzes the linguistic performances of Black Jews in order to focus on how speakers "make selective use of elements of the distinctive linguistic repertoires associated with African Americans and with Jewish Americans" to accomplish diverse goals. Building upon her theorizing of *ethnolinguistic repertoires* (2010), Benor argues that we move from speaking about ethnolects and focus on ethnolinguistic repertoires as "pools of distinctive linguistic resources" that become associated with a group over time, a process that Agha (2003) refers to more generally as *enregisterment*. Like Williams, Roth-Gordon, and Chun (this volume), she demonstrates how speakers use language in highly performance-based contexts to "mock essentialist understandings of language and identity, as well as ideologies of biraciality as additive (Race A + Race B = Race A + B)."

In a direct intertextual conversation with Blake, Benor writes about how some Black Jews use language to indicate their multiple identifications, while others resist using particular racialized forms of speech in order to *prove* themselves to others as "authentic" members of Black or Jewish ethnoracial groups. In one case, a Black Jew with Jamaican ancestry uses language in such a way that indicates "her ideology that proudly identifying as African American does not entail using elements of the linguistic repertoire associated with African Americans." In another case, a Black Jewish Hip Hop artist rejects the idea that "you're supposed to give up your Black identity and transform that into . . . a Jewish identity." The raciolinguistic ideologies (Flores and Rosa 2015) in conflict here are evident. When this speaker uses speech marked as African American, "the reaction of other Jews implies, 'That's ghetto, that's something you should give up. If you're going to speak in a broken English, speak it with Yiddish.'" Despite sometimes reifying hegemonic notions of "broken English," these speakers "serve to contest common constructions of authenticity, in which an authentic member of a group must use linguistic features commonly associated with that group."

Whereas Benor focuses on Black Jews' construction of enthoracial identities through the use of enthnolinguistic repertoires, Gafter concentrates on the use of two minute and seldom-used—but *highly* salient and contested—raciolinguistic variables in Israeli society. Specifically, Gafter uncovers the social meaning of the Hebrew pharyngeal segments [ħ] (a voiceless pharyngeal fricative) and [ʕ] (a voiced pharyngeal approximant) in the context of social and economic inequality between *Ashkenazi* Jews (European descent, usually lighter-skinned) and *Mizrahi* Jews (Middle Eastern descent, often darker-skinned, sometimes raced as "Arab"). Gafter builds upon studies of Israeli mass media that come to the "bleak" conclusions that Israeli cinema normatively portrays Ashkenazi Jews as "just Israelis," while portraying Mizrahi Jews in a stereotypically Orientalist fashion—"they are uneducated, primitive, vulgar, sexist, and violent; they are also warm, hospitable, and have good food" as well as innocent and kind but "irrational and quick to get angry." His analysis shows that through raciolinguistic ideological links created between language use and racial stereotypes, these features of Mizrahi speech become iconic (Irvine and Gal 2000) representations of Mizrahi-ness or what it means to be Mizrahi. These raciolinguistic ideologies further link Mizrahi identity with undesirable Arab identities as a means by which Ashkenazi Jews reproduce racist discourses of Othering by "challenging the place Mizrahis get to occupy in Israeli society."

Importantly, for students of sociolinguistics, Gafter's research complicates the very neat lines drawn by Labovian sociolinguistics between class, style, prestige, and sound change, "with the move from more casual to more careful speech in intraspeaker variation reproducing the class differences observed in interspeaker variation." While the pharyngeal segments used by Mizrahis index lower class, status, and prestige, they also occupy a special position as the "correct" and "authentic" pronunciations due to their proximity to original Hebrew pronunciation (many Mizrahi Jews speak Arabic and so these sounds are part of their linguistic repertoire whereas Ashkenazi Jews lack them, or choose not to learn them). Given the fluidity and instability of social meaning presented by these pharyngeals, Gafter draws on Eckert's model of *indexical fields*, where meanings are located in a "dynamic structure [that] is created by the constant linking of form and meaning, without the previous reconstruals disappearing" (see Ochs 1992; Silverstein 2003; Reyes 2007 on indexicality). In drawing upon these models, he argues that sociolinguistic studies must consider in depth the historical context of specific linguistic features, their immediate context of use, as well as the locally significant stereotypes of race and ethnicity in order to understand their multilayered, raciolinguistic meanings.

The last two chapters, considered together, further represent the analytic and methodological strengths of variationist sociolinguistics to the project of raciolinguistics. Both Podesva ("Stance as a Window into the Language-Race Connection: Evidence from African American and White Speakers in Washington, DC") and Sharma ("Changing Ethnicities: The Evolving Speech Styles of Punjabi Londoners") represent the future of sociolinguistic variation studies within raciolinguistics in that they: (1) integrate the delicate and rigorous quantitative analysis of sociolinguistic variables with qualitative (ethnographic and interactional approaches) analysis to theorize race and language together; (2) demonstrate the intersectionality of race and ethnicity with gender, class, local politics, generation, immigration, and community history; and (3) acknowledge the fundamental complexities of ethnoracial styles of speaking and draw on relevant research on race and ethnicity to strengthen their particular linguistic projects. Working across vastly different communities—Podesva's African American and White speakers in a rapidly gentrifying Washington, DC, and Sharma's Punjabi Londoners in the changing ethnic community of Southall—both point the field toward useful analytic directions.

Podesva's analysis of (-t/d) deletion and falsetto illustrates how minute sociolinguistic features and discursive acts can be associated with African American ways of speaking, but also how they can be used by speakers to take *stances* about race and racially charged issues such as gentrification. As Podesva puts it, by analyzing stancetaking, we can argue that these features not only index African American identity, "but rather that they are also powerful resources for carrying out many other kinds of identity work." Podesva argues that analysts should not "expect African Americans to pattern together uniformly, given that gender may not play out in the same ways in the African American community as it does in other cultural contexts." In thinking across race and gender, for example, he was able to demonstrate that African American women used falsetto at much higher rates than African American men and Whites—and that this fact had particular social implications for the politics of race and gender in this changing urban context.

Similarly, in Sharma's analysis of the naturally occurring speech of Punjabi Londoners, she demonstrates how the "evolving uses and meanings of ethnic speech features can only be understood if factors such as gender, history, and class are taken into account"; in fact, as Alim and Reyes (2011) argued, she ultimately finds race and ethnicity "to be inseparable from these other dimensions of social life." We learn that "gendered uses of ethnic forms pointed to a gradual development of more British-like gender roles in the community," and similarly, "the influence of class on the use of accent features was shown to increase over time, with the youngest group once again showing the greatest resemblance to their British counterparts." Rather than disappear, however, Sharma argues that ethnoracial forms are used quite robustly by newer generations, who display distinctive ways of using them and imbue them with new, local meanings. Sharma, building upon her work together with Rampton (2015), ultimately points a way forward that highlights how various axes of differentiation (race, class, gender, for example) "come to vary in their salience over time in different communities and for different individuals."

Finally, these chapters illustrate the analytic insights gained from an approach that both *races language* and *languages race*. In considering how linguistic analysis can enrich the study of race and ethnicity, both studies demonstrate how fine-grained accounts of the broad distributional patterns of given sociolinguistic variables enable us to disambiguate the effects of linguistic (phonological or morphosyntactic considerations, for example) and social constraints (race, gender, class, etc.) on language use. As Podesva notes, it is imperative that linguistic analyses be informed and guided by ethnographic and theoretical understandings of race and ethnicity. As he explains, "the knowledge that gentrification, which most speakers conceptualize as a racial issue in Washington, DC, emerged as such a salient issue across the corpus of interviews," impacted his decision to analyze how (-t/d) deletion varies depending on whether speakers were talking about gentrification or not.

Similarly, in drawing on Crenshaw's (1989) theorizing of intersectionality, he was able to bring to light heretofore unacknowledged gendered patterns in his data. And, in turn, while the theoretical concept of intersectionality inspired him to analyze African American women separately from African American men, "it is the difference in falsetto patterns for these two groups" in the first instance that served as the motivation "to think more deeply about why African American women might experience race differently from African American men." These studies demonstrate that racing language and languaging race—or the simultaneous theorizing of language and race—can yield fruitful insights for both scholars of language and scholars of race and ethnicity.

LANGUAGE, RACE, AND EDUCATION IN CHANGING COMMUNITIES

In the third and final section of this volume, authors continue raciolinguistics' collective aim of producing research that enhances our understanding of linguistic racialization. Importantly, however, this set of contributors is explicitly motivated by a desire to transform policy, pedagogy, and practice in the language education of youth of Color. Chapters in this section not only theorize language and race but also provide implications for transforming traditional ways of educating ethnoracially and linguistically marginalized youth, and offer forward-looking suggestions that counteract the regressive ideologies and policies that inhibit youth of Color from reaching their full potential. This research is conducted across a rich array of school contexts and communities—including the experiences of African American, Latino, and Pacific Islander youth in the rapidly diversifying and gentrifying neighborhoods in the San Francisco Bay Area; indigenous immigrant Zapotec, Mixtec, and Purepecha youth in Los Angeles; *transfronterizo* ("border-crossers") Mexican and Mexican American youth living near the 2,000-mile border that separates Mexico from its former territories (California, Arizona, New Mexico, and Texas); Korean American youth in "cram schools" in New York City; and Moroccan and Roma students in an increasingly heterogeneous small town in southwestern Spain.

Paris's "'It Was A Black City': African American Language in California's Changing Urban Schools and Communities" and Perez, Vasquez, and Buriel's "Zapotec, Mixtec, and Purepecha Youth: Multilingualism and the Marginalization of Indigenous Immigrants in the United States" are conceptual chapters that represent the most recent advancements in pedagogical theory, what Paris (2012; see also Paris and Alim 2014; Alim and Paris 2015; Paris and Alim 2017) has termed *culturally sustaining pedagogy* (CSP). Paris's analysis expands and revises conventional ideas about "how young people in our changing communities, schools, and nation enact race and ethnicity through language" and updates traditional definitions of "English Language Learners." Paris's analysis of *language sharing* (Paris 2011; as opposed to Rampton's *language crossing* and *Styling the Other*, 1999)—how Latina/o and Pacific Islander youth participate widely in linguistic practices traditionally associated with African Americans (and, to some extent, vice versa)—challenges all-too-common assumptions "about relationships between language, race, and ethnicity" that "imagine a one-to-one-mapping of, for instance Spanish use only among Latinos/as or AAL use only among African Americans." These complex, multidirectional language practices lead Paris to rethink both "*how* languages are learned and *which* languages are learned in changing urban landscapes." Paris shows how Latino and Pacific Islander immigrant and first-generation students are not socialized into varieties of English associated with White Americans; rather, many are socialized into and through the linguistic practices of African Americans—or what Ibrahim (2014) similarly describes as "Black English as a Second Language (BESL)" in his studies of African immigrant youth in Canada. By taking into account the "Englishes" that urban immigrant youth are *actually* learning, Paris posits that they are often "Learners of American Englishes (LAEs) rather than simply learners of some monolithic language called 'English.'"

Perez, Vasquez, and Buriel similarly discuss linguistic practices in communities of Color that are invisible—and inaudible—to most educators. Their chapter is the first scholarly account of *trilingual language brokering* (the complex process of how trilingual speakers codeswitch between and translate multiple languages at once) among indigenous immigrant youth from Mexico. These youth face complex, multidirectional forms of racism, classism, and xenophobia: "They are often treated as 'illegals' in an increasingly hostile American political and legal climate, as 'Mexicans' or 'Latinos' by those who don't know enough to distinguish their indigenous background, and as 'inferior' by nonindigenous Mexicans because of their cultural, linguistic, and geographic roots as indigenous peoples." Ironically, for these youth, the three-way convergence of "mainstream American society's general, English monolingualism, combined with their parents' monolingualism, and their peers' bilingualism (English-Spanish)," has produced "a generation of indigenous youth who function as trilingual language brokers." As Perez, Vasquez, and Buriel argue, indigenous youth who are supported by their parents and peers "have learned to navigate social life in the United States through an impressive display of language learning that is not often recognized" by American educational institutions. They have accomplished this despite being labeled as linguistically "deficient," being assumed to be Spanish-speaking learners of English as a Second Language, and experiencing widespread raciolinguistic stigmatization and discrimination from Americans, Mexicans, and Mexican Americans alike.

When taken together with Zentella's analysis of the complex and innovative linguistic practices of youth who live along the U.S.-Mexico border, all three authors advocate for a U.S. educational system that recognizes, encourages, supports, and develops the bi- and multilingualism that students of color often bring to the classroom (and that monolingual Americans can learn from). In the first sociolinguistic ethnography of a "border school" in California (" 'Socials,' 'Poch@s,' 'Normals' *y los demás*: School Networks and Linguistic Capital of High School Students on the Tijuana–San Diego Border"), Zentella's fieldwork reveals "a wealth of linguistic diversity and skills that often go unnoticed and are sometimes disparaged, even by the students." Chief among the raciolinguistic challenges that these students face "is the racialization processes that stigmatize Mexicans as non-White and imagine them, their region, and their schools as violent and out of order, and the varieties of English and Spanish that they speak as incorrect and/or impure."

As discriminatory discourses about the languages of ethnoracially minoritized groups are still commonplace and acceptable (as opposed to overt remarks about race or phenotype), Zentella describes how "race has been mapped onto language," or how language serves as a proxy for racism. Zentella informs raciolinguistic studies by powerfully integrating her long-standing call for an *anthropolitical linguistics* with new calls for what educators have termed "border pedagogies" (Venegas-García and Romo 2005). Her analysis of school networks and linguistic capital along the border provides data that help to illuminate "a stigmatized group's attempts to construct a positive self within an economic and political context that relegates its members to static and disparaged ethnic, racial, and class identities, and that identifies them with static and disparaged language codes and practices."

The raciolinguistically discriminatory practices described by Zentella and Perez, Vasquez, and Buriel are made manifest in the content, organization, and uptake of talk in the studies of classroom discourse and interaction by Bucholtz ("On Being Called Out of One's Name: Indexical Bleaching as a Technique of Deracialization"), Reyes ("The Voicing of Asian American Figures: Korean Linguistic Styles at an Asian American Cram School"), and García-Sánchez ("Multiculturalism and Its Discontents: Essentializing Ethnic Moroccan and Roma Identities in Classroom Discourse in Spain"). While most chapters in the previous sections of this volume analyzed indexical meanings as evolving and expanding over time, Bucholtz highlights the concept of *indexical bleaching* ("whereby an index sheds part of its social meaning") as a "technique of deracial- ization, or the stripping of contextually marked ethnoracial meaning from an indexical form." In this case, Bucholtz analyzes an "all-too-common practice in American classrooms": the phonological mutilation and raciolinguistic violence enacted by White (and other) Americans who symbolically dominate racialized Others by renaming, disnaming, and misnaming them. For Bucholtz, in situa- tions where ethnoracialized groups come into contact, names become "sites of negotiation and struggle over cultural difference, linguistic autonomy, and the right to self-definition."

We see these precise processes occurring more broadly in García-Sánchez's raciolinguistic ethnography of Moroccan and Roma children in a fourth grade classroom in southwestern Spain and in Reyes's year-long ethnographic study of classroom discourse and interaction in a fifth grade English language arts class in a supplementary school run by Korean immigrants in New York City. In her detailed interactional analysis of "precisely how students' narratives are elicited" by well-meaning teachers, García-Sánchez reveals how "teachers are involved (often inadvertently) in reproducing monolithic and artificial, yet authorita- tive, versions of *authenticity* for immigrant and minority students." Despite the school's dedication to "multicultural diversity" and "inclusive pedagogical mod- els"—even garnering two prominent awards, one by a prestigious human rights organization—teachers often relied on essentializing notions of race, ethnicity, and culture, which "unwittingly identified minority children as culturally differ- ent and exotic." Given Spain's (and Europe's more generally) increasing multi- lingualism and ethnoracial diversity, García-Sánchez's linguistic anthropological research joins calls from critical multicultural educators to "disrupt ideologies that frame diversity as suspect and problematic" or risk reproducing them even "by those who genuinely struggle to address racial and ethnic inequalities."

In contrast to García-Sánchez, who primarily focused on teacher-student interaction, Reyes closely examined the talk between and among *students* in a middle-class Queens neighborhood "of which Asian Americans—primarily Korean Americans and Chinese Americans—reportedly comprise about a quarter of the population." Reyes's theoretical contribution to raciolinguistics brings the Bakhtinian concept of *voicing* (Bakhtin 1981) together with Bucholtz and Hall's (2005) theorizing of language and identity, Agha's (2005) "figures of personhood," and Inoue's (2006) focus on "the listening subject." Her theoretical synthesis informs her detailed analysis of how Korean American children draw "on four recognizable figures of Koreanness" in order to "sort out the available ways to be identifiably Korean; locate themselves in this complex milieu; accomplish specific kinds of interactional work; and contribute to circulating racial ideologies."

Importantly, Reyes demonstrates how these children created Korean American group membership by voicing and aligning with or against two contrasting figures—"the ideal Korean American" and "the Korean immigrant fob" (see Chun, this volume). In an interplay with Bucholtz (this volume), the children voice "the ideal Korean American" by mispronouncing Korean names and mocking Chinese language, while "the fob" figure was voiced through derisive mispronunciations of English and was represented mockingly "as a linguistically incompetent first-generation" Korean. According to Reyes, "voicing the fob figure reproduces racial ideologies that question Asian American national belonging and that understand languages in nation-state terms (i.e., 'speak American')" as well as produces "a recognizable Asianness that conforms to ideas that those understood as Asian are also expected to be foreign and nonnative English speaking." Reyes deftly shows how these children's small-scale voicing routines create divisions between Korean immigrants and Korean Americans. The students' voicing of "the fob" reproduces the large-scale "forever foreigner" stereotype of Asian Americans, while their voicing of the "ideal Korean American" reproduces linguistic practices (Anglicized Korean and Mock Chinese) that allow the children to position themselves as linguistically competent Americans. As we saw with Asian American adults in Lo's study of Laurelton, California, these young children exhibit similar anxieties around race, language, and national belonging, which are mediated by dominant raciolinguistic stereotypes that link "Asianness" and Asian languages with "foreignness" and "Whiteness" and "unaccented" English with "Americanness."

Taken together, the authors in this section present new research that uncovers continuing raciolinguistic challenges across changing societies. They have shown collectively that schools are not merely sites of learning, but are, as

García-Sánchez writes, "crucial sites through which issues of national identity and linguistic diversity" are continually "contested and reproduced." Through their detailed, discourse-analytic focus on language in interaction, these authors have contributed much to our theoretical understanding of how raciolinguistic ideologies (Rosa and Flores 2017) are formed and how classroom discourse continues to be a fruitful site of exploring the complex relationships between race, ethnicity, and language.

Moving Forward

LANGUAGE AND RACE IN "THE NEW AMERICA" AND BEYOND

In thinking about moving forward—or the proverbial question, "Where do we go from here?"—it is my hope that raciolinguistics can continue to impact and complicate interdisciplinary explorations of the new and emerging problems of race and ethnicity in "the new America" and beyond. As evidenced by the growing impact of CCSRE (Center for Comparative Studies of Race and Ethnicity) at Stanford University, for example, race scholars are beginning to ask new questions that address America's shifting racial landscape. These scholars critique traditional approaches to race and ethnicity as often decontextualized from evolving demographic contexts. While conventional approaches have been important, as many studies in this volume have pointed out, these approaches miss the fact that the United States, for example, has already entered into a particular historical moment of rapidly changing racial demographics and politics.

It is becoming clear that rather than a marginal enterprise, the study of America's racialized "minorities" is, in fact, *central* to the study of American culture, language, politics, and education. Put another way, high school dropout rates (or high unemployment and low home-ownership rates, etc.) of ethnoracially minoritized Americans means one thing when they together constitute 13 percent of the population, and something *altogether different* when they comprise a much larger share of the American population, for example. Demographers agree that White Americans will become a minority in the United States by 2050. Already, People of Color are a majority of live births. In so-called majority-minority states like California, for example, Latinos (see Mendoza-Denton, Bucholtz, and Zentella, this volume) have overcome Whites as the largest ethnic group (coming in around 40%), while Asian Americans (see Lo and Chun, this volume) continue to expand (approximately 13%). African Americans hold steady or shrink; in California, Blacks comprise 6 percent of the population and "mixed race" Americans comprise 5 percent (see Paris, this volume). Notably, African American majority cities (Washington, DC, for example; see Podesva, this volume) are now met with an increasing racial diversity that threatens African Americans' majority status. Of course, for those of us living and researching in California, we have witnessed *all* of these shifts in just the last ten years.

These demographic shifts are linguistic shifts, and they necessitate new approaches to the study of race and ethnicity. It is my hope that this volume can help guide scholars of race and ethnicity to look forward, not backward, toward America's evolving racial future. What is needed in this "new America" is not just research that attempts to solve the enduring racial problems of the past, but rather, new approaches to solve the emerging racial problems of the future. The need to consider America's—and the world's (Brazil, South Africa, Spain, Israel, Mexico, the Pacific Islands and the Caribbean, and other contexts with increasingly multiracial and multilingual populations)—racial problems with a new multiracial lens could not be more evident when one considers the contexts and communities covered in this book. I want to suggest that we do this by taking a closer look at the youth discussed in the pages of this volume, and by reflecting forward through the eyes of our future. In this volume, we have documented their struggles in contexts of linguistic racism, classism, and xenophobia, but what can we learn from their resistance to these multiple forms of oppression?

In the remainder of this introduction, I want to look toward youth—not to fetishize youth as "the solution" to our complex racial problems, but rather to discuss and develop counterhegemonic strategies that resist (and avoid reproducing) dominant narratives of race, ethnicity, and language. In considering the innovative raciolinguistic strategies of diverse youth, I hope to point a way forward for our field as we attempt not just to theorize linguistic racialization but to minimize its destructive impact on our lives.

Youth in these studies resisted being racialized through language in at least four ways: (1) small-scale interactional means, (2) conscious raciolinguistic performances, (3) raciolinguistic activism, and (4) transracialization. For example, fourth grade Moroccan and Roma children in Spain, where they are often stereotyped by teachers through Orientalist discourses (Said 1978) as racial Others, resisted multiple forms of misrecognition by often taking "advantage of open-ended interactional sequences to contest essentialist cultural characterizations and to assert more realistic perspectives of themselves and their communities" (García-Sánchez, this volume). The Mexican and Puerto Rican youth in Rosa's chapter, who are often framed as inassimilable or linguistically deficient, used complex translanguaging strategies to navigate and transform linguistic boundaries. Their use of what Rosa refers to as Inverted Spanglish "voiced in-group knowledge of Spanish and English" at the same time as it parodied the school leadership's imposition of the assimilationist, monolingual figure of "Young Latino Professional." These practices sometimes presented complex critiques of White racial and monolingual hegemonies. In both of these cases, youth use language to navigate and sometimes interrupt essentializing, xenophobic discourses.

While these youth used small-scale interactional sequences as moments to disrupt linguistic racism(s) (see Kroskrity 2014; Hill 2008; van Dijk 1987), others used conscious linguistic performances and activism (from satire to Hip Hop) to present counterhegemonic perspectives on language and race. For example, Chun writes about the use of satire in direct response to racist language like *ching-chong*, aimed at constructing Asian Americans as rude, unintelligible, and perpetually foreign. The antiracist YouTube video drew on an implicit set of antiracist assumptions invoked through absurd transformations: "a racist rant reimagined as the inspiration for a love ballad, a white racist reimagined as an object of sexual desire, and a victim of racial prejudice reimagined as a womanizing charmer." Importantly, as Chun points out, the meaning of language like *ching-chong ling-long ting-tong* was not fixed as a racist insult "but used here as a tool for critiquing racist ideologies" (even as the same youth potentially reproduced sexist discourses).

Youth involved in Hip Hop culture, locally and globally, are known for critiquing dominant ideologies of race and language directly or indirectly through their fluid linguistic practices (Alim et al. 2009)—and we have two examples of that in this volume from Williams and Perez, Vasquez, and Buriel. The South African youth in Williams's chapter resist racist descriptions of themselves through their linguistic choices. In a raciolinguistic context where their language (Cape Afrikaans) is stigmatized across nearly all social domains, "these youth registers challenge the supposed inferiority of this variety," with its very use resisting "long-held stereotypes about Cape Afrikaans—and its speakers, mostly working-class Coloureds—as unintelligent, lazy, and criminal." Further, in a context where the nation-state espouses multilingualism, yet hegemonic raciolinguistic ideologies continue to frame South Africans of Color as "illiterate," youth are creating an agentive multilingual citizenship through their performances (see Alim 2011 on "global ill-literacies"; and Alim et al. 2010 on how boys and young male Hip Hop heads often reproduce problematic masculinist and heteronormative ideologies).

In Perez, Vasquez, and Buriel, we see that, increasingly, indigenous youth in the United States are creating youth groups that create their "own terms of engagement" around issues of linguistic racism. One of these groups, Autónomos, founded by Oaxacan indigenous youth in Fresno, California, explicitly provides a space for youth "to reclaim their indigenous identity." These youth hosted a performance by Oaxacan Hip Hop artist Bolígrafo, who performed his now very well-known trilingual Mixtec-Spanish-English anthem, *UNA ISU* ("Mixteco Is a Language"). In the context of severe linguistic and racial discrimination and degradation, Bolígrafo not only proudly proclaims his indigenous Mixtec language but his trilingualism encourages indigenous youth to preserve their culture and language in the face of immense social pressure to assimilate.

The next example comes from the group of Chicanas in Santa Barbara, California, who experience forms of raciolinguistic "violence in the form of phonological mutilation or wholsale erasure" on a regular basis. These youth are often renamed, disnamed, or misnamed through processes of mispronunciation or deliberate anglicization that "indexically bleaches the original name of its ethnoracial specificity and renders it safely deracialized and normative." These young women recognized, critiqued, and engaged in social activism around the issue of renaming. Their YouTube video production subverted this hegemonic practice by engaging in what Mason Carris (2011, 476) refers to as *la voz gringa*, a counterform of mock language that she argues serves to "disrupt the dominant sociolinguistic order and elevated status of white Mainstream English with respect to Latina/o language practices; and ... challenge racial/ethnic power dynamics between whites and Latinas/os." As Bucholtz describes, the girls further reverse "the relative political positionality of English and Spanish phonology" by revealing "the correct Spanish pronunciation of their names in the International Phonetic Alphabet, authoritatively invoking a technical notation system in order to reject hegemonic anglicized pronunciations." These girls' sociopolitical critique, as with the antiracist YouTube video described by Chun (this volume), reached an audience well beyond their peer group and thus succeeded in publicly challenging the hegemonic raciolinguistic ideologies of their schools and societies.

Finally, we move beyond small-scale interactional disruptions and conscious linguistic production (through satire or Hip Hop), and witness a fourth raciolinguistic strategy of resistance—*transracialization*. Alim described these youth—whether Dominican American (as in Bailey 2000) or multiracial/White (as in Pollock 2005)—as *transracial subjects*, whose raciolinguistic strategies enabled them not only to move "across" racial groups but also to alternately disrupt and exploit the process of racial categorization. Pollock's (2005) observations of these youth in the Bay Area suggested that rather than full-on "race changes," these youth opted for "race-bending" strategies, which required alternately making race matter (when fighting for racial equality) and not matter (when resisting racial categorization). Much like "gender-bending" practices, these youth allowed us to imagine a level of sophistication in our race thinking that went beyond both the blind adherence to racial categorization *and* the total dismantling of racial categorization.

Whether engaged in micro-interactional forms of resistance, deliberate counterhegemonic performances, social activism, or the transgressive, destabilizing practices of transracialization, these youth have a lot to offer theorists of race, ethnicity, and language moving forward. As scholars, we, too, can interrupt oppressive interactions around race and language in our universities and broader disciplinary fields; we, too, can produce work that deliberately disrupts hegemonic ideas through widely circulating technologies; we, too, can develop new transracial politics in order to produce a cross-racial coalition of progressive researchers in raciolinguistics. These youth were transgressive not only because they crossed racial borders and resisted categorization but also because their simultaneous rejection and acceptance of racialization allowed them to potentially open up spaces for progressive cross-racial coalition building.

As we reach across disciplinary communities and engage in bidirectional dialogue with mainstream scholars of "language and gender," "language and sexuality," and "language and identity" writ large (some of whom are contributors in this very volume), raciolinguistics, as evidenced within these pages, has in fact already built a multiracial coalition of scholars who are committed to antiracist research and analysis. This coalition-building is necessary because the demographic changes discussed at the beginning of this section have created new racial and ethnic problems and divisions, as well as new opportunities for crossracial coalition and collaboration. As we have done in this volume, scholars must work collaboratively to explore not just the problems of one particular group, or that group as measured against the performance of Whites, but rather, the relations between America's racialized minorities and the possibilities for building a new racial future for the United States. As I hope we have demonstrated, if our efforts are to be most productive, we need to think more broadly and comparatively across ethnoracial "groups," not simply within them, to address how the role of racialization is fundamental to questions of citizenship and belonging.

Rather than erasing race, we must work as a collective to produce knowledge that eradicates racism, linguistic or otherwise, at home or abroad. Given that race continues to covertly and overtly structure the lived experiences of millions of People of Color around the world—as well as hegemonically dominant populations (even if unbeknownst to them)—our work must continue to resist and transgress the overwhelmingly White fields of anthropology and linguistics that continue to, at worst, marginalize and, at best, sidestep issues of race and racialization. While the fields of "language and gender" and "language and sexuality" have long been established, we seek to put forth raciolinguistics as both a field that foregrounds race and as an intersectional project that views race in conjunction with various forms of social differentiation (and urges other scholars to view gender and sexuality as always intersecting with race).

For many of us, this is not merely an academic interrogation but a question of life and death, particularly for the most vulnerable in our communities. Perhaps few of us understand this process more intimately than queer Black trans women and trans women of Color. Even in the era of "marriage equality," the connection between discursive and physical violence against these particular queer communities continues to be as underdiscussed as it is alarming. Activists on Twitter (#BlackTransLivesMatter), for example, have been the primary drivers of increased awareness about the 19 trans women of Color murdered in 2015 alone (a number that is very likely to be underreported; see Dalton 2015).

Raciolinguists have shown that pejorative, discriminatory language can have real-life consequences. For example, we have worried about the coincidence of the rise in the use of the term "illegals" and the spike in hate crimes against all Latinos. As difficult as it might be to prove causation in this instance, the National Institute for Latino Policy reports that the FBI's annual Hate Crime Statistics show that Latinos comprised *two-thirds* of the victims of ethnically motivated hate crimes in 2010. When racist speech is prevalent in mainstream U.S. political arenas—such as the poisonous, fear-mongering, racializing discourses of Donald Trump, Ted Cruz, and other Republicans in the 2016 presidential primary (simultanously anti-Black, anti-Latino, and anti-Muslim, not to mention misogynist and homophobic)—the possibility for violence increases, as we've seen with the recent attacks on U.S. Muslims.

In late 2015, after the Paris attacks, and in the same month that Trump and Cruz and others fomented anti-Muslim sentiments, violence against Muslims (and other People of Color mistaken for Muslims, such as Sikhs and Indian women who wear headscarves) *tripled*, according to California State University's Center for the Study of Hate and Extremism. According to reporting by Rizga (2016), in American schools, the number of students reporting bullying based on Islamophobia was *twice* the number of those who reported being bullied based on gender and race nationwide. In fact, even before the attacks in Paris and San Bernardino, Rizga reports that a 2014 survey by the Council on American Islamic Relations found that "52 percent of Muslim students in California reported being the target of verbal abuse and insults." Many of these students are being labeled "ISIS." As is the case with the anti-Latino slur "illegal," when some*one* is repeatedly described as some*thing*, language has quietly paved the way for violent action.

As argued throughout this volume, raciolinguistics concerns itself with more than just the words we use; we should work toward eliminating all forms of language-based racism and discrimination. In the legal system, CNN reported that the U.S. Justice Department alleges that Arizona's infamous Sherrif Joe Arpaio, among other offenses, has discriminated against Latino inmates with limited English by punishing them and denying critical services. In education, as many of the contributors in this volume have shown, hostility toward those who speak "English with an accent" (Asians, Latinos, and African Americans) continues to be a problem. In housing, the National Fair Housing Alliance has long recognized "accents" as playing a significant role in housing discrimination against African Americans. On the job market, language-based discrimination intersects with issues of race, ethnicity, class, gender, sexuality, and national origin to make it more difficult for well-qualified applicants with an "accent" to receive equal opportunities.

In the face of such widespread language-based discrimination, raciolinguistics can be more than just an academic field of inquiry but also a critical, progressive linguistic movement that exposes how language is used as a means of social, political, and economic oppression. By adopting a raciolinguistic lens, we can work to expose how educational, political, and social institutions use language to further marginalize racialized and minoritized groups; to resist colonizing language practices that elevate certain languages over others; to push for bilingual and multilingual education policies that don't just tolerate but value, support, and sustain the diverse linguistic and cultural practices of communities of Color; to resist attempts to define people with terms rooted in negative stereotypes; to refocus academic discourse on the central role of language in racism and discrimination; and, importantly, to reshape discriminatory public discourses about racially and linguistically marginalized communities. As Roth-Gordon concluded from her account of Brazilian youths' experience of deeply entrenched racism and classism, speakers of oppressed groups, whether in U.S. ghettos, South African townships, Brazilian favelas, or elsewhere, "cannot afford to ignore language as a critical resource for the construction of racial meaning"—and neither can scholars of race and ethnicity.

Note

1. To our knowledge, Nelson Flores and Jonathan Rosa (2015), in "Undoing Appropriateness: Raciolinguistic Ideologies and Language Diversity in Education," were the first scholars to use the term "raciolinguistic ideologies" in print to describe ideologies that "produce racialized speaking subjects who are constructed as linguistically deviant even when engaging in linguistic practices positioned as normative or innovative when produced by privileged white subjects." (150). Citing Paris and Alim (2014, 86), who themselves cited Toni Morrison's interview with Charlie Rose in 1998, their perspective built upon "the critique of the white gaze–a perspective that privileges dominant white perspectives on the linguistic and cultural practices of racialized communities." (150–1). Alim, along with Smitherman, have used the terms "raciolinguistic practices" or "raciolinguistic performances" to describe the simultaneous production of language and race in Barack Obama's political performances. Scholars are now using related terms in various ways. In this introduction, we are building upon the work of these scholars, and yet, using the term *raciolinguistics* in a different way, that is, as an umbrella term to refer to an emerging field dedicated to bringing to bear the diverse methods of linguistic analysis–discourse analysis, ethnographic linguistic anthropological studies, quantitative variationist sociolinguistics, applied linguistics and language educational analyses, etc.–to ask and answer critical questions about the relations between language, race, and power across diverse ethnoracial contexts and societies.

References

Agha, Asif. 2003. The social life of cultural value. *Language and Communication* 23: 231–73.

Agha, Asif. 2005. Voicing, footing, enregisterment. *Journal of Linguistic Anthropology* 15(1): 38–59.

Alim, H. S. 2004a. *You Know My Steez: An Ethnographic and Sociolinguistic Study of Styleshifting in a Black American Speech Community.* Durham, NC: Duke University Press.

Alim, H. S. 2004b. "Hip Hop Nation Language." In E. Finegan and J. R. Rickford, eds., *Language in the USA*, 387–409. Cambridge: Cambridge University Press.

Alim, H. S. 2009a. "Racing Language, Languaging Race." Paper presented at the University of California, Los Angeles Symposium on Race and Ethnicity in Language, Interaction, and Culture. February 27.

Alim, H. S. 2009b. "Translocal Style Communities: Hip Hop youth as cultural theorists of style, language, and globalization." *Pragmatics* 19(1): 103–27.

Alim, H. S. 2011. "Global ill-literacies: Hip Hop cultures, youth identities, and the politics of literacy." *Review of Research in Education* 35(1): 120–46.

Alim, H. S., A. Ibrahim, and A. Pennycook, eds. 2009. *Global Linguistic Flows: Hip Hop Cultures, Youth Identities, and the Politics of Language.* London: Routledge.

Alim, H. Samy, J. Lee, and Lauren Mason Carris. 2010. "Short, fried-rice-eating Chinese emcees and good-hair havin Uncle Tom niggas": Performing race and ethnicity in freestyle rap battles. *Journal of Linguistic Anthropology* 20(1): 116–33.

Alim, H. S., and D. Paris. 2015. "Whose Language Gap?: Critical and Culturally Sustaining Pedagogies as Necessary Challenges to Racializing Hegemony." Invited forum, "Bridging 'the Language Gap.'" *Journal of Linguistic Anthropology* 25(1): 66–86.

Alim, H. S., and A. Reyes, eds. 2011. *Complicating Race: Articulating Race across Multiple Social Dimensions*, special issue of *Discourse & Society* 22(4).

Alim, H. S., and G. Smitherman. 2012. *Articulate While Black: Barack Obama, Language, and Race in the U.S.* New York: Oxford University Press.

Anzaldúa, Gloria. 1987. *Borderlands/La Frontera: The New Mestiza.* San Francisco: Aunt Lute Books.

Bailey, B. 2000. "Language and the Negotiation of Ethnic/Racial Identity among Dominican Americans." *Language in Society* 29(4): 555–82.

Bakhtin, Mikhail. 1981 [1935]. *The Dialogic Imagination.* Austin: University of Texas Press.

Barreto, M. and G. Segura. 2014. *Latino America: How America's Most Dynamic Population Is Poised to Transform the Politics of the Nation.* New York: Public Affairs.

Baugh, J. 2003. "Linguistic profiling." In S. Makoni, G. Smitherman, and A. K. Spears, eds., *Black Linguistics: Language, Politics and Society in Africa and the Americas*, 155–168. London: Routledge.

Benor, Sarah Bunin. 2010. Ethnolinguistic repertoire: Shifting the analytic focus in language and ethnicity. *Journal of Sociolinguistics* 14(2): 159–83.

Boas, F. 1940. *Race, Language, and Culture.* Chicago: University of Chicago Press.

Bucholtz, M. 1995. "From Mulatta to Mestiza: Language and the reshaping of ethnic identity." In K. Hall and M. Bucholtz, eds., *Gender Articulated: Language and the Socially Constructed Self.* New York: Routledge.

Bucholtz, M. 2011. *White Kids: Language, Race, and Styles of Youth Identity.* Cambridge: Cambridge University Press.

Bucholtz, Mary, and Kira Hall. 2005. Identity and interaction: A sociocultural linguistic approach. *Discourse Studies* 7(4–5): 585–614.

Crenshaw, Kimberlé. 1989. Demarginalizing the intersection of race and sex: A black feminist critique of antidiscrimination doctrine, feminist theory, and anti-racist politics. *Chicago Legal Forum* 140: 139–67.

Cross, J., T. DeVaney, and G. Jones. 2001. "Pre-service teacher attitudes toward differing dialects." *Linguistics and Education* 12: 211–27.

Dalton, Deron. 2015. "The 22 trans women murdered in 2015." October, 15th. http://www.dailydot.com/politics/trans-women-of-color-murdered/.

Dick, H., and K. Wirtz, eds. 2011. *Racializing Discourses*, a special issue of the *Journal of Linguistic Anthropology*, 21(1).

Eberhardt, J. L., P. A. Goff, V. J. Purdie, and P. G. Davies. 2004. "Seeing Black: race, crime, and visual processing." *Journal of Personality and Social Psychology* 87: 876–93.

Flores, Nelson, and J. Rosa. 2015. "Undoing Appropriateness: Raciolinguistic Ideologies and Language Diversity in Education." *Harvard Educational Review* 85(2): 149–71.

Fought, Carmen. 2006. *Language and Ethnicity*. Cambridge: Cambridge University Press.

Goff, P. A., J. L. Eberhardt, M. J. Williams, and M. C. Jackson. 2008. "Not yet human: Implicit knowledge, historical dehumanization, and contemporary consequences." *Journal of Personality and Social Psychology* 94: 292–306.

García, O., and L. Wei. 2014. *Translanguaging: Language, Bilingualism, and Education*. London: Palgrave Macmillan.

Hill, Jane H. 2008. *The Everyday Language of White Racism*. Malden, MA: Wiley-Blackwell.

Ibrahim, A. 2003. "Whassup, Homeboy? Joining the African Diaspora: Black English as a Symbolic Site of Identification and Language Learning." In S. Makoni, G. Smitherman, and A. Spears, eds., *Black Linguistics: Language, Society, and Politics in Africa and the Americas*, 169–185. New York: Routledge.

Ibrahim, A. 2014. *The Rhizome of Blackness: A Critical Ethnography of Hip-Hop Culture, Language, Identity, and the Politics of Becoming*. New York: Peter Lang.

Inoue, Miyako. 2006. *Vicarious Language: Gender and Linguistic Modernity in Japan*. Berkeley: University of California Press.

Irvine, Judith T., and Susan Gal. 2000. "Language ideology and linguistic differentiation." In Paul Kroskrity, ed., *Regimes of Language*, 35–83. Santa Fe, NM: School of American Research Press.

Kroskrity, P., ed. 2000. *Regimes of Language: Ideologies, Polities, and Identities*. Santa Fe, NM: School of American Research Press.

Kroskrity, P. 2014. "On Producing Linguistic Racism." Paper and Society of Linguistic Anthropology Presidential Conversation (B. Meek, J. Rosa, H. Alim, A. Lo, R. Gaudio, B. Perley), American Anthropological Association, Washington, DC, November.

Labov, William. 1972. *Language in the inner city: Studies in the Black English Vernacular*. Philadelphia: University of Pennsylvania Press.

Makoni, S., G. Smitherman, and A. Spears, eds. 2003. *Black Linguistics: Language, Society, and Politics in Africa and the Americas*. New York: Routledge.

Markus, H., and P. Moya. 2010. *Doing Race: 21 Essays for the 21st Century*. New York: W. W. Norton.

Mason Carris, Lauren. 2011. "La Voz Gringa: Latino Stylization of Linguistic (In)Authenticity as Social Critique." *Discourse & Society* 22(4): 474–90.

Mendoza-Denton, N. 2008. *Homegirls: Language and Cultural Practice among Latina Youth*. Malden, MA: Blackwell.

Morgan, J. 2009. "Black Like Barack." In T. Denean Sharpley-Whiting, ed., *The Speech: Barack Obama's "A More Perfect Union"*, 55–68. New York: Bloomsbury.

Obama, B. 2004. *Dreams from My Father: A Story of Race and Inheritance*. New York: Broadway Books.

Ochs, Elinor. 1992. "Indexing Gender." In A. Duranti and C. Goodwin, eds., *Rethinking Context: Language as an Interactive Phenomenon*, 335–58. Cambridge: Cambridge University Press.

Orfield, G., and C. Lee. 2007. *Historic Reversals, Accelerating Resegregation, and the Need for New Integration Strategies*. UCLA Civil Rights Project/Proyecto Derechos Civiles, August 29.

Orfield, G., and J. Yun. 1999. *Resegregation in American Schools: The Civil Rights Project*. Cambridge, MA: Harvard University Press.

Paris, D. 2011. *Language across Difference: Ethnicity, Communication, and Youth Identities in Changing Urban Schools*. Cambridge: Cambridge University Press.

Paris, D. 2012. Culturally sustaining pedagogy: A needed change in stance, terminology, and practice. *Educational Researcher* 41(3): 93–97.

Paris, D., and H. S. Alim. 2014. What are we seeking to sustain through culturally sustaining pedagogy?: A loving critique forward. *Harvard Educational Review* 84(1): 85–100.

Paris, D., and H. S. Alim. 2017. *Culturally Sustaining Pedagogies*. New York: Teachers College Press.

Pennycook, A. 2007. *Global Englishes and Transcultural Flows*. London: Routledge.

Pollock, M. 2005. *Colormute: Race Talk Dilemmas in an American School*. Princeton: Princeton University Press.

Purnell, Thomas, William Idsardi, and John Baugh. 1999. "Perceptual and Phonetic Experiments on American English Dialect Identification." *Journal of Language and Social Psychology* 18: 10–30.

Rampton, Ben. 1995. *Crossing: Language and Ethnicity among Adolescents*. London: Longman.

Rampton, Ben. 1999. "Styling the other: Introduction." In B. Rampton, ed., *Styling the Other*, special issue of *Journal of Sociolinguistics* 3(4): 421–27.

Reyes, Angela. 2007. *Language, Identity, and Stereotype among Southeast Asian American Youth: The Other Asian*. Mahwah, NJ: Lawrence Erlbaum.

Reyes, A., and A. Lo, eds. 2009. *Beyond Yellow English: Toward a Linguistic Anthropology of Asian Pacific America*. New York: Oxford University Press.

Rickford, J. R. 1999. *African American Vernacular English: Features, Evolution, Educational Implications*. Oxford: Blackwell.

Rickford, J. In press. "Ain't no justice: Race, Dialect Prejudice, and Inequities in U.S. Courts and Schools: A linguistic analysis of the testimony of Rachel Jeantel in the Florida vs. Zimmerman case." *Language in Society*.

Rickford, J., G. J. Duncan, and L. A. Gennetian. 2015. "Neighborhood effects on use of African American Vernacular English." *Proceedings of the National Academy of Sciences*, 112(38): 11817–22.

Rizga, Kristina. 2016. "The chilling rise of Islamophobia in our schools." January 26. http://m.motherjones.com/politics/2016/01/bullying-islamophobia-in-american-schools.

Rosa, Jonathan. 2017. *Looking Like a Language, Sounding Like a Race: Inequality and Ingenuity in the Learning of Latina/o Identities*. New York: Oxford University Press.

Rosa, Jonathan, and Nelson Flores. 2017. "Do You Hear What I Hear?: Raciolinguistic Ideologies and Culturally Sustaining Pedagogies." In D. Paris and H. S. Alim, eds., *Culturally Sustaining Pedagogies*. New York: Teachers College Press.

Roth-Gordon, Jennifer. 2016. *Race and the Brazilian Body: Blackness, Whiteness, and Everyday Language in Rio de Janeiro*. New York: Palgrave Macmillan.

Said, E. W. 1978. *Orientalism*. New York: Pantheon Books.

Sapir, E. 1921. *Language: An Introduction to the Study of Speech*. New York: Harcourt, Brace.

Schieffelin, B., K. A. Woolard, and P. Kroskrity, eds. 1998. *Language Ideologies: Theory and Practice*. New York: Oxford University Press.

Sharma, Devyani, and Ben Rampton. 2015. Lectal focusing in interaction: A new methodology for the study of style variation. *Journal of English Linguistics* 43(1): 3–35.

Silverstein, Michael. 2003. Indexical order and the dialectics of sociolinguistic life. *Language and Communication* 23: 193–229.

Smitherman, G. 1977. *Talkin and Testifyin: The Language of Black America*. Boston: Houghton Mifflin.

Smitherman, G. 2000. *Talkin that Talk: Language, Culture, and Education in African America*. New York: Routledge.

Spears, A., ed. 1999. *Race and Ideology: Language, Symbolism, and Popular Culture*. Detroit: Wayne State University Press.

Steele, C. 2010. *Whistling Vivaldi: And Other Clues to How Stereotypes Affect Us*. New York: W. W. Norton.

Talmy, Steven. 2010. Achieving distinction through Mock ESL: A critical pragmatics analysis of classroom talk in a high school. *Pragmatics and Language Learning* 12(1): 215–54.

Urciuoli, Bonnie. 1996. *Exposing Prejudice: Puerto Rican Experiences of Language, Race, and Class*. Boulder, CO: Westview Press.

Van Dijk, Teun. 1987. *Communicating Racism: Ethnic Prejudice in Thought and Talk*. Newbury Park, CA: Sage.

Venegas-García, M., and J. Romo. 2005. Working Paper for Border Pedagogy Conference, USD, October.

Zentella, Ana Celia. 1997. *Growing Up Bilingual*. Malden, MA: Blackwell.

Part I

LANGUAGING RACE

1

Who's Afraid of the Transracial Subject?

Raciolinguistics and the Political Project of Transracialization

H. SAMY ALIM

In the summer of 2015, when news broke out that a "White" woman, Rachel Anne Dolezal, who was chair of a local chapter of the National Association for the Advancement of Colored People (NAACP) in Spokane, Washington and an Africana studies professor, had misrepresented her "race" and "pretended" to be Black, all race-theoretical hell broke loose.[1] All of a sudden, in a rage/rush to critique whiteness, some of the nation's top minds were reifying oppressive, exclusionary, and essentialist notions of race. While many were irate, and understandably so, given the historically oppressive relations between whiteness and blackness, Jelani Cobb (2015) took a more reasoned approach in the *New Yorker*, highlighting race as both a socialization process and a fiction: "In truth, Dolezal has been dressed precisely as we all are, in a fictive garb of race whose determinations are as arbitrary as they are damaging. This doesn't mean that Dolezal wasn't lying about who she is. It means that she was lying about a lie."

Cobb further captured the moment with characteristic clarity:

> Rachel Dolezal is not black—by lineage or lifelong experience—yet I find her deceptions less troubling than the vexed criteria being used to exclude her. If blackness is simply a matter of a preponderance of African ancestry, then we should set about the task of excising a great deal of the canon of black history, up to and including the current President. If it is simply a matter of shared experience, we might excommunicate people like Walter White, whose blue eyes were camouflage that could serve both to spare him the direct indignity of racism and enable him to personally investigate and expose lynchings.

In this chapter, I build upon Cobb's argumentation and push it a little bit further. I am well aware that most race theorists, and some theorists of language, will find the arguments that I make herein wildly unpopular, yet I believe that when we theorize race along with language there are new opportunities to interrogate the racial project and perhaps transform it altogether.

It should become clear by the end of this chapter that my conceptualization of *transracialization* is far more complex than Dolezal's performance of race, which does not explicitly critique or undo race in any way; rather, it merely recreates it. But can someone change their race? Linguistic anthropologists have written about the instability and fluidity of race and language for decades (see the introduction in this volume), and the literature certainly includes examples of speakers who "passed" for one race or another. But what does recent research and theorizing tell us about the complex relations among language, race, and phenotype in this troubling racial moment? Despite the fact that Dolezal indeed crossed over into blackness (after all, however problematic, hundreds of people over the span of *years* believed her to be "Black"), we need a focused interrogation of what it means to be *transracial*. Can someone be transracial?

Pushing past Dolezal, and leaving her behind for now, my aim is to theorize transracializion by considering those who do more than move across racial formations. Rather, I am interested in transracialization as a political project performed by those whose racial enactments and commitments challenge racial hierarchies. In the following pages, I argue that not only can transracial subjects change their "race" but also that their raciolinguistic practices have the potential to transform the oppressive logic of race itself. This chapter, then, represents both a search for the transracial *subject* and an attempt to theorize a transracial *politics*.

Transracialization: Rethinking Language and Race in Language Studies

In recent years, a critical mass of scholars in the area of *raciolinguistics* (the study of language and race) has developed across sociolinguistics, linguistic anthropology, and other language-related fields. The stage is now set to shift our collective thinking about language and race by considering how the fluidity of racial identification leads us to challenge systems of racial categorization. Perhaps most critical in this endeavor is our theorizing of *transracialization*, our aim to theorize racialization as a dynamic process of *translation* and *transgression*. Important, for me, is the goal of productively theorizing race in ways that speak to *both* the abstract, theoretical sensibilities of our field and the tangible, lived experiences of people ideologically positioned and racialized as "people of color."[2] This chapter raises more questions than it answers, offering observations of a specific and unique set of social practices that are consequential to how I—and a growing number of "multiracial" and "racially ambiguous" people, especially but not exclusively the "ambiguously brown"—move through the world.

This chapter critiques the discourses of emerging postrace theories (Touré 2011) in relation to the growing focus on language and race by scholars of language. Beginning with an analysis of President Barack Obama's raciolinguistic performances, and moving toward an autoethnographic narrative of being racialized nine different ways in the span of five days, I demonstrate that, rather than being fixed and predetermined, racial identities can shift across contexts and even within specific interactions (Bailey 2000; Bucholtz 1995; Sweetland, 2002; Bucholtz and Hall 2004). I conclude by suggesting a need to move beyond postrace and language and race theories and toward theories of *transracialization*.

Postrace theories soundly critique public discourses of a postracial America as naïve. Whereas White public discourses of postracial America remain colorblind—arguing that race is irrelevant—postrace theorists of color argue for the need to redefine and expand race groups beyond traditionally narrow conceptions (see Chang 2014 for a thorough discussion). Both strategies of avoidance and redefinition, however, leave race groups intact. Thinking transracially, as opposed to postracially, we can move beyond attempts to demonstrate our loyalty and belonging to particular racial categories and work toward problematizing the very process of racial categorization itself. Drawing on Pennycook's (2007, 55) productive reworking of translation, transracialization is not simply how race is coded and decoded across "different" racial formations but also about *resisting codifications*. While not attempting to flatten the distinctions among race, gender, and sexuality, I am adapting Butler's (2004) work on gender and sexuality and Pennycook's (2007, 36; emphasis in original) work on culture specifically in terms of race, claiming that "to think and be *trans* is not only to cross over, to transcend the bounded norms of social and cultural dictates, but also to question the ontologies on which definitions" of race are founded. The transracial subject is transgressive because crossing borders becomes central to disrupting race.[3]

Pennycook (2007) discusses the need for any critical project to carry both a political agenda *and* a commitment to question its inherent concepts. To take a small step in this direction, I want to theorize language and race together, paying particular attention to how both social processes mediate and mutually constitute each other. I want to *race language* and *language race* (Alim 2009), not just to view racial politics through the lens of language but also to theorize race by drawing upon our most advanced theories of language: those calling for an antifoundationalist perspective of language that interrogates notions of purity, fixity, and discreteness (see Makoni and Pennycook 2006; Pennycook

2007). Critical to this work is a commitment to theorizing and speaking against public discourses (which I think is where we too often stop), as well as finding ways to *speak to the public* (which I think is necessary to the advancement of transracial work).

This chapter builds upon the work of Alim and Smitherman (2012), which discusses how Barack Obama *translates* himself as "Black" through his mostly successful (that is, ratified) raciolinguistic performances. As with this entire volume, my goal in this chapter is not only to engage the public but also to push academic thinking forward, as many leading scholars of race continue to reify "the lie" that is race in response to public media outcries involving (trans)racialization. I share an autoethnographic narrative of my own experiences of repeated racializations to show how *transracialization* is not only about translating oneself but also about being translated in radically different and unexpected ways—and with an unbelievable amount of certainty on the part of those doing the translation. Transracialization is not about unfettered agency. The narrative I share below allows us to think about the ways that various interpretive frames come to be placed upon the same individual—that is, how my body (phenotype, comportment) and language (my use of particular linguistic resources, in particular ways, including gestures) are translated racially.[4]

After showing how we translate ourselves and how we are translated racially, I end with a search for the *transracial subject*. I do this with the goal of inching toward the development of a more nuanced, sophisticated way to deal with the reality of racism in contemporary American society. My goal is to theorize race forward by demonstrating, and then pushing back against, the insistence that the social construction of race is diametrically opposed to the idea that race has a real, tangible impact on the lives of people of color. As I argue in the introduction to this volume, these two ideas are equally valid and equally needed to bring about social transformation. I want to move toward thinking transracially, as opposed to postracially, so that our thinking, research, and dialogue can move beyond attempts to demonstrate our allegiance or belonging to particular racial categories (or pretending they don't matter), and rather work toward problematizing the very process of racial categorization itself.

I propose the transgressive figure of the transracial subject as one who knowingly and fluidly crosses borders while resisting the imposition of racial categories—calling into question the very existence of the oft-heard question: *What are you, really?* The transracial subject pushes back against the need to know, against the imposition of racial categories as real. It would be naïve to argue that transracial subjects can undo the logic of race, which took centuries to build and continues to evolve, simply through raciolinguistic performances. As

I argue throughout, transracialization must also be a collective process of social transformation.

Barack Obama and the Process of Racial Becoming

Barack Obama can be said to *translate* himself as "Black" through his mostly successful raciolinguistic performances of blackness. In recent years, we have come into a new understanding that language varieties are not just lists of features that belong to a given race. Further, more scholars are questioning the notion of a fixed "language variety," preferring to use more terms like "linguistic resources" that capture the fluidity of language use (see Garcia and Wei 2013 on the development of the concept *translanguaging*). We now view linguistic resources as being employed by speakers as they shape and engage in processes and projects of identification. President Barack Obama's use of what comes to be racialized as "Black Language," for example, is very much a conscious raciolinguistic project. In *Articulate While Black*, we analyze several videotaped examples of Barack Obama's diverse raciolinguistic performances that highlight the process of *becoming Black*.

In the same way that the president selected "Black" on the U.S. Census to mark a racial identity, he also selects particular linguistic resources to be employed in the multifaceted project of *becoming Black* (Ibrahim 2003) or in the process of *racial becoming* more generally. In fact, Obama's book, *Dreams from My Father*, chronicles his search for "a Black identity." He writes, "Away from my mother, away from my grandparents, I was engaged in a fitful interior struggle. I was trying to raise myself to be a black man in America, and beyond the given of my appearance, no one around me seemed to know exactly what that meant [calling attention to the role of phenotype]" (2004, 76). Many Americans who are racialized as Black, particularly those on the margins of what most Americans see as a normative Black identity (take the sons and daughters of Caribbean immigrants as discussed in Blake, this volume, for example), know this process well. Awad Ibrahim, Sudanese professor of education at the University of Ottawa, describes the process like this: "To become black is to become an ethnographer who *translates* and searches around in an effort to understand what it means to be black in North America." It is a process of "entering already pronounced regimes of Blackness" (2003, 154; emphasis added). Feminist and cultural critic Joan Morgan, who identifies as Jamaican, described the process of *becoming Black* in America in these terms: "As a matter of both acclimation and survival, we learn [African American] history. We absorb the culture. Some of us even acquire the *accent*" (2009, 63; emphasis added).

For both of these scholars, *racial translation* is a bidirectional process: (1) being positioned as "Black" by others in society and experiencing anti-Black racism; and (2) positioning yourself as "Black" by acquiring "Black" ways of speaking and being in the world. I have referred to this process in the past as the "dialectic of positionality" (Alim 2004). Speaking in terms of racial translation— and processes of racial becoming—moves us closer to challenging racial ways of thinking by positing race as not a neutral/linear translation from discrete language A to discrete language B, but a process that is imbued with active choices and political consequences. Rather than neutral and linear, racial translation is political and multidirectional; the process questions the purity and fixity of race A and race B (and as Benor in chapter 9, this volume, argues, the logic that "biracial" identities are additive, Race A + Race B = Race A + B).

Nine Moments of Racial Translation across Five Language Varieties

In this section, I use personal narrative to demonstrate how racial translation can also be multidirectional and draw on multiple linguistic resources. I also highlight the role of both language and phenotype in racial categorization, with language being, usually, the more malleable of the two resources. In this autoethnographic narrative, I briefly describe nine moments of racial translation across at least five "language varieties," in five days and three countries, by one speaker (me). I am translated—and, through my use of language and my silence, translate myself—into "Indian," "Algerian," "Mexican," "Turkish," "American Latino," "Columbian," "Arab," and "Black," and later as "Coloured" or "Cape Malay." (Although not widely recognized, race is always enmeshed with notions of ethnicity and nationality.) This is not only a narrative of racial translation but also a narrative of the beginnings of the denial of racial categorization and hegemonic race discourse. Let me take it back to the beginning of the story.

It's a mild autumn afternoon in the San Francisco Bay Area: Mountain View, California to be exact. I'm standin on my front porch, waitin for the cab to come pick me up and give me a ride to the airport. Not even a minute later, I hear this upbeat, friendly voice, marked by what most Americans would refer to as an "Indian accent" (an accent that is still widely mocked in U.S. media and society in general):

"You are Indian, my friend?"
"Oh, no I'm not, but a lot of people ask me that."
"Oh, you look Indian [looking in the rearview mirror
    and gesturing with an open hand up and down his face]."

"Oh, yeah? I've heard that a lot, especially around here."
As he insisted, I said, "Well, who knows, maybe I am
and I just don't know it!" adding a laugh.

Later that same day, I'm on a plane, on a ten-and-a-half-hour flight to Paris. I find my row and there, greeting me with a gigantic smile, is a portly, middle-aged (and as it turned out, *unbelievably* garrulous) man. I didn't realize it at the time, but I had raced him as "White." Turns out he identified as "Native American," as I discovered from his long, winding, passionate tales of his involvement with the American Indian Movement *and* the Black Panthers, his years of battling drug and alcohol addiction, his trouble with French women, and on and on and on. Although we had already introduced ourselves, later during the flight, he turned to me and said, "What was your name again?"

"Samy." [Choosing the most "harmless," Anglo name I got! See chapter 15, this volume, on the deracialization involved in the indexical bleaching of names.]

"Oh, you're an Osama?" he asked me.

"What?" I said, confused.

"Are you an Osama?"

"What?" I was stunned.

Homie asks me the same fuckin question a third time, "Are you an Osama?"

At this point, I'm like, is dude tryna clown me? Is he makin some real bad terrorist joke or something? I responded, "I don't understand what you're trying to ask me."

"Is Samy short for Osama?" he asked, and then, feeling the need to explain, he said, "I have an Algerian friend of mine whose name is Osama and he goes by Samy for short, you know, to avoid all the drama . . . I thought maybe that was something Algerians were now doing."

At this point, it's not even worth it to tell dude that I'm not Algerian—after all, we were on our way to France, which has a sizable Algerian community, and I wasn't trippin anyway.

"No, that's it, man, Samy, S-A-M-Y." Then I joked to lighten things up a bit, "My parents didn't know how to spell; they shoulda put another 'm' in there!"

Later, I noticed two women, one whom I assumed was "Asian" and the other whom I assumed was "Latina." At some point midflight, I struck up a conversation with Mimi (the "Asian" one) immediately on my right. I don't remember exactly how it got started, but I do remember her asking me, "What do you do in the Bay Area?" and we were off chatting. When I told her that I spoke English, Arabic, and Spanish, with reading knowledge in Swahili, she gasped again, "Oh!" and tapped her friend María, the "Latina," on the arm to bring her into the conversation. "He speaks Spanish!" María turned and asked me quickly, almost hopefully, "Are you Mexican?" Then, explaining her directness, she added, "I mean, how do you speak Spanish fluently?" "Well, I have a lot of Mexican and other Spanish-speaking friends and family, and that's how I learned Spanish." She then told me that she was a Mexicana *también* (a fellow "co-ethnic"), but felt terrible because she couldn't speak Spanish.

Fast-forward to the second leg of my flight—from Paris to Berlin. I always find it fascinating the way that flight attendants, seemingly instinctively, switch back and forth between languages as they greet passengers. They quickly take in all of the contextual cues—phenotype, dress, gesture, bodily comportment, and so on—and decide on a language of address. They almost always addressed me in English. However, as I made my way to my seat, on more than one occasion, some passengers, whom I raced vaguely as of "Arab" or "Middle Eastern" ancestry, spoke to me in a language that I assumed was "Turkish." (My assumption was based on two admittedly simple factors: one, we were on our way to Berlin, which had a sizable Turkish population; and two, it wasn't Arabic.) I had no way of understanding Turkish so I smiled and shrugged politely.

So, I land in Berlin, excited to get to my destination—ironically, the "Translating Hip Hop" conference and festival—and wonder if I would have time to connect with my German cousins, some of whom I hadn't seen in over two decades. I was *starving*, so I went on the hunt for food, eager to see what the food culture was like. Once I'd found an Italian place, I walked up to the counter and was greeted in German by the cook, whom I assumed was Italian (which he later confirmed). I responded in English, "Are you still open?"

> In response to my English, he looked at me and said in Italian-accented English, "Ah, American Latino. Español."
> To which I said, in a sigh of relief, "Sí, sí, español es mejor porque no hablo alemán yo."
> He smiled and said in a Spanish of a nonnative speaker, "Yo no hablo ingles. Qué quierés comer, amigo?"
> "No tienes una pastita caliente con pollo o algo así, algo bien caliente?" (Germany was cold, man!)
> "Sí," me dijo, "Número nueve."

While the food was cooking, we continued to chit-chat in our new lingua franca. At the end of my meal, I thanked the cook and we exchanged warm smiles. "Gracias, amigo," he called out, as I headed back out into the cold and wondered what my Italian former sister-in-law's family would make of the whole exchange!

At the conference, there were many more moments of racial translation. One event, in particular, stands out to me. During an intermission, I noticed the rapper from Bogotá, Diana Alleva. I stood at the side of her table for a minute, waitin for her to finish up her current conversation. At a natural break, she turned, looked up to me and said, "Hola," and smiled. At this point, my curiosity was heightened after the diverse moments of racial translation on this trip thus far.

"Hola," I said to her, and asked, "Cómo supiste que yo hablo español?"

"Por tus rasgos. Pareces a un miembro de mi familia o cualquier persona de Colombia," she said confidently, and added, "Eres Colombiano."

"No, no soy Colombiano, pero sí tengo mucha familia que habla español, allí in California, en los Estados Unidos."

"Ohhhh," she said. "Pero para mí, eres Colombiano," she laughed.

At the end of our talk, she said, "Quiero presentarte a mi amiga de Líbano, Malikah. Es una artista también." As we walked over to Malikah, I noticed that Diana introduced me to her in Spanish, "Malikah, Samy es un profesor de los Estados Unidos."

I remember thinking, "This Lebanese artist speaks Spanish?" I asked her, "Hablas español también?"

"Sí," me dijo, "wa 3arabi. Inta 3arabi, right?"

I responded to her in the variety of Spanish-Arabic (Lebanese)-and English that she was kickin, "Sí, tengo familia min Misr, but I'm from the States."

"Bti7ki 3araby?"

"Aywa, ba7ki 3arabi, bas bil lahga al-Misriyyah," I said with a smile.

"Mish mushkila, kollo tamam," she responded and laughed, flexing her Egyptian variety of Arabic (that is, in addition to her Lebanese variety).

The three of us conversed mostly in Spanish, with two varieties of Arabic and English mixed in, and ended the conversation with a combination of, "Mucho gusto," "Tasharrafna" ("pleased to meet you"), and the universal Hip Hop salutation, "Peace/Salam." To talk about these languages as discrete in this conversation would be strange, both interpersonally and theoretically. What "language" is "Sí, wa 3araby. Inta 3araby, right?"

In just a few short moments, in addition to "Indian," "Mexican," or "American Latino," I was raced specifically as "Colombian" and more broadly as "Arab." On one occasion, I was identified as a Spanish-speaking Colombian before I even opened my mouth, highlighting the role of phenotype. And on the other, I was identified as "Arab" after being introduced as "Samy" (which could be Arabic, Spanish, Anglo, or African American); and, despite my speaking Spanish, again highlighting how the same phenotype can be raced in different ways. The diversity of linguistic resources in this moment of racial translation offers us a unique window into the fluidity of race, racial identification, and the complex, interrelated roles of language and phenotype in the process.

On the last night of the conference . . . I was hangin with a group of Americans, two of whom I identified as "Latino." The conversation was mostly in what I would call an East Coast variety of Hip Hop Nation Language, which becomes associated mostly with Blacks and Latinos. We linked up with an emcee from New York who identified as Black, who was tellin us about this "White German" scholar who had the courage/nerve to roll up in the hoods of Los Angeles and do a research paper on Black men's hairstyles. The audience jumped all over her for what was, to them, her obvious fetishization of Black men. The Black emcee from New York turns to me and says, "You know they're *intriiigued* by us, man. They're *intriiigued*." Then he turned to me and joked, "She comin for *you* next!" And everybody cracked up!

So, by the end of these four days, less than 96 hours, I had been raced and reraced at least eight times: "Indian," "Algerian," "Mexican," "Turkish," "American Latino," "Colombian," "Arab," and "Black." My race began on the other side of the world in South Asia, traveled through North Africa and across the Pacific, back again to Eurasia, to the United States, Latin America, the Arabian Peninsula, and "ended up" in African America. That's one helluva transracial journey. And it's not over yet.

Several months later, I was sitting in a bar with a group of mainly American friends in the Sea Point neighborhood of Cape Town, South Africa, when the semiotics of language and race came together to reconstruct me yet again. The conversation was in English, but someone made a joke that required knowledge of "Spanish" for its comprehension. Upon my laughing at the joke, the one Capetonian member of the group turns to me and says, a bit surprised, "Oh, you understand Spanish, too? I didn't know you were Latino. When you walked into the lobby, I said to myself, 'Who is this Coloured Muslim man?'" Sea Point is an exclusive, extremely wealthy "White" section of this so-called post-Apartheid city, so in his imagination we were the only two "Coloured" folks in sight. In this exchange, language and phenotype came together anew to racialize me in very specific, but very different, ways. At once I was both Latino and Coloured—and due to my beard (my new Capetonian friend informed me), I further became a "Coloured Muslim," which as a racioreligious category has specific local connotations of a particular socioeconomic class of "Coloured" persons in Cape Town.

With this exchange, it began making sense to me why so many "Coloured" Capetonians would greet me in Afrikaans or use typical Muslim phrases with me, such as "As-salaamu alaikum" and "shukran." While I am sometimes raced as Black in the United States—as just recently happened on three different occasions in San Francisco ("You're Black, but you're not all the way Black," said one "White" dude, while his "Black" friend says, "I know you're Black, but maybe with a little Latino mixed in, right?", and another says, "I took one look at you and knew you were Black, your nose, lips, forehead")—in South Africa, I was hardly ever explicitly raced as Black. U.S. racial categorization allows for "mixedness" under the label "Black," while the South African system places "mixedness" under "Coloured"; this is complicated because progressive "Coloured" folks sometimes identify themselves—and me—as "Black," preferring to transgress rather than reinforce apartheid racial categories (Erasmus 2001). Further, while some Black South Africans are Muslim, the only discrimination from a person of color that I sensed in my entire three months came from a Black South African who, after only looking at me, informed me that it wasn't Friday and that I shouldn't be downtown (lots of mosques downtown). This is an instance of how various signs—linguistic and phenotypic (from skin color to beard)—come to take on multiple social meanings across race, class, and, in this case, religion as well. Nah, this shit ain't complicated.[5]

As we see from this autoethnographic narrative, for many of us, race is so fluid that we can change our race—and, in particular, have our race changed for us—with a simple plane ride, or even a night in a local bar. One need not even get on a plane to have these transracial experiences. Speaking for myself, I negotiate this transracial dialectic on a daily basis right here at home. In the same day, or stretch of days, I might hear a combination of: "Oh, I knew you had some Black in you; that chest is Black." "Hey, us Latinos gotta stick together, homes." "You have to discover your Arab identity." "Eres Caribeño, no?" "You look like Jason Kidd, so you're half-White, half-Black." "Just remember, it was *Black* folks who got you here." "Oh, it's *you*; that beard—I thought it was some Middle Eastern dude!" "What are you? She thinks you're Hispanic; I think you're Black." "Samy, that's Indian, right?" "You're Mexican, right? Eres de Mazatán [small town in Mexico, not Mazatlán]?" "You're Black and Puerto Rican like me." "Oh, I didn't know you were Brazilian?"

There are extremely uncomfortable examples as well, where people of color corral me into their racism against other ethnoracially minoritized groups; being recruited into racism is certainly one of the limits of transracialization. Recruitment into racism happens even in academic contexts, and within them, even with scholars who study race and ethnicity. In the sadly all-too-familiar territorial, zero-sum-game politics of minority faculty hiring, one Black colleague of mine pulled me into her office to privately express her anger about how the university was expected to hire one Black and one Latino faculty, and "now the Latinos wanna hire *two*; oh no, not two Latinos! They can't come in here and take over everything like they always do!" I stood quietly, and met her anger with silence, refusing to ratify her anti-Latino discourse. On another occasion, a "Latino" man who spoke what I identified as a Mexican variety of Spanish said to me, attempting to enlist me into his racist complaint, "Estos *pinches* chinos!" (He had grown furiously impatient while waiting for an "Asian" man to finish using the air dryer.) On yet another occasion, I was being ignored and treated poorly by a Palestinian convenience storeowner in East Palo Alto until I read aloud a Qur'anic verse written in Arabic behind his register. He exclaimed with surprise, "Oh, I thought you were one of *them*!" motioning toward a group of African American Muslims by the door. After talking at length with the storeowner, essentially shaming him for holding anti-Black beliefs while claiming to be a member of an antiracist faith, I never set foot inside that store again, for obvious reasons.

In addition to being corralled into racism against people of color, and in order to not fetishize the "multiracial" or "racially ambiguous" experience, the limits of transracialization can manifest themselves in terribly racist contexts. For me, as a brown-skinned man with a beard, that context was northern Italy, where I endured three weeks of the most horrifying and psychologically damaging racist terror I have ever experienced in my life.[6] In Rome and Venice, I understood viscerally what life in the 1950s must have been like for Black folks in America: I was kicked out of establishments and denied service in cafes, bars, and first-class trains; I was screamed at (multiple times), laughed at, ridiculed, threatened, and followed by White men who made monkey and ape noises behind me. Those are just a few examples. I'll never forget the red, angry, distorted face of that café owner as she yelled at the top of her lungs for me to go eat somewhere else; I wouldn't be exaggerating to say it was traumatic. To many Italians, especially those who hold strong racist, xenophobic beliefs (much of the country's right wing), it mattered not one iota that I was racially "ambiguous"; I was identified as a racial Other to be expelled from the country no matter what language I spoke or how I dressed.

To be clear, I am aware of the limits of transraciality, as I know for certain that: (1) millions of people cannot escape being targets of this kind of flat-out, hate-filled overt racism; and (2) even more cannot move so fluidly across racial, linguistic, and national boundaries. Nevertheless, as I illustrate below, there is value to pushing forward and critically thinking through the subversive potential of transracialization.

Transracialization as a Dynamic Process of Translation and Transgression

In the United States, there is sometimes a noticeable sense of discomfort when we don't know how to race someone. For example, upon meeting a Black octogenarian—famed African American jazz musician Chris Columbo!—for the first time, he looked at me and smiled widely, saying, "Hope you're not Cablanasian." (It was a straight-up, hilarious reference to Tiger Woods's racial self-identification, but also perhaps a phenotype-based challenge to my racial loyalty given Woods was considered suspect by the majority of African Americans.) And then there's this most recent comment from a new colleague of mine: "You're like the campus Rosario Dawson or Jessica Alba—no one knows what you are!" And in these comments is embedded the sometimes anxious question, one that multiracial or racially ambiguous folks hear a lot, *But what are you, really?*

Transracialization could simply be about the way that the same body is raced and reraced—the way we are continuously translated and continuously translate ourselves and others into various racial formations. But in relation to the question, *What are you, really?* I want to suggest that the previous narrative begins to take the *trans* in *transracialization* beyond conventional definitions of *translation* and toward a mode of being where the *translation* functions as *transgression* (following Pennycook 2007, 40, leaning on hooks 1994). I realized throughout my narrative that there were moments—especially when I had the ability to speak "the language" that mapped onto "my race"—where I resisted racial identification either through silence or through appeals to "my family." These strategies allowed me to move fluidly through communities that are always already constituted by racial/ethnic/national/linguistic identification. But more than moving fluidly between these formations, I believe that these practices are *transracial* not just in the sense that one moves *across* "groups" but that this movement across serves as a basis by which we can begin to question hegemonic ideas about both "language" and "race" and about the relationship between language and phenotype.

I want to offer two examples of *transracialization* in order to make the concept a little more concrete. Specifically, I want to talk about two *transracial subjects* found in the linguistic anthropological literature. The first is Wilson, a Dominican American youth in Rhode Island (Bailey 2000), who is part of the community of youth who refer to themselves as "Spanish" or "Hispanic" and find themselves at odds with the phenotype-based racial terms "Black" or "African American," which are applied to them in the U.S. context. Bailey writes, with wonderful detail, about how Wilson, who is "phenotypically indistinguishable" from other "Black" youth, uses language to negotiate identity and "resist ascription to totalizing phenotype-racial categories." Many Afrolatinos living in the United States can readily identify with Wilson's raciolinguistic fluidity.

The ambiguity of his identity—a function of his phenotype and his multi-variety language proficiency—leads to a number of explicit identity claims: an earnest claim of Dominican identity ("No, I'm Dominican"), as well as playful claims that he is Haitian (*Yo nací en Haití, pero me crie en Santo Domingo* 'I was born in Haiti, but I grew up in Santo Domingo (the Dominican Republic)' or that he is Black American ("Cause I'm Black"). Wilson "actively and explicitly claims, rejects, and exploits for humor" these diverse racial translations (2000, 574). This creates ambiguity for those who might ask Wilson the question *What are you, really?*, seeking to impose a system of racial categorization upon his body. This example demonstrates that transracial subjects not only can change their "race" but also their raciolinguistic practices have the potential to transform the oppressive logic of race itself.

It is commonly assumed that one cannot undergo a "race change," for example, in the same way that one might undergo a "sex change" (as it is popularly referred to) or engage in transgender practices. But these transracial subjects suggest otherwise. "Individual Dominican Americans, through speaking Spanish, ARE frequently able to transform their race status, from Black or White to Spanish. . . . The ongoing negotiation of identity" by these individuals "contributes to the transformation of existing social categories as well as the constitution of new ones where they might otherwise have not existed" (Bailey 2000, 575). This point has its predecessors as well. Specifically, see Allyson Hobbs's *A Chosen Exile* (2014), which contains groundbreaking research on African American "passing," a transracial project with life-and-death stakes and consequences if there ever was one.

But the real transgressive potential for transracial subjects lies not in their ability to translate themselves into existing racial categories, or to create new racial categories; these practices still carry the weight of hegemonic systems of racial categorization. Transracial subjects can be truly transgressive if and only if their raciolinguistic practices highlight the fallacy of normative, hegemonic ideas of race that rest on the shaky ground of biology, genetics, ancestry, and so on.

Lastly, I want to move from Wilson in Rhode Island to a diverse group of youth in the San Francisco Bay Area featured in Mica Pollock's (2005) ethnography of race talk dilemmas. I use this example below to return to my initial concern: the goal of productively theorizing race in ways that speak *both* to the abstract, theoretical sensibilities of our field and to the tangible, lived experiences of "people of color." This example, and Pollock's work more generally, helps us think through the question: How can we destabilize restrictive and regressive notions of race when the struggle for racial equality requires racializing oneself in order to be treated justly; to be "counted" and to "count"; and to receive resources, aid, legislation, educational reform, and so on?

Pollock's observations of these youth in the Bay Area suggested that rather than full-on "race changes," these youth opted for "race-bending" strategies, which required alternately making race matter and not matter, alternately reifying and destabilizing racializing discourses. According to Pollock (2005, 14), these race-bending strategies allowed students to strategically interrogate "the very notion of 'racial' difference even while keeping race labels available for inequality analysis." Much like "gender-bending" practices, these youth allowed us to imagine a level of complexity in our race thinking that went beyond either the blind adherence to racial categorization or the total dismantling of racial categorization. In a racially stratified society—where certain groups remain unequal to others, along so many social dimensions—we can imagine a multilayered, fluid, and situational strategy that switches between upholding and dismantling racial logic, according to the complex, political demands of the situation.

In this sense, this example from Bay Area youth—who recognize "race" as a concept with negative consequences, one that pits "groups" against each other in a struggle for social equality—offers a rejoinder to abstract theorizing that might not be grounded in the pressing and urgent concerns of everyday folks who are racialized as Others. *Transracialization* is productively viewed as the transgressive practice of not only resisting racial categorization but also *employing it—boldly—in struggles for racial justice* (think how #BlackLivesMatter activists vocally affirm the value of Black life in the context of widespread state violence against Black bodies). As long as societies continue to be organized racially, and differential outcomes are produced along racial lines, *transraciality* necessitates the alternative subversion and maintenance of racial categorization. The idea that *transracialization* should always be about destabilizing the idea of race—no matter the context—is naïve, at best, and counterproductive at worst. To *think transracially* requires a level of sophistication, a recognition that racially discriminatory contexts require simultaneous/alternating strategies of transracialization with moments of strategic racialization.

Who's Afraid of the Transracial Subject?

Transracialization is not about doing away with race altogether; it's about both doing race and undoing race in an effort to develop a subversive transracial politics. The transracial political project is about developing a more nuanced, strategic stance that requires us to know when (and when not to) uphold, reject, and exploit racial categorization. This is, for many, a terrifying level of sophistication. So, here is my answer to the question in the title of this chapter, "Who's afraid of the transracial subject?": We all should be. That includes those of us who, despite wonderfully theorizing race as performative, as a social construct, or as a myth, cling to outdated notions of race based on genetics, ancestry, or essence; those who move through the world with an uncritical "race loyalty"; those who espouse "colorblind" ideologies; those academics who seek to "help" racial minorities by claiming we are "postracial," or who repeat the tired old claim that "it's really about class, not race"; those rabid racists who cling to race at least as hard as they cling to their proverbial "guns and religion"; those well-meaning liberals who demand that racial justice activists stop using race labels to fight for equality;

the Rachel Dolezals of the world, who rather than stand with their allies stand on top of them by uncritically reproducing racial categories and hierarchies; and, yes, even committed racial justice activists, particularly those whose "one-race-at-a-time" activism inhibits the development of progressive multiracial coalition politics by failing to seek justice for groups other than their "own."[7] Be afraid, but not very.

Notes

1. The ideas in this paper were first presented at the annual meeting of the American Anthropological Association meetings in San Francisco in November 2012 as part of a panel organized by me and Angela Reyes on "Transracialization: Rethinking Language and Race in Linguistic Anthropology." As will become clear in the chapter, I am theorizing from a very specific subject-position, that of the multilingual, "ambiguously brown," or as a colleague has referred to me, "the racially interstitial" subject (i.e., millions, if not billions, of people worldwide). That said, this work is applicable, albeit to a lesser degree, even to those who are viewed to fit more neatly into categories like "White" and "Black" (see Saperstein and Penner 2012), and those rarely considered in U.S. discourses on race (see Harpalani 2013, on the "racial ambiguity" of South Asian Americans; and Ocampo 2016 on Filipinos as "racial chameleons").

2. I am using the term "people of color" to refer to those who are discussed as "racial minorities" in much of the social science literature. While I recognize the problematic nature of locating "color" within only particular racialized bodies, my aim here is to avoid terms that relegate the majority of the Earth's population to "minority" status as well as terms like "non-White" that define "people of color" by what "we" lack. Sometimes I use the term "ethnoracially minoritized" groups, as Bucholtz has in the past (2015) to point toward racialization as a process, but I know, still problematic all the way around.

3. I am deeply indebted to Awad Ibrahim's and Alastair Pennycook's thinking on the concepts discussed in this chapter. While Ibrahim theorizes race explicitly, and is cited throughout this chapter, Pennycook does not explicitly discuss race. However, I have not only benefited tremendously from both of their writings but I learned a great deal from the workshops Pennycook gave as the Center for Race, Ethnicity, and Language's CREAL Distinguished Visiting Fellow in 2012, as well as our many conversations where I fumbled clumsily through early versions of these ideas (and I'm sure both he and Awad would say that I'm still awkwardly making my way). Props to Mica Pollock, too, whose painstakingly detailed ethnography of race labels provided a breakthrough into *transracialization* as political strategy. Thank you.

4. Miyako Inoue (2006) has written powerfully about what she refers to as "the listening subject" in an effort to critique linguistic anthropology's focus on speaker agency. Her work has been taken up productively by Jonathan Rosa and colleagues (Flores and Rosa 2015; Rosa and Lo 2015) to focus not just just how language can transform race but also on "the other side of the equation—when racialized signs come to transform linguistic ones. Whereas linguistic anthropologists are sensitive to the ways that empirically observable signs can be interpreted in a range of ways based on the ideologies through which they are construed, we seek to direct attention to the semiotic processes through which signs are not simply interpreted or valued in multiple ways, but also potentially (re)materialized and (trans)formed" (Rosa and Lo 2015). This work is becoming an increasingly important focus in linguistic anthropology and has much to offer the growing field of raciolinguistics.

5. I share an interesting anecdote here from Paris regarding how the semiotics of the beard come together with race, religion, and sexuality. My first time in Paris, I learned that I was almost always raced as "North African," and specifically as "Algerian," "Tunisian," or "Moroccan." My beard, however, added the extra religious dimension of being categorized as "Muslim." Since my first visit was during Ramadan, I remember one taxi driver (Tunisian) automatically assuming that I was Muslim and reciting the Qur'an with me in the cab, asking me how my fasting was going, etc. The beard, however, was read in wildly different (and in most cases, divergent?) ways as well. While one driver took my beard as a sign of my Muslim piety, for example, another made reference directly to my beard, and my belly, hoping that they were markers of a particular type of gay male subculture known as "bears," usually but not always large, hairy, heavyset, or muscular men. Yup, can't make this shit up.

6. And I am no stranger to overt racism. I grew up in Jersey in the 1980s and 1990s where White people called me everything from "nigger boy," "sand nigger," "spic," "pyramid builder," to the hurtful, childhood color-coded term "boogie" and being yelled at to "go back south of the border, amigo," endured "race riots" in high school, heard anti-Black jokes about lynching made by my athletic coaches and teachers, and was even shot at in an anti-Muslim, White terrorist attack on our local mosque. Just to give you an idea. Again, I am not in any way fetishizing the experience of multiracial, racially ambiguous, or "ambiguously brown" folks. But while maneuvering through multiple communities certainly has its benefits, we are also faced with multiple racisms from the anti-Black crowd, the anti-Latino/anti-immigrant crowd, the xenophobic/Islamophobic crowd, etc.

7. Angela Davis argues this throughout *The Meaning of Freedom* (2012); further, her work consistently reminds us that transracialization is not just about building coalitions of concerned and committed political actors across race, but across gender, sexuality, class, religion, and other axes of social differentiation. None of us are free until all of us are free.

References

Alim, H. S. 2004. *You Know My Steez: An Ethnographic and Sociolinguistic Study of Styleshifting in a Black American Speech Community.* Durham, NC: Duke University Press.

Alim, H. S. 2009. "Racing Language, Languaging Race." Paper presented at the University of California, Los Angeles Symposium on Race and Ethnicity in Language, Interaction, and Culture, February 27.

Alim, H. S., and G. Smitherman. 2012. *Articulate While Black: Barack Obama, Language, and Race in the U.S.* New York: Oxford University Press.

Bailey, B. 2000. "Language and negotiation of ethnic/racial identity among Dominican Americans." *Language in Society* 29: 555–82.

Bucholtz, M. 1995. "From Mulatta to Mestiza: Language and the reshaping of ethnic identity." In K. Hall and M. Bucholtz (eds.), *Gender Articulated: Language and the Socially Constructed Self.* New York: Routledge.

Bucholtz, M., and K. Hall. 2004. "Language and Identity." In Alessandro Duranti (ed.), *A Companion to Linguistic Anthropology.* Oxford: Basil Blackwell, 268–94.

Butler. J. 2004. *Undoing Gender.* New York: Routledge.

Chang, J. 2014. *Who We Be: The Colorization of America.* New York: St. Martin's Press.

Cobb, J. 2015. "Black Like Her: Rachel Dolezal and Our Lies about Race." *The New Yorker*, June 15. (http://www.newyorker.com/news/daily-comment/rachel-dolezal-black-like-her)

Davis, A. 2012. *The Meaning of Freedom: And Other Difficult Dialogues.* San Francisco: City Lights.

Erasmus, Z. 2001. *Coloured by History, Shaped by Place: New Perspectives on Coloured Identities in Cape Town.* Cape Town: Kwela Books.

Flores, Nelson, and J. Rosa. 2015. "Undoing appropriateness: Raciolinguistic ideologies and language diversity in education." *Harvard Educational Review* 85(2): 149–71.

Garcia, O., and L. Wei. 2013. *Translanguaging: Language, Bilingualism, and Education.* New York: Palgrave Pivot.

Harpalani, V. 2013. "DesiCrit: 'Theorizing the Racial Ambiguity of South Asian Americans.'" *Annual Survey of American Law* 69(1): 77–184.

Hobbs, A. 2014. *A Chosen Exile: A History of Racial Passing in American Life.* Cambridge, MA: Harvard University Press.

hooks, b. 1994. *Teaching to Transgress: Education as the Practice of Freedom.* New York: Routledge.

Ibrahim, A. 2003. "Whassup, Homeboy? Joining the African Diaspora: Black English as a Symbolic Site of Identification and Language Learning." In S. Makoni, G. Smitherman, and A. Spears (eds.), *Black Linguistics: Language, Society, and Politics in Africa and the Americas.* New York: Routledge.

Inoue, Miyako. 2006. *Vicarious Language: Gender and Linguistic Modernity in Japan.* Berkeley: University of California Press.

Makoni, S., and A. Pennycook, eds. 2006. *Disinventing and Reconstituting Languages.* Clevedon: Multingual Matters.

Morgan, J. 2009. "Black Like Barack." In T. Denean Sharpley-Whiting (ed.), *The Speech: Barack Obama's "A More Perfect Union."* New York: Bloomsbury, 63.

Obama, B. 2004. *Dreams from My Father: A Story of Race and Inheritance.* New York: Random House.

Ocampo, A. 2016. *The Latinos of Asia: How Filipino Americans Break the Rules of Race.* Stanford, CA: Stanford University Press.

Pennycook, A. 2007. *Global Englishes and Transcultural Flows.* London: Routledge.

Pollock, M. 2005. *Colormute: Race Talk Dilemmas in an American School.* Princeton: Princeton University Press.

Rosa, Jonathan, and A. Lo. 2015. "Towards a semiotics of racialization: Ontologies of the sign." Paper presented at the American Anthropological Association, Denver, CO, November 19.

Saperstein, A., and A. Penner. 2012. "Racial Fluidity and Inequality in the United States." *American Journal of Sociology* 118(3): 676–727.

Sweetland, J. 2002. "Unexpected but authentic use of an ethnically-marked dialect." *Journal of Sociolinguistics* 6: 514–36.

Touré. 2011. *Who's Afraid of Post-Blackness: What It Means to Be Black Now.* New York: Atria Books.

2

From Upstanding Citizen to North American Rapper and Back Again

The Racial Malleability of Poor Male Brazilian Youth

JENNIFER ROTH-GORDON

Introduction

Before the election of President Barack Obama in 2008, there were several national discussions about his race. This included commentary on what it would mean to have the first nonwhite president or whether to describe him as "biracial" or "African American"; the question also arose as to whether he was "really black" at all. Here the discussion ignored traditional U.S. definitions of race that foreground biology (the color of one's skin and other physical features) and ancestry (whether the individual in question has an ancestor of known African heritage). Instead, at the heart of this particular debate lay questions about Obama's upbringing and everyday habits: How did Barack Obama dress? What kind of music did he listen to? Could he play basketball? But of all the attention paid to his daily behaviors, most salient was the issue of how he spoke. As Alim and Smitherman (2012) point out in *Articulate While Black: Barack Obama, Language, and Race in the U.S.*, Obama's ability to styleshift in and out of what is considered "standard" English received abundant media play.

In this chapter, I expand on the linguistic notion of styleshifting and embrace the concept of "racial malleability" (Roth-Gordon 2013) to explain how cultural and linguistic practices (what people actually do and how they speak) matter to our everyday assessments of someone's race. In keeping with the theme of this volume, I suggest that race is not something that you "see" through visual cues alone—but it is, in no small part, constructed through how people "sound." One of the most tangible ways that people make sense of race—in terms of understanding themselves and evaluating others—is through language. Here, I illustrate the relevance of language to the construction of racial meaning through fieldwork conducted in a *favela* (shantytown) in Rio de Janeiro, Brazil, where poor male youth deliberately engaged in linguistic and other cultural practices to shift the racial appearance of their bodies.[1]

Borrowing Whiteness

Despite its international reputation as a "racial democracy" (Sheriff 2001), Brazil has for centuries treated nonwhiteness as something to be feared and minimized—not just within the Brazilian body politic but also within the individual Brazilian body itself. Brazilian policies of racial assimilation have encouraged miscegenation (or race mixture) and marrying someone of a lighter skin so that Brazil could progressively "whiten" through future generations of racially mixed Brazilians (Skidmore 1993). Along similar lines, Brazilians were encouraged to manage their own personal bodily appearance through the request for *boa aparência* (lit., "a good appearance"). Up until recently, this requirement was commonly mentioned in job ads to indicate a preference for whiteness that included not only physical appearance but also "proper" comportment and manners (Caldwell 2007; see also Sansone 2003). Racial "improvement" thus involved "behavioral whitening: that is, discarding African and indigenous cultural practices" (Dávila 2003, 27). The implicit imperative for people of color to act "whiter" to reduce the effects of racism is, of course, widespread throughout the Americas and a pillar of white supremacy (see, for example, Carbado and Gulati 2013). And yet, despite this strong push toward whitening, the male youth I met in Rio de Janeiro in the late 1990s attempted to manage their racial appearance by moving both *toward and away from* linguistic and cultural practices associated with whiteness.

For example, in Excerpt 1, a dark-skinned male youth nicknamed Blue,[2] who lived in a favela that I call Cristo,[3] told me about one of his run-ins with the police in which an officer attempted to illegally search him. Though Brazilian citizens are legally required to carry identification, it is not obligatory within a certain distance of your home, and few wealthy Brazilians carry their personal documents as they walk through Rio's South Zone on their way to the beach. Dark-skinned shantytown residents cannot afford to be so carefree and secure in their rights to walk the streets of their own neighborhoods (Goldstein 2003; Sheriff 2001). Poor male youth complain about these frequent police searches, and it is a common topic taken up in rap songs. In order to avoid the humiliation and potential violence of a bodily search, Blue tells the police officer that he is a second-year law student at a well-known, private, and expensive law school. (In fact, he is not a law student; he had just told me that he dropped out of school after the seventh grade.) As he tells this story to me and to friends in his community, he presents himself as speaking in a fairly "standard" Portuguese with the officer, as would befit the typical white wealthy student who could afford to attend such an exclusive school in Rio.

Excerpt 1: "*Eu sei dos meus direitos*" [I know my rights][4]

1	Blue:	*O cara agarrado-eu falei, "Vou botar*	Blue:	The guy was clutching— I said, "I'm going
2		*advogado. 'Tô fazendo meu segundo*		to get a lawyer. I'm doing my second
3		*ano de advocacia da Universidade*		year of law school at Gama Filho
4		*Gama Filho e pá. Sei todos dos direitos,*		University and all. I know all of my rights,
5		*eu sei dos meus direito (?). Eu moro aqui*		I know my rights (?). I live here
6		*na comunidade e a menos de cinqüenta*		in the community and less than fifty
7		*metros da minha casa eu não sou*		meters from my house I am not
8		*obrigado a mostrar documento."* [. . . .]		obligated to show my documents." [. . . .]
9		*E aí o sargento, "Não, 'tá*		And then the sergeant [said], "No, it's
10		*certo."*		okay."
11	Cachaça:	*Caralho.*	Cachaça:	Shit.
12	CW:	*Porra.*	CW:	Damn.
13	Blue:	*Não, é que eu 'tô certo não.*	Blue:	No, it's not that he thinks that I'm right.
14		*Porque eles pensam, eles pensam que*		Because they think, they think that
15		*"todo mundo que mora aqui é favela. Aqui*		"everyone who lives here is ghetto. Here
16		*não tem um intelectual, não tem um*		there isn't an intellectual, there isn't an
17		*oficial, não tem um sargento*		official, there isn't a sergeant,
18		*Não tem nada. Aqui só tem o quê?*		There isn't anything. What is there here?
19		*A classe de burro." E não é isso.*		The class of idiots." And that's not right.
20		*Aqui tem pessoas bem educadas.*		There are very well educated people here.

In order to demand respect and defend his civil rights—including the rights to freedom and privacy—Blue's strategy of self-defense requires that he establish himself as a legitimate, upstanding citizen. In Brazil, where citizenship rights are unequally distributed according to race and class positions in an "entrenched regime of differentiated citizenship" (Holston 2008), this entails demonstrations of racial "improvement," through which Blue must associate himself with white spaces and whiter speech. Indeed, preferential treatment remains codified in Brazilian law, which offers special consideration by the police and prison system to anyone with a college degree.

Regardless of how he spoke in the actual encounter with the officer, it is striking that, during this retelling among friends, Blue speaks to the officer in what would be considered more "standard" Portuguese;[5] and he reports that the officer responds to his flaunting of legal knowledge, "proper" Portuguese, and mention of imaginary personal contacts by letting him go. Blue also evokes the white voice of privileged Brazilian citizenship through his invented association with elite white spaces such as Gama Filho University, one of the most important, expensive private universities, known not just in Rio de Janeiro but also throughout Brazil. Here Blue embraces the speech style and the embodied posture of white entitlement, answering the police officer's legal challenge with a legal challenge of his own. It is not that he pretends that he *is* white; it is that he embraces practices associated with whiteness in an attempt to distance himself from the stigma of blackness.[6] He takes on the trappings of whiteness to pull rank, to garner additional privileges, and to distinguish himself as someone who deserves respect and better treatment. Other shantytown male youth similarly shared with me their own personal linguistic strategies, such as excessive politeness, that they used to protect themselves from the police. These strategic attempts to "improve" their appearance rely on the fact that bodies do not come pre-labeled with racial categories and, in fact, are constantly being assessed for a range of racial cues. And as these youth know all too well, there are physical consequences to being perceived as darker-skinned by police officers (Mitchell and Wood 1999).

I am interested in looking at Blue's story through the lens of racial malleability to foreground the role of linguistic practices in the racial shifts that are made possible through daily interactions. In his narrative, Blue embraces both referential and pragmatic functions of language to avoid being searched by the officer: He talks about the law, lawyers, and law school (using the *referential* function of language—the ability to describe something with words). Blue answers the police officer's verbal challenge with a verbal challenge of his own—"I'm going to get a lawyer" (in lines 1–2)—which bravely asserts a linguistic confidence that causes the police officer to let him go (illustrating the *pragmatic* function of language—what one can accomplish through what and how you say something). I am interested not only in how Blue uses language to get himself out of this potentially dangerous situation but also in how language has an actual effect on his racial appearance. Language does not offer permanent and/or tangible forms of bodily change, of course. It's not the same as straightening one's hair or getting a nose job,[7] which are two common ways to "whiten" one's body in Brazil (Edmonds 2010). And yet, language offers speakers an incredibly affordable, portable, and abundant set of resources to "improve" one's racial appearance.

During his encounter with the police, Blue cannot run home and change his clothes or grab a briefcase to present a more respectable, citizen-like appearance, nor can he literally transport himself out of the racializing space of his shanty-town to associate himself with whiter neighborhoods or establishments. But his ability to draw on the respect and prestige accorded to speakers of a "standard" language (as opposed to the slang he more commonly speaks with friends; see Roth-Gordon 2007b) offers opportunities to link himself to racialized people, places, and ideas and to change the racial appearance of a body that must ultimately be "read" or interpreted by others. In effect, Blue has "borrowed" white-ness; he would not readily be recognized as a white person in Brazilian society, nor would he identify himself as such. But in this situation, he has successfully embraced a particular set of raciolinguistic ideologies (Flores and Rosa 2015)— racialized ideas about language and how certain people speak—to change the officer's reaction to him. In real-life, face-to-face communication, there is no way to separate out how people *sound* from the visual cues we normally associate with race (such as skin color, hair texture, facial features, etc.). This example thus illustrates how language shapes the racial differences that people "see."

Evoking Blackness

While whiteness is associated with citizenship, privilege, and respectability (among other positive attributes), these same youth also use language to shift away from whiteness—particularly when they seek to affiliate with popular youth subcultures such as politically conscious Brazilian Hip Hop. During the time of my fieldwork in Rio de Janeiro in 1998, the São Paulo–based rap group Racionais MC's (The Rationals) achieved national success with their platinum album *Sobrevivendo no Inferno* (Surviving in Hell). Though the group had been around since the start of Brazilian Hip Hop in the 1980s, this album took politi-cally conscious rap in Brazil to new heights, winning national MTV awards and launching the success of like-minded rap groups from Brasilia to Rio de Janeiro. Unlike the more commercially driven rappers who became especially success-ful after 2000, Racionais MC's fill their lyrics with searing condemnations of Brazilian racism and socioeconomic inequality. Politically conscious rap groups like Racionais MC's are especially influenced by North American civil rights–inspired themes and encourage fans to racially identify as black—an idea that is highly controversial in Brazil, where many people think of themselves as racially mixed and/or *moreno* (brown) (see Goldstein 2003; Sansone 2003; Sheriff 2001).

Politically conscious Brazilian Hip Hop's bold rejection of whitening is articulated most clearly in its embrace of a U.S. black–white binary and is personified in the male figures of the *mano* (black brother) and his rival, the *playboy* (white, wealthy male youth). The male youth I knew all oriented to these local interpretations of blackness and whiteness—taking on different bodily practices that allowed them to look more like the desirable *mano*. This included transforming their bodies through bodily aesthetics and clothing choices: *manos* most often wore either short or braided hair, baseball or ski caps, and oversized baggy clothing—all drawn from the imagery of urban African Americans as portrayed in popular culture. Indeed, the Yankees logo was highly valued on caps and clothing, not for its reference to baseball (a sport that is poorly understood and not highly regarded in Brazil), but because it is a common marker of Hip Hop fashion and blackness in the United States. As I will illustrate, rappers and their fans engaged in both visual and linguistic transformations to make their bodies appear blacker.

At one rap concert I attended in April 1998, I spoke with rappers before the show and then recorded the segments between songs, in which performers spoke directly to the audience either to introduce an upcoming song or to energize the crowd. In Excerpt 2, Mano Brown (Brother Brown), the lead singer for Racionais MC's, addresses his *carioca* (Rio de Janeiro–based) audience, predominantly other poor male shantytown youth, before singing one of their older and more well-known songs, "Hey [Play]boy" (1990). He lays out clearly for his audience the elements of Hip Hop or *mano* style:

Excerpt 2: *"Nós somos todo uma revolução"* [We are all a revolution]

1	*Nós somos todo uma revolução, só, faló mano?*	1	We are all a revolution, that's it, right brother?
2	*A revolução da attitude, tá ligado?*	2	The revolution of attitude, you know what I'm saying?
3	*Eu tenho um maior orgulho, morô? De usar minha*	3	I take a lot of pride, okay? In wearing my
4	*bombeta, de usar minha jaqueta, morô, mano?*	4	cap, in wearing my jacket, okay, brother?
5	*De cortar o cabelo assim, porque essa é minha vida,*	5	In cutting my hair like this, because this is my life,
6	*tá ligado? Eu não preciso usar*	6	you know what I'm saying? I don't need to have a

7	*topete para imitar playboy,*	7	wavy forelock of hair to imitate a *play-boy* [white, middle-class male youth],
8	*[gritos, aplausos] morô mano? Tá*	8	[shouts, applause] okay brother? You know what
9	*ligado, [ovação] minha vida é essa, môro?*	9	I'm saying, [loud applause] my life is this, okay?

I am interested in these stylistic lessons because they reveal how youth strategically interpret ideas about whiteness and blackness in order to influence how their own bodies are perceived. As I have suggested here, their racial appearance is determined not only by the physical features they have biologically inherited but also by the daily choices they make in terms of how they look and how they sound to others (see also Haney-López 1998).

In Excerpt 3, Mano Brown continues to address his audience at the show as he explicitly critiques the cultural practices he associates with black people who "sell out" through their embrace of whiteness. He warns his audience about what he views as a lamentable recent shift toward whitening among shantytown youth:

Excerpt 3: *"Paz entré nós"* [Peace amongst us]

1	*De lá pra cá mano? De lá pra cá, vários preto*	1	Since then brother? Since then, a lot of blacks
2	*se vendeu. Vários preto alisou o cabelo, morô*	2	sold out. A lot of blacks straightened their hair, okay
3	*mano? Vários preto curtia*	3	brother? A lot of blacks started listening to
4	*New Wave. Vários preto virou roqueiro.*	4	New Wave. A lot of blacks turned into rock fans.
5	*Vários mano traiu nação morô mano?*	5	A lot of brothers betrayed the nation okay brother?
6	*Mas então é o seguinte, porque o rap é a minha vida,*	6	But the thing is, rap is my life,
7	*morô? É minha gíria, minha bombeta, meu estilo de*	7	okay? It's my slang, my cap, my lifestyle.
8	*vida. É o que eu sei fazer. É o que me deu*	8	It's what I know how to do. It's what gives me the

9	*força para tá aqui até hoje, morô?*	9	strength to be here today, okay.
10	**Paz entre nós. Foda-se os playboys!**	10	**Peace amongst us. Fuck the playboys!**
11	[*começo da música*: "Hey [Play] Boy"]	11	[start of song: "Hey [Play]Boy"]

"Selling out," according to these rappers, involves straightening one's hair to achieve what is commonly called *cabelo bom* (good hair), in contrast to *cabelo ruim* (bad or kinky hair—the type of hair associated with people of African descent), as well as consuming white music, such as rock and roll or New Wave. In another rap song entitled "Stop Sucking Up (to Playboys)," Rio rapper M. V. Bill (1999) sharply criticizes youth who "look black but act white" due to their participation in sports such as surfing and their choice to hang out in spaces such as expensive dance clubs.[8] *Playboys*—wealthy white youth who follow others—are thus defined as the opposite of racially conscious and proud black brothers (Roth-Gordon 2007a). As we will see, poor shantytown youth can also be accused of trying to act like *playboys*.

In addition to dress, bodily aesthetics (such as hairstyle), and choice of activities (including the kinds of music one listens to and the sports one participates in), one's posture and demeanor send racial messages in terms of one's attitude toward whiteness. The aggressive stance of the *mano*—most clearly expressed in Mano Brown's parting shot in line 10 above: "Peace amongst us. Fuck the *playboys*!"—is meant to signal his opposition to *playboys* and to whiteness. The posture and comportment of a racially empowered *mano* is also juxtaposed with the *negro comportado/acomodado* (unassuming, assimilated, and well-behaved black person). In most cases, the album covers of politically conscious Brazilian rap groups showcase rappers in tough, irreverent, and "hard" poses that are typical of North American rappers. As Derek Pardue notes of Brazilian rap, "hip hop masculinity is about fashioning and displaying hard bodies and hardened faces" (2008, 146). In the photo that graces the cover of his debut CD, M. V. Bill stands unsmiling with no shirt on, displaying a muscular chest and a large tattoo. As with the aggressively cold and distancing stares Mano Brown is famous for, M. V. Bill's physical posture is uncompromising and threatening in order to foreground the challenge he poses to "the system." Here we have the opposite situation from Blue's example above, where Blue fakes an affiliation with a white law school in order to be seen as an upstanding member of Brazilian society. In fashioning anti-establishment bodies, rappers and rap fans must move away from whiteness and take on practices that are readily (and stereotypically) associated with blackness.

Nonconformist and irreverent stances are also conveyed linguistically. Politically conscious rappers fill their lyrics with what some consider to be aggressive profanity and slang, both of which violate the grammar and discourse rules taught in schools and defended by more privileged members of Brazilian society. Here rappers' linguistic "rebellion" can be interpreted by others as characteristic of the lack of discipline often associated with non-whiteness. In Excerpt 4, taken from the song *Diário de um Detento* (Diary of an Inmate) by Racionais MC's (1998), Mano Brown narrates the voice of a criminal who has second thoughts about his life and his actions, voicing the inmate through the use of speech considered to be highly "nonstandard."

Excerpt 4: *"Não tem pá, não tem pum"* [There's no pá, there's no pum]

1	*Não, já, já, meu processo tá aí*	1	No, it's done, it's done, my life is like this
2	*Eu quero mudar, eu quero sair*	2	I want to change it, I want to get out
3	*Se eu trombo esse fulano, não tem pá, não tem pum*	3	If I take out [kill] this guy, there's no *pá* [sound of a gunshot], there's no *pum* [another gunshot sound]
4	*E eu vou ter que assinar um cento e vinte e um.*	4	And I will have to sign [plead guilty to] the 121.
	[lei contra homicídios]		[law against homicide]

The use of sound words such as *pá* and *pum* (representing gunshots) as lexical placeholders (similar to "this" or "that" in English) is just one example of how rappers linguistically take up an anti-establishment stance that is intended to darken their appearance—in part by associating them with the sounds of criminality and in part by distancing themselves from the proper speech associated with Brazilian schools, "high" culture, and "a good appearance." While Brazilian youth cannot often understand the lyrics of North American rap songs due to their lack of English, they are well aware that African American rappers fill their songs with slang and profanity to create a different "sound" from white entertainers (both musically and linguistically). Brazilian rappers—and the rap fans who embrace their lyrics and their style through their daily practices—do not connect themselves to African Americans and U.S. urban spaces through visual appearance alone. They also draw on language in order to manipulate the racial appearance of their bodies.

To illustrate how rap fans use language to change how they racially appear to others, I offer an example of everyday conversation from three rap fans who all lived in the same shantytown as Blue (from Excerpt 1 above). In Excerpt 5, two male youth nicknamed "CW" and "Smoke" ask to listen to a friend's walkman—but the friend, called "Bad Dog," refuses to hand it over, embarrassed by what he has been listening to. A verbal—and racial—struggle ensues. To defend himself against the accusation that he is "acting white," Bad Dog engages in a practice that I call "conversational sampling," quoting rap lyrics in his response (Roth-Gordon 2009). The quoted lyrics are in bold.

Excerpt 5: "Periferia é periferia" [Periphery is periphery]

1	CW:	*Deixa eu ver [o aparelho]. Deixa eu*	CW:	Let me listen [to the walkman]. Let me
2		*mariar. Deixa eu mariar. Não. Deixa*		check it out. Let me check it out. No. Let
3		*eu mariar. Só pra mim criticar.*		me check it out. Just so I can make fun.
4	Bad Dog:	*(?) Não, tem nada pra tocar aí.*	Bad Dog:	(?) No, there's nothing good playing.
5	Smoke:	*Cho ver, cho ver, cho ver.*	Smoke:	Lemme see, lemme see, lemme see.
6	CW:	*Porra, tá com uma marra de*	CW:	Shit, you have the attitude of a
7		*playboy fudida heim.*		fucking *playboy*, huh.
8		*[. . . .]*		[. . . .]
9	Bad Dog:	*Tá me confundindo com quê?*	Bad Dog:	You are confusing me with what?
10	Smoke:	*Playboy.*	Smoke:	*Playboy.*
11	CW:	*Daqui a pouco tu tá usando*	CW:	Soon you'll be wearing your hair
12		*topetinho aí.*		with a little forelock.
13	Smoke:	*É.*	Smoke:	Yeah.
14	Bad Dog:	*Sou é **"periferia é periferia,"***	Bad Dog:	What I am is **"periphery is periphery,"**
15		*rapá.*		man.
16		*[. . . .]*		[. . . .]
17		***"Periferia é periferia, Racionais no***		**"Periphery is periphery, Racionais on**
18		***ar, filha da puta, plá plá plá."***		**the air, son of a bitch, uh uh uh."**[9]

In this conversation, the negotiation of what or who Bad Dog "is" fuses the consumption of music and hairstyle with a stance toward whiteness: The wrong song can imply whitening or "selling out." In order to defend himself from this racialized attack (in lines 6–7, then in 10–13), Bad Dog linguistically equates himself with the title of a famous politically conscious rap song in lines 14–15, and then continues on to sing lyrics from two different songs—ending with verbally "aggressive" profanity and the onomatopoetic "*plá plá plá*" (also meant to represent gunshots; see Roth-Gordon 2007b). To reject the racialized insult of *playboy*, Bad Dog must quickly display the comportment, sensibilities, and consumption practices of the "black brother" or *mano*. To affirm his toughness and his rejection of whiteness, Bad Dog transforms his body through the aggressive stance of rappers using linguistic features such as profanity, sound words that implicitly reference violence, and direct quotes from rap songs. These strategic linguistic choices all work to shift his racial appearance away from whiteness and toward the tough blackness these youth positively associate with North American and Brazilian rappers. As these examples reveal—and as the participants are well aware—skin color and other physical features do not solely determine racial meaning. In this moment, Bad Dog can't change any of his physical features (and, though he clearly wishes to, he can't change the song he has been listening to either)—but by shifting his physical posture and carefully choosing the language that he uses in his response, Bad Dog can embrace the racial malleability of his body to change how he appears to others. He helps demonstrate my point that one's racial appearance and one's stance toward (or against) whiteness are constantly negotiated through daily practices that include language.

In arguing that Bad Dog's racial appearance must constantly be "negotiated," I do not seek to locate him within an "official" Brazilian racial category (black, brown, or white), nor am I referring to how he might choose to racially describe himself (as black or brown, for example). Indeed, I am less concerned with questions of what we might call "racial classification" or "racial identity" and more interested in revealing the instability of race as it is lived on a daily basis. In this example, Bad Dog "evokes" blackness, not because he really "is" black, but because he wishes to identify himself with a racialized persona (the rapper or the black brother) that is highly desirable among his peer group. The *mano* is tough, cool, and well-respected; his counterpart, the white wealthy *playboy*, is a wannabe. In the various excerpts presented above, famous rapper Mano Brown and Rio rap fans Blue and Bad Dog hint at the fact that we all constantly manage our racial appearances (consciously or not) through language.

Conclusion

In this chapter, I have argued that bodies are not only given racial meaning but also remain racially malleable—able to be read as more or less white, based on a range of daily practices that include bodily aesthetics, patterns of consumption (from clothing to music), and, critically, language use. My desire to call attention to how the instability of race is negotiated through language does not include an assessment of racial identities or experiences. As I examine how Brazilian male youth shift between whiteness and blackness in their daily lives, I do not view them as "really black" or seek to accuse them of acting "too white." Instead, I am interested in how they draw on contrasting racial associations in order to craft a positive, desirable image of themselves in different situations. Sometimes this means taking on the role of the "upstanding" white citizen in order to gain full Brazilian citizenship. Other times, this means performing the part of a famous Hip Hop celebrity in order to gain some of the prestige and respect associated with black male "toughness." These racial shifts—enacted through language—remind us that speakers play an important role in constructing a global racial hierarchy that links whiteness with notions of rationality, discipline, and respectability and associates blackness with characteristics such as coolness and toughness as a few of its "positive" attributes (Bucholtz 2011; Hill 2008). And yet, these shifts should remind us that race is daily remade by speakers who must reconcile powerful linguistic ideologies with the social interactions that make up the substance of our everyday lives. Speakers cannot afford to ignore language as a critical resource for the construction of racial meaning, and neither can scholars of race.

Notes

1. While the examples I will present show speakers playing with notions of blackness and whiteness, the process of racially locating oneself is not limited to people of African descent (see, e.g., Montoya 1998).
2. Pseudonyms have been chosen to reflect the wide range of nicknames used by Brazilians and these youth in particular, including initials for celebrities they admired (both American and Brazilian). I have translated some of these names for the English reader.
3. This pseudonym references their clear view of the Christ the Redeemer statue that is a famous landmark in Rio de Janeiro and their contested occupation of desirable land in Rio.
4. Transcription conventions are as follows:

(?)	transcription not possible
(word)	uncertain transcription
[laughter]	transcriber's note (includes background noise as well as clarifications for the reader)

...	noticeable pause (untimed)
[....]	excerpt cut
Underline	emphatic stress or increased amplitude
::	vowel elongation
-	self-interruption; break in the word, sound abruptly cut off
//	simultaneous speech (noted before speech of both participants)
.	sentence-final falling intonation
,	phrase-final intonation
?	question rising intonation
Bold	indicates lexical items or example to be illustrated

5. Though Blue speaks primarily in "standard" Portuguese here, there is some slippage in his use of the slang form *e pá* in line 4 (see Roth-Gordon 2007b) and a lack of nominal agreement on *dos meus direito* in line 5.

6. The connections between race and class are strong here, and many Brazilians would equate "correct" and more educated speech with socioeconomic class as well. And yet his behavior cannot be explained by class alone. A common Brazilian saying describes darker-skinned individuals as *socialmente branco* (socially white) when they display higher levels of education and behavioral refinement.

7. Rhinoplasty, in which the nose is narrowed and raised to conform to white aesthetic standards, is a commonly requested plastic surgery by people of African descent in Brazil (see Edmonds 2010 for more).

8. In Portuguese, the song is titled "Pare de Babar (o ovo de Playboy)" and the exact lyric is *"preto por fora, branco por dentro"* or "black on the outside, white on the inside" (M. V. Bill 1999).

9. Here Bad Dog mixes the title of the Racionais MC's song *Periferia é Periferia* (Periphery Is Periphery) with a refrain from the popular song *Capítulo 4, Versículo 3* (Chapter 4, 3rd Verse).

References

Alim, H. Samy, Geneva Smitherman. 2012. *Articulate While Black: Barack Obama, Language, and Race in the U.S.* New York and London: Oxford University Press.

Bucholtz, Mary. 2011. *White Kids: Language, Race, and Styles of Youth Identity.* Cambridge: Cambridge University Press.

Caldwell, Kia Lilly. 2007. *Negras in Brazil: Re-envisioning Black Women, Citizenship, and the Politics of Identity.* New Brunswick, NJ: Rutgers University Press.

Carbado, Devon W., and Mitu Gulati. 2013. *Acting White? Rethinking Race in "Post-Racial" America.* New York: Oxford University Press.

Dávila, Jerry. 2003. *Diploma of Whiteness: Race and Social Policy in Brazil, 1917–1945.* Durham, NC: Duke University Press.

Edmonds, Alexander. 2010. *Pretty Modern: Beauty, Sex, and Plastic Surgery in Brazil.* Durham, NC: Duke University Press.

Flores, Nelson, and J. Rosa. 2015. "Undoing appropriateness: Raciolinguistic ideologies and language diversity in education." *Harvard Educational Review* 85(2): 149–71.

Goldstein, Donna M. 2003. *Laughter Out of Place: Race, Class, Violence, and Sexuality in a Rio Shantytown.* Berkeley: University of California Press.

Haney-López, Ian. 1998. "Chance, Context, and Choice in the Social Construction of Race." In *The Latino/a Condition: A Critical Reader,* edited by Richard Delgado and Jean Stefancic, 9–16. New York: New York University Press.

Hill, Jane H. 2008. *The Everyday Language of White Racism*. Malden, MA: Wiley-Blackwell.

Holston, James. 2008. *Insurgent Citizenship: Disjunctions of Democracy and Modernity in Brazil*. Princeton, NJ: Princeton University Press.

M. V. Bill. 1999. *Traficando Informação*. São Paulo: BMG International.

Mitchell, Michael J., and Charles H. Wood. 1999. "Ironies of Citizenship: Skin Color, Police Brutality, and the Challenge to Democracy in Brazil." *Social Forces* 77(3): 1001–1020.

Montoya, Margaret E. 1998. "Masks and Acculturation." In *The Latino/a Condition: A Critical Reader*, edited by Richard Delgado and Jean Stefancic, 435–441. New York: New York University Press.

Pardue, Derek. 2008. *Ideologies of Marginality in Brazilian Hip Hop*. New York: Palgrave Macmillan.

Racionais MC's. 1990. *Holocausto Urbano*. São Paulo: Zimbabwe.

Racionais MC's 1998. *Sobrevivendo no Inferno*. São Paulo: Zambia.

Roth-Gordon, Jennifer. 2007a. "Racing and Erasing the Playboy: Slang, Transnational Youth Subculture, and Racial Discourse in Brazil." *Journal of Linguistic Anthropology* 17(2): 246–265.

Roth-Gordon, Jennifer. 2007b. "Youth, Slang, and Pragmatic Expressions: Examples from Brazilian Portuguese." *Journal of Sociolinguistics* 11(3): 322–345.

Roth-Gordon, Jennifer. 2009. "Conversational Sampling, Race Trafficking, and the Invocation of the *Gueto* in Brazilian Hip Hop." In *Global Linguistic Flows: Hip Hop Cultures, Youth Identities, and the Politics of Language*, edited by H. Samy Alim, Awad Ibrahim, and Alastair Pennycook, 63–77. New York: Routledge.

Roth-Gordon, Jennifer. 2013. "Racial Malleability and the Sensory Regime of Politically Conscious Brazilian Hip Hop." *Journal of Latin American and Caribbean Anthropology* 18(2): 294–313.

Sansone, Livio. 2003. *Blackness without Ethnicity: Constructing Race in Brazil*. New York: Palgrave Macmillan.

Sheriff, Robin E. 2001. *Dreaming Equality: Color, Race, and Racism in Urban Brazil*. New Brunswick, NJ: Rutgers University Press.

Skidmore, Thomas. 1993. *Black into White: Race and Nationality in Brazilian Thought*. New York: Oxford University Press.

3

From Mock Spanish to Inverted Spanglish

Language Ideologies and the Racialization of Mexican and Puerto Rican Youth in the United States

JONATHAN ROSA

In April 2012, Linda Chavez, a widely recognized Latina conservative political figure,[1] penned a column titled "Why So Few Latinos ID Themselves as 'American'." Chavez cites a 2012 Pew Hispanic Research Center report based on a nationwide survey of Hispanic adults, and ponders why "only 8 percent of immigrant [Hispanics], 35 percent of second-generation Hispanics, and 48 percent of third-generation Hispanics" identify themselves first and foremost as American. She constructs a historical narrative in which the predominantly European immigration cohort in the early twentieth century was "encouraged to 'Americanize'" and "public schools saw it as their primary responsibility to help form the children of these immigrants into new Americans." Chavez distinguishes between the assimilationist ethos surrounding European immigration and "the advent of multiculturalism and ethnic solidarity, beginning in the 1960s," which coincided with dramatic increases in immigration from Latin America.

For Chavez, "if the children and grandchildren of Hispanic immigrants still see themselves as a group apart, it's because we've encouraged them to do so." As examples of how racial and ethnic identities are continually promoted, she points to affirmative action policies that require ethnoracial self-identification on government forms, educational entrance exams, and applications for colleges, jobs, and mortgages or bank loans. Shifting gears, Chavez assures readers that "the news on the assimilation front in the Pew Hispanic Center's study is not all bad." She explains that "Hispanics overwhelmingly believe in the importance of learning English; 90 percent think English fluency is crucial to succeeding in the United States." Doubling-down on this point, Chavez repeats the study's finding that "nearly all U.S.-born Hispanics say they speak, read and write English well." Thus, for Chavez, ideas about language—namely, proficiency in English—figure centrally in determining whether U.S. Latinas/os will join an unmarked, assimilated American "melting pot" or remain a racialized group, separate and apart from white Americans.

Chavez's views are characteristic of popular discourses surrounding U.S. Latinas/os. Such discourses are often anchored in the powerful relationships among ideologies of language, race, and nation. These linked ideologies are reflected in longstanding and contemporary debates about immigration, citizenship, English-only legislation, and ethnoracial categories and classifications. In this chapter, I analyze the ways that language ideologies shape the racialization of U.S. Latinas/os. I focus specifically on raciolinguistic ideologies (Flores and Rosa, 2015) and practices in the context of a predominantly Latina/o Chicago public high school and its surrounding communities. In particular, I analyze the relationship between linguistic practices that Jane H. Hill describes as "Mock Spanish" (1998, 2005, 2008) and what I call "Inverted Spanglish." I draw on theories of language ideologies and processes of racialization to complicate Hill's claim that Mock Spanish stigmatizes "historically Spanish-speaking populations" (2008). In contrast, I suggest that Mock Spanish stigmatizes populations *racialized* as U.S. Latinas/os regardless of their linguistic practices. I conclude by showing how U.S. Latinas/os appropriate the meaningfulness of Mock Spanish through the use of Inverted Spanglish by inverting both pronunciation patterns associated with Spanish lexical items and the ethnolinguistic identities associated with these linguistic forms. I will demonstrate how U.S. Latinas/os not only navigate but also transform linguistic boundaries. In order to frame this analysis of the relationship between Mock Spanish and Inverted Spanglish, the following section provides an overview of language ideologies and the racialization of U.S. Latinas/os.

Racing Language and Languaging Race in the Context of U.S. Latinas/os

One of the primary ways in which U.S. Latinas/os are imagined as a recognizable ethnoracial group, from in-group and out-group perspectives alike, is through language ideologies that position Spanish-English hybridity as the clearest sign of Latina/o identity. The 2002 book by Ed Morales, *Living in Spanglish*, provides an illustration of this ideology:

> Why Spanglish? There is no better metaphor for what a mixed-race culture means than a hybrid language, an informal code. . . . Spanglish is what we speak, but it is also who we Latinos are, and how we act,

and how we perceive the world. It's also a way to avoid the sectarian nature of other labels that define our condition, terms like Nuyorican, Chicano, Cuban American, Dominicanyork. (Morales 2002, 3)

In Morales's take on what many autobiographers have described as a fractured Latina/o identity (Rodriguez 1982; Anzaldua 1987), *Spanglish* is proposed as a unifying force among Latinas/os. Mobilizing prevailing language beliefs that "*a* culture" must speak "*a* language," Morales equates Latinas/os as members of a "mixed-race culture" with *Spanglish*, "a hybrid language." Note here the fascinating play on the ideology of "one people, one language," in that the "one language" of Latinas/os is a Spanish-English hybrid.

While Morales voices his position from an in-group perspective, his views align with what Ana Celia Zentella has described as "*chiquita*-fication" (2003; emphasis in original), the process whereby U.S. Latinas/os are simultaneously romanticized and otherized. Zentella has suggested that this process "is central to Hispanophobia because it reduces Hispanics to an undifferentiated and uncomplicated but huge and threatening mass" (2003, 52). Zentella complicates romanticized images of unity by questioning their simplicity and pointing to the stigmatization of Latina/o ethnolinguistic difference. She asserts that the negotiation of ambiguity and mixedness is neither a particularly Latina/o phenomenon nor a specifically contemporary emergence. Stigmatization occurs through the policing of English-language use by U.S. Latinas/os. Signs of accents and Spanish-language use are regarded as reflections of abject foreignness, regardless of the long history of Spanish-language use across the Americas.

Within the context of a U.S. regime of English-language standardization, the Spanish language is positioned as an emblem of identity (Silverstein 2003) that signals ethnolinguistic and ethnoracial difference. The act of speaking Spanish publicly is a subtle marker of this difference. As the political stakes of codes, registers, and styles associated with U.S. Latinas/os become heightened, the public display of linguistic difference is alternately celebrated or stigmatized depending on the speaker's social position. Language use and race come to be constructed and interpreted in relation to one another.

In the U.S. context, Pierre Bourdieu's notion of "strategies of condescension" (Bourdieu 1991, 19) is interesting to consider in relation to race. Think of many American political candidates' common practice of speaking a phrase or two of stilted Spanish in front of Spanish-speaking audiences. Their legitimate public use of the Spanish language is secured in relation to their racial positions and/or the subordination of Spanish to English in White public space (Hill 1998). For many U.S. Latinas/os, public usage of Spanish or "accented" English is prohibited and/or understood as an index of primordial inferiority (i.e., racial difference). This policing of Spanish vis-à-vis English is evident in the requirement of English-language "proficiency" in order to qualify for permanent legal status and U.S. citizenship as part of proposed immigration reform legislation. Thus, in line with other chapters in this volume, ideologies of race and language work together to structure our ideas (and our laws) regarding who counts as a U.S. citizen.

For U.S. Latinas/os, the racialization of language results in the stigmatization and differentiation of their Spanish and English linguistic practices. In their analysis of "Latino crossings" between Mexicans and Puerto Ricans in Chicago, De Genova and Ramos-Zayas explain that while "the apparent commonality of the Spanish language … is presupposed as a basis for unification among Latino groups…Mexican migrants' and Puerto Ricans' shared language was instead an especially salient object around which to produce their difference" (2003, 145). Language ideologies alternately position the Spanish language as an emblem of imagined unity across, and difference among, U.S. Latina/o national subgroups. De Genova and Ramos-Zayas point out that "Mexicans and Puerto Ricans in Chicago not only drew distinctions between themselves based on the identifiable type and 'quality' of Spanish spoken by each group … but also evaluated and hierarchically ranked each other's English" (2003, 173). U.S. Latinas/os are faced with *and* participate in the double-stigmatization of their English and Spanish linguistic practices. The interplay between ideologies surrounding Spanish and English, on the one hand, and the differentiation of Latina/o national subgroups, on the other, links language practices such as "Mock Spanish" to the racialization of U.S. Latinas/os.

Rethinking Mock Spanish

Jane Hill's analysis of Mock Spanish focuses on the everyday ways that White racial hegemony is reproduced through syncretic Spanish and English language use (2008). She defines Mock Spanish as a set of discursive practices involving the incorporation of "Spanish-language materials into English in order to create a jocular or pejorative 'key'" (Hill 1998, 682), such as Arnold Schwarzenegger's famous "Hasta la vista, baby" from the film *Terminator 2: Judgment Day*. Hill cites several examples to demonstrate how the same "language mixing" that is heavily policed for U.S. Latinas/os is received as legitimate (and even prized) for Whites. Such analyses of Mock Spanish characteristically link these linguistic practices to existing ethnoracial categories (i.e., "White") rather than analyzing the role that language use plays in constructing ethnoracial categories. However, can only non-Latina/o White people effectively use Mock Spanish? What about non-Latinas/os in general, such as African Americans? What about Spaniards? These questions require a reanalysis of the ways Mock Spanish participates in the dynamic, joint construction of categories of language, race, and ethnicity.

Hill describes the "major functions" of Mock Spanish as "the elevation of Whiteness and the pejorative racialization of members of historically Spanish-speaking populations" (1998, 682). This description raises several important questions: How might a range of ethnoracial groups participate in "the elevation of Whiteness," and how might different usages of Mock Spanish potentially elevate a range of ethnoracial groups? Can only the practices of White people (whom Hill sometimes glosses as Anglos) contribute to the elevation of whiteness? If Mock Spanish is to be understood in terms of processes of racialization, then who exactly are the "members of historically Spanish-speaking populations"? Does Mock Spanish necessarily participate in the racialization of *all* Spanish speakers? Can one be positioned simultaneously as a member of a historically Spanish-speaking population *and* White?

In different treatments of Mock Spanish, Hill seems to equate "historically Spanish-speaking populations" with non-whiteness in straightforward ways. Citing examples of Mock Spanish in several texts, Hill (2005) analyzes the functions of Mock Spanish; yet, Hill's analysis of "Spanish persons" as the racialized and stigmatized targets of Mock Spanish overlooks the different positions of Spain-oriented Spanish speakers and U.S. Latina/o Spanish-speakers. If racialization is a central function of Mock Spanish, then it is important to develop a more precise explanation of the nature of "Latina/o" as a racialized category and its connections to language ideologies in general and to the Spanish language specifically.

Hill argues that Mock Spanish is a "covert racist discourse" that "accomplishes racialization of its subordinate-group targets through indirect indexicality, messages that must be available for comprehension but are never acknowledged by speakers" (Hill 1998, 683). In other words, Mock Spanish invokes stigmatizing stereotypes about Latinas/os without making such stereotypes explicit. The most profound aspect of this process, however, is not that it frames "Spanish speakers" (regardless of national background and ethnoracial identity) in particular ways, but that it specifically produces "Latina/o" as a U.S. racial category. Thus, Mock Spanish must be analyzed specifically in relation to U.S. Latinas/os rather than all Spanish speakers or "members of historically Spanish-speaking populations" in any national context.

These language ideologies need not correspond to actual linguistic practices. People who are racially stigmatized in this process may speak little to no Spanish; recognizing this fact, Hill describes stigmatized targets as "historically Spanish-speaking populations." Yet, the racializing effects of Mock Spanish do not apply to a large number of the individuals who would seem to fit into this category, namely many Spaniards and other "historically Spanish-speaking populations" that are not racialized as non-White in the ways that millions of U.S. Latinas/os are. The complex nature of the relationship between ideologies of language and race makes linguistic practices such as Mock Spanish difficult to parse in relation to broader questions about the (re)production of ethnoracial and ethnolinguistic categories in specific contexts.

In comparing Mock Spanish to African American English (AAE) "crossover" (Smitherman 1994), Hill points out that "while the 'Black' indexicality of 'What's happening' is easily suppressed, it is virtually impossible to suppress the 'Spanish' indexicality of 'Nada,' which has in 'Mock Spanish' the semantically pejorative sense of 'absolutely nothing, less than zero'" (Hill 1998, 685). For Hill, the common difference between AAE and Spanish is the frequent indeterminacy of AAE (i.e., the suppression of "Black" indexicality) as opposed to the explicit Spanish indexicality of Mock Spanish usages. Note the way in which AAE and Spanish are made comparable here (even if differentially so). While African American English seems to point toward particular speech communities within the United States, does Spanish do the same? Hill positions "Black" and "Spanish" as analogous racial categories, thereby confining the practice of Mock Spanish as a racializing project to U.S. Latinas/os only—rather than generalizable to all Spanish-speakers.

Through an ethnographic case study of language ideologies and linguistic practices within a predominantly Latina/o Chicago public high school and its surrounding communities, I take up these issues and analyze the specific ways that typifications of whiteness and "Latina/o-ness" are enacted in Mock Spanish and related language use.

Mexican and Puerto Rican Language Ideologies and Practices in Chicago

New Northwest High School (henceforth NNHS)[2] is a Chicago public high school located near the borders of several predominantly Latina/o communities and a predominantly African American community. Because it is a neighborhood high school and not an application-based selective enrollment school, it draws its students from these nearby communities. More than 90 percent of NNHS's roughly 1,000 students are Latina/o; the vast majority of the remaining students are African American. The school's Latina/o student population consists of almost equal numbers of Mexicans and Puerto Ricans; some of these students are of mixed-Latina/o parentage, such as those with one Mexican parent and one Puerto Rican parent.

I conducted ethnographic and sociolinguistic research in NNHS and its surrounding communities between 2007 and 2010. When Dr. Baez, the Puerto Rican principal of NNHS, initially introduced me to the school, she explained her goal of transforming the students from "at risk youth" into "young Latino professionals." I was interested not only in Dr. Baez's critical awareness of her students' shared experiences of spatial, racial, and class exclusion but also in the question of what a Young Latino Professional might sound like. Dr. Baez's project of youth socialization sought to drive a wedge into the raciolinguistic binary of assimilation and multiculturalism. That is, the category Young Latino Professional combines mainstream notions of professionalism with Latina/o identity maintenance. Still, this effort was situated within a neighborhood public high school; the school was required to uphold English language hegemony mandated at the district, state, and national levels. This meant that while Spanish was spoken regularly by NNHS students and employees, students officially designated as "English Language Learners" (about 10% of the student population) were required to participate in a transitional bilingual education program that framed the Spanish language as a handicap to overcome rather than a resource to develop.

Mainstream students (i.e., those not classified as "English Language Learners") alternately reproduced this stigmatization of the Spanish language and embraced it as an object of cultural pride. The following student identity portraits include self-identified English-dominant and/or bilingual students, and focus on their raciolinguistic ideologies and practices:

1. Jimmy (PR, Gen. 3, Gr. 12), [3] a 17-year-old senior, self-identified as a monolingual English speaker, yet demonstrated both speaking and comprehension skills in Spanish. For example, while wondering aloud about the sexuality of another male student at NNHS, Jimmy questioned whether the student preferred "pincho," a Puerto Rican–style shish kebab that in this instance euphemistically referred to the male genitalia. Additionally, Jimmy's standard phone greeting is "bueno," which is stereotyped in the Chicago context as the telephone greeting for Spanish-speaking Mexicans. Still, Jimmy was frustrated by situations in which he was unable to communicate effectively in Spanish. He joked that this was especially troublesome during the summer months at the home improvement and construction store where he worked. He said that as the weather warmed up his skin tanned to a darker color and this prompted more customers to speak to him in Spanish. Jimmy's White bosses also continually asked him to help Spanish-dominant customers. Latinas/os and non-Latinas/os alike expected Jimmy to speak Spanish. In one of our tutoring sessions, I asked Jimmy to choose a written character that we could use as a variable when writing out algebraic equations. Jimmy chose "ñ." When I asked him how he could choose a Spanish orthographic character despite his self-proclaimed English monolingualism, he jokingly replied, "Spanish lives in my soul, bro."

2. Victor (Mex/PR, Gen. 3, Gr. 11), a 16-year-old "MexiRican" junior, was born to a bilingual Mexican mother and a bilingual Puerto Rican father, but was

taken in by a Spanish-dominant Puerto Rican foster family at the age of 10. He had not seen his birth father since he was a baby, but he visited his biological mother (a Chicago-born Mexican) regularly. Victor described himself as an English-dominant bilingual; he claimed that he could speak both Mexican and Puerto Rican Spanish, but that he spoke more Puerto Rican Spanish because this was the dominant variety spoken in his foster home. Victor told me that Puerto Rican Spanish is better than Mexican Spanish because Puerto Rican Spanish is "what's up" (i.e., cool), but that Mexican Spanish is more correct. Despite his strong valorization of Puerto Rican Spanish and his self-identification as a bilingual English-Spanish speaker, I rarely heard Victor speak Spanish with other students. In one interaction, Victor responded to a Mexican friend's Spanish-language greeting, "¿Que pasó, güey?" (What's up, man?), by telling him, "speak to me in English, I don't mess with that Spanish." He later clarified that he didn't like to be called "güey," an intimate, masculine term of address in Mexican Spanish (Bucholtz 2009). Victor told me that his friend should "take that güey and go on his way," playfully utilizing the homophony of Spanish "güey" and English "way."

3. Carlos (Mex, Gen. 2, Gr. 9), a 15-year-old Mexican freshman, was born in Chicago; both his parents were born in Mexico. A self-described bilingual, Carlos said he spoke Spanish with his parents and mostly English with his younger siblings (he is the oldest). He was Spanish-dominant until he entered elementary school and began learning English. In the classroom in which I observed him most closely, he sat with a boisterous group of Mexican students (three boys and three girls); he spoke English, Spanish, and Spanglish with these students, codeswitching intersententially and intrasententially, but also pronouncing Spanish words with English phonology and vice versa. When I asked Carlos about Mexican and Puerto Rican Spanish, he initially voiced an egalitarian perspective, simply claiming that every Latino national subgroup has its own variety of Spanish. He pointed to my paleto-velar pronunciation of /r/ as /l/ in the word /verdad/ (really) as an example of how Puerto Rican and Mexican Spanish differ. Upon further questioning, Carlos went on to say that Mexican Spanish is probably a little bit better than Puerto Rican Spanish because it is more correct. He also joked with me about the fact that he had only recently learned from friends at NNHS that some of his favorite Spanish words, such as "chévere" (cool/awesome) and "bochinche" (gossip), were in fact Puerto Rican, not Mexican Spanish terms.

4. Mayra (Mex, Gen. 1.5, Gr. 11), a 16-year-old junior, was born in Mexico City and came to the United States with her parents and baby brother at the age of 8. She described herself as bilingual, but said that Spanish is her main language. She worried that she still had a "Mexican" accent when speaking English. Her parents were monolingual Spanish speakers and her brother,

now 11, was bilingual. During an interview, Mayra joked about how it is not fair that her younger brother can speak English "without an accent." In contrast to Mayra's anxieties about her English-language skills, she spoke confidently about her Spanish-language abilities and about the Spanish language in general. She said that one of the main differences between Mexicans and Puerto Ricans is "the language." She provided examples such as the Mexican and Puerto Rican Spanish words for "sidewalk," *banqueta* and *concreto*, respectively[4]. Mayra also talked about her appreciation of Spanish slang, such as *cuaderno* (notebook) for "friend," and idiomatic phrases such as *de bolón pin pon* (of a Ping-Pong ball) to tell someone to hurry up. She said that she used to think that the best Spanish is spoken in Spain, but that changed when she heard that the best Spanish is actually spoken in Mexico. She also said that she definitely would not go to Puerto Rico to hear good Spanish because Puerto Ricans "don't say the words right . . . they miss some words . . . like sometimes they lose the 'r,' sometimes they lose the 's,' and it's really weird . . . and with Mexicans . . . they know how to talk!" Mayra explicitly articulated the stereotype that Puerto Rican Spanish is nonstandard. Similar to Carlos above, she highlighted the alternates of /r/ and /s/ in Puerto Rican Spanish. Mayra also described the shift from Spain (Castilian as spoken in Madrid) to Mexico (Mexico City) in the standard Spanish variety spoken and taught in the United States.

These students differ in age, gender, Latino national subgroup, and self-described language proficiency. Yet, their language ideologies and linguistic practices demonstrate a shared investment in the ability to speak unmarked or "unaccented" English, as well as intimate familiarity with and affinity for Puerto Rican and Mexican varieties of Spanish. Specifically, the students draw on local language ideologies that emphasize the "correctness" of Mexican Spanish and the "coolness" of Puerto Rican Spanish (Rosa 2014a, 2014b). These ideologies challenge the notion that the Spanish language unifies U.S. Latinas/os in straightforward ways. A simultaneous commitment to demonstrating "unaccented" English ability and intimate Spanish familiarity would seem to present these students with competing linguistic demands. In the following section I show how Latina/o NNHS students reconfigure Mock Spanish usages in order to reconcile this contradiction.

From Mock Spanish to Inverted Spanglish

In dialogue with Hill's work on Mock Spanish, Zentella (2003) and Mason Carris (2011) provide evidence of U.S. Latinas/os drawing on mock-language practices to parody the speech of Whites. I build upon this work to suggest that in addition to the mocking quality of the voicing involved here, U.S. Latinas/os use these language practices to meet the demand that they speak Spanish *in* English without being heard to possess an accent. These usages transform Mock Spanish into what I call "Inverted Spanglish," a set of language practices that function as a unifying component of the ethnoracial experiences of many U.S. Latinas/os (1.5 generation and beyond). I refer to these practices as "Inverted Spanglish" because they invert both pronunciation patterns associated with Spanish lexical items and the ethnolinguistic identities associated with these linguistic forms. Whereas Mock Spanish involves the production of whiteness through the combination of Spanish linguistic forms and English pronunciation, Inverted Spanglish appropriates similar linguistic patterns to produce U.S. Latina/o ethnolinguistic identities that signal intimate familiarity with both English and Spanish.

In one private classroom exchange, two sophomore boys—one Puerto Rican, Pedro (PR, Gen. 3, Gr. 10), the other MexiRican, Miguel (PR[m]/Mex[f], Gen. 2, Gr. 10)—traded Inverted Spanglish insults[5]:

Excerpt 1: *Inverted Spanglish insults*

Pedro: What's up, cuhbron? /kʌbɹoʊn/ (Spanish, /kaβɾon/, "cabrón," "bastard")

Miguel: Not much, pendayho! /pɛndeɪhoʊ/ (Spanish, /pendexo/, "pendejo," "dumbass/asshole")

In this instance, Inverted Spanglish transformed Spanish vulgarities that might otherwise operate as serious provocations into jovial play.[6] By pronouncing these words with conventional English phonology, the would-be offenses took shape as jocular exchanges. The voicings involved here are more complicated, however, as *cabrón* and *pendejo* index Latina/o in-group knowledge of Spanish insults. These items are not available to most non-Latina/o Mock Spanish users. Inverted Spanglish, as opposed to Mock Spanish, allowed Pedro and Miguel to accomplish multiple goals simultaneously: (1) highlight a shared Latina/o identity that involves critical distance from whiteness, (2) lay claim to a "cool" Americanness through English-language dexterity, and (3) display their insider knowledge of Spanish.

Inverted Spanglish was ubiquitous at NNHS; it was used in interactions among Latina/o teachers, Latina/o students, and between Latina/o teachers and students. This U.S. Latina/o–based linguistic register consists of Spanish lexical items pronounced with English phonology; what might be described as "saying Spanish words in English." The particular type of English phonology varies. In some cases, the Spanish word is pronounced with the same phonology that speakers conventionally use in their English speech. These usages generally take place in predominantly U.S. Latina/o settings and involve in-group Spanish tokens (i.e., usages that are not familiar to most non-Latinas/os and/or are not part of Mock Spanish repertoires).

Other Inverted Spanglish usages consisted of hyper-anglicized pronunciation of widely understood Spanish words in the course of English-dominant interactions. These tokens of Inverted Spanglish involved neither intimate Spanish vulgarities nor private conversations. In one case, a teacher began the day in a sophomore study skills classroom by asking students to remind her of the date. One student yelled out, "November **quatro**" [/kwɒtɹoʊ/] (Spanish, /kwatɾo/, *cuatro*, "four"). Later in the class, another student responded to the teacher's request for a volunteer to answer a question on a worksheet: "I've got the answer to **numerow trace**" [/num3·ɹoʊ/ / tɹeɪs/] (Spanish, [/numeɾo/ /tɾeis/], *numero tres*, number three). These cases differ from the previous examples because they appear to be similar to standard Mock Spanish usages. That is, they do not index intimate knowledge of Spanish. Instead, these usages more directly parodied the speech of Whites and others who might know and use basic Spanish words such as the numbers in this example. I commonly heard students draw on these usages outside of school, particularly in contexts that involved interactions between White people and Latinas/os.

One such context was a Mexican restaurant near NNHS. The NNHS students who went to eat at this restaurant with me were annoyed by the way that White customers addressed Latina/o employees. In a familiar scene in U.S. restaurant settings (Barrett 2006), these customers were dismissive of waiters and waitresses and loudly expressed their annoyance at being forced to communicate in Spanish. Diana (Mex, Gen. 2, Gr. 12) and Walter (PR, Gen. 2, Gr. 12) drew on hyper-anglicized Inverted Spanglish usages to parody these customers' behavior:

Excerpt 2: *Hyperanglicized inverted Spanglish*

Diana: **Donday esta el banyo**? /doʊndei ɛsta ɛl banjoʊ/ (Spanish, /dondei esta el baɲo/, "*¿Dónde está el baño?*", "Where is the bathroom?")

(Walter points in the direction of the bathroom.)

Diana: **Moochus Gracias**. /mʊtʃʌs gɹɔsiʌs/ (Spanish, /mutʃas gɾasjas/, "*Muchas gracias*," "Thank you.")

Walter: **Di nada**. /dɪ nɑdʌ/ (Spanish, /dei naða/, "*De nada.*", "It's nothing.")

Diana and Walter ostentatiously staged an impromptu performance that they intended to be overheard by the White people whose behavior they were parodying and the employees with whom they empathized. Unlike the examples of Inverted Spanglish above, Diana and Walter did not use their normative English phonology when pronouncing Spanish words. Instead, they drew on the hyper-anglicized "Whitey voice" (Alim 2004). These students actively sought to make the disgruntled customers feel uncomfortable about their behavior by turning the linguistic tables and marking their language practices. In order to do so, it was crucial that the Spanish words referenced by Diana's and Walter's hyper-anglicized Inverted Spanglish usages were widely recognizable by non-Latinas/os and were even commonly part of Mock Spanish usages.

Restaurants and other contexts in which Spanish-dominant Latinas/os provide services to non-Latinas/os are prime sites for the production of these tokens of Inverted Spanglish. This is similar to Mason Carris's (2011) analysis of what she calls "La Voz Gringa," in which Latina/o employees use "Valley-Girl-esque" phonology to perform in-group impersonations of the Spanish language use of a White employee in a Southern California Mexican restaurant. An important distinction here is that Diana and Walter staged their performance in relation to White customers and Latina/o restaurant employees, and their ability to speak "unaccented English" was central to their performance and ongoing presentation of self.

Inverted Spanglish becomes a way for U.S.-based Latinas/os to claim Spanish and English as their own, and to call into question negative in-group views of their Spanish proficiency and out-group views of their English proficiency. Importantly, the use of English phonology in Inverted Spanglish usages down-plays the indexical significance of Mexican–Puerto Rican Spanish phonological difference, thereby contributing to the creation of shared U.S. Latina/o ethno-linguistic identities. In the context of NNHS, Inverted Spanglish takes on addi-tional indexical meanings. If the school principal's category of Young Latino Professional corresponds to English-dominant speech that somehow acknowl-edges Latina/o identity, then Dr. Baez and her students would seem to be on the same linguistic page. However, Young Latino Professional is not only a cat-egory that lives in this particular school. In fact, categories such as Young Latino Professional are often promoted by aspirationally middle-class and/or upwardly mobile Latinas/os, as well as those who embrace hegemonic assimilationist perspectives more broadly. Inverted Spanglish, which parodies speech associ-ated with professionals, represents students' satirical response to this range of viewpoints. Inasmuch as a category such as Young Latino Professional attempts to balance assimilation and cultural identity maintenance by inflecting main-stream notions of professionalism with "Latina/o-ness," Inverted Spanglish is students' playful way of saying, "we get it."

Inverted Spanglish simultaneously voices these Latina/o students' ethnolin-guistic and ethnoracial experiences, playfully responds to the principal's project of socialization within NNHS, and pushes back against broader assimilation-ist perspectives that circulate in popular discourses surrounding U.S. Latinas/os. These assimilationist perspectives are evident in the views of Linda Chavez discussed at the beginning of this chapter, which promote assimilation to hege-monic Americanness through the embrace of the English language. U.S. Latinas'/os' transformation of Mock Spanish into Inverted Spanglish reflects an aware-ness of the racializing forces that position them on the margins of Americanness. These language practices represent a complex set of interrelations among U.S. Latinas/os that must be carefully analyzed in specific ethnographic contexts and the broader scales to which they are linked.

Conclusion

Inverted Spanglish language practices, which in many ways seem strikingly simi-lar to Mock Spanish usages, present neither a straightforward critique of hege-monic whiteness and monolingual English dominance nor a straightforward embrace of these hegemonies. Instead, Latinas/os transform Mock Spanish into Inverted Spanglish in order to meet competing institutional demands that require them to speak Spanish *in* English without being heard to possess an accent. Inverted Spanglish allows Latina/o students to make "the linguistic statement that they have acquired a practical insight or a linguistic mastery of their socio-linguistic environment" (Jaspers 2005, 296). In order to gain insight into these interactional dynamics, both Mock Spanish and Inverted Spanglish usages must be analyzed in context, with a specific focus on the racialization of U.S. Latinas/os. The failure to do so leads to the conflation of U.S. Latinas/os with categories such as "historically Spanish-speaking populations" and "Spanish persons."

My analysis of Inverted Spanglish is not intended to provide a general model of English-Spanish bilingualism among students at NNHS. There were many other ways in which students moved within and between varieties of English and Spanish, many of which mirrored existing accounts of monolingual style-shifting and bilingual codeswitching. My research highlights the ways that NNHS students not only navigated but also transformed linguistic boundaries. This perspective presents an analytical framework that can be used to under-stand the translingual practices of students who might otherwise be approached separately as monolingual or bilingual. The categories of monolingual and bilin-gual were crucial inside NNHS. Depending on the variety, language ideologies in this context positioned monolingual English speech as a sign of deviance (i.e., monolingual nonstandard English) or selling out (i.e., monolingual standard English). Meanwhile, monolingual Spanish speech was often viewed as uncool and a barrier to full participation in everyday school life. Inverted Spanglish resolves this bind by voicing in-group knowledge of Spanish and English, while simultaneously parodying the category of Young Latino Professional.

It is important to locate the category Young Latino Professional in relation to Linda Chavez's discussion of assimilation, language, and Hispanic/American identity with which this chapter began. For Chavez, assimilation is a straightforward matter of self-identification as American or Hispanic, and English is a straightforward sign of assimilation to normative Americanness. The comparison that Chavez draws between Latinas/os and earlier waves of predominantly European immigrants overlooks the ways that European immigrants came to be racialized as White and included in hegemonic constructions of Americanness. Thus, assimilation is not simply a matter of self-identification, but instead a reflection of structural inequalities that position populations as more or less ideally American regardless of their self-identification. For U.S. Latinas/os, these inequalities are reflected in housing, employment, health care, education, and criminal justice. An embrace of the English language has done little to guarantee equal access to these institutional settings for the millions of U.S. Latinas/os, any more than other racialized peoples who identify as monolingual English speakers yet still face profound experiences of exclusion. Thus, we must pay close attention to the racialization of U.S. Latinas'/os' Spanish- *and* English-language use. This involves a critique of the promotion of English-language learning as the magic bullet that will eradicate Latina/o societal marginalization, as well as a critique of assimilation more broadly as a racializing process that ranks groups as more and less worthy of full citizenship.

This chapter demonstrates the complex relationship between language ideologies, linguistic forms, and power-laden cultural contexts of usage. It also questions racialized assumptions about U.S. Latina/o ethnolinguistic authenticity and stigmatization. U.S. Latinas'/os' naturalized relationship to the Spanish language highlights ways that "authenticity" can simultaneously valorize and stigmatize languages and their speakers in specific cultural contexts. Inverted Spanglish, despite all its sociolinguistic complexity and savvy, is by no means a straightforward signal of one's institutionally sanctioned Latina/o personhood. The language ideologies and linguistic practices analyzed in this chapter raise new questions about relationships between ethnolinguistic and ethnoracial categories. Future research focused on these issues must track the ways that minute linguistic forms are aligned with ethnoracial categories across contexts and scales. Such an approach will make it possible to analyze the ways in which large-scale processes of racialization are made visible—indeed audible—in everyday interactions.

Notes

1. Throughout this chapter, I use the terms "Latina/o," "Latinas/os," and "Hispanic" interchangeably to refer to U.S.-based persons of Latin American descent. This is how these terms were conventionally used in the ethnographic context that is the focus of this chapter.

Chavez has served as part of various Republican presidential administrations and currently authors a weekly syndicated column that circulates nationally. Her column can be accessed here: http://www.dallasnews.com/opinion/latest-columns/20120405-linda-chavez-why-so-few-latinos-id-themselves-first-as-american.ece.

2. The names of the school and individuals associated with it are pseudonyms to protect anonymity.

3. Students are coded using abbreviations of self-ascribed Latina/o national subgroup categories such as "Mexican" (Mex) and "Puerto Rican" (PR), as well as generation cohort with respect to (im)migration and grade year in school. For example:

Pedro (PR, Gen. 3, Gr. 10)
Name (self-ascribed identity, immigration cohort, grade year)
Generation 1: born and raised outside of the U.S. mainland until the age of 12 or older
Generation 1.5: born outside of the U.S. mainland, but raised within the U.S. mainland before the age of 12
Generation 2: born and raised within the U.S. mainland by parents who were born and raised outside of the U.S. mainland
Generation 3: born and raised within the U.S. mainland by parents who were born and raised within the U.S. mainland

I use the phrase "U.S. mainland" to distinguish between the continental United States and its territories and possessions; Puerto Rico is a U.S. Commonwealth. Thus, someone born in Puerto Rico is born "outside of the U.S. mainland." This allows for a unified designation for people born in Puerto Rico or anywhere else in Latin America.

4. Mayra provided other examples such as *pato*, which is Puerto Rican slang for "gay," but simply means "duck" in Mexican Spanish; she also pointed out the counterexample of *puñal*, which means "gay" in Mexican slang, but simply means "knife" in Puerto Rican Spanish.

5. Inverted Spanglish usages are bolded, italicized, and transcribed informally in English for nonlinguists, followed by phonetic transcriptions in brackets. The corresponding Spanish versions of these usages are also presented with Spanish phonology, written with Spanish orthography, and translated into English. For example:

numerow trace [numɜ˞ɹou treɪs] (Spanish, [numeɾo tɾeis], *numero tres*, number three).

6. One student told me about an uncle of his from Puerto Rico who got into a fight with his Mexican employer who called him a *cabrón* (bastard). The inversion of *cabrón* from an insult to a compliment was not communicated in the shift from Mexican Spanish to Puerto Rican Spanish. The use of *cabrón* in unaccented Spanglish avoids these conflicts.

References

Alim, H. Samy. 2004. *You Know My Steez: An Ethnographic and Sociolinguistic Study of Styleshifting in a Black American Speech Community*. Durham, NC: Duke University Press.

Anzaldúa, Gloria. 1987. *Borderlands/La Frontera*. San Francisco, CA: Aunt Lute Books.

Barrett, Rusty. 2006. "Language Ideology and Racial Inequality: Competing functions of Spanish in an Anglo-Owned Mexican Restaurant." *Language in Society* 35(2): 163–204.

Bourdieu, Pierre. 1991. *Language and Symbolic Power*. Cambridge, MA: Harvard University Press.

Bucholtz, Mary. 2009. From Stance to Style: Gender, Interaction, and Indexicality in Mexican Immigrant Youth Slang. In A. Jaffe, ed. *Stance: Sociolinguistic Perspectives*, 146–70. Oxford: Oxford University Press.

Chavez, Linda. 2012. "Why so few Latinos ID themselves first as 'American.' *Dallas News*. http://www.dallasnews.com/opinion/latest-columns/20120405-linda-chavez-why-so-few-latinos-id-themselves-first-as-american.ece. Accessed June 30, 2013.

De Genova, Nicholas, and Ana Y. Ramos-Zayas. 2003. *Latino Crossings: Mexicans, Puerto Ricans, and the Politics of Race and Citizenship.* New York: Routledge.

Flores, Nelson and J. Rosa. 2015. "Undoing Appropriateness: Raciolinguistic Ideologies and Language Diversity in Education." *Harvard Educational Review,* 85(2): 149–71.

Hill, Jane H. 1998. "Language, Race, and White Public Space." *American Anthropologist* 100(3): 680–89.

Hill, Jane H. 2005. "Intertextuality as Source and Evidence for Indirect Indexical Meanings." *Journal of Linguistic Anthropology.* 15(1): 113–24.

Hill, Jane H. 2008. *The Everyday Language of White Racism.* Malden, MA: Wiley-Blackwell.

Jaspers, Jürgen. 2005. "Linguistic Sabotage in a Context of Monolingualism and Standardization." *Language & Communication* 25: 279–927.

Mason Carris, Lauren. 2011. "La Voz Gringa: Latino Stylization of Linguistic (In)Authenticity as Social Critique." *Discourse & Society* 22(4): 474–90.

Morales, Ed. 2002. *Living in Spanglish.* New York: St. Martin's Griffin.

Rodríguez, Richard. 1982. *Hunger of Memory: The Education of Richard Rodriguez.* Boston: D. R. Godine.

Rosa, Jonathan. 2014a. "Learning Ethnolinguistic Borders: Language and Diaspora in the Socialization of U.S. Latinas/os." In *Diaspora Studies in Education: Towards a Framework for Understanding the Experiences of Transnational Communities,* edited by Rosalie Rolón Dow and Jason G. Irizarry, 39–60. New York: Peter Lang.

Rosa, Jonathan. 2014b. "Language as a Sign of Immigration?" *American Anthropologist* 116(1): 11–12.

Silverstein, Michael. 2003. "The Whens and Wheres—as well as Hows—of Ethnolinguistic Recognition." *Public Culture* 15(3): 531–57.

Smitherman, Geneva. 1994. *Black Talk: Words and Phrases from the Hood to the Amen Corner.* Boston: Houghton Mifflin.

Zentella, Ana Celia. 2003. "'José, Can You See?' Latin@ Responses to Racist Discourse." In *Bilingual aesthetics,* edited by Doris Sommer. Durham, NC: Duke University Press.

Zentella, Ana Celia. 2009[2002]. "Latin@ Languages and Identities." In *Latinos: Remaking America,* edited by Marcelo M. Suárez-Orozco and Mariela M. Páez, 21–35. Berkeley: University of California Press.

4

The Meaning of *Ching-Chong*

Language, Racism, and Response in New Media

ELAINE W. CHUN

During a two-day period in March 2011, over a million people witnessed a self-described "polite, nice American girl" named Alexandra Wallace engaging in a three-minute monologue of complaint about Asians who lacked American manners. The following excerpt is taken from the climax of this monologue.

Example 1 **Wallace's rant against Asians**

You know what they don't also teach them is their manners, which brings me to my next point. Hi. In America we do not talk on our cell phones in the library, where every five minutes I will be—okay not five minutes, say, like fifteen minutes—I'll be like deep into my studying, into my political science theories and arguments and all that stuff, getting it all down, like typing away furiously, blah blah blah. And then all of sudden, when I'm about to like reach an epiphany, over here from somewhere, "Ooooh. ching-chong? ling-long? ting-tong? Ooooh." Are you freaking kidding me? In the middle of finals week.

This European American student at the University of California, Los Angeles (UCLA) was largely unknown on YouTube prior to her video rant, but she emerged in public space as a captivating example of "white racism" and as the target of mockery in subsequent videos. Her nationwide notoriety as a racist spectacle speaks not only to the cultural reach of new media tools but also to the complex contours of ideologies of language and racism in the United States.

While various factors contributed to interpretations of Wallace's performance as problematic, public discourses often focused on her use of *ching-chong*, a word that straddles an important boundary between "Oriental talk" and English. On the one hand, it represents non-English speech; yet on the other hand, it is composed of English sounds (*ch, i, o, ng*) [tʃ, ɪ, ɑ, ŋ] and follows an English pattern of "antiphony," in which repeated syllables differ by a single vowel. Specifically, the "I" [ɪ] followed by "o" [ɑ] is found in other words of English, such as *ding-dong, king-kong, ping-pong, sing-song, flip-flop, hip-hop, tip-top*, and *tick-tock*.[1] Yet this "bivalent" word (Woolard 1998), which belongs to two languages at once, serves less to disrupt this linguistic boundary than to reify it. *Ching-chong* is the language of racial others, reminding *us* of *their* difference. Wallace's performance thus aligned her with other figures in U.S. popular culture, including Shaquille O'Neal in 2002, Rosie O'Donnell in December 2005, and Rush Limbaugh in January 2011, who have been critiqued as racist users of this word.

Specifically, public responses to the use of *ching-chong*, like that of other pejorative racial terms, have ranged from characterizing the word as racist to denying its status as problematic. Debates have swirled around whether the word should be eradicated, whether it should be allowed but only in special circumstances, and whether users should be condemned. Importantly, these discussions reflect popular ideologies of racist meaning as well as ideologies of language meaning more generally. For example, some have focused on the definition of *ching-chong: What does the word mean?* Others have examined its immediate context of use: *What was the situation? Who was present? What kind of person said it? What was intended?* Still others have focused on the broader socio-cultural context: *What does this say about today's societal beliefs and race relations?* Additionally noteworthy is that these explicit discussions have had a paradoxical effect: they have required *ching-chong*'s repeated "speaking" in order to define it as "unspeakable" (Butler 1997; Fleming and Lempert 2011; Hill 2008), arguably reestablishing a racist tool through the very attempts to dismantle it. In recent years, the effects of such discussions may be intensifying through tools of new media, whether YouTube, Twitter, or Facebook, increasing the speed at which words move across communities. In this pivotal moment of discursive shifts and expansions, a crucial issue to consider is how, if at all, the public should respond.

In this chapter, I thus draw on linguistic and anthropological tools to examine ideologies of racist language in the United States and to explore how responses to *ching-chong* incidents may themselves reflect, reinforce, and shift these ideologies. My analysis focuses primarily on an illustrative subset of the 10,410 viewer comments responding to Wallace's video within the month that followed its posting.[2] I propose two axes of linguistic meaning that inform these public discussions and interpretations of *ching-chong*, namely the *locus* of meaning (where linguistic meaning is located) as well as its *temporality* (when meaning happens). I then discuss how seven antiracist strategies—*eradication, regulation, quotation, euphemism, rehistoricization, reappropriation*, and *satire*—differently foreground these axes of linguistic meaning and variably succeed in achieving antiracist goals. In particular, I show how each of these strategies usefully raises public awareness of racist language but how each also encounters certain important pitfalls.

Ideologies of Language and Racism

This chapter examines ideologies of language and racism, including what scholars refer to as a "folk" perspective (Hill 2008), such as the commonly espoused notion that racism is embedded either in people's minds (e.g., conscious and unconscious beliefs about racial inferiority) or in specific words (e.g., racial epithets and code words). Yet I also address ideologies among scholars themselves, who typically understand racism to be a cultural, structural project: racism is maintained through institutional and everyday practices that reproduce racial hierarchies (Hill 2008). My own view aligns with this latter perspective, but I also believe that "scholarly theories" are not wholly separable from "folk beliefs." I regard it as important to delineate the similarities and differences between various cultural theories of language and meaning when considering antiracist responses to racist language.

As such, the first part of my analysis illustrates how interpretations of racism in language, among scholars and nonscholars alike, reflect diverse assumptions about how language relates to meaning more generally. These assumptions can be described in terms of two basic axes (Figure 4.1). The first (horizontal) axis

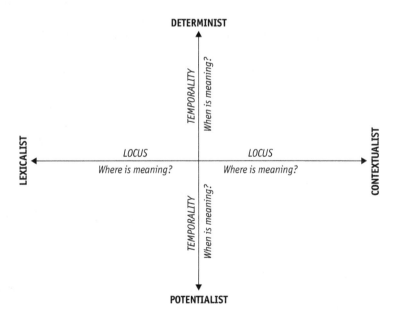

Figure 4.1 Two axes of language meaning.

addresses the issue of *where* linguistic meaning lies (*locus of meaning*), namely whether meaning is embedded in words themselves (*lexicalism*) or whether it depends on the contexts in which these words are used (*contextualism*). The second (vertical) axis concerns the issue of *when* meaning happens (*temporality of meaning*), that is, whether meaning is fixed (*determinism*) or whether it is necessarily open to change (*potentialism*).

Axis of Locus: Where Is Racist Meaning?

Our claims about whether language is racist can vary in terms of where we assume meaning to lie. Under a view of lexicalism, the locus of meaning is the linguistic form itself as each form is tightly linked to its semantics; each word carries a set of true meanings. When Alexandra Wallace uttered *ching-chong*, it was interpreted as Mock Asian (Chun 2004), or a mimicry of the speech of East Asians, and the racism of her performance was understood as embedded, at least in part, in the "racist" word itself. While *ching-chong* remains absent from widely used English dictionaries, it is more extensively recognized among English speakers than many obscure words that do appear, given that it circulates widely in everyday public encounters among youth in multiethnic communities. It is due to the cultural recognizability of the word as a vessel of racist meaning that public discourses can erupt when it is used in public space.

Interestingly, the perceived racism of *ching-chong* also derives from a particular brand of lexicalism that scholars refer to as "referentialism" (Hill 2008), according to which words count as words only as long as they have semantic reference (Samuels 2004), subsequently becoming listable in a dictionary and usable in a game of Scrabble.[3] Under this view, *ching-chong* has a questionable status as a "real" word: it conveys linguistic sounds yet remains void of semantic meaning, similar to speech-based onomatopoeias such as *blah-blah-blah* and *yada-yada-yada*. By lying at the boundary between sense and nonsense, it transgresses the boundaries of real, meaningful language. Yet more similar to forms such as *derka-derka* and *click-clack*, used in U.S. popular culture to represent the "otherness" of Arabic and African languages respectively, *ching-chong* remains outside real language as well as subordinate to it. As such, it iconically conveys Asian "inscrutability," invoking an American Orientalism, whereby "the East" is imagined as racially and linguistically alien (Said 1978).

Adopting this belief, a large number of YouTube commenters pointed to the inauthenticity of *ching-chong* as meaningful words of Chinese, implying that its linguistic inauthenticity was the source of its racist status.

Example 2 **Ching-chong** as inauthentic Chinese

COMMENTER	COMMENT
brittxlin	Asians don't speak like ching chang chong, it's more complex then that you ugly piece of shit.
chazferrari	btw WE ASIANS DON'T SPEAK CHING CHANG CHONG!
MYMProcks	chinese people don't speak ching chong chang whatever you just said. you dumb ass!

Commenters' interpretation of *ching-chong* as a racist insult can be inferred from their confrontational tone. In the first example, brittxlin notes that "it's more complex [than ching chang chong]" and then adds "you ugly piece of shit," an insult that presumably reciprocates Wallace's prior insult. Additionally, chazferrari and MYMProcks also use exclamation points and uppercase letters, conveying the kind of heightened emotion that a racist act might provoke.[4]

An ideology of contextualism, on the other hand, takes a very different view, privileging the surrounding context—whether the situation, speaker, or culture—as the locus of linguistic meaning. Those who defend cases of "racist" language often appeal to this view, noting that the usage was "funny" rather than "racist," thus distinguishing between situational contexts that orient to humor from those that orient to insult. Wallace herself appealed to a contextualist ideology when she defended herself in a press release: "In an attempt to produce a humorous YouTube video, I have offended the UCLA community and the entire Asian culture" (Parkinson-Morgan 2011). While YouTube is an online space in which humor is frequently performed, most viewers rejected her defense, since her use of *ching-chong* was embedded in a presumably serious rant rather than playful humor. This ideology of contextualism is also at play above (Example 2) in which brittxlin, chazferrari, and MYMProcks each use a potentially racist term without risk of being accused of being racist themselves; the situational and interactional context of interpretation—that is, their frame (Goffman 1974)—clearly diverges from Wallace's.

A related contextual factor when interpreting a linguistic act concerns the speaker. Scholars describe this specific contextualist ideology as "personalism," or the idea that the beliefs, intentions, and qualities of a speaker are central to what gives words their meaning (Hill 2008). Wallace's self-defense, in fact, additionally invoked this contextual dimension by suggesting that her intent (implied by her use of the term "attempt") had been to be humorous. In her press release, she further conveyed a morally upright persona by claiming sincere regret: "I am truly sorry for the hurtful words I said" (Parkinson-Morgan 2011).

While Wallace drew on this personalist-contextualist ideology to defend herself, it was primarily adopted by Wallace's critics, who characterized her words as racist by depicting her as a morally deficient individual. According to this ideology, the morality of speakers is inseparable from the meanings that emerge from their mouths: good people say good things; bad people say bad things. In addition to being directly described as racist, Wallace was often critiqued as ignorant and promiscuous.

Example 3 **Wallace as a morally deficient person**

Ignorant (236 comments)
she's ignorant
she's a fucking idiot
she's just a dumb blonde!

Promiscuous (45 comments)
She is just plain WHORE-ible.
She must've sucked alot of dick to get into UCLA
I think she slept with the dean to get into UCLA.

Racist (40 comments)
she's a racist
She's definitely racist.
she's hitler.

Importantly, commenters' characterizations of Wallace as immoral were not exclusively based on antiracist ideologies. Rather, commenters invoked highly problematic racist and sexist ideologies in order to depict Wallace as immoral on the basis of her presumed intellectual deficiency and sexual promiscuity, characteristics that derive from a stereotype of young, white femininity ("the vacuous Valley Girl"). Commenters also presume a sexist ideology according to which female sexuality must be critiqued and controlled, in this case because of its threat as an immoral tool of manipulation ("sle[eping] with the dean to get into UCLA").

In addition to situational and personal contexts, the broader cultural context may be invoked when interpreting language meaning: institutional and everyday discourses about race. This is a perspective that many scholars, including myself, have taken. According to this view, the use of *ching-chong* is inseparable from how Asians have been historically represented in

U.S. mainstream discourses. Discourses of Asian "foreignness" unsurprisingly emerged in some comments.

Example 4 **Discourses of Asians as "foreign"**

COMMENTER	COMMENT
frigginfreddy	Despite the Valley Girl delivery, she is right on. Foreigners need to learn and practice OUR ways. They are fortunate to be here, show it by respecting our culture.
bunniesgopop	if u foreigners hate americans, especially after this video: Go TO YOUR OWN FUCKING COUNTRY. this girl has the right to express her feelings and plus SHE WAS BORN HERE.
trailblazer225	Agreed! Enough is enough!! Foreigners who come here NEED to learn to respect the American culture! Period. Or, go back to where they came from and disrespect their own culture and fellow citizens.

Yet as seen in the following set, some comments invoked this same discourse in order to critique it as problematic.

Example 5 **Counterdiscourses to Asians as "foreign"**

COMMENTER	COMMENT
xbluanchovyx	Not All Asian are foreign some of us are born here.
Sugar0Tits0	There is no such thing as american manners. This is a country that is made up of foreigners, which also include white americans who have european ancestry.
kayla13311	this is why I hate some white people . . . they treat us as if we're foreigners . . . I was born and raised in amerca, I'm as american as you people, so don't always point out that we're asian. fucking racist cunts

---

Axis of Temporality: When Is Racist Meaning?

A second axis of meaning concerns when racist meaning takes place. In the examples presented thus far, debates about whether Wallace's act was racist focus on linguistic and contextual dimensions that have contributed to shaping the act's meaning. According to this determinist ideology, linguistic meaning derives from an identifiable source, or set of sources, whether the word (lexicalism), the context (contextualism), or some combination of the two. While a linguistic act's meaning can be complex because of multiple sources of determination, such as the simultaneous presence of relevant linguistic, situational, personal, and cultural factors, each linguistic act is defined by determinable, preexisting realities. Discussions that focus on whether a racist act "is" or "isn't" racist take this perspective.

In contrast to a determinist ideology, a potentialist perspective, which I adopt here, focuses on the potential effects of language use as part of its meaning. This perspective overlaps with what Hill (2008) refers to as a "performativitist" ideology, drawing on J. L. Austin's (1975) understanding of how speech acts have real-world consequences. Under this view, linguistic interpretation must consider the effects of a linguistic act, such as the kind of personal injury that may result or the increasing recognizability of language over time. Meaning is not limited to predefined linguistic or contextual factors but is necessarily mutable and partly unpredictable (Butler 1997); words not only shape the very contexts they newly enter but also become newly shaped themselves. A potentialist perspective thus considers language meanings in terms of their possible trajectories over time and space, as well as the linguistic and social consequences of this trajectory.

Commenters' descriptions of language as potentially "hurtful" or "offensive" partly adopt this ideology; words are problematically racist if they cause harm to people, according to the following examples.

Example 6 **Racism defined by hurtfulness**

COMMENTER	COMMENT
eleanorhel-enakwan	even if you didnt mean to sound racist, or to offend anyone . . . the things you said DOES offend people. it makes you look like an idiot.
liltabajudna	Cmon if your gonna say that dont say it on YouTube because that can hurt people i was very offended by this
Spotook	My God how rude!!!! Ching Chong ling long ting ton? Seriously. . . . . . . I am Asian and I am very offended by this . . . . How can't she not see this is offensive????

As seen in these three cases, Wallace's performance is defined as racist because of the offense that resulted. For commenters such as eleanorhelenakwan, Wallace's intended meaning, as might be considered from a determinist perspective, was less important ("even if you didnt mean to sound racist") than the consequences of her language use. The result was not only personal offense ("the things [she] said DOES offend people") but also Wallace's tarnishing of her own reputation ("it makes [her] look like an idiot"). Similarly, commenter liltabajudna frames Wallace's act as a personal offense ("i was very offended by this"), and Spotook notes her own racial identity ("I am Asian") to claim the legitimacy of her interpretation that Wallace has offended her ("and I am very offended by this"), noting the transparency of this interpretation ("How can't she not see this is offensive????").

Responding to *Ching-Chong*: Strategies of Antiracism

In both scholarly and popular discussions of racist words, numerous strategies have been proposed to curtail their potentially racist effects. In the rest of this chapter, I describe some key strategies that antiracists have offered in response to racist language, and I discuss how lexicalist, contextualist, determinist, and potentialist ideologies underlie them. By making explicit popular assumptions about language meaning, I wish to illuminate the ideologies that we may

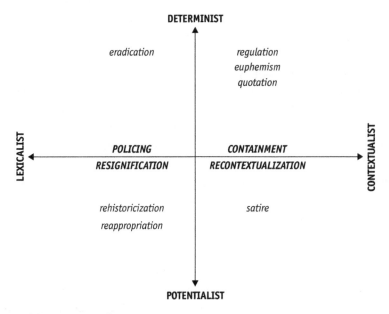

Figure 4.2 Strategies of antiracism.

reproduce in engaging in these strategies as well as their potential effectiveness as antiracist practice.

Any antiracist strategy necessarily orients, at least in part, to a potentialist ideology by assuming that the effects of racist acts can be subverted; the racist act itself is never the final act of discourse. Yet most are also heavily determinist in their assumption that meaning is more fixed than fluid. In Figure 4.2, I present four sets of strategies. The upper-left quadrant includes a *policing* strategy (*eradication*), the upper-right quadrant includes three *containment* strategies (*regulation, euphemism,* and *quotation*), the lower-left quadrant includes two *resignification* strategies (*rehistoricization* and *reappropriation*), and the lower-right quadrant includes a *recontextualization* strategy (*satire*).

Determinist Strategies: Policing and Containment

Two sets of strategies presume language meaning to be largely fixed. The first is policing, which involves the complete authoritative control of language use. Eradication, which is a kind of policing, assumes that racist meaning is located so centrally in words—that is, words are weighed down by unshakable "baggage"—that "all uses . . . are wrongful and hurtful" (Kennedy 2003, 126), regardless of the context of usage. As such, the only solution is the banishment of racist words, or "verbal hygiene" (Cameron 1995). Perhaps the most recognizable object of eradicationists' focus in U.S. public discourse has been the slur *nigger*, which is typically viewed as risking a racist interpretation—of lexical "leakage" (Hill and Irvine 1993)—regardless of how careful its packaging, for example, within the quoted speech of another speaker in a printed essay on language. Given the inseparability of sound and meaning in this case, the utterance of similar-sounding terms can even be interpreted as racist practice, as evidenced by the public debate that erupted after the word *niggardly* was used by a European American mayoral aide in the presence of an African American aide (Hill 2008; Woodlee 1999). Similarly, the symbolic "burial" of the term *nigger* at the National Association for the Advancement of Colored People (NAACP) Convention in 2007, which called on people to put an end to this term's usage in any form, suggested that racist meanings were encapsulated in words themselves (Williams 2007).

Another set of determinist strategies are those that may permit the use of words linked to racism as long as they are placed in a "safe" context. One such strategy of containment (Irvine 2011) is language regulation, as seen in hate speech codes that typically recognize that context plays a role in shaping language meaning. As noted by Kennedy, regulationists draw a distinction between the use of racial terms "as insult" and their use as in-group "affection" or "word play" (126). A second containment strategy is euphemism, or the replacement of a tabooed term with a non-tabooed one (e.g., *n-word*), though still making reference to the tabooed term. A final strategy of containment is quotation, or the use of a term as belonging to another speaker (e.g., "Wallace said *ching-chong*"); when potentially racist words are quoted, they may be regarded as occupying a safe space that precludes racist intepretation.

While policing and containment practices are often used to take antiracist stances, it is unclear how effective they are as antiracist strategies. On the one hand, these strategies may be successful to the extent that they align with popular ideologies of racist meaning as determined by words and their contexts. On the other hand, determinist strategies necessarily ignore potential linguistic consequences. First, restrictions on a word's usage through eradicationism can potentially endow an unspeakable word with greater potency when it becomes spoken. Second, even when words are "safely" contained in euphemisms or quotations, "unsafe" racist meanings are always lurking in "safe" contexts and may potentially "leak" into those contexts (Hill and Irvine 1993). Finally, explicit prohibitions are likely to be viewed by many as incompatible with ideologies of free speech, as reflected in the U.S. legal system (Kennedy 2003), generating debate about whether problematic terms should be restricted, and if so, in which contexts (Butler 1997; Hill 2008). In other words, from a potentialist perspective, one can see how the power, preoccupation, and proliferation of racist words may intensify through attempts to police or contain them.

Potentialist Strategies: Resignification and Recontextualization

Another set of strategies adopts the view that meanings are not fixed but emergent through new uses over time and space. Such strategies thus attempt to steer linguistic trajectories, either by endowing words with new meanings (resignification) or shaping new contexts through the use of these words (recontextualization). A prominent resignification strategy in public settings is that of reappropriation, through which speakers who belong to the targeted racial group use the derogatory word in a nonderogatory sense. It is believed that such in-group usage will incrementally "defang" words of their negative connotations, ultimately reshaping the lexical content of the word itself. This strategy can be witnessed in the in-group usage of terms such as *nigger, chink,* and *fob* ("fresh-off-the-boat" Asian immigrants), which are sometimes used endearingly by African Americans and Asian Americans,[5] respectively.

This particular strategy has both potential and limitations. Its potential lies in its recognition of the performative nature of language; as noted by Butler (1997), language includes both its use and its consequences. Under this view, words endowed with hegemonic meanings can subsequently enter an "unanticipated political future for deconstructive thinking" (161). A commonly cited example is the term *queer*, reappropriated by those who reject heterosexist ideologies, despite once reflecting these ideologies; the term has thus moved from serving as a homophobic epithet to a potentially nonderogatory descriptor used in scholarly and public discourse (e.g., the academic field of queer theory and the television show *Queer Eye for the Straight Guy*). Yet similar examples of reappropriation are scarce, given that the success of this strategy depends on the authority of a marginalized group to persuade the public of its resignified usage. In the case of *queer*, reappropriation seems to have been possible because other existing slurs (e.g., *fag* or *dyke*) more saliently serve heterosexist functions; that is, the struggle over the usage of *queer* is less contentious than *nigger* and *chink*, which serve as "the" prevailing terms of racist derogation in public space.

Interestingly, a complementary strategy of resignification moves in the other direction, shifting the lexical content of a word toward, rather than away from, its negative connotations by providing a narrative of racist lexical origins. This strategy of rehistoricization is often adopted by scholars who claim the authority to excavate linguistic histories. An example of this strategy can be seen when the verb *gyp*, commonly used to mean "to cheat," is identified as deriving from a racist stereotype of gypsies as swindlers (e.g., Davidson 1973, 83), or when the term *squaw* is defined as a "destructive slur [that] dates back at least 150 years" (Hill 2008, 59), contrary to the "mistaken" belief that it is a "technically correct expression" for a Native American woman (62). Likewise, in my own work, I have drawn upon this strategy of rehistoricization by citing historical evidence that *ching-chong* appeared in the genre of childhood rhymes as early as the late nineteenth century. According to historian Henry Carrington Bolton, some children's counting-out rhymes (e.g., "*Ching, Chong, Chineeman, Oh! that is too dear! Ching, Chong, Chineeman, Clear right out of here!*") reflected prevailing anti-Asian sentiment on the Pacific Coast. Rehistoricization strategies assume that producing public knowledge of links to racist historical origins, words such as *gyp*, *squaw*, and *ching-chong*, will eventually become unacceptable in public space.

Finally, I discuss the potentialist strategy of recontextualization, which alters the ideological context of usage, that is, the ideological assumptions that underlie linguistic meaning. Unlike the strategies mentioned earlier, it is an indirect strategy of political or cultural persuasion that does not directly shape lexical meanings or cultural contexts, but indirectly—and thus perhaps seductively—encourages listeners to align with antiracist assumptions. This strategy was exemplified when Yao Ming, a rookie star from China in the National Basketball

Association, responded to reports of *ching-chong* mockery by Shaquille O'Neal, a seasoned star who is African American. Yao was reported as having playfully said, "Chinese is hard to learn. I had trouble with it when I was little" (January 10, 2003, Associated Press), playfully transforming O'Neal into an aspiring student of Chinese. Yao's tongue-in-cheek response managed to indirectly critique O'Neal's act, based on the public presupposition of its racism, thus reinforcing the public's antiracist stance.

A related strategy of recontexualization is satire, or an artfully playful parody serving as moral cultural critique (Gray et al. 2009). Four days after Wallace's video, Jimmy Wong, an Asian American man in his early twenties, posted a folksy love ballad video as a satirical response, playfully translating *ching-chong* as words of romance ("I love you").

Example 7 **Wong's love ballad to Wallace**

1   ((Speaking)) Ew Alexandra Wallace. Damn girl you so feisty. You so feisty they should call you Alexandra Great Wall. Ace.

2   Now don't pretend I didn't see you watch me talk on my phone yesterday. All sexy. **Ching-chong wing-wong**.

3   Baby it's all just code. It's the way I tell the ladies it's time to get funky.

4   ((Singing)) I hope one day you can meet my mother, my brothers, sisters, grandmothers, grandpas, and cousins. Ooh.

5   Cause what they're really doing on those Friday nights is showing me how to cook and dress

6   Cause baby I wanna take you out and blow your freakin mind. Eww.

7   And underneath the pounds of makeup and your baby blue eyes

8   I know there's a lot of pain and hurt for such a big brain to spend all night studying poli sci.

9   I pick up my phone and sing

10   **Ching-chong**. It means I love you. **Ling-long**. I really want you. **Ting-tong**. I don't actually know what that means.

11   **Ching-chong**. It's never ending. **Ling-long**. My head is spinning. **Ting-tong**. Still don't know what that means.

Through satire, Wong playfully defines *ching-chong ling-long ting-tong* (lines 10–11), transforming its semantic absence and pejorative connation into semantic presence and sexualized romance ("I love you. . . . I really want you. . . . It's never ending. . . . My head is spinning"). Yet the antiracist effect of his video lies not in sincere lexical redefinition but in the context he created, namely, the set of antiracist cultural assumptions he invoked to achieve humor in his performance (Hill 1998). He never mentioned these assumptions explicitly, but invoked them through ludicrous transformations: a racist rant reimagined as the inspiration for a love ballad, a white racist reimagined as an object of sexual desire, and a victim of racial prejudice reimagined as a womanizing charmer. As in the case of Yao, the implicitness of Wong's critique was important, as it invited listeners to share an assumed antiracist stance in order to understand why he was funny, and his act was unlikely to be rejected as "hypersensitivity," as explicit antiracist discourses sometimes are. The satirical performance served as pointed critique of these implicit racist assumptions, yet his antiracist stance remained shielded from opposition (compare Mitchell-Kernan 1972).

Wong thus depended on the potential for language to take on new meanings; *ching-chong* was not fixed as a racist insult but used here as a tool for critiquing racist ideologies. In addition, his performance was aesthetically sophisticated, showcasing his musical and comical virtuosity and propelling his video across his audience. The video currently has over five million views, and Wong's redefinition of *ching-chong* as "I love you" has been playfully adopted on Urban Dictionary, a popular youth-oriented website where members of the public collaborate on the definition of slang terms. Importantly, his antiracist act took effect not only during the moment of his original performance but also across the millions of moments of its viewing. The immense success of his performance, as a vehicle for aligning the public against Wallace, speaks to satire's potential as a powerful antiracist strategy.

It is important to note, however, that Wong's success in circulating a video that critiqued racism did not preclude his own participation in recirculating racist and sexist representations. Although his purported sexual desire for Wallace, expressed by his plan to "blow [her] freakin mind" (line 6), is clearly tongue-in-cheek, he depends on a stereotype of hypersexualized white femininity by referring to her "pounds of makeup," "baby blue eyes," and "big brain" as a means of discrediting her morality and intellect. Likewise, when he asserts, "Damn girl, you so feisty" (line 1), using the African American address term *girl* and copula (*be*) absence, he potentially invokes a stereotype of black male sexual prowess. In addition, the humor of the stereotype of black masculine excess may derive in part from its ironic juxtaposition with an assumption of Asian masculine inadequacy (Fung 1991). In other words, despite the satirical framing of the images depicted in his performance, racist and sexist ideologies are necessarily invoked and left uncontested.

Conclusion

I have shown how public discourses about *ching-chong*, and other racializing terms, depend on two key axes of language meaning. The first axis concerns where meaning lies and the second concerns when meaning happens. I have suggested that while my own perspective recognizes that language meaning is always shaped by the context of use and that it may often take unpredictable paths, diverse public understandings of racist words, including both "folk" and "scholarly" theories of language (Hill 2008), are important to acknowledge. In addition, by evaluating antiracist strategies in terms of how they engage with these language ideologies, we can explore why certain strategies, such as satire, carry a potential to significantly shift public consciousness, particularly as new media technologies continue to change how we experience words and their meanings. We have seen that in this public space, *ching-chong* may seem bereft of meaning, but it can ultimately bear immensely important and complex cultural significance.

Notes

1. Similarly, *ching-chang-chong*, a variant of *ching-chong*, recalls an alternation pattern characteristic of some English verbs: *sing-sang-sung, ring-rang-rung, swim-swam-swum,* and *drink-drank-drunk.*
2. Wallace's original video, posted on March 11, 2011, was removed two days later (Huffington Post, March 14, 2011), so the comments analyzed in that paper respond to the same video reposted by another YouTube user on March 15, 2011. The reposted video (https://www.youtube.com/watch?v=Johj5WEYzZo) has since been removed.
3. Scholars themselves are not immune to this belief, often providing their own linguistic descriptions that may disprove popular belief but still presume that abstract forms and meanings can be truthfully described.
4. Perhaps it is ironic that each commenter quotes Wallace as having said "ching chang chong," although my own transcription shows "*ching-chong.*" They succeed in displaying Wallace's racism, however, by connecting her speech to a similar form that is also recognized in U.S. culture as racist (see n. 1).
5. The term *fob* is also used among Middle Eastern and North African groups (p.c. H. Samy Alim).

References

Austin, J. L. 1975. *How to Do Things with Words*. Cambridge, MA: Harvard University Press.

Butler, J. 1997. *Excitable Speech: A Politics of the Performative*. New York and London: Routledge.

Cameron, D. 1995. *Verbal Hygiene*. London: Routledge.

Chun, Elaine. 2004. Ideologies of legitimate mockery: Margaret Cho's revoicings of Mock Asian. *Pragmatics* 14: 263–89.

Davidson, G. W. 1973. "GYPSIES": People with a Hidden History. *Soundings: An Interdisciplinary Journal* (56): 83–97.

Fleming, L., and M. Lempert. 2011. Introduction: Beyond Bad Words. *Anthropological Quarterly* (84): 5–13.

Fung, R. 1991. Looking for my penis: The eroticized Asian in gay video porn. In *How Do I Look?: Queer Film and Video,* ed. Bad Object-Choices, Seattle: Bay Press, 145–68.

Goffman, E. 1974. *Frame Analysis: An Essay on the Organization of Experience*. Boston: Northeastern University Press.

Gray, J., J. P. Jones, E. Thompson. 2009. *Satire TV: Politics and Comedy in the Post-Network Era*. New York: New York University Press.

Hill, J. H. 1998. Language, race, and White public space. *American Anthropologist* (100): 680–89.

Hill, J. H. 2008. *The Everyday Language of White Racism*. Malden, MA: Wiley-Blackwell.

Hill, J. H., and J. T. Irvine. 1993. Introduction. In *Responsibility and Evidence in Oral Discourse*, ed. J. H. Hill. Cambridge: Cambridge University Press, 1–23.

Huffington Post. 2011. Alexandra Wallace, UCLA Student, Films Racist Rant. *Huffington Post*, March 14.

Irvine, J. T. 2011. Leaky Registers and Eight-Hundred-Pound Gorillas. *Anthropological Quarterly* (84): 15–39.

Kennedy, R. 2003. *Nigger: The Strange Career of a Troublesome Word*. New York: Vintage.

Mitchell-Kernan, C. 1972. Signifying and marking: Two Afro-American speech acts. In *Directions in Sociolinguistics: The Ethnography of Communication*, ed. J. J. Gumperz and D. H. Hymes. New York: Holt, Rinehart & Winston, 161–79.

Parkinson-Morgan, K. 2011. Alexandra Wallace apologizes, announces she will no longer attend UCLA. *Daily Bruin*, March 18, University of California, Los Angeles.

Said, E. W. 1978. *Orientalism*. New York: Pantheon.

Samuels, D. 2004. Language, meaning, modernity, and doowop. *Semiotica* (149): 297–323.

Williams, C.2007. NAACP Symbolically Buries N-Word. *Washington Post*, July 9.

Woodlee, Y. 1999. D.C. Mayor Acted "Hastily," Will Rehire Aide. *Washington Post*, February 4.

Woolard, K. A. 1998. Simultaneity and bivalency as strategies in bilingualism. *Journal of Linguistic Anthropology* (8): 3–29.

5

"Suddenly Faced with a Chinese Village"

The Linguistic Racialization of Asian Americans

ADRIENNE LO

In recent years, glowing portraits of Asian American immigrants have circulated widely in the American press. "Not only are Asian Americans the fastest-growing racial group in the country, but they have the highest incomes, are the best-educated and are happier with their lot in life compared with other groups," announced the *San Francisco Chronicle* in October 2012 (Garofoli 2012). Building upon a Pew Research Center report noting that the number of immigrants from Asia who arrived in the United States in 2010 surpassed the number of Latino immigrants that year ("The Rise of Asian Americans," cited in Garofoli 2012), several articles have contrasted these two groups. For example, one *Wall Street Journal* (WSJ) article cast Latinos in the image of an "unstoppable wave of unskilled, mostly Spanish-speaking workers—many illegal." For the WSJ (and many others; see chapters 3 and 18, this volume), Latinos embodied widespread anxieties that "today's immigrants" were "less ambitious, less skilled, less willing and able to assimilate." Asian Americans were instead depicted as the polar opposite of Latinos: "The world's best, the world's hardest-working and the world's most ambitious are still coming our way" (Mead 2012). The Pew report itself celebrated this image of Asian Americans as the "model minority," celebrating measures of income, intermarriage, and residential patterns as evidence of their assimilation:

> A century ago, most Asian-Americans were low-skilled, low-wage laborers crowded into ethnic enclaves and targets of official discrimination. Today they are the most likely of any major racial or ethnic group in America to live in mixed neighborhoods and to marry across racial lines. ("The Rise of Asian Americans" 2012, 1)

As scholars of race have noted, discourses like these, which pit Asian Americans against Latinos and African Americans, divert attention away from the structural forces of White racism that underlie racial inequalities (Abelmann and Lie 1995; Kim 1999; Palumbo-Liu 1999; Prashad 2000). By framing the racialization of Asian Americans as a thing of the distant past and no longer present today, such narratives imagine Asian Americans as "honorary Whites" (Tuan 1998). When contemporary racial discrimination is acknowledged at all in these depictions, it is often cast as something that is on the verge of disappearing.

But does this idyllic portrait of wealthy, happy, high-achieving, educationally successful, fully assimilated Asian Americans actually describe what life is like on the ground? As research in Asian American studies has demonstrated, the fact that Asian Americans have largely achieved parity with Whites in arenas like educational achievement can be read as a *response* to racialization, not as evidence of its absence (Sue and Okazaki 1990; Suzuki 1977). Indeed, relatively little work has explored the lives of those who seem to have all of the stereotypical qualities of the "model minority." Instead, researchers have attempted to document the broad socioeconomic, ethnic, religious, and cultural diversity of those who are lumped together under the term "Asian American" (Espiritu 2003; Ong 2003; Reyes 2007). In this chapter, I look specifically at the experiences of suburban, upper-middle-class Asian Americans who were living in a community in California that I call Laurelton.

I argue that Asian Americans were strongly racialized by White residents through language, as Whites positioned Asian Americans discursively as racial others, while interpreting their linguistic production through racializing frames. This work builds upon research in linguistic anthropology, which has looked at how racialization can manifest through subtle discursive patterns, not simply in words that are, in and of themselves, considered "racist" (Alim and Smitherman 2012; Bucholtz 2011; Chun 2009; Hill 2008; Reyes 2007). I consider the interworkings of race and language at two levels. First, I examine how Whites located themselves and Asian Americans in moral and social space through talk about "newcomers" and "oldtimers." At the discursive level, these forms of covert racialization situated Asian Americans as illegitimate, peripheral members of the community and centered Whites as legitimate residents. Asian Americans who fit the model minority stereotype, and who are often imagined as leading fully assimilated lives, are covertly racialized through discourses about language. Through their pronoun use and the ways that they associated categories like "Asian," "newcomer," and "oldtimer" with moral positions, Whites portrayed themselves as the rightful, central members of Laurelton.

I examine how Whites read the linguistic production of Asian Americans, interpreting their language use as an emblem of their foreignness. This ethnographic approach illustrates the fact that class does not always trump race, as upper-middle-class Asian Americans who lived near Whites did not find themselves especially welcomed by them. I argue that linguistic racialization is central to analyzing the place of Asian Americans in the changing American racial landscape. Popular culture imagines Asian Americans as essentially White. On the ground, however, Whites in Laurelton strenuously distanced themselves from Asian Americans through language.

White Raciolinguistic Imaginaries: How White Americans Imagine Asian Americans and "Their Language"

Images of Asian Americans and their linguistic production have been extensively investigated in scholarly research on race and racism. Robert Park's (1950) influential work on assimilation, for example, read group processes of assimilation through a family narrative of the Oriental parent and child (Yu 2001). In this downscaling project, the centuries-old dichotomy of Asians as both "dangerous threat" and "inspirational model" in the gaze of the West (Clarke 1997; Said 1978) is mapped onto immigrant parents and second-generation children. In his model, language was the key criterion that Whites could use to tell one kind of Asian American from the other. Since outward signs were unreliable (the "mask of the Oriental"), with clothing and the like being read as only "costumes" or "disguises," spoken English became the definitive sign that Whites could rely upon to distinguish unassimilated Asian Americans from assimilated ones.

Park's theory of assimilation is thus centered not just on the figure of the Asian American but specifically upon their *linguistic* signaling as perceived by Whites. These two figures—the immigrant who will never lose her grating accent and the descendant of immigrants whose English supposedly bears no trace of accent—embody both the totalizing power and transcendence of a core linguistic ideology. It is an ideology that associates "standard" English with White speakers and nonstandard varieties of English with racialized speakers (Bonfiglio 2002; Jones 1999; Lippi-Green 1997). This "passage" from accented speaker of a vernacular form of English to speaker of an impeccable standard (Gal 2012) positions the family as a crucible of language learning. It further defines language as a kind of racialized inheritance, illustrating how raciolinguistic imaginaries anchor the theory of assimilation.

The Idyllic Suburb?

Laurelton was the kind of place many immigrants hope to live in. It had comfortable tree-lined streets, generous playgrounds and parks, and a thriving public school system. The prototypical Laurelton household was a two-parent, dual-income family with school-aged children. While many Laurelton residents spoke of a sharp change in demographics (pointing to the fact that the percentage of Whites had declined from over 90% to near 50% over the past thirty years), this was only the latest in successive waves of immigration over the past few hundred years. Some moved to the area when it was a flourishing agricultural region; others came in the post–World War II era, when modest California bungalows, condos, and apartments replaced farms. Many arrived when the low-priced starter homes of the fifties and sixties had risen in value and had become highly desirable.

The high housing prices in Laurelton meant that most of its residents were well-paid professionals. Laurelton was adjacent both to more upscale communities and to less upscale ones, and it bordered several communities with greater racial diversity. The majority of its residents were White or Asian American. I lived in a (less upscale) community adjacent to Laurelton from 2001 to 2004 and watched as racial dynamics helped fuel White flight from Laurelton and from its schools. As Asian Americans became increasingly visible in Laurelton's political, civic, and commercial arenas, the community gained a reputation among some Whites for being "too Asian." Some local White realtors began to steer White home-buyers away, recommending other nearby communities where they might feel more "comfortable." The Asian Americans who lived in Laurelton were, demographically speaking, "model minorities." They were, for the most part, well-educated, professional, dual-income families where parents and children were highly proficient speakers of English. Yet, through language used to describe them, they were frequently positioned by others in ways that located them as essentially different and foreign.

Positioning Self and Other

Both Whites and Asian Americans created racial boundaries by delineating categories of people, locating themselves in relation to categories, and endowing these categories with social and moral meaning. For example, through their use of pronouns and terms for people, many White speakers created landscapes in which "Asians" were different from and opposed to "us." Both White and Asian American Laurelton residents used the term "Asian" to refer to anyone of Chinese, Japanese, Korean, Vietnamese, Thai, Cambodian, and other types of descent, while "Indian" was used largely by Whites to speak about people who could trace their ancestry to India, Pakistan, Bangladesh, Sri Lanka, or Nepal. While the Asian American population was diverse, Chinese Americans were the largest subgroup. It was common for Whites to use "Chinese" and "Asian" interchangeably. Most Whites did not distinguish between ethnic Chinese from

Taiwan, Hong Kong, or China; those who had come from the Chinese diaspora in Southeast Asia, Indonesia, or the Philippines; or those whose families had been in the United States for several generations—all of these were lumped into one group, "Chinese," in both print and in conversation.

Although White Laurelton residents spoke readily about "Asians" and "Chinese," they did not usually use the word "White" to refer to themselves. Nor was this a very common term used by Asian Americans, who usually called people of European descent "American." Both groups used terms like "African American," "Mexican," or "Hispanic" for people not racialized as White.

While the relevant local terms were thus "Asian" versus "American," I use "Asian American" in this chapter to refer to anyone of Asian descent who was living in the United States, and "White" to refer to those of European descent living in the United States. I do this in part because I am uncomfortable with the ways that local categories position Asian Americans in opposition to and as incommensurate with "American." I recognize that "White" and "Asian American" are racializing terms that erase ethnic, socioeconomic, and religious difference. I use these terms not in support of this racializing project, but as a way of highlighting the ways that Laurelton residents themselves organized the world.

Claims to Place: "Oldtimers" and "Newcomers"

Fieldnote: I drove past one of Laurelton's many mini-malls and ducked into a Japanese supermarket to grab a quick snack. Elaborately coiffed young Korean American moms held the hands of their stylish tots; Japanese American kids whined to their grandmothers to buy them sweet packaged pastries, and workers from nearby companies ordered bowls of steaming ramen. Signs in both English and romanized Japanese were found throughout the store. I grabbed a prepackaged tuna fish sandwich on airy white bread and went down the street to the Laurelton Historical Society to learn more about the history of the community. Tom, an elderly White man who had moved to Laurelton with his wife as a young married couple, told me that he was an "oldtimer" and offered to lead me, a "newcomer," around the current exhibit, which traced the history of Laurelton. Historical pictures featured locally prominent families of European descent, shopkeepers, teachers, and agricultural laborers. As I left the historical society and drove past a Japanese American–owned business which was run by third- and fourth-generation Laurelton residents, I couldn't help thinking about how the exhibit made it seem as though life in the good old days was purely White.

In interviews and in the local newspaper, local White residents presented themselves as legitimate members of the community and Asian Americans as illegitmate ones. Whites routinely referred to themselves as "oldtimers" or "longtime residents," stressing their ties to nostalgic visions of Laurelton's rural past. They spoke longingly of the bountiful harvests and "neighborly" interactions of this supposedly more carefree time. Both those whose ancestors were actually involved in agriculture, as well as later arriving White professionals, evoked these images.

Local White residents used the term "oldtimers" in opposition to the term "newcomers." Newcomers were not seen as rightful residents of Laurelton, but as usurpers who were "taking over" the community. Their "selfish" pursuit of their own interests was linked to their unhealthy relationship with money and property. Whereas "oldtimers" were imagined as people who cared about the land and about their neighbors, "newcomers" were just out to make a quick buck and cared only about themselves. They claimed more than their fair share of public resources and demanded "special treatment" like foreign language classes that were a waste of public money. The discourse of the "newcomer" framed Asian Americans as having come *from* somewhere else to the United States and pointed to their inescapably foreign origins. It linked Whites to the genteel persona of the farmer who lived in a "more relaxed" nostalgic time and space, while linking Asian Americans to the rabidly hypercompetitive neoliberal student/homeowner.

Asian Americans were associated with the more recent and discomfiting changes of suburbanization, overcrowding, and commercialization (Lye 2005; Mitchell 2004). This racializing discourse, however, erased the substantial connection Asian Americans had to Laurelton's agricultural past. Although Asian Americans had been agricultural laborers and owners of stores that sold produce from the fields, "newcomer" discourses cast them as the primary agents of the unwelcome social changes that had taken place across California over the past decades.

Local White residents created categories of people through the use of pronouns that established moral boundaries. At a city council meeting, one longtime White resident said, "I welcome them to our community, but it is them coming to our community. I don't want it to change into their community." Similarly, a White city council member said of an Asian philanthropist, "What do we know about these people?" By drawing distinctions between "our community" and "their community," and "we" and "these people," speakers drew moral boundaries between one set of people who were bonafide members of the community and another set of people who were unknown, suspect interlopers. Dismissive references to "these people" and "them" positioned White speakers as morally superior to Asian Americans. Whites used similar forms of evaluative language to talk about local Asian American politicians. One speaker described an Asian American political candidate with the sentence, "His agenda is more about 'my people.'" Here, Asian Americans are presented as interested only in advancing the narrow interests of the racially exclusive "my people," not in the welfare of the wider community of Laurelton.

Stereotypes of Asian Americans as unfriendly and exclusive were extended not only to immigrants but to their American born children as well. Public schools were imagined as being filled with "overly competitive" Asian American kids. When one realtor told a White family who was considering purchasing a home in the area, "[your] child might be the only Caucasian in the class," it reinforced the idea that being surrounded by Asian Americans was not something to which you should subject your children. It didn't take much for Whites to feel that there were "too many" Asian Americans; White flight from the public schools was already apparent by the time Asian Americans comprised a mere third of the overall population.

Asian Americans were surprised by the extent to which they lived separate but unequal lives from Whites in Laurelton. They told me that they participated in racially divided sports leagues, Boy Scout troops, and PTA organizations. In reaction to a reporter's question about racial tension in a local high school, one Asian American school administrator said, "There is no racial tension because there is no interaction [across racial boundaries]." Recently arrived teens from South Korea told me that they had a difficult time making "American" (e.g., White) friends and were considering transferring to schools in other parts of the state where they thought things might be better.

Many Asian Americans also seemed to resent the presumption that they did not belong in Laurelton regardless of how long they had lived there. When I was at a reception for a local civic organization, I met a South Asian American whom I had just read about in the organization's newsletter. I asked her a question alluding to her recent hiring: "Oh, so how long have you been here?" I remember being rather taken aback by her curt response informing me that she had lived in the area for over thirty years. When I asked how long she had been "here," I meant to refer to her time at the organization, not her time in California or the United States. The fact that she read my question as being stereotypically about her presumed foreignness revealed resentment about being constantly positioned as someone who was not "from here."

When I asked a woman, an immigrant from Taiwan, how she felt about Laurelton's racial climate, she told me that she was not entirely prepared for how "Chinese" Laurelton felt to her. According to her, this was at times a disadvantage: "In some ways, it's just like Taiwan here. All the kids are always studying. . . . . Sometimes I think we should move to someplace really American, like Seattle. Then the kids could just play outside after school instead" (translated from Mandarin). In fact, when I asked Asian Americans why they had decided to move to Laurelton, they gave many of the same reasons Whites did: stable real estate values, proximity to work, its reputation as a "nice" community. Very few specifically mentioned a desire to be near other Asian Americans as a key reason. The racial segregation that Asian Americans experienced in Laurelton did not happen because Asian Americans voluntarily chose to associate only with other Asian Americans; instead, they were held at arm's length by White residents who did not welcome their presence.

Reading the Linguistic Landscape

Fieldnote: Laurelton's town green was a large public space frequently used for festivals of various kinds. Such events featured vendors, music, kids' activities, performances by school groups, and booths by local civic organizations. On festival days, grandmothers would chase after their grandkids, children would dart around scarfing down whatever sweet treat was on sale, and the cries of vendors hawking sunglasses, mobile phone accessories, hats, and kids' trinkets filled the air. Many of these were generically themed events (e.g., the "food and wine festival") but occasionally, a festival that was ethnically or racially specific would come along as well (e.g., Oktoberfest, Lunar New Year, Diwali). While Oktoberfest never raised much concern, several of the Asian-associated festivals prompted angry letters to the local newspaper about their "exclusionary" nature. In some cases, vendors in the "international" section were required to sign a pledge that they would not represent any other country in a negative way. In other cases, festivals that had been dedicated to particular Asian groups or holidays were instead converted to "international" festivals. By surrounding attractions such as children doing aikido and Korean drumming troupes, with attractions like firefighters, men in kilts, and high school bands, such festivals were deracialized and made unthreatening. They were transformed into events that were, in the words of those who insisted on these reforms, "welcoming to all."

Some Whites in Laurelton objected strongly to displays of Asian languages in Laurelton public space. The public presence of Asian Americans, apparent in the stores and restaurants that lined Laurelton's commercial thoroughfares, was a sharp point of tension. Adjacent communities that had comparable percentages of Asian Americans did not suffer the same kind of friction as there was in Laurelton, partly because of the ways that some residents read public space. In this section, I focus on how some residents interpreted both spoken and visual displays of Asian languages as "foreign" and linked to deception. I understand these not as features of the codes themselves, but as cultural frameworks of interpretation that positioned some kinds of writing and speech as illegible or incomprehensible.

Many White residents were concerned about the ways that Laurelton's commercial spaces had become "Asian." Laurelton did not have a quaint downtown, a pedestrian area lined with upscale children's boutiques, wine bars, and cafes, like some communities in the area. Instead, it had mini-malls, where several small businesses, visible from the street, were clustered around a parking lot in front (see Figure 5.1). The main commercial thoroughfares were packed tightly

Figure 5.1 A California mini-mall.

with restaurants, insurance companies, markets, banks, gas stations, hardware stores, car dealerships, and fast food establishments. It was not uncommon to hear languages other than English being spoken in these places, as well in the public library or the post office. I often spoke Mandarin, Cantonese, or Korean in Laurelton stores and restaurants.

Many Whites objected to the ways that commercial spaces in Laurelton catered to Asian American customers, with visual displays of Asian languages seen as especially inappropriate. Some who explicitly mentioned their long residence in the community wrote letters to the editor of the local paper complaining about the "appalling" number of store signs and delivery trucks with writing in a "foreign language." A study was then commissioned by the town council, which in fact only found a handful of instances in which a sign did not also include an English translation. In these letters, visual displays of Chinese characters were most highly salient in the imagination as "foreign"; signs that used roman letters but whose meaning might have been opaque to English monolinguals nonetheless (e.g., *nước mắm, cup ramen shoyu menraku hikari*) were not singled out. Chinese characters could be found on outdoor signs for insurance companies, banks, restaurants, and stores; in posters in store windows; and on printed menus, handwritten strips of paper taped to walls of restaurants, signs inside stores, and labels for food items (see Figure 5.2).

Figure 5.2 Chinese in public space.

One market in town was singled out by some Whites as a particularly uninviting space because of its visual displays of language:

> MS. HARPER: Just going down to the [Asian supermarket]
>   And um- you look at that.
>   What do you see?
>   I don't- I don't understand any of the language in that.
> MS. WILKINS: I'd really like to go there [a local Asian supermarket]
>   But I have no clue what they have.
>   And so if it's also in English
>   Maybe more people would go.

In these descriptions, the market is represented as a place where there is no English writing. The experience of being in the market is described as one of utter lack of comprehension for someone who is not literate in Chinese ("I have no clue what they have" "I don't understand any of the language in that"). In fact, when I went to take a look, I found mostly multilingual signs that featured English alongside writing in Chinese characters. There were some signs that were in Chinese only, such as advertisements for Chinese newspapers or concerts. Yet most of the labels for products were in both English and Chinese, with occasional uses of Vietnamese (which is written with roman letters) and Korean (which uses its own alphabet) (see Figure 5.3).

Yet many White residents nevertheless imagined the market as a place with no English. In such descriptions, the mere presence of non-Roman writing alongside English made certain spaces illegible.

Asian Americans were linked not only to undecipherable writing but also to undecipherable speech. As one resident said, "On my block 90 percent [of my neighbors] are Asian. I can't talk to them." Here, being "Asian" itself makes someone unable to interact with non-Asians. Such perceptions ignored the fact that most Asian Americans in Laurelton were highly proficient multilinguals who used English on a daily basis at work or at school. By creating a space in which there are "Asians" who are framed in general as linguistically incomprehensible, and by locating himself in opposition to that category, the speaker here covertly replicates stereotypes of Chinese as bad speakers of English and non-Asians as good speakers of English.

Lastly, speaking in a language other than English was also sometimes publicly linked to attempts at deception and secrecy, echoing "yellow peril" discourses that have been used to describe crafty Chinese and devious Japanese among others (Lye 2005). In one letter to the editor, a resident expressed her feelings about the development of a local mini-mall:

> There has been quite a bit of publicity lately in [the local paper] regarding the future of the city center. City officials and [the] director

Figure 5.3 Signs at the Chinese market.

of community development were quoted as being delighted with the new ownership.

When I met with [the director of community development] and questioned him regarding the new owners' plans regarding the city center, he stated that the city had no jurisdiction regarding the usage of the acquired property.

That explains how Laurelton was suddenly faced with a "Chinese Village" at the corner of [. . .] roads, which was originally billed as a supermarket but blossomed into the present enclave after negotiations were carried out in Chinese and with a "hands-off" attitude by the city.

The new owners, Mr. Wong and his Asian partners, have denied that their international restaurant would cater exclusively to Asian clients, but his credibility would be increased if some European flavor would be included in his planning and the veil of secrecy so dear to his business planning [. . .] would be lifted.

In this letter, the languages that people speak make them more or less trustworthy.

"Mr. Wong and his Asian partners" are depicted as conducting business negotiations in Chinese, thereby creating a "veil of secrecy" around their plans to develop a local mall. Just as Spanish speakers are sometimes prohibited from speaking Spanish on the job because they are thought to be trying to hide something from English monolinguals, carrying on "negotiations in Chinese" is here associated with attempts to deceive the good citizens of Laurelton (who are thus implicitly positioned as not Chinese). Specifically, the words of "Mr. Wong and his Asian partners" are not to be trusted; they might claim that they are not building a restaurant that will serve only Chinese, but we should not really believe them because there are no Whites (e.g., "European flavor") involved in this project. Here, speaking Chinese is associated with plotting nefarious deeds and making false public promises. Similarly, spaces associated with Chinese are deemed inherently exclusionary to others.

This letter is written in the hyperbolic style that was common in letters to the editor in this newspaper. The local newspaper was a place where passionate opinions were expressed; people that I interviewed in person did not make statements that were nearly as forceful. Nevertheless, such texts covertly racialized Asian Americans in Laurelton by evoking stereotypes of the Chinese language as less "straightforward" than Western languages, and as linked to "convoluted" modes of writing and expression. They also upheld English as the language of honesty, transparency, and candor.

Conclusion

In this chapter, I have shown how Asian Americans who fit the model minority stereotype, and who are often imagined as leading fully assimilated lives, are covertly racialized through discourses about language. In local discourses that recalled the "yellow peril," Whites portrayed well-educated, multilingual Asian Americans as nefarious businessmen; as greedy "newcomers" who did not "care" about the community; and as hypercompetitive students who were not well-rounded. Attempts by Asian Americans to revitalize commercial areas, to get involved in local politics, or to remodel their homes were seen as threatening and exclusionary, unseemly displays of wealth that contrasted with oldtimer Whites' genteel relationships to the land. Through their pronoun use and the ways that they associated categories like "Asian," "newcomer," and "oldtimer" with moral positions, Whites portrayed themselves as the rightful, central members of Laurelton.

At the same time, discourses that associated speaking an Asian language with deception and secrecy, and that depicted written displays of Asian languages in public spaces as illegible and inappropriate, circulated in letters to the editor of the local paper. In such letters, writers voiced strong opposition toward public celebrations of Asian-identified holidays on the town green or towards "special services" like classes at the library in languages other than English. Just as World War II helped to speed language loss among German-speaking and Japanese-speaking American communities, associations in Laurelton between speaking in an Asian language and dishonesty promoted English monolingualism.

While statistics may lead us to believe that Asian Americans are being readily accepted by Whites, a closer look shows that merely living among Whites is not the same as being accepted by them. This should not be surprising. Many communities the world over are characterized by both close proximity *and* sharp divisions along ethnic, religious, or racial lines. Indeed, the residential concentration of highly educated, high-income Asian Americans in U.S. metropolitan areas actually increased from 1990 to 2000 (Iceland and Wilkes 2006). These patterns may not be due to Asian Americans voluntarily "choosing" to live among other Asian Americans. It may very well be that racializing discourses like the ones described above, where Whites linguistically portrayed Asian Americans as toxic and unwelcome neighbors, help to spur White flight from communities that have become "too Asian" (Zhou, Tseng, and Kim 2009).

References

Alim, H. Samy, and Geneva Smitherman. 2012. *Articulate While Black: Barack Obama, Language, and Race in the U.S.* New York: Oxford University Press.

Abelmann, Nancy, and John Lie. 1995. *Blue Dreams: Korean Americans and the Los Angeles Riots.* Cambridge, MA: Harvard University Press.

Bonfiglio, Thomas Paul. 2002. *Race and the Rise of Standard American.* New York: Mouton de Gruyter.

Bucholtz, Mary. 2011. *White Kids: Language, Race, and Styles of Youth Identity.* Cambridge: Cambridge University Press.

Chun, Elaine. 2009. Ideologies of legitimate mockery: Margaret Cho's revoicings of Mock Asian. In Angela Reyes and Adrienne Lo (Eds.), *Beyond Yellow English: Toward a Linguistic Anthropology of Asian Pacific America*, 261–87. New York: Oxford University Press.

Clarke, J. J. 1997. *Oriental Enlightenment: The Encounter between Asian and Western Thought.* New York: Routledge.

Espiritu, Yen Le. 2003. *Home Bound: Filipino Lives across Cultures, Communities, and Countries.* Berkeley: University of California Press.

Gal, Susan. 2012. Sociolinguistic regimes and the management of "diversity." In Monica Heller and Alexandre Duchene (Eds.), *Language in Late Capitalism: Pride and Profit*, 22–37. New York: Routledge.

Garofoli, Joe. 2012. Asian American immigrants outpace Latinos. *San Francisco Chronicle*, June 19. Retrieved from http://www.sfgate.com/politics/joegarofoli/article/Asian-American-immigrants-outpace-Latinos-3643191.php.

Hill, Jane H. 2008. *The Everyday Language of White Racism.* Malden, MA: Blackwell.

Iceland, John, and Rima Wilkes. 2006. Does socioeconomic status matter? Race, class, and residential segregation. *Social Problems* 53(2): 248–73.

Jones, Gavin Roger. 1999. *Strange Talk: The Politics of Dialect Literature in Gilded Age America.* Berkeley: University of California Press.

Kim, Claire Jean. 1999. The racial triangulation of Asian Americans. *Politics & Society* 27(1): 105–38.

Lippi-Green, Rosina. 1997. *English with an Accent: Language, Ideology, and Discrimination in the United States*. New York: Routledge.

Lye, Colleen. 2005. *America's Asia: Racial form and American literature, 1882–1945*. Princeton, NJ: Princeton University Press.

Mead, Walter Russell. 2012. America's New Tiger Immigrants. *Wall Street Journal*, June 30. Retrieved from http://online.wsj.com/article/SB10001424052702303561504577494831767983326.html.

Mitchell, Katharyne. 2004. *Crossing the Neoliberal Line: Pacific Rim Migration and the Metropolis*. Philadelphia: Temple University Press.

Ong, Aihwa. 2003. *Buddha Is Hiding: Refugees, Citizenship, the New America*. Berkeley: University of California Press.

Palumbo-Liu, David. 1999. *Asian/American: Historical Crossings of a Racial Frontier*. Stanford, CA: Stanford University Press.

Park, Robert Ezra. 1950. *Race and Culture*. Glencoe, IL: Free Press.

Prashad, Vijay. 2000. *The Karma of Brown Folk*. Minneapolis: University of Minnesota Press.

Reyes, Angela. 2007. *Language, Identity, and Stereotype among Southeast Asian American Youth: The Other Asian*. Mahwah, NJ: Lawrence Erlbaum Associates.

The Rise of Asian Americans. 2012. Washington, DC: Pew Research Center.

Said, Edward W. 1978. *Orientalism*. New York: Vintage.

Sue, Stanley, and Sumie Okazaki. 1990. Asian-American educational achievements: A phenomenon in search of an explanation. *American Psychologist* 45(8): 913–20.

Suzuki, Bob H. 1977. Education and the socialization of Asian Americans: A revisionist analysis of the 'model minority' thesis. *Amerasia Journal* 4(2): 23–51.

Tuan, Mia. 1998. *Forever Foreigners or Honorary Whites?: The Asian Ethnic Experience Today*. New Brunswick, NJ: Rutgers University Press.

Yu, Henry. 2001. *Thinking Orientals: Migration, Contact, and Exoticism in Modern America*. New York: Oxford University Press.

Zhou, Min, Yen-fen Tseng, and Rebecca Y. Kim. 2009. Suburbanization and new trends in community development: The case of Chinese ethnoburbs in the San Gabriel Valley, California. In Min Zhou (Ed.), *Contemporary Chinese America: Immigration, Ethnicity, and Community Transformation*. Philadelphia: Temple University Press.

6

Ethnicity and Extreme Locality in South Africa's Multilingual Hip Hop Ciphas

QUENTIN E. WILLIAMS

Global Hip Hop cultural studies demonstrate that youth around the world have used global and local linguistic resources to forge local Hip Hop cultures that speak to their specific contexts and life experiences. These "global linguistic flows"—from Brazil to Japan to Tanzania—often involve a mixing and remixing of local varieties and some forms associated with African American Language (AAL; see Alim et al. 2009). In some contexts, the use of AAL represents an empowered transnational blackness, a nod to Hip Hop's "origins" as an African American form, and a cosmopolitan engagement with a global cultural movement. In other contexts, the use of AAL has been viewed as an uncritical and inauthentic adoption of hegemonic American linguistic forms in a cultural practice that privileges the local ("the hood comes first" in Hip Hop) and the real (the cultural mandate is to "keep it real"). This cultural and linguistic imperialism is also sometimes seen as an extension of American political and economic imperialism.

While these contested ideologies exist simultaneously in many scenes, it is generally the case that the more established Hip Hop becomes in any given context, the more it consistently foregrounds local styles. As Hip Hop is indigenized, efforts are made not only to reframe this global art form in local cultural contexts but also to reinvent and align local cultures with global youth's cultural and linguistic practice. When it comes to the languages of local Hip Hop cultures, youth use local varieties in ways that index local identities, such as ethnicity, gender, region, linguistic knowledge, and street affiliation. As we see below, the use of AAL in some Hip Hop ciphas (the circular arrangement of emcees who perform improvised rhymes) in Cape Town, South Africa—at the expense of local languages and styles—can cause an emcee to lose a freestyle rap battle (an improvisational verbal duel). This chapter demonstrates how youth forge a local variety of Hip Hop Nation Language (Alim 2004) that relies on the strategic and creative use of linguistic resources associated with English, Cape Afrikaans (*Kaaps* or Cape Afrikaans is a variety of Afrikaans predominantly spoken in the Cape Flats), the local street variety Sabela (an admixture of isiXhosa, Kaaps, Zulu, and nonverbal gang signs), and AAL. In the process, youth jointly produce ethnicity and extreme locality by forming linguistic registers, creating an agentive multilingual citizenship. In a linguistic context where Cape Afrikaans is stigmatized across nearly all social domains related to power and upward mobility (from education to politics to the job market), these youth registers challenge the supposed inferiority of this variety; its very use resists long-held stereotypes about Cape Afrikaans—and its speakers, mostly working-class Coloureds—as unintelligent, lazy, and criminal.

Introducing Cipha Performances in Cape Town

The study of Hip Hop in South Africa has traditionally focused on narratives of race, resistance, and counterhegemonic agency in the context of apartheid and the early days of postapartheid. However, Hip Hop cipha performances, an integral part of Hip Hop cultural practice, remain relatively underresearched (see, for instance, Haupt 1996; Warner 2007; Watkins 2000). In this chapter, I show that analyses of discursive features of cipha performances are not only of particular interest to Hip Hop in the Cape Flats (the geographical area outside the city of Cape Town where the majority of Coloured and Black folks live), but also engage core issues around multilingualism, agency, and performance.

The cipha event at the center of the present analysis was collected as part of a yearlong (2008–2009) ethnographic study resulting in a considerable archive of observations, interviews, and over one hundred hours of video and audio recordings. In the South African context, Coloured emcees generally use two or more languages to convey place, identity, and rap style and also to interact with the audience. As these particular youth are generally marginalized in South African society, they deploy innovative and inventive configurations of multilingual resources to establish local identities and cultural practices both within and outside of Hip Hop cultural spaces.

Ethnographies of Language in Hip Hop Cipha Performances

Recent sociolinguistics of globalization research focuses on how global genres are performed locally for purposes of stylization, appropriation, and identification (Alim et al. 2009; Pennycook 2010). Since the inception of Hip Hop in

New York (see Chang 2005; Forman and Neal 2004), rap (especially) has grown over the last forty years into a global phenomenon. It continues to be appropriated in creative ways for different local contexts that have shaped its local expression (Osumare 2007). In her studies on "conversational sampling" in Brazilian Hip Hop, for example, Roth-Gordon (chapter 2, this volume) notes how Hip Hop influences everyday language practices, and how the integration of certain Hip Hop language registers in the daily language practices of fans imbues spaces and places with new meaning. Similarly, Higgens (2009) shows how kiSwahili (a local language in Tanzania) is mixed with AAL and other varieties in performing indigenous as well as transnational identities.

Omoniyi (2009) underscores how Hip Hop not only provides the space for developing various sorts of alternative, yet local, identities but also serves as a cultural reference system that offers youth access to global identities. Omoniyi notes that Hip Hop heads in Nigeria sometimes refer to those who rhyme solely in English and AAL as sounding like "yankees," that is, inauthentic Hip Hop artists who mimic African Americans rather than using Nigerian Pidgin and local varieties.

Writing about the South African context, Shaheen Ariefdien, cofounder of the pioneering Hip Hop crew Prophets of da City, describes the "courtship" with U.S. Hip Hop as conflicted. According to Ariefdien, a major reason why South African youth identified with U.S. Hip Hop was its unabashed and counterhegemonic use of a "Black American" variety of English and "its emergence from a context that established language as a marker of race/class hierarchy" (2011, 236). Yet at the same time:

> Certain crews refuse to rhyme in English or with American accents. Instead they choose to flaunt what is perceived as a uniquely Cape Town or South African sound. Hip Hop took the language of the "less-thans" and embraced it, paraded it, and made it sexy to the point that there is an open pride about what constituted "our" style. *Gamtaal*, a dialect consisting of a mixture of Afrikaans, English, Xhosa, and Arabic, spoken mostly in Cape Town, and *spaza* rhymes, a mixture of Xhosa, Afrikaans, and very little English, are used to express local reworkings of Hip Hop. . . . Even some local emcees who rhyme with an American accent [understood here as AAL] get dissed in some quarters. (Ariefdien and Abrahams, 2007, 266).

In Cape Town, Hip Hop youth created a spatial niche not only to communicate to the global Hip Hop nation the racial subjugation of Coloured and Black people but also to highlight the poverty and the extent of racial discrimination in township spaces under apartheid. Cape Town became the locality where the struggle against Whiteness and linguistic chauvinism took root, as Hip Hop youth revisited what it meant to be "Coloured" in a transforming multilingual polity (Haupt 1996). Within this context, I provide a raciolinguistic analysis of how Coloured rappers position themselves with respect to their "Colouredness," stereotypes of "racial mixed-ness," and their linguistic status.

The Ethnography of Club Stones

Hip Hop spaces in Cape Town are typically racialized as Black or Coloured spaces, depending on the township or suburb. Club Stones ("Stones", see Figure 6.1), the venue for the performance cipha analyzed in this chapter, is located in the Northern Suburbs (Kuilsriver). Regularly, on a Wednesday night

Figure 6.1 Club Stones in Kuilsriver.

Figure 6.2 Promotional poster for "Stepping Stones to Hip Hop" at Club Stones.

between 10:00 p.m. and 2:00 a.m., Stones hosts a gathering of mainly Coloured youths: rappers, DJs and Hip Hop heads who are there to enjoy the show, "Stepping Stones to Hip Hop" (see Figure 6.2). In 2008, a group called Suburban Menace approached Club Stones' management in Kuilsriver and negotiated the hosting of a Hip Hop show. A young Coloured group, their main purpose was to gain experience performing in front of an audience in a club. The highlight of their show was the performance of cipha.

The staff employed by Club Stones is predominantly Coloured and male (Figure 6.3). The audience and patrons who attend the show are usually multilingual, speaking at least Afrikaans and English. While most of the employees live in the historically Coloured area cordoned off by the apartheid-era Group

Figure 6.3 The staff at Club Stones.

Areas Act, many of the audience members who frequently attend the show are from areas beyond the community of Kuilsriver. Many travel from as far afield as Mitchell's Plain, Bellville, central Cape Town, and even Johannesburg.

Every Wednesday night I attended the show in Club Stones, talking to patrons, rappers, b-boys, b-girls, turntablists, graffiti writers, Hip Hop heads, entertainment journalists, and curious onlookers who came to the club for the first time. I conducted audiotaped interviews with Hip Hop heads, rappers, and the management of Club Stones. I also gathered promotional posters, mixtape CDs, and photographs of the show. My observations were initially recorded in a notepad, but subsequently all rap performances, danceoffs, and drinking competitions and DJ (or turntablist) performances were captured on video. Below I demonstrate how two rappers, both Coloured, along with cipha audience members in Club Stones, worked together to construct ethnicity and *extreme locality* through a variety of semiotic means. I demonstrate how the two emcees articulate Colouredness and stereotypes of Coloured identities differently, not only in relation to each other but to the audience as well.

The term *extreme locality* emphasizes how the performance of a cipha battle, and its locality, are mutually constituted. The present analysis shows how aspects of space, both local-spatial coordinates and nonlocal spatial elements, are *entextualized* in the actual performance of a rap cipha between two emcees. Another core feature in the construction of the extreme local is how language varieties, styles, gestures, and audience interaction are variously referenced multilingually and incorporated into the performance.

Performing Ethnicity and Extreme Locality
ROUND ONE: VERBAL CUEING, BITING RHYMES, AND REPRESENTIN

On the night of the cipha battle between rappers Keaton and Phoenix, Club Stones attracted a large audience of youths for the Suburban Menace Hip Hop show. The audience is mainly made up of males, dressed according to the poster requirements: baggy jeans, hoodies, and Hip Hop caps. Before every cipha performance, rappers sign up on a clipboard but do not necessarily know who their opponent will be. Only at the start of the cipha performances will a cipha mediator (or timekeeper) call the cipha competitors on stage. Each performer is given 60 seconds to outperform their opponent.

Keaton and Phoenix are two Coloured emcees who had never met prior to their lyrical duel that night at Club Stones. However, as rappers they shared a great deal in terms of creativity, lyrical style, and Hip Hop musical tastes. Keaton, on the one hand, is in his early 20s and has rapped since his early school days, but only recently started to freestyle battle. Born and raised in the historically demarcated area for Coloureds and Blacks in Kuilsriver, he is fluent in Cape Afrikaans and Coloured South African English, is able to rap in both varieties, and understands the street language Sabela. Phoenix, sometimes known as Charlie Raplin, is also in his early 20s and has been actively involved as a rapper and a battle emcee for more than eight years in the Hip Hop community of Kuilsriver. A fluent speaker of Cape Afrikaans and Coloured South African English, Phoenix (like Keaton) has been exposed to Sabela in the community of Kuilsriver.

At the beginning of the first round of the cipha performance, Mseeq (the cipha mediator) called Keaton and then Phoenix to the stage. Phoenix won the coin toss, electing Keaton to begin the lyrical duel:

Round 1 of Cipha

Keaton:

1 Yo, yo . . . yo, yo

2 Ek gat Engels spit, nuh
   I'm going to spit in English, nuh

3 Julle verstaan SMEngelS
   You understand SMEngelS

4   Hie' gat ek
     Here I go

5   [...]

6   My favourate colour is red

7   Like a bloodshed

8   With purple haze

9   When I shoot the sucker dead

10   I'm rolling in a

11   Shish kebab

12   When I woke this morning I was a lost soul

13   Cause I got [inaudible]

14   And a sore throat

15   A wardrobe with an army robe

16   In a [inaudible] signing autographs

17   I just remembered that I'm absent-minded [inaudible]

18   That it crossed my mind

19   I can't rhyme it

20   I freestyle every verse I spit

Keaton began his performance with a verbal cue used commonly as a turn-taking element in cipha battles, "Yo, yo . . . yo, yo" (line 1). The use of this particular verbal cue is commonly associated with AAL. In his attempt to promote himself as a credible emcee, Keaton's use of this verbal cue in this context suggests that he is attempting to purchase the transnational capital of African American Hip Hop. Despite this attempt, he violates a basic rule requiring him to perform *battle* rhymes, comprising a personal attack on his opponent (that is, disrespecting him), including insulting commentary on his opponent's verbal or nonverbal comportment. Although clearly expected of a cipha battle, Keaton does not do this. He rhymes about being a pro-tagonist in a series of events, where: (1) he talks about his favorite color, other colors, and his ability to draw color through violence against others (lines 6–9); (2) that he is driving around in a vehicle that is as attractive as a shish kebab dinner (lines 10–11); (3) that he is lost because of a "sore throat"; (4) that he has a wardrobe full of choices, even his coat of arms (lines 12–15); and (5) that even though he is able to think off the top of his head, he still performs freestyle lyrics (lines 16–20). Noticeable is the constant metareflection on his person rather than the expected deployment of inter-personal and combative disses.

Importantly, the lyrical content is managed largely through the use of English, although from his opening it is evident that Keaton is attempting to engage both English and Afrikaans speakers in the audience. In lines 2 to 4, he rhymes: "ek gat Engels spit [*I'm going to perform in English*], nuh, julle verstaan [You understand] SMEngelS. Hie' gat ek. [*Here I go*]." The form SMS (short message service) is commonly associated with the linguistic practices of texting (the combination of acronyms, short phrases, and icons usually used in social networking *Real Time Chats* [RTC]). Keaton builds his lyrical content around this form, thus assuming that those in the audience who practice tex-ting or frequently visit social networking sites such as Facebook will relate. ("julle verstaan [You understand] SMEngelS" [line 3]). This is an important line as the emcee recognizes interaction with audience members figure as an important part of cipha battles. As Alim et al. (2010 and 2011) have shown, audience members are both assessors and significant co-constructors of good cipha performances.

An important feature of Keaton's performance is that many of the lyrics that he performs are from rapper Eminem's song "Cum on Everybody" off the *Slim Shady LP* (1999)—a point surely not lost on the audience. Rappers frown on this practice of *biting rhymes* (plagiarism) and those who do it inherit the dubious reputation of "spitting writtens" (Lee 2009; Smitherman 2006). This audience, through its censorship and monitoring, is intrinsically involved in the ongoing emergences of Keaton's cipha performance. Toward the end of his performance, many of the audience members started to *boo* him off stage. His attempt to be lauded as an emcee was slowly slipping beyond his grasp. To make matters worse, Keaton's competitor Phoenix added insult to injury by turning his back on Keaton while he was rhyming, whereupon Keaton was *booed* even louder. And while the music faded into the background, Mseeq had this to say to Phoenix:

Mseeq:

---

21   Ooh, djy draai jou rug.

Ooh, you turn your back

22   Lyk my djy wil in die hol geëet word.

It looks like you want to be fucked in the ass

23   Waar's 28?

Where's 28?

24   Is 28 in die building?
Is 28 in the building?

25   [Laugh]

26   Dai's 'n facebook joke.
That's a facebook joke

27   Ok, Phoenix is djy gereed?
Ok, Phoenix are you ready?

28   Is djy gereed Phoenix?
Are you ready Phoenix?

29   Ok, [name of DJ] sit die man se mic hard genoeg.
Ok, [name f DJ] increase the volume for the man's mic.

Mseeq says *Ooh, you turned your back. It looks like you want to be fucked in the ass. Where's 28? Is 28 in the building? [Laugh]* [lines 21 to 25]. With his words, he is entextualizing practices and knowledge associated with street ciphas and the heteronormative encounters of the Number gangs in Cape Town. (The Number gangs are a well-known feature of South African prison life. There are three groupings: the 28s, 26s and 27s [compare Steinberg 2004].) He continues with the statement: *"That's a facebook joke"* [line 26], thereby recognizing the function of the social networking site to link locals and friends. In his interruption, Mseeq makes reference to a variety of features essential to the contribution of extreme locality, namely: (1) the identification with 28 (in the use of the number 28) and the use of Sabela; and (2) the language and discursive practices used on Facebook by locals. Thus in a single linguistic interchange, Mseeq entextualized both linguistic and nonlinguistic aspects for extreme local spatialization by drawing on features associated with (not unproblematic) versions of Coloured masculinity in the townships. Countering Keaton's use of AAL, this communicative action recentered the discursive practices that remain locally relevant for constructions of "Colouredness" and "Coloured multilingualism."

With respect to each of the features highlighted in Mseeq's interruption, Keaton is guilty of violating some of the fundamental principles of rap performance. Not only does he choose to rap in AAL instead of Cape Afrikaans, he *spits writtens*. This latter feature suggests how *improvisation* contributes critically to the production of extreme locality. Improvisation of course is by its very nature a situated practice, dependent upon the local context. And finally, by erasing all references to the immediate context—such as choosing not to refer abusively to his protagonist—Keaton once again fails to contribute to the construction of extreme locality. It is precisely his failure to anchor his performance in the local that earns Keaton the audience's derision.

It was now Phoenix's turn to respond to Keaton:

Phoenix:

30   Yo, yo, is ja
     Yo, yo, yes

31   Kuila ruk die ding ja
     Kuila keeps it rocking yes

32   Kuila ruk die ding ja
     Kuila keeps it rocking yes

33   Kuila ruk die ding ja
     Kuila keeps it rocking yes

34   Jy! Jy!
     Yes! Yes!

35   Ek kom met 'n sword in
     I come with a sword

36   Ek druk hom binne 'n bord in
     I'll drive it through you like through a wooden board

37   Ek sal die bra hop-tail
     I will jump on this guy

38   Dan kap sy gevriet in by Jordon
     And slice his face like [Michael] Jordon

39   Ja, tjek 'it uit, ja
     Yes, check it out, yes

40   Kyk hoe lyk djy my broe'
     Look at you brother

41   Djy het nie eens geld nie
     You don't even have money

42   Vir jou sal ek wen soes Liverpool teen Chelsea
     I will win against you like Liverpool against Chelsea

43   Is ja
     Oh, yes

44   Djy's gefok ja
     You're fucked yes

45   My broe djy kan kans drobba
     My brother, you can't even drobba

46   My broe djy lyk met 'n fake hare amper soes Drogba
     My brother, you have fake hair like Drogba

Like Keaton, Phoenix initiates his performance through verbal cues (evident in lines 30, 34, 39, and 43). However, from the outset, what makes his performance different from Keaton's is a sampling of African American verbal cueing *combined* with a local form of verbal cueing in Afrikaans (see lines 30, 34, and 39). He begins the performance with "Yo, yo" and ends the verbal cue with "ja," thereby introducing Cape Afrikaans into a position in cipha battles that has not been experienced before. In other words, Phoenix (re)entextualized the previous use of AAL verbal cueing by Keaton by using a clear, local anchoring. Phoenix entextualized the phrase intentionally to enact, what is commonly referred to in global Hip Hop communities as, *representing your place* (see Smitherman 2006).

Phoenix continues rhyming in Cape Afrikaans. His use of phrases such as "Ek kom met 'n sword in" [I come with a sword] (line 35), "druk hom" [drive it through you] (line 36), and words such as "hop-tail" (line 37) and "smash" (line 38) are lyricized to exact the necessary violence commonly expressed in cipha battles through Cape Afrikaans. For example, he draws on the discourse of poverty to denigrate Keaton's rap identity by comparing him to someone who has poor taste in clothes and no money (lines 40–41); always backing the losing team of a match (line 42). Buoyed by his lyrical creativity—and cheered on by members of the audience—Phoenix continued to assail his opponent, depicting him as forlorn [Djy's gefok ja] (see line 44) and unable to bounce back ['...kan kans drobba] (line 45).

Phoenix formulated the lyric in line 42 with direct reference to Keaton's prior performance. Initially, Phoenix turned his back and looked up to the television set, watching the football game between Liverpool Football Club (FC) and Chelsea FC. The lyric in line 45 is inspired by the dribbling ability and running passes of footballer Didier Drogba—an aspect of the match that Phoenix quickly studied and inserted into his cleverly improvised rhymes, thereby importing an instance of extreme local space into his performance. This lyrical attack in Cape Afrikaans implies that Keaton is unable to respond to his battle rhymes because he "kan kans drobba"; Keaton is identified in line 45 as a fake emcee whose lyrical performances (presumably "writtens") are comparable to the fake hair on football star Didier Drogba's head.

In this first round, Phoenix focuses in on the stereotypical and racialized features of Coloured lifestyle often associated with Coloured identities: socioeconomic class and the Coloured body. In lines 38, 45, and 46, for example, his opponent's face and hair are made an issue in the cipha space. Furthermore, Phoenix suggests his opponent does not dress well (see line 40), suggesting he may be a poor Coloured by the look of his clothes, cleverly following up with a lyric that he also has no money (see line 41). These lyrical comments by Phoenix on his opponent's socioeconomic standing and body are a specter of racial subjugation that haunts Coloured multilingual speakers in South Africa.

As noted above, Phoenix *spit* his rhymes in Cape Afrikaans, highlighting both ethnicity and extreme locality in his lyrical performance. His use of verbal cues in this variety is unique and currently an emerging performative discourse in Cape Town's multilingual Hip Hop community. Furthermore, on the one hand, we see that both emcees test the limits of using racialized varieties: AAL and Cape Afrikaans, respectively. On the other hand, we also see entextualized particular stereotypical features of Colouredness put on display. They do so with the knowledge of the history of racial subjugation that has provided them the conditions to enregister such stereotypes since its creation in colonialism and transformation in apartheid (Erasmus 2001).

Coloured identities (as much as African identities) are products of colonial South Africa, created to fortify the virtues of White European, mainly English and Dutch speakers, in a hierarchy that came to privilege a form of transatlantic whiteness (Seekings 2008). This hierarchy defined public discourse on Colouredness, persisting over time (Adhikari 2005) while allowing for revising the meaning of what whiteness would mean, and what Blacks (classified as Africans during colonialism) should be (see Posel 2010). Through the construction and reconstruction of Colouredness as a marginalized identity in colonial and apartheid society, the social life of Coloured identity has suffered innumerable stereotypes. The people who were, and are, so-called Coloureds remain subjugated in space, language, and practice. It is then no surprise that we see our two Coloured emcees use Cape Afrikaans and AAL, with the exception of Mseeq drawing on the discourse practices of the Numbers, representing a type of multilingualism typical of Coloured multilingual speakers on the Cape Flats.

ROUND 2: ENTEXTUALIZING DISRESPECT (DISSING)

In the previous performance, Keaton and Phoenix performed very different verses. For Keaton, the "upscaled" and global use of AAL was thought to be more useful to gaining the appreciation of audience members. However, this was not well received, and his opponent, Phoenix, used his failure to score a win. In the next round, Keaton's performance reveals two things: (1) his understanding that he must perform battle rhymes, and not merely rap about himself; and (2) his realization that he must perform in a language variety that would earn him a win.

In the following, the audience attempts to influence the rappers' performance even more explicitly than before (see lines 38, 40–42). Their goal is to put pressure on Keaton to perform in what they consider to be the "appropriate" language. Below, Keaton begins the second round by drawing upon the discourse of disrespecting (*dissing*) with an excessive use of what would be considered expletives in Cape Afrikaans (see phrases in bold):

Round 2 of Cipha

Keaton:	*Audience Members:*
	38 Afrikaans man!
39 Is julle reg?	
Are you ready?	
	40 Ja!
	41 Doen Siebela!
	Do Sabela!
	42 Djy jou naai!
	You Mothafucka!
43 Vir hom ek sal sy **Masse Poes**	
For him I'm going to Muthafucking	
44 se **fokking** bek ba's	
Fuck his mouth up	
45 Ek sal sy **fokken** afkap	
I will fucking axe him up	
46 en dan smetterig smeer	
And grease him good	
47 Ek **fokking** rhyme	
I fucking rhyme	
48 want ek probee'	
Cause I try	
49 Ek reppie/	
I don't just rap	
50 want ekke rep soe' **fokkien** wheck	
I rap so fucking whack	
51 Wat?	
What?	
52 hie' kom ek deur	
I'm coming through	

53 ek kom deur met respek
    I'm coming through with respect
54 ek briek sy **fokking** nek
    I break his fucking neck
55 ek slat my skoen somme binne
    I kick my shoe till
56 in sy bek
    In his mouth
57 Ek worry nie
    I don't worry
58 want ekke nie worry
    Cause I don't worry
59 en hy's **fokking** geworried
    Cause he's fucking worried
60 want hy is dik gesplif aan die Darry
    Cause he's high on the hash
61 ja
    yes
62 die **fokking** . . .
    The fucking . . .

In this round, Keaton appeared to have become aware of how freestyle battle-rhyming in AAL was limiting his ability to get the audience members to engage with him. His response is thus to introduce linguistic forms in Cape Afrikaans and use the register of intimidation through Sabela to disrespect Phoenix. He uses phrases such as *cunt* (Poes) and *breaking your fucking mouth* (fokking bek ba's) to violently attack his opponent: "Vir hom ek sal sy Masse Poes se fokking bek ba's / Ek sal sy fokken afkap en dan smetterig smeer / Ek fokking rhyme want ek probeer" (Translation: *For him I'm going to muthafucking fuck his mouth up. I will fucking axe him up and grease him good. I fucking rhyme 'cause I try*). What is particularly salient about Keaton's lyrical content in the second round is that he employs forms of language perceived to be more masculine and street-affiliated, indexical of the extreme locality of Club Stones and the use of Cape Afrikaans. His lyrical jibes on the body of his opponent are not only a matter of dissing but also cut to the core of how Coloured bodies are perceived in the South African imagination; violence is constructed as a hallmark of "tough" Coloured masculinity.

Keaton thus attempts to accommodate what he perceives to be his audience's wishes, thus hoping to negate the impact of his weak first-round performance. The increased audience response indicates that he had some measure of success, although Mseeq once again policed Keaton's language use:

Mseeq:

63	Whoooo!
64	Keaton
65	as djy Afrikaans rap
	If you're going to rap in Afrikaans
66	dan moet djy wiet wat djy sê jong
	Then you must know what you are going to say
67	Jou Masse frikken . . .
	Your Motha freaking. . .
68	djy is dan net net dit . . .
	You are this this and that . . .
69	kom Pheonix let's go
	Come Pheonix let's go

Mseeq admonishes Keaton when he points out that there are norms to rapping and rhyming in Cape Afrikaans, when he emphasizes, *"Keaton, if you're going to rap in Afrikaans then you must know what you going to say, brother. Your Motha freaking . . . you are this and that."* To Mseeq and some others, Keaton's use of Cape Afrikaans appeared inauthentic and exaggerated as he overcompensated for his lackluster first-round rhymes.

Below, Phoenix continued to skillfully finish off the cipha (and his opponent):

Phoenix:	**Audience Members:**
70 Uh, tjek 'it uit. Tjek 'it uit	
Uh, check it out. Check it out	
71 Kuila!	
	72 Hosh!
73 Hosh, o's represent	
Cool, we represent	
	74 Jy!

75 Met die pen
With the pen

76 met die slet
With the slut

77 Tsais!

78 djy moet ken
You must recognize

79 Uh

80 djy's 'n disaster
You're a disaster

81 ek is die Master
I'm the Master

82 As ekke klaa' is
When I'm done

83 dan lien djy by iemand 'n plaster
You'll need a plaster

84 [. . .]

85 Hy is die flow
He's the flow

86 djy moet onthou
You must remember

87 vir jou gooi ek soes vleis op die braai
I'll throw you like meat on the braai

88 want djy is rou
Because you're raw

90 [. . .]

91 Djy bly my gryp
You grab me all the time

92 djy is 'n meit
You're a whore

93 lyk my ek moet hom weer hop-tail
It seems I'll have to hop-tail him again

94 en vir hom die keer ryp
And rape him again

Phoenix's final performance above is relatively bare of expletives. He started his second-round performance in an almost identical way to his first round, as can be seen from his verbal cueing in lines 70 and 79. With the exception of a few omissions in lines 84 and 90, the performance here shows a clever form of improvisation. In the first round, Phoenix performed "representing." In this round, he initially appears to be preparing a repeat of "representing" (see line 71), but instead of producing intimidating rhymes and lyrics, he switches instead to a lyrical metareflection on the creative process preceding a cipha performance.

Audience engagement and co-construction in Phoenix's performance is evident in the way they offer greetings in Cape Afrikaans and Sabela, the two most common varieties on the Cape Flats. "Hosh!" (line 72) is a socially acceptable greeting among multilingual youth on the Cape Flats, and used to announce a person's presence. On the other hand, it is also an invitation to engage in talk commonly associated with the street language Sabela. The use of the lexical form "Tsais!" has multiple meanings but is here used by audience members to emphasize that Phoenix must push Keaton "off-stage" because he fails to construct good rhymes. The manner in which "tsais" is used is further suggestive of the audience's desire to have Cape Afrikaans as a central part of this evolving Hip Hop register.

The penultimate lyrical turns in Phoenix's final performance are innovative and improvised to further denigrate Keaton. In clearly organized turns of four stanzas, Phoenix reflects on Keaton's previous rhymes in the cipha (lines 80–83); that he is much too young to rhyme against him (Phoenix) (lines 85–88); and that he has been feminized (lines 91–94). Phoenix makes it clear that any rapper who battles him will always be a disaster ("djy's n disaster," line 80) because he is the better emcee ("n Master," line 81). His performance is always threatening and insulting ("As ekke klaa' is / dan lien djy by iemand 'n plaster," lines 82–83). He informs the audience that Keaton thinks he can rhyme ("hy is die flow," line 85) but that he *will* fail ("djy moet onthou/vir jou gooi ek soes vleis op die braai/want djy is rou," lines 86–88). In the last lines of his performance, Phoenix feminizes Keaton. He does this by making reference to how Keaton was pulling on his clothes in order to add "paralinguistic value" to his use of expletives. Phoenix implies that Keaton in reality just wanted to hold him ("Djy bly my gryp," line 91); that he is a woman ("djy is 'n meit," line 92); and because Keaton continued with the action Phoenix must win the second round ("lyk my ek moet hom weer hop-tail/en vir hom die keer ryp," lines 93–94). In this way, Phoenix thus ended the cipha performance as the winner.

What Phoenix demonstrates in the end provides evidence that "feminizing" one's opponent through the use of heteronormative discourses is widely observed in Hip Hop ciphas. In fact, Alim et al. (2010, 2011) documented an almost identical discourse in freestyle battle ciphas in Los Angeles, California (see Alim et al. 2017 for a comparative analysis of U.S. and South African Hip Hop ciphas). As those researchers noted, it is not uncommon for youth (and humans, in general) to be progressive on some dimensions (language, for example) and regressive on others (gender, sexuality).

Discussion and Conclusion

This chapter demonstrated how ethnicity and extreme locality are jointly produced through language. I showed how youth in Club Stones entextualize local Coloured identity, while simultaneously enregistering the discourse genre of the cipha. As a local place, Stones offered a local stage for the enactment of local speech genres and language practices of the youth who gathered there. Coloured youth construct the extreme local through their performances, which deploy references to local coordinates, recontextualizing local and global linguistic resources, and incorporating local proxemics and audience response and commentary.

The extreme local is accomplished partly through the use of particular language varieties and partly by indexical reference to spatial and nonspatial coordinates. Features such as context-dependent improvisations, and references to local discourses such as the Number Gangs and sports teams, for example, all figure in the coproduction of ethnicity and the extreme local. What came to be excluded and banned from the (joint) performance was the appropriation (by Keaton) of lyrics from Hip Hop artists outside of the local context and the use of AAL (rather than Cape Afrikaans). Though the notion of an empowering transnational "Blackness" or "connective marginalities" with African Americans appeals to some (see Osumare 2007), local audiences are not always interested in one's connection to a kind of "first-world" (African) Americanness. Rather, local ethnicities—being Black and Coloured in the Cape Flats—are constructed linguistically through the ("appropriate") use of varieties that index membership in these groups. Ethnicity and extreme locality are jointly produced through forms of multilingualism that are built around local varieties of Cape Afrikaans and Sabela. As we witnessed, Phoenix's use of Cape Afrikaans and Sabela was aligned with audience insistence and contributed both to his victory and to the construction of local ethnicities and identities.

Though not equally progressive on gender and sexuality, and sometimes ambivalent about race/class identities, the entextualization of the local gave legitimacy to multilingual practices that created conditions favorable to the expression of marginalized racial and ethnic identities. While questions remain about the use of heteronormatively masculinist discourses to challenge a colonial ethnolinguistic legacy, a grassroots practice of multilingualism has the potential for youth agency in the form of multilingual citizenship. As South African Hip Hop continues to develop its awareness of these issues (see Ariefdien and Burgess 2011), an inclusive, progressive multilingualism needs to be supported in order to thrive.

References

Adhikari, Mohamed. 2005. *Not White Enough, Not Black Enough: Racial Identity in the South African Coloured Community*. Athens: Ohio University Press.

Alim, H. Samy. 2004. Hip Hop Nation Language. In E. Finegan and J. R. Rickford, eds., *Language in the USA: Themes for the 21st Century*. Cambridge: Cambridge University Press, 387–409.

Alim, H. Samy, Awad Ibrahim, and Alastair Pennycook, eds., 2009. *Global Linguistic Flows: Hip Hop Cultures, Youth Identities, and the Politics of Language*. London: Routledge.

Alim, H. Samy, J. Lee, and Lauren Mason Carris. 2010. "Short, fried-rice-eating Chinese emcees and good-hair havin Uncle Tom niggas": Performing race and ethnicity in freestyle rap battles. *Journal of Linguistic Anthropology* 20(1): 116–33.

Alim, H. Samy, J. Lee, and Lauren Mason Carris. 2011. Moving the crowd, "crowding" the emcee: The coproduction and constestation of Black normativity in freestyle rap battles. *Discourse & Society* 22(-4): 422–39.

Alim, H. Samy, J. Lee, L. Mason Carris, and Quentin E. Williams. 2017. Linguistic creativity and the production of cisheteropatriarchy: A comparative analysis of improvised rap battles in Los Angeles and Cape Town. *Language Sciences*.

Ariefdien, Shaheen, and Nazli Abrahams. 2007. Cape Flats Alchemy: Hip Hop Arts in South Africa. In Jeff Chang, ed., *Total Chaos: The Art and Aesthetics of Hip Hop*. New York: Basic Civitas Books.

Ariefdien, Shaheen, and Marlon Burgess. 2011. Putting two heads together: A cross-generational conversation about Hip Hop in South Africa. In P. Khalil Saucier, ed., *Native Tongues: An African Hip Hop Reader.* Cape Town: Africa World Press.

Chang, Jeff. 2005. *Can't Stop, Won't Stop: A History of the Hip-Hop Generation.* New York: St. Martin's Press.

Erasmus, Zimitri, ed. 2001. *Coloured by History, Shaped by Place: New Perspectives on Coloured Identities in Cape Town.* Cape Town: Kwela Books.

Forman, Murray, and Mark Anthony Neal, ed. 2004. *That's the Joint! The Hip Hop Studies Reader.* New York: Routledge.

Haupt, Adam. 1996. *Rap and the Articulation of Resistance: An Exploration of Subversive Cultural Production during the Early 90s, with Particular Reference to Prophets of da City.* Master's mini-thesis, University of the Western Cape.

Higgens, Christina. 2009. *From da Bomb to Bomba: Global Hip Hop Nation.* In H. Samy Alim, Awad Ibrahim, and Alastair Pennycook, eds., *Global Linguistic Flows: Hip Hop Cultures, Youth Identities, and the Politics of Language.* London: Routledge.

Lee, Jooyoung. 2009. *Escaping Embarrassment: Face-work in the Rap Cipher. Social Psychology Quarterly* 72(4): 306–24.

Omoniyi, Tope. 2009. *"So I Choose to do am Naija Style": Hip Hop and Postcolonial Identities.* In H. Samy Alim, Awad Ibrahim, and Alastair Pennycook, eds., *Global Linguistic Flows: Hip Hop Cultures, Youth Identities, and the Politics of Language*, 113–35. London: Routledge.

Osumare, Halifu. 2007. *The Africanist Aesthetic in Global Hip-Hop: How Power Moves.* New York: Palgrave Macmillan.

Pennycook, Alastair. 2010. *Language as a Local Practice.* London: Routledge.

Posel, Deborah. 2010. Races to consume: revisiting South Africa's history of race, consumption and the struggle for freedom. *Ethnic and Racial Studies* 33(2): 157–75.

Seekings, Jeremy. 2008. The continuing salience of race: discrimination and diversity in South Africa. *Journal of Contemporary African Studies* 26(1):.1–25.

Smitherman, Geneva. 2006. *Word from the Mother: Language and African Americans.* London: Routledge.

Steinberg, Jonny. 2004. *The Number: One Man's Search for Identity in the Cape Underworld and Prison Gangs.* Johannesburg: Jonathan Ball.

Warner, Remi. 2007. *Battles over Borders: Hip-Hop and the Politics and Poetics of Race and Place in the New South Africa.* Unpublished dissertation. Toronto, Ontario: York University.

Watkins, Lee. 2000. *Tracking the Narrative: The Poetics of Identity in the Rap Music and Hip-Hop Culture of Cape Town.* Unpublished Master's Dissertation. Durban: South Africa.

7

Norteño and Sureño Gangs, Hip Hop, and Ethnicity on YouTube

Localism in California through Spanish Accent Variation

NORMA MENDOZA-DENTON

The globalized culture of Hip Hop and the emphasis on local forms of language play important roles in other chapters in this volume (see chapters 2 and 6, for example).[1] In this chapter, my analysis of localism and the politics of territory in the constitution of various California language varieties adds multiple semiotic dimensions to this work. Below, I build upon my long-term ethnographic research among Latino gangs in California to highlight various kinds of Chicano/ Mexican identity work through language. As I will demonstrate, the language ideological fault lines between Norteños and Sureños positioned the former as mostly speakers of Chicano English from Northern California and the latter as Spanish speakers from either Southern California or possibly of recent immigrant Mexican background. I build upon Hill's (2008) analysis of Mock Spanish as well as Talmy's (2010) use of "Mock ESL," as a mock register "surrounding the widely stigmatized acquisition of English as a Second Language," to uncover further layers of complexity in U.S. Latino language use in transnational, mass-mediated contexts. In the process, I examine cyberspace as a potential context where young people become political analysts (and actors) and synthesize their understanding of the larger processes of race (various forms of *Latinidad*), language (multiple regional, ethnic, and mock varieties of both English and Spanish), capital structures, and global power relations.

Recent work in sociolinguistic variation has examined the role of both the mass media (Coupland 2009; Stuart-Smith 2005) and of the Hip Hop/rap genre on language in various locales (Alim 2006 for the Northern California Bay Area; Morgan 2009 for Los Angeles; Blake and Shousterman 2010 for St. Louis; Taylor 2011 for Austin, Texas). Attention has increasingly focused on the role of new media such as YouTube (see Schieffelin and Jones 2009). YouTube users post videos in what serves as a *call*; subsequently, this call brings *responses* either in video format, or as text commentary on the original posting. This call-response format provides a unique combination of data that allows for the simultane- ous investigation of language, metalanguage, and their relationships to space and place.

Although new media have traditionally been thought of as delocalized, I draw on prior discussions of localism and politics of territory in the constitution of subaltern California language varieties, analyzing how stylistic variation and dimensions of proficiency in Spanish acquire a symbolic, localistic dimension for new media users. I argue that hemispheric localism is a projection onto the hemispheric political-stage of processes that began locally in the history of groups of Latinos in California, and that this meaning system becomes projected as a wider political analysis. Young people involved in Norte and Sur become political analysts and actors, organizing their experience through the lens of their participation in these groups. Their participation provides opportunities to make sense of broader racial, linguistic, and economic structures and rela- tions of power.

This analysis draws on a small subset from a corpus of forty YouTube music- fan video postings and their associated responses collected between April 2008 and December 2012. The videos represent rap music claiming association with the California gangs[2] Norteños and Sureños (Mendoza-Denton 2008). A mul- tilayered methodological approach utilizing discourse analysis and semiotic analysis is used to analyze the content and structure of images and language in the videos. As worn on T-shirts, as traded in figurines, and as circulated in hand-drawn artwork, recurrent historical symbols shown in the videos help to set the discursive chronotopes (Bakhtin 1981). These include the space/time intersectional frame of California in the 1960s and 1970s, invoked partially through the iconography of the United Farm Workers (UFW) movement (for example, pictures of the UFW symbol of an angular black eagle against a red background, known as the *Huelga/Welga* [Strike] Bird), and of prison-scapes and barrio-scapes, consistent with an imaginary of the prison as the place where gangs began.

If we agree with Tuan (1977, 6) that places are pauses in historical time, it is less obvious that meaning is embedded in physical space, or that there exist some objective coordinates on the earth's surface onto which webs of meaning are woven, as some definitions of space/place by political geographers would lead us to believe (Agnew 1987; see discussion in Cresswell 2004). *Places* on YouTube can be as ephemeral as a temporary electronic comment-board, or as durable as the well-established and recurrent pattern of references to both the prison- and barrio-scapes, constructed discursively and graphically anew in the text and images uploaded by fans.

This chapter focuses on the post–mass media phenomenon of fan video remixes, where not only are traditional physical spaces represented with map-making zeal, but new place distinctions are created. For example, while *banging* usually means "carrying out gang-related activities," there is a sharp distinction between *banging* on the streets versus *banging* on the Internet (sometimes called *e-banging*, regarded as less credible).

The data I present here are from new media mixed by fans from materials produced by Chicano rappers who claim to have involvement in gangs. As I have noted elsewhere (Mendoza-Denton 2008), an important division among Latino gangs in California involves the Norteños (Northerners) and Sureños (Southerners). Among youth in the 1990s in my Northern California ethnographic high-school study, Norteños saw themselves as Chicanos from Northern California, while Sureños represented themselves as either Southern Californian and urban, or possibly recent immigrant Mexicans. In each case, the group aligned more closely with a particular language. Chicano English was more emblematic of Norteños, while Spanish use was often interpreted as indexing Sureños. Although I don't claim that the situation I found is wholly replicated on YouTube, I offer examples that will allow us to explore continuities across the symbolic aspects of English and Spanish language use, and their relationship to space and place.

In fan-produced YouTube videos, images of California, North America, representation of area codes, and territorializing devices around language are specifically highlighted. Despite pervasive and native English-Spanish codeswitching in the rap lyrics and commentary, fan videos remixed by Norteños make use of Mock Spanish, Mock ESL, and boldly mispronounced codeswitching to portray Sureños as rural, backward, Spanish-accented immigrants, in line with discourses identified by Hill (2008) in her analysis of Mock Spanish, but notably deployed intraethnically. Elsewhere I have analyzed other linguistic devices in these samples including creaky voice (Mendoza-Denton 2011).

Working with YouTube: Fan Videos in the Post–Mass Media

YouTube, currently the largest online video-sharing website, has grown from its inception in 2005 to more than six billion video streams across the world. Lemos (2010) calls its participatory structure the *post–mass media*, and distinguishes it from our traditional understanding of mass media, which is supported by advertising and editorially controlled by corporations and by the state. Here I focus on semiotic/content analysis of four fan-uploaded videos. Table 7.1 lists the downloaded videos, stills, or music in the order in which each will be discussed in this chapter:

Table 7.1 **Videos discussed in this chapter**

Video number (subcategory)	Hypotext/Source: Remix of song, artist
Video 1. Brown Pride Norte (Revolutionary Rap)	"559" by PBC
Video 2. La Vida de un Sureño (Revolutionary Rap)	"La Vida de un Sureño," by Tongo
Video 3. Sur Trece Pela	Homemade track
Video 4. SK (Revolutionary Rap)	Untraceable song, but with recognizable sample from "Corazón de Madera" by Mexican Ranchera-genre music group Mister Chivo

YouTube users and commenters were not contacted for this research, and their identities or involvement as gang affiliates were not ascertainable from their posts. I do, however, identify broad discursive and thematic patterns common across online images that exhibit commonalities with material artifacts collected in fieldwork conducted among high school students in Northern and Southern California in the late 1990s–early 2000s (Mendoza-Denton 2008), and with material artifacts described in research carried out in Los Angeles neighborhoods in the 1970s and 1980s (Moore 1978; Vigil 1988; Moore 1991). In some cases, these artifacts are found in research dating back to the 1940s and 1950s (i.e., zoot suits; see Molina 2002).

These aspects of material culture often reference Mexican-American/Chicano history, bringing to life places and spaces—that is, chronotopes—at a particular, historically significant time. When graphic sequences do include stills, they may depict 30- or 40-year-old archival photographs of some of the founding members of the Nuestra Familia and the Mexican Mafia prison gangs, demonstrating fans' attention to historical context, consciousness, and continuity. These stills exploit well-known iconicities that can be read by members with knowledge of Mexican-American/Chicano civil rights and gang history.

Consider the image presented in Figure 7.1, found in fan-uploaded video #1 for the PBC song "Don't Wanna be a Playa." The image depicts a red puppeteer's hand manipulating the words "Bay Area," presented on the left panel, side-by-side with its hypotext, the movie poster for *The Godfather*, shown on the right. The localistic claim about Norteños controlling the Bay Area through a red puppeteer's hand references not only local gang ideology and the Hollywood movie but also the fact that both Norteños and Sureños gangs envision their structure as replicating that of the Italian Mafia (Mendoza 2005; Mendoza-Denton 2008).

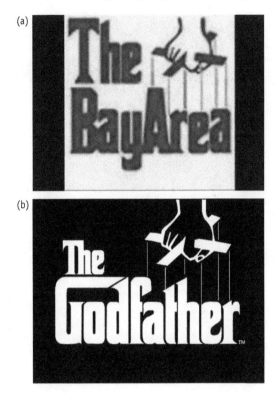

Figure 7.1 Comparison of Norteños "The Bay Area" image from a fan-uploaded video, and the image from the movie poster for *The Godfather*.

Animated Graffiti: History, Localistic Ideologies, and Linguo-Visual Semiotics

> Place is how we make the world meaningful and the way we
> experience the world. Place is space invested with meaning in
> the context of power. (Cresswell 2004, 12)

The gangs as depicted in the fan videos show localistic ideologies, claiming control of geographic areas as small as specific streets within neighborhoods, but most frequently representing claims with area codes and maps of various territories. In this way, fan videos extend the material practice of gang graffiti to the Internet. As gangs claim physical space, the chronotopic nature of the videos allows them to claim place as well. *Place* on these YouTube fan videos is linked to history in quite explicit ways. A Sureño-aligned video (#2) repro-duces an advertisement that ran only in Mexico by the vodka company *Absolut* (Figure 7.2). The graphic lays claim to the historical territory that used to be Mexico in the early nineteenth century, depicted with the slogan "In an Absolut

Figure 7.2 "In an Absolut World" image from a Sureño-aligned video.

World"—presumably Absolut here means "ideal"—overlain on a map of Mexico and the United States before the Mexican Cession of 1848, the Gadsden purchase of 1853, and the annexation of Texas in 1845. This map is projected in quick succession after a map of the territory claimed by Sureños (Figure 7.3)

The map of territory claimed by the Sureños in video #2 looks very similar to the Absolut/historical map except that it is animated. The two-second animation begins with the territorial outlines of an early-nineteenth-century Mexico map and eventually shows the entire United States, Mexico, and Central America as blue—Sureño—territory. Not only does the map reflect a historical connection with the prior territorial claims of Mexico, but it also has much in common with law enforcement and other time-series maps depicting the spread of gangs. This type of broad time-series geographic mapping of gangs has been used within police departments and in the media (Mendoza-Denton 2008). The homemade animated videos reflect both an awareness of the history of the territories in question and are intertextual with gang-related materials commonly issued by police departments.

Places in more circumscribed areas of the United States, such as specific cities in Northern California (see Figure 7.4), are represented by their telephone area codes. Known by everyone who lives in the region, they mark the user as

Figure 7.3 Map of the territory claimed by Sureños.

Figure 7.4 Places in California represented by telephone area codes.

being local to that area. In addition, sometimes the area codes appear as material objects through gang tagging (graffiti) or on bodily tattoos. People and objects are associated with particular places by their inclusion in the fan-videos or in the lyrics of the rap songs. For example, Tongo's "La Vida de Un Sureño" rap claims the 813 area code in Florida, "ocho uno tres/ ésta area me pertenece, [*eight one three / this area belongs to me*]," while PBC's (2000) song "559" finds its title in the area code currently given to PBC's home city of Lemoore in Kings County, California, which in 1998 changed from the 209 to the 559 area code. Even these prior area codes make their way onto songs: lyrics from PBC's song "4-Life" are given below:

---

(1) We're just some crazy little bald-headed
Mexicans
representing for Lemoore city
and when we put in work we do it
and show no fucking pity.
We used to be from the 209
Kings county, 559.

In the case of area codes, the poster of a video has the power to represent their vision of what places are to be interpellated. These call-outs are supported or challenged by commenters reacting to the clips: here I suggest that the comments are akin to the repeated crossings-out of graffiti, with claims being posted, challenged, and reasserted. Since much of the claiming has to do with space outside the YouTube forum, a tension emerges through participants' claims of legitimacy in physical, localistic space; at the same time users appear to distance themselves from "e-banging," that is to say, presumably inauthentic (or at least unverifiable) gang-related behavior on the Internet. Nonetheless, geographic claims made online encompass broad swaths of territory, as is the case in Figure 7.5.

In both Figures 7.4 and 7.5 we encounter the chronotope of Chicano Civil Rights and of California in the 1970s through the Huelga Bird. Chronotopes put together the historical, intergenerational memory of California as a place where the farmworker struggle originated, and serve as an invocation and reminder of the roots of the gangs. This memory is richly accessorized with references to material cultural objects, semiotically bundled (Keane 2003) in their participation through various modalities. Memorialization in the "virtual landscape" consists of displaying images of historical, prison-related, and barrio-related iconography, overlain with sonic hypotexts such as Original Oldies ("Oldies"). These semiotic bundles serve as both memory and metaphor, and are participants in an epiphenomenal process: when appearing simultaneously, they trigger a new

Figure 7.5 "From Texas 2 th4 Bay, Nortenos run thizz $hit."

context. Because the iconography presented in the videos is also available in figurines, jewelry, t-shirts, drawings, magazines (like *Lowrider*), and other symbols outside of the virtual world of YouTube, they are multiply redundant and immediately interpretable to participants. Technologization and globalization of the post–mass media allow for fans' documentation and broadcast of local aspects of their material culture: when fans upload images of homemade art, or videos synced to popular rap songs, they participate in what I call an episemiotic intertextuality that transcends their local space and time.

So far I have discussed how aspects of locally recognized material cultures can be broadcast and made available to like-minded fans. Producers seek out, recombine, and manufacture their own music and images, pushing the limits of the technology (creating video channels and allowing other fans to follow them), effectively sending out privately coded public messages that echo some of the strategies—like the radio station dedication, and the scrawl of graffiti— available to their parents and grandparents, the original listeners of 60s Oldies, and originators of many of the intertextual icons being manipulated.

But how does a post–mass mediated technology like YouTube, allowing for the combination, indefinite storage, and simultaneous broadcast of music, text, and images, enable new kinds of language production and new kinds of localisms? And how do producers and commenters engage in metapragmatic stereotypes (Agha 2007, 150) that hinge on the overt identification of language ideologies? I proceed with a discussion of language ideologies, followed with one of Mock Registers and an analysis of fan-uploaded video samples deploying these registers for ideological effect.

Ideologies of English and Spanish Use

On fan-uploaded videos as well as in rap songs themselves, *language use is contested*, with English generally regarded as unmarked in videos originating in the United States (recall that both YouTube and the gangs are transnational). In videos claiming to originate in the United States, English-Spanish codeswitching is regarded as unmarked, while exclusive Spanish use is normatively classified as Sureño. For example, in video #2, the following lyrics from "La Vida de un Sureño" by the rapper Tongo are commented on by YouTubers:

(2) La vida de un Sureño	*The life of a Sureño*
Con el uno y el tres	*With the one and the three*
Te canto esta rola	*I'm singing (for) you this song*
En español	*In Spanish*
No en inglés.	*Not in English*

As is common in this genre of video, many of the commenters express agreement with the message of the fan-uploaded video, while some of them thunder invective. One commenter, a native Spanish speaker (his lexical choice in swear words and pronouns suggests he could be Colombian), uses mostly Spanish but also some English in codeswitching to make derogatory remarks toward Mexicans, referring to them as "beaners" and saying "come mow my lawn." A commenter responds in Spanish: "[. . .] seguro eres uno de e[s]os babosos k por k hablan un poco d ingles se creen una verga. *(I'm sure you're one of those idiots that just because they speak a little bit of English think they are the shit [meaning: excellent].)*" Another commenter responds: "porque [h]ablas asi de estos vatos. mejor no uses el espanol si no te gustan los mexicanos. (Why do you talk like that about these guys? Better not to use Spanish if you don't like Mexicans.)" These comments suggest that in this ideological context Spanish use is indicative of alignment with Mexicans, even if one is a native Spanish speaker from somewhere else. The lyrics of the rap song by Tongo, reproduced above, also allude to specific linguistic selection. By creating a contrast between Spanish and English, and aligning Spanish use with Sureño membership, rapper and commenters alike take a semiotic stance, one that is common on the streets (here I mean to contrast "the streets" with both prisons and the Internet) among Norteño- and Sureño-affiliated youth (Mendoza-Denton 2008; Bettie 2003).

Other examples reinforce the perceived alignment between being a Sureño and Spanish use, and between being a Norteño and English use. In the comments section on fan-uploaded pro-Norteño video #3, a photomontage over rap from a rapper in Polk County, Florida, all in Spanish (00:39-00:50), the commenters erupt:

(3) comment1: o hell no this bitch ass video is a big disrespect for the surenos and the mexicans. fake ass video never put spanish on ur videos ur a bitch. this is big sur 13 m3x1can for life [. . .]

comment2: why the fuck is dat foo buster ass chapete rapping in spanish, fucking gringo bitch

comment3: Your Fucken Clueless! No Doubt Your A Wannabe! If You Knew What You Were Saying You'd Know We'z Mexicans Too Fucken IDIOT!! Never Seen A White Norteno Before! And Learn To Type You Fucken Little Kid.

comment4: mutha fuckin $crap$ alway$ think we nortenoz r muthafuckin guero$ putoz we muthafuckin chicano$ eh. fuckin $crapa$ pinche pai$a$ putoz [3]all bout NORTE XIV

comment5: mexico is in north america tho u fucking stupid ass skraps

comment6: iam reping all polk kounty and palmbeach kounty nortenos, lakeland, winter heaven, plantcity, hanincity, westpalm, lakeworth, and doverlocos puro norte XIV

In these examples, a contradiction emerges. On the one hand, the structure of YouTube has allowed the transcendence of strictly California-based interpretations of Spanish-language ideologies: both of the examples shown above are from Florida-based rappers, where the local meanings of Spanish use are clearly different from those in California. By using Spanish as emblematic of both Sureños and Norteños, and using specific types of Spanish to align with Mexicans, YouTube participation has deeply unsettled the original language ideologies surrounding the divisions between Norteños and Sureños.

From Interethnic Mock Spanish to Intraethnic Mock ESL

Hill (2005, 2008) identifies Mock Spanish as "a set of tactics that speakers of American English use to appropriate symbolic resources from Spanish" (2008, 128). It is a discursive register that borrows Spanish words and morphology and is used by Whites and other non-Hispanics (or non-Latinas/os) to display *covert* racism toward people of color. Crucially in Hill's account, the mockery is interethnic. It is also part of a long history of Spanish language use in the United States, a history that includes conflict with Mexico and the systematic and pervasive oppression of Spanish-speaking people in the United States, especially in the Southwest.

According to Hill, Mock Spanish goes largely unnoticed and is broadly accepted by the majority society, giving the impression that the speaker is a relaxed, easy-going sort of person with a surface familiarity with another culture. However, the retrieval of this easygoing persona relies on accessing negative stereotypes about Spanish speakers—that they are lazy, for instance. This particular stereotype begets the pejorative use of the Mock Spanish *mañana* ("tomorrow"), while stereotypes of sexuality may beget Mock Spanish usage such as *mamasita* ("beautiful woman"; misspelling of Spanish *mamacita*, lit., "little mama") or "caliente" [lit., "hot"], taken in Mock Spanish to mean "sexy."

Hill outlines four tactics in the borrowing of Spanish words into the Mock Spanish register of English:

1) Semantic pejoration.
2) Euphemism.
3) Addition of Spanish morphology (*el* and *lo* articles and *-a* and *-o* suffixation).
4a) Hyper-anglicization and 4b) bold mispronunciation. (Hill 2008, 134–40)

Hill argues that the covert nature of racism in the examples she has collected allows for the portrayal of the speaker as jocular and relaxed, the kind of sophisticated person who may know Spanish but who might deliberately hold back that knowledge (Barrett 2006), peppering phrases with ungrammatical, anglicized Spanish to simultaneously show a distance from actual Spanish and its speakers as well as to convey pejoration toward Spanish speakers. In ethnographic work, Barrett (2006) conducted a study of a restaurant in Chicago that he calls *Chalupatown*, where Anglo servers used Mock Spanish toward the Mexican kitchen staff even though it caused misunderstandings among them in the fulfillment of customer orders and in the general operation of the restaurant. Ironically, the ungrammaticality of Mock Spanish perpetuated confusion in both spoken and written orders, but the misunderstandings were blamed on the Spanish speakers only, who were suspected of willful miscomprehension. Barrett bolsters Hill's conclusions that Mock Spanish is primarily used interethnically (across ethnicities) to convey and effectuate degradation and pejoration (see chapter 3, this volume, for an expanded discussion).

The research conducted here is also closely related to other investigations of dialect and register mockery, including the discussions by Ronkin and Karn (1999) and Rickford and Rickford (2000) of Mock Ebonics; Thompson's (2010) study of Kenyan ethnic parody; Chun's (2004, 2009) studies of the ways in which a Mock Asian register was used in the speech of a famous stand-up comic, and also in a Texas high school; and Hiramoto's (2009) investigation of how different dialects of Japanese were used to marginalize and stereotype racialized persons in the Japanese translation of the script of *Gone with the Wind*. As in Hiramoto's study of movie scripts, rap songs can be viewed as a type of scripted speech that is subject to performance and evaluation for audiences.

In the analysis of these data, I have in practice found it difficult to delineate among bilingual speakers a consistent boundary between Mock Spanish as described by Hill and Barrett, and what Steven Talmy has termed Mock ESL (Talmy 2010), which we might define here as the mock register surrounding the widely stigmatized acquisition of English as a Second Language (ESL).[4]

This discussion of the semiotic stances of YouTubers vis-à-vis Spanish and English brings us back to our consideration of mock registers, where these are used to a different effect than that documented in the previous literature. Here I take up the question of what happens when the mocking takes place intra-ethnically rather than interethnically. In the case of the YouTube fan videos I analyze below, there is no "foreign culture" at play over which to display one's easygoing nature. Speakers (rappers/fans) and listeners (comment-writers) are bicultural and bilingual, and their usage of Mock ESL/Mock Spanish provides evidence of native English and native or near-native command of Spanish, with the ability to deploy fine phonetic details of Spanish in their mocking registers. The mocking register I describe here is an English-based Mock ESL/Mock Spanish with primarily English syntax and Spanish loanwords as described by Hill and by Barrett, though what I call here Mock Regional Spanish has interspersed sociophonetic features drawn from lower-prestige targets within nonstandard regional Spanish (like Mexican Rural Spanish, or Salvadoran Spanish). In traditional sociolinguistic terms this practice would fall under dialect crossing (Rampton 2009) or styleshifting (Rickford and McNair Knox 1994; Alim 2004).

Below are the lyrics from the audio track of a video titled "GB." This audio is layered on a static image showing a parental-advisory sign proclaiming "Warning: Norteños Puttin' it down." This is how the video self-identifies as a Norteño video. In this sequence two purported Sureños (PS) get beat up by some Norteños (N). The voice actors portraying them strain to produce their utterances in a higher pitch, and with features of Rural Mexican Spanish (*in italics*) and Mock ESL (underlined):

(at 00:58–01:27 Mexican Cumbia music plays)

1 PS1: Hey Joker, turn it up! That's my favorite song *ey!*
2 PS2: *Órale* homes, *órale.*
3 PS1: You know we gotta <u>show</u> these chapetes *ey*, <u>we gotta [ch]show them</u>!
4 PS2: Wear your paño proud! Wear your paño proud!
5 PS1: Ey! ah! Ey!
6 PS1: It's just under it ey? What you trippin' off of?
7 PS2: Los chapetes, dos chapetes, they're coming!
8 PS1, PS2: <u>Oh they're coming, they're coming!</u>
9 N: Who are these fools?
10 <u>Hey no bang, no bang. No bang, no bang.</u>
11 <u>No, no, no! Don't do that ey?</u>
12 [Sounds of violence]

(end at 01:27)

In these videos, a corollary to being able to identify an area code is being able to distinguish what is and is not normal variation within the language of your interlocutor. Playing with that, overexaggerating (as in line 3, *ch* as a Mock ESL pronunciation of "show"), or alternately an allusion to the well-known *sh~ch* alternation in Spanish and some dialects of Chicano English, as documented by Flores-Bayer (2013); and underemphasizing the targets, either in the form of Mock Spanish or Mock ESL, relies on a very finely calibrated understanding of the interlocutor and of the mapping between language and space. In other words, it is a joke at the expense of the target, but the target has to "get it." The last insult heaped on Sureños in this sequence is the idea that they would switch to an even less fluent version of English to try to back down from a fight. If bold mispronunciation of Spanish is a hallmark of Mock Spanish, this bold mispronunciation and ridicule of L2 English is meant as a dig against Sureños, transparent at all levels of exaggeration to the intended targets. Fan video posters assume a particular model of an extended speech community that can encompass rural Mexican Spanish, deploy it in exaggerated ways, and make fun of it. Levels of proficiency in Spanish and English thus acquire symbolic and localistic dimensions.

Conclusion

Street political organizations—gangs—find an outlet on the Internet, a "network of networks" that has been likened to an idealized public sphere. Aspects of locally recognized material cultures can be broadcast and made available to like-minded fans. I have shown that content producers seek out, recombine, and manufacture their own music and images, effectively sending out privately coded public messages. Most of the videos that make up this corpus rely heavily on prior familiarity with the symbols known to the communities, and neither recruit (contra Arquilla and Ronfeldt 2001) nor welcome outsiders to comment on the opposing claims or the opposing parties already involved.

Core aspects that emerge are the negotiation of (a) language use and language ideologies; (b) various levels of localism, both California-centered and hemispheric; and (c) various kinds of Chicano/Mexican identity work, all mediated through sets of symbols that video-mixers tacitly agree on as representing their common concerns. Further work in this area will address the gendered dimensions of the economies of affect within the videos. I consider the present analysis as contributing to the call for a semiotics that analyzes "the ways in which systems and codes are used, transformed or transgressed in social practice" (de Lauretis 1984, 167). Lastly, semiotic analyses of the use, transformation, and transgression of particular varieties can greatly complicate our understanding of language, race, and ethnicity across continually evolving, technological means of communication.

Notes

1. This chapter owes a debt of gratitude to many of my colleagues and friends who encouraged me. Most notable among those are Aomar Boum, Maggie Boum-Mendoza, Ashley Stinnett, Terry Woronov, Bambi Schieffelin, Miriam Meyerhoff, Brendan O'Connor, Jane Hill, Rudi Gaudio, Perry Gilmore, and colleagues and audiences at the University of Arizona, Copenhagen University, University of Edinburgh, and the Australian National University. I am also deeply grateful to H. Samy Alim and to John R. Rickford for editorial input, and to the Australian National University's Humanities Research Center for providing the time and space for me to complete this work.
2. I adopt the following definition of a gang from Brotherton and Barrios (2004, 23): "A street political organization is a group formed largely by youth and adults of a marginalized social class which aims to provide its members with a resistant identity, an opportunity to be individually and collectively empowered, a voice to speak back to the dominant culture, a refuge from the stresses and strains of barrio or ghetto life and a spiritual enclave within which its own sacred rituals can be generated and practiced."
3. The Spanish invective *pinches paisas* roughly translates to "stupid country bumpkins."
4. Many thanks to Rudi Gaudio for discussing this distinction with me.

References

Agha, Asif. 2007. *Language and Social Relations*. New York: Cambridge University Press.

Agnew, J. 1987. *The United States in the World Economy*. Cambridge: Cambridge University Press.

Alim, H. Samy. 2004. *You Know My Steez: An Ethnographic and Sociolinguistic Study of Styleshifting in a Black American Speech Community*. Durham, NC: Duke University Press.

Alim, H. Samy. 2006. *Roc the Mic Right: The Language of Hip Hop Culture*. New York: Routledge.

Arquilla, John, and David F. Ronfeldt. 2001. *Networks and Netwars: the Future of Terror, Crime, and Militancy*. United States Dept. of Defense. Office of the Secretary of Defense. Santa Monica, CA: Rand.

Bakhtin, M. M. 1981. Forms of Time and of the Chronotope in the Novel. In *Dialogic Imagination*, trans. C. Emerson and M. Holquist. Austin: University of Texas Press, 259–422.

Barrett, Rusty. 2006. Language ideology and racial inequality: Competing functions of Spanish in an Anglo-owned Mexican restaurant. *Language in Society* 35(2): 163–204.

Bettie, J. 2003. *Women without Class: Girls, Race, and Identity*. Berkeley: University of California Press.

Blake, Renee, and Cara Shousterman. 2010. Diachrony and AAE: St. Louis, Hip Hop, and Sound Change outside of the Mainstream. *Journal of English Linguistics* 38(3): 230–47.

Brotherton, D. C., and L. Barrios. 2004. *The Almighty Latin King and Queen Nation: Street Politics and the Transformation of a New York City Gang*. New York: Columbia University Press.

Chun, Elaine. 2004. Ideologies of legitimate mockery: Margaret Cho's revoicings of Mock Asian. *Pragmatics* 14: 263–89.

Chun, Elaine. 2009. Speaking like Asian immigrants: Intersections of accommodation and mocking at a U.S. high school. *Pragmatics* 19(1): 17–38.

Coupland, Nikolas. 2009. The Mediated Performance of Vernaculars. *Journal of English Linguistics* 37(3): 284–300.

Cresswell, Tim. 2004. *Place: A Short Introduction*. Oxford: Blackwell.

de Lauretis, Teresa. 1984. *Alice Doesn't: Feminism, Semiotics, Cinema*. London: Macmillan.
Flores-Bayer, Isla. 2013. CHare the CouSH: Insights into the ch/sh alternation in Chicano English. Paper presented at the Forty Second Annual Conference on New Ways of Analyzing Variation [NWAV42], University of Pittsburgh.
Hill, Jane. 2005. Intertextuality as Source and Evidence for Indirect Indexical Meanings. *Journal of Linguistic Anthropology* 15: 113–24.
Hill, Jane. 2008. *The Everyday Language of White Racism*. Malden, MA: Blackwell.
Hiramoto, M. 2009. Slaves Speak Pseudo-Toohoku-ben: The Representation of Minorities in the Japanese Translation of Gone with the Wind. *Journal of Sociolinguistics* 13/2: 249–63.
Keane, Webb. 2003. Semiotics and the Social Analysis of Material Things. *Language and Communication* 23: 409–25.
Lemos, Andre. 2010. Post-Mass Media Functions, Locative Media, and Informational Territories: New Ways of Thinking About Territory, Place, and Mobility in Contemporary Society. *Space and Culture* 13: 403–20.
Mendoza, R. 2005. *Mexican Mafia: From Altar Boy to Hit Man*. Corona, CA: Whitley & Associates.
Mendoza-Denton, Norma. 2008. *Homegirls: The Making of Latina Youth Styles*. Malden, MA: Blackwell.
Mendoza-Denton, Norma. 2011. The Semiotic Hitchhiker's Guide to Creaky Voice: Circulation and Gendered Hardcore in a Chicana/o Gang Persona. *Journal of Linguistic Anthropology* 21(2): 261–80.
Molina, Ruben. 2002. *The Old Barrio Guide to Low Rider Music, 1950–1975*. Los Angeles: Mictlan Publishing.
Moore, J. 1978. *Homeboys: Gangs, Drugs, and Prisons in the Barrios of Los Angeles*. Philadelphia, PA: Temple University Press.
Moore, J. 1991. *Going Down to the Barrio: Homeboys and Homegirls in Change*. Oxford: Blackwell.
Morgan, Marcyliena. 2009. *The Real Hiphop: Battling for Knowledge, Power, and Respect in the LA Underground*. Durham, NC: Duke University Press.
Rampton, Ben. 2009. Interaction ritual and not just artful performance in crossing and stylization. *Language in Society* 38: 149–76.
Rickford, John R., and Faye McNair-Knox. 1994. Addressee- and Topic-Influenced Style Shift: A Quantitative Sociolinguistics Study. In D. Biber and E. Finegan, eds., *Sociolinguistic Perspectives on Register*. New York: Oxford University Press, 235–76.
Rickford, John R., and Russell J. Rickford. 2000. *Spoken Soul: The Story of Black English*. New York: John Wiley.
Ronkin, Maggie, and Helen Karn. 1999. Mock Ebonics: Linguistic racism in parodies of Ebonics on the internet. *Journal of Sociolinguistics* 3(3): 360–80.
Schieffelin, Bambi, and Graham Jones. 2009. Talking Text and Talking Back: "My BFF Jill" from Boob Tube to YouTube. *Journal of Computer-Mediated Communication* 14(4): 1050–79.
Stuart-Smith, J. 2005. Is TV a contributory factor is accent change in adolescents? Final Report on ESRC Grant No. R000239757. http://www.researchcatalogue.esrc.ac.uk/grants/R000239757/read/outputs/title. Last accessed: June 8, 2016.
Talmy, Steven. 2010. Achieving distinction through Mock ESL: A critical pragmatics analysis of classroom talk in a high school. *Pragmatics and Language Learning* 12(1): 215–54.
Taylor, Chris. 2012. *Power to Represent: The Spatial Politics of Style in Houston Hip Hop*. Doctoral dissertation, University of Texas–Austin.
Thompson, Katrina Daly. 2010. "I am Maasai": Interpreting ethnic parody in Bongo Flava. *Language in Society* 39(4): 493–520.
Tuan, Yi-Fu. 1977. *Space and Place: The Perspective of Experience*. Minneapolis: University of Minnesota Press.
Vigil, J. D. 1988. *Barrio Gangs: Street Life and Identity in Southern California*. Austin: University of Texas Press.

Part II

RACING LANGUAGE

8

Toward Heterogeneity

A Sociolinguistic Perspective on the Classification of Black People in the Twenty-First Century

RENÉE BLAKE*

As a young Black scholar in the late 1990s, I was struck by the fact that once language scholars found out I grew up in the United States as the child of Trinidadian and Venezuelan immigrant parents, I was rarely sought after for my intuitions as a native speaker of African American English or Creole English for that matter. Questions went from "Can you say . . . ?" to "Have you ever heard . . . ?" I was no longer considered an "authentic" speaker of the languages within the cultures in which I had grown up. At the very least, linguistically, I existed on the periphery. Despite my own feelings of belonging, I accepted my assigned position and continued my academic pursuits, in many ways buying into the ideology of not belonging. Approximately a decade later, at the very beginning of the twenty-first century, my sentiments were echoed by members of Black communities in New York City, evidenced in an exchange with Dana,[1] a Black second-generation West Indian, twenty-one years of age:

(I)NTERVIEWER: Um. Where's your mom from?
(D)ANA: Jamaica.
I: And your dad?
D: Jamaica.
I: Oh. And . . . but you were born here?
D: Yeah.
I: And what do you consider yourself?
. . .
D: . . . I consider myself a Jamerican. Because if I tell the American kids that both of my parents are Jamaican, they tell me I'm Jamaican. And if I tell the Jamaican kids

that both of my parents are Jamaican, some of them will
tell me I'm Jamaican, but for the most part, all you hear
is you're a Yankee, and that means that you're American.
[LAUGH] But, yeah. So I just say I'm a Jamerican.

Spears (1988) argues that the sorely underestimated social and linguistic heterogeneity of the Black population in the United States needs to be considered in studies of the language of Black speakers.[2] For instance, in New York
City, Caribbean Americans, Afrolatinos, and more recent African immigrants
and their children reside alongside and commingle with long-standing African
American communities, and are often identified with African Americans socially,
racially, and linguistically (Zentella 1997; Waters 1999; Blake and Shousterman
2010). Waters (1994) notes that the "straight line" assimilationist model that
generally applied to earlier European immigrants to the United States (compare
Warner and Srole 1945) does not apply to Black immigrants (and their children).
She says (1994, 799), "if these immigrants assimilate they assimilate to being
not just Americans but Black Americans." Further, "given the ongoing prejudice
and discrimination in American society, this represents downward mobility for
the immigrants and their children." Here we see how the classifications Black
and African American are inextricably linked such that to be Black in America is
eventually to be African American. Such linking is evident in our national ideology. It is in fact commonplace for scholars, politicians, cultural critics, community members, and individuals to use the term "Black" synonymously with
"African American." Moreover, this linking is hardwired in the U.S. Census and
other official documentation. While scholars have problematized the inter-
changing of the terms "Black" and "African American," we continue to be caught
in it (compare Dodson 2007).

At its core then this chapter is about highlighting diversity within Black communities in the United States, and implications for sociolinguistics and the study
of communities more generally in the twenty-first century.[3] By studying the
sociolinguistic behavior of other Black[4] ethnics (e.g., non–African Americans)
in the United States, we can illuminate the ways in which individuals from these
communities use and manipulate language, consciously and unconsciously,
as a resource to mark their identification relative to their African American–
identified counterparts. This chapter argues that language scholars should go
beyond social categories defined in the national imagination and incorporate
the nuances of how groups and individuals understand themselves without the
imposition of a national ideology of race.[5]

Walk the streets of New York City over the past decade and you can easily
hear a group of darker-skinned children who would be phenotypically identified
as Black benignly asking the question of each other, "Are you Black or Hispanic?"

Now, this seems like an odd question for children of varying shades of Brown and Black. But one would also be surprised by the ease with which this question is answered. On the surface, it may be a question about whether at least one parent is an immigrant from a Spanish-speaking nation or you grew up speaking Spanish in the home. So, the question, are you Black or Hispanic, is in fact a language question that seems to be informed by and informing racial ideologies (i.e., *racing language/languaging race*, as framed by Alim 2009). Thus, if you are phenotypically Black *and* Hispanic as delineated above, then you are somehow *not* Black, consequently *not* African American. This raciolinguistic dynamic is supported by our institutionalized structures, themselves perhaps the result of ideologies upheld by our institutions.[6] Such distinctions are further reified when Black people in the United States are asked if they are Black/African American/non-Hispanic. What gets lost here are the ways in which phenotypically Black people, like African Americans, can be marginalized regardless of class, language, culture, and so on.

Race/Ethnicity in Sociolinguistics

Fought, in her 2006 book, *Language and Ethnicity*, notes that with few exceptions, the field of sociolinguistics has given little attention to the definition of ethnic categories.[7] She (2006, 4) points out that while the definitions of race and ethnicity are elusive and "not based on any objectively measurable criteria," it is agreed that they are socially constructed.[8] And although socially constructed, ideas and beliefs about race and ethnicity inform and are informed by our lived experiences. She further states (2006, 9), "most works on race and ethnicity acknowledge the important roles of *both self-identification and the perceptions and attitudes of others* in the construction of ethnic identity."[9] For sociolinguistics, there is a parallel here with Irvine and Gal (2000, 35–36), who argue that representing language is not ideologically neutral. They say that linguistic ideologies are held by the immediate participants in a local sociolinguistic system, as well as by other observers, such as linguists and ethnographers, who have mapped the boundaries of languages and peoples and provided descriptive accounts of them, which has been the case for African American English (AAE) and its speakers, for example.

According to Morgan (2014, 2), "speech communities are one way that language ideologies and social identities are constructed." Within sociolinguistics, while there is not a consensus on definition of speech community, there is a general notion of shared symbolic or interactional norms by community members. Guy (2001), borrowing from Judaism, Book of Judges, told of the beheading of the Ephraimites by the Gileadites. Although the Ephraimites were members of the same Semitic community (i.e., Tribe), at the moment of reckoning, after a military defeat, they pronounced the word *shibboleth* with *s* instead of *sh*, thereby identifying themselves as not belonging to the victors. Guy joked that if the Ephraimites could have only had more time they could have perhaps proven to the Gileadites that they were one of them. They could have generated enough linguistic data to prove that their sibilant, [s], was part of their context-free variation, and therefore they were in fact very much like the Gileadites. Allegorizing this biblical story to the present, one could argue that the Gileadites are like community members able to determine the boundaries of a community through linguistic means. But returning to the idea of observers mapping boundaries onto communities, modern-day sociolinguistics could also be equated to evolved Gileadites in that in our work we have the power to determine how community lines are drawn, with the choice of deciding to consider or not consider the oftentimes idiosyncratic categories and delineations generated or offered by community members.

Over a decade ago, Eckert (2003) explicitly addressed one of the elephants in the room within the field of sociolinguistics, the notion of the Authentic Speaker, namely those who naturally speak the local vernacular spontaneously and unconsciously. In the case of AAE, with only a few exceptions (e.g., Mitchell-Kernan 1971; Rickford 1992), sociolinguistic studies focused on young urban African American *males*, who were viewed as the "real" speakers of the vernacular and authentic members of core Black culture, that being street culture of the inner cities (compare Labov 1972; Morgan 1994; Cutler 1999; Eckert 2003). While Labov (and others) have produced work that counters arguments that the language of African Americans is somehow deficient or deviant, Morgan (1994, 28) argues that his description of AAE and its speakers has been problematic for the field:

> This description of vernacular or core black culture constructs authentic African American membership and language as male, adolescent, insular and trifling. By default, everyone else in the black community, regardless of age, is a lame. Because lames do not participate in core culture, having "suffered a loss of some magnitude" in terms of verbal skills, do not use AAE features in ways significantly related to vernacular members, and speak some version of AAE, they are not culturally African American.[10]

While language scholars have since produced many other studies that systematically describe AAE in terms of variation across and within speakers with regards to many social factors (Alim 2004),[11] when it comes to ethnicity and race, African Americans are still treated as a monolithic group (i.e., descendants of enslaved

Africans in the United States). And again, the label *African American* is used interchangeably with *Black*. From the 1960s to the present, sociolinguists have worked within the fixed racial binary categories of White (Anglo/Caucasian) and Black (African American/Negro), which are directly linked to a history of racial inequities. As Alcoff (2000, 24) states, "racialized identities in the United States have long connoted homogeneity."

Towards Heterogeneity: Semiotic Changes for Black People in the United States

Smitherman (2000) provides a schemata for the historical framing of African American English alongside the Black experience in the United States and the evolution of ethnic/racial labels over a 400-year period. She makes a clear distinction between African Americans and other Black ethnics, stating (2000, 43):

> Notwithstanding historical, cultural and cosmological linkages with Continental and Diasporic Africans and, further, notwithstanding similarities between American slavery and slavery in other historical epochs, the African American, as James Baldwin once put it, is a unique creation. Whereas other African peoples lay claim to national identity in countries where the population is "Black"—e.g., Jamaicans, Ghanaians, Bajans, Nigerians—African Americans claim national identity in a country where most of the population is non-Black.

Table 8.1 is adapted from Smitherman (2000, 36; also 41–56) and shows the alignment of key events or social forces that she argues would have affected the development of AAE. Alongside this are the changing racial referents for Africans (i.e., Black people) in the United States over time. I add an assessment for the beginning of the twenty-first century (see new row 11).

As Smitherman (2000, 34) notes, "in historical moments of racial progress, the language [of African Americans] is less Ebonified; in times of racial suppression, the language is more Ebonified." Her argument here is that when the racial climate is such that Blacks in America feel their vested interests are being acknowledged and addressed, their linguistic codes tend to correspond and move closer to the codes used by Whites, as shown in columns 2 and 3 of Table 8.1.

Critical to the discussion of the categorization of African Americans/Blacks is column 4, which shows the racial referencing among people of "African" descent in America. The earliest self-referent "African" seems to have been generated *from within* as a way to reflect a "a distinct African consciousness." The term "colored" emerged in the nineteenth century and reflected a shift from generations

Table 8.1 **Historical trajectory of the Black Experience, African American Language, and semantic classification of Black People in the United States**

Year	Relevant historical event(s)	Related Linguistic developments	Ethnic group name	Attested uses for events and organizations
1557	Beginning of African use of English	**Pidgin**		
1619	20 African slaves/ indentured servants arrive at Jamestown on a Dutch ship		**African**	African Episcopal Church
1661	Beginning of slave codes circumscribing activities and lives of slaves	**Creole**		
1808	Outlawing of slave trade; rise of anti-slavery movement	**De-Creolization**	**Colored**	National Association for the Advancement of Colored People (NAACP)
1863	Emancipation	**De-Africanization**		
1877	Reconstruction ends; institutionalization of "separate but equal"	De-Creolized forms solidify, especially among under-class/"field" slave descendants	**Negro**	American Negro Academy
1914-45	World War I & II; vast urban migration of Blacks out of the South	**De-Creolization continues**		
1966	Black Power Movement; push for integration comes to a halt	**Re-Creolization Re-Africanization** De-creolization halted; conscious attempt to recapture earlier Black Language forms and create new ones	**Black**	Black History Week

(continued)

Table 8.1 **Continued**

Year	Relevant historical event(s)	Related Linguistic developments	Ethnic group name	Attested uses for events and organizations
1990s	Capitalist, post-industrialist crises creating severe problems for some blacks; unparalleled prosperity for others	Emergence of bilingual consciousness; linguistic experimentation	**African American**	National Museum of African American History
2000s	*Capitalism and continued racial injustices and inequality for many Black communities; Globalization; Trans-nationalism*	*Multilingual and multidialectal consciousness; Linguistic experimentation continues*	*African American; Black; African descendant (of African Descent)*	*World Summit of African Descendants*

Source: Adapted from Smitherman 2000, 36, 41–56.

of Africans arriving from Africa to generations born on American soil with the hope of emancipation and citizenship through struggle. In another attempt at creating an identity that would usher in dignity and citizenship came the label "negro," which was further articulated through the capitalization of the first letter around the 1920s. Smitherman notes (2000, 47) that a new sociolinguistic construction of reality came in 1966 with the Black power movement. While Negro was viewed as a label *from outside* imposed through slavery, "Black signaled an ideological shift, a repudiation of whiteness and the rejection of assimilation." And while the label "African American" emerged around the same time as "Black," it did not gain currency until the 1980s/1990s. In fact, it did not make it onto the U.S. Census as a racial category until 2000. Interestingly, the argument for the shift in paradigm to African American is that it indicates something about Black Americans in the world. According to Smitherman (2000, 49), the new semantic constructs an identity of unified global struggle against race domination, linking Africans in North America with continental Africans and with other Diasporic African groups.[12]

In the twenty-first century, African American and Black are used interchangeably, but with the influx of Black people from around the globe into the United States, we are now at a crossroads of determining how to shift discourses of ethnicity within race. Afrolatino activists threw down the gauntlet at the 2001 United Nations (UN) world conference in Durban, South Africa, calling for a radical joining of forces of Blacks globally living under racist ideologies. These activists acknowledged parallel histories and systematic problems experienced by Black people in the United States with Black people outside of the United States, and the critical impact Black Americans have made on antiracist struggles throughout Latin America (compare Turner 2002). Some Blacks across the United States have slowly begun to answer the call of the label "African descendant" or "of African descent." (compare Román and Flores 2010; Blake 2014).

In the next section, I examine how the language of Black ethnics in New York City may give us insights into questions of the racial/ethnic diversity. The individuals interviewed are the members of the social and familial networks of two undergraduate students at New York University who are friends, and who were hired and trained to conduct sociolinguistic interviews. The interviewers are both women in their early twenties and from New York who identify as Black, with one closely linked to a social network of Caribbean Americans and the other closely linked with African Americans historically anchored to the United States.

Empirical Case Study: African American Language in New York City

Here, I present a summary of the results of two early sociolinguistic studies of Black New Yorkers[13]—second-generation Caribbean Americans (SGCAs) whose parents migrated from the English-speaking Caribbean (i.e., West Indies) to the United States, and their African American counterparts of U.S.-born parentage (U.S. African Americans or USAA).[14] I present their use of three linguistic variables: postvocalic /r/ in words like *floor*, the tensing and raising of the vowel /ɔ/ in words like *talk* (referred to as BOUGHT raising in this paper), and the realization of the vowel in words like *boat* (referred to as BOAT word class in this paper). As these variables have come to be associated with either New York City, African American, or Creole English speech, an examination of them can shed light on the ways in which Black New Yorkers make use of linguistic features in creating their social identities.

The complexity of race, culture, and ethnicity for second-generation Caribbean Americans is evident in the earlier excerpt from Dana, the Jamerican. According to Kasinitz et al. (2008, 15) "second generation young people may see themselves as very 'American' compared to their immigrant parents and yet still feel—and seem—very much like foreigners compared to the children of natives." What is also evident for Black second-generation Caribbean Americans is the racial link that they have with native African Americans who are their "clearest reference group" and the group with whom they are most likely to interact in school, at work, and in their neighborhoods (Kasinitz et al. 2008, 16).

Recent studies have shown that /r/ varies regionally in AAE. In dialects that do vocalize /r/, a historical /r/ in syllable coda position is deleted or realized vocally as schwa. /r/-fulness is the prestige form both in New York City and many (but not all) Anglophone countries in the Caribbean.[15] BOUGHT raising is a well-known feature of New York City speech, often parodied in the media, for example on *Saturday Night Live*'s "Coffee Tawk" with Linda Richmond. This variable has traditionally been associated with White speakers of New York City English, although it appears robustly in New York City African American English as reported by Becker (2010).[16] Thus, BOUGHT raising indexes New York City speech. The vowel in the BOAT word class has distinctive realizations in American English versus various dialects of Creole English, which gives it geographical, and in some cases stylistic, distinctiveness. As shown in Figure 8.1, for Caribbean speakers of English, the BOAT vowel has a markedly different pronunciation from American English, which typically starts back with a glide offset that is out- and up-gliding (see [1] in Figure 8.1; the arrow indicates the direction of the glide). The Caribbean English realizations of BOAT tend to either start back with little or no glide ([2] in Figure 8.1), or start high and glides downward ([3] in Figure 8.1).

The data analyzed are from eight young men and women in their twenties or early thirties. They are equally divided by gender and parental origins (the United States or the Caribbean), and are all of similar socioeconomic backgrounds— lower-middle-class. The speakers interviewed were born and raised in New York City, and live in various neighborhoods in Manhattan, Brooklyn, Queens, and the Bronx. The parents of the SGCAs in the sample were born in Jamaica or St. Thomas.[17] All of the SGCAs have some competency in the English-lexifier Caribbean Creole spoken by their parents, in addition to dialects of American English.

As shown in Table 8.2, Blake and Shousterman (2010, 39) found quantitative differences in postvocalic /r/ vocalization in the speech of USAAs and SGCAs, with SGCAs retaining postvocalic /r/ more than USAAs.[18] The difference in their

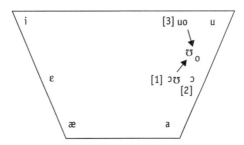

Figure 8.1 Schematic representation of realizations of BOAT word class.

Table 8.2 **Effect of ethnicity on retention of constricted postvocalic /r/.**

Ethnicity	Factor Weight	Frequency (%)	N
Second-Generation Caribbean Americans [SGCAs]	.55	49	1,225
U.S. African Americans [USAAs]	.45	40	1,101
Total N			2,326
Overall Frequency (%)			45
Corrected Mean			.445
Log Likelihood			−1,433.374

Source: Adapted from Blake and Shousterman 2010.

respective frequencies is statistically significant (p< .0001 by Fisher's Exact Test and Chi Square).

As Blake and Shousterman (2010, 39) note:

> This finding provides evidence that second generation West Indians are doing at least some linguistic work to differentiate themselves from native African Americans and vice versa. It is not, however, the insertion of a Caribbean Creole linguistic feature into West Indian American dialects of English, since /r/-fulness is typically not associated with the language of their parents. Rather, second generation West Indians may be attaching new meaning to /r/-fulness in their American dialects of English to identify as something "other" than African American, but still different from someone who was born and raised in the West Indies.

The authors also argue that higher rates of /r/ retention among SGCAs may be tied to notions of class and prestige, as was the case in Labov's (1966) department store study in New York City. Specifically, these speakers may be producing postvocalic /r/ to create or maintain a higher social class identity.

Blake et al. (2012) acoustically analyzed BOUGHT raising and the vowel in the BOAT word class in the speech of the same two groups of speakers whose /r/ productions were studied in Blake and Shousterman (2010). Normalized speaker means for sixty vowel tokens per speaker are illustrated in Figures 8.2 and 8.3.

In Figure 8.2, all speakers have the characteristic New York City raised BOUGHT, with normalized mean F1s that are less than 700 Hz (the cutoff point for BOUGHT raising as defined by Labov et al. 2006). The glides produced by

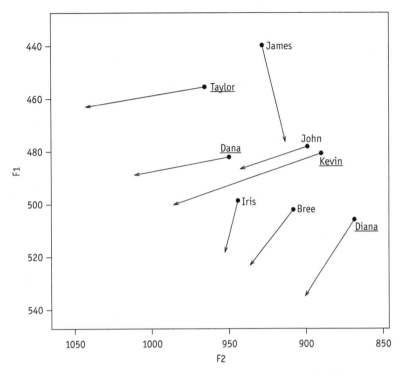

Figure 8.2 Normalized means for BOUGHT realizations for Second Generation Caribbean Americans (SGCAs, underlined) and U.S. African Americans (USAAs).

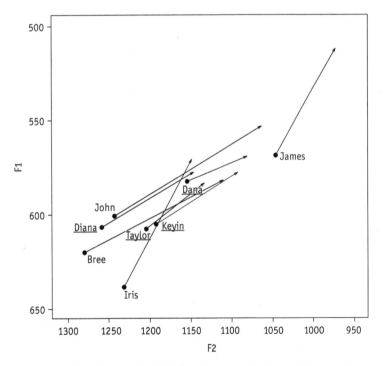

Figure 8.3 Normalized means for BOAT realizations for Second Generation Caribbean Americans (SGCAs, underlined) and U.S. African Americans (USAAs).

almost all speakers are down- and in-gliding, as indicated by the direction of the arrows. Some individual differences do exist, however. For example, one USAA, James, produces glides that average out as down- and out-, rather than inglid-ing. A further examination of speaker means for BOUGHT indicates that signifi-cant differences exist between SGCAs and USAAs, with the SGCAs (underlined in Figure 8.3) producing larger (in terms of length) glides than USAAs, suggest-ing a slightly less raised BOUGHT.

The results in Figure 8.3 show that all speakers have the typical New York City BOAT that is backed, with a vowel offset that is out- and upgliding, illustrated by the direction of arrows. However, the vowels produced by these two groups differ in terms of vowel height, with the SGCAs having a higher starting tongue position with significantly smaller changes in the F1 suggesting some monoptho-nigizing of the BOAT vowel.

The findings for /r/, BOUGHT, and BOAT in this study provide evidence that Black New Yorkers are using linguistic resources available to them to do iden-tity work on multiple levels (compare Le Page and Tabouret-Keller 1985). For instance, place identity is particularly salient, as speakers' linguistic choices and practices seem linked to a representation of New York (compare Myers 2006). /r/-fulness is on the rise in New York City English, to which both Black ethnic groups are attuned and performing at higher rates than Whites in New York. Higher rates for SGCAs may be tied to notions of class and prestige as well. Raised BOUGHT also suggests place identity for both groups, as well as ethnic differentiation evidenced by subtle qualitative differences. For SGCAs, it can be an expression of "I'm a Black New Yorker, who is somewhere in between African American and West Indian." Both groups appear to have the American realization of BOAT, but more recent work shows that plotting all tokens can reveal a more complicated picture wherein a range of realizations, including Creole English real-izations, is evident and connected to changes in topic of conversation (compare Blake, Shousterman, and Newlin-Łukowicz 2015).

Conclusion

In 2011, the highly successful singing competition TV show, *The X Factor*, fea-tured its eventual winner, Melanie Amaro. It was two days before Thanksgiving, and Melanie had the nation abuzz with the spontaneous big reveal of her "authentic self," or as many news outlets called it, her "true self" through lan-guage. Up until this moment, she was a Black woman with an American accent. Suddenly overcome with emotion, she *became* Caribbean with an unmistakable (British Virgin Islands) Caribbean accent. The nation applauded her for letting go and being herself, and delighted in her accent. But it is also important to remember that Melanie moves in and out of her many authentic selves. Along these lines, Eckert (2000) explains social practice in the sense of individuals in a community constructing and representing themselves in a particular time and space, with these acts connected to linguistic choices as well as to sociocultural and psychological phenomena within a community. Along these lines, one SGCA in the study above reminds us, "you know [pause] identities are so fluid, so they kind of go back and forth." And another says, "I have loads of identities and they're all fine with me."

Pennycook (2000, 2003; see also chapter 1, this volume) invokes the notion of performativity, suggesting that people do not use language based on their identity, but rather use their language to *perform* identity. And as García and Zakharia (2010, 524), drawing on Pavlenko and Blackledge (2004, 27), note:

> Languaging and ethnifying options may be limited or not, or nego-
> tiable or not, depending on particular sociohistoric contexts, but
> individuals are agentive beings, "constantly in search of new social
> and linguistic resources which allow them to resist identities that
> position them in undesirable ways, produce new identities and
> assign alternative meanings to the links between identities and lin-
> guistic varieties."

African American/Black communities have been and are becoming more diverse across the United States and this is having an impact and being impacted at a global level. Black ethnics in the United States express themselves in linguistically complex ways. And while they may come to behave similarly in terms of linguistic code, subtle distinctions are evident in language, suggesting that language is being used to perform acts of identity (LePage and Tabouret-Keller 1985, 5).

I argue that sociolinguists, and social scientists more generally, should consider thinking about Black communities in the twenty-first century within broader categories, like people of African descent, which would allow for more complex discussions of race and identity in the United States. And it is from here that we can talk about Black ethnics, of which U.S. African Americas are a critical and dynamic community. Johnstone (2000) notes that we, as social scientists, should think about our research methodology more carefully, given that we are now asking additional and differing questions, and need new ways of answering them. This is precisely the case as we move away from working with identity as a set of fixed categories toward viewing it as an ongoing social and political process (Bucholtz and Hall 2005). African American/Black people will continue to reinvent themselves and their language(s), and what is needed is a roadmap for more nuanced analyses of Black ethnics. The interplay between race and ethnicity can be observed throughout Black communities. We will need to think deeply about the ramifications of the methods we use to define and delineate the speech communities. Who gets included? Who gets excluded? And for what reasons? What are the ideologies that we as researchers bring to the work and how does this impact the work?

The onus is on the researcher to learn about the everyday lives of community members to better understand sociohistorical and ideological forces affecting individuals and communities. While we couch our analyses within social categories defined in the national imagination, we also need to gain deeper understandings of how groups and individuals define themselves, both in and out of national ideologies of race and ethnicity. It behooves us to ask community members about ethnic backgrounds in relation to language and the perception of ethnic differences (or lack thereof). Such information can be correlated with the linguistic patterns found in the data and/or judgments given by community members about particular linguistic constructions. And finally, it is imperative that language scholars engage with research in various disciplines (e.g., Race and Ethnic Studies, Anthropology, Psychology, Political Science, Sociology, History, and Cultural Studies) to develop a more comprehensive analytical framework, and to understand critical aspects of our data that might otherwise be missed.

Notes

* Thank you to H. Samy Alim and John Rickford who first invited me to present this work at the "Racing Language, Languaging Race: New Approaches to the Study of Race, Ethnicity and Language" symposium at Stanford University in 2012. Malcah Yaeger-Dror and Christopher Cieri's forums on the subject "critically thinking about identity in the field of sociolinguistics" were also helpful. Finally, I am grateful to Kenneth Saunders, Selanthia Griffiths, Shedia Small, and the graduate students and faculty of the Sociolinguistics Lab Group at New York University for engaging me in informative discussions of this work.

1. All names used in this study are pseudonyms.
2. This is explicitly evident in the work of Nero (2001), Pratt-Johnson (2006), and Zéphir (1996) for Black communities in the United States from the Anglophone and Francophone Caribbean.
3. See Greer 2013 for treatment of Black ethnics from a political science perspective.
4. I am using *Black* and *White* as both adjectives and nouns to describe and refer to individual people and groups. Both are capitalized throughout the paper.
5. This paper also draws from earlier works including Blake et al. 2015, Blake 2014, and Blake and Shousterman 2010.
6. See Blake 2014 for further discussion.
7. See Zéphir 1996 and 2001; Dubois and Melançon 2000. Rickford 1985 discussed the need for sociolinguistics to consider ethnicity as a sociolinguistic boundary, referring to contact and distance between Black and White speech communities as two of several factors potentially helping to inscribe or maintain ethnolinguistic differences.
8. There are many definitions of race and ethnicity, some overlapping, some separate, some unclear. One definition offered by Fought (2006, 10) is from Bobo (2001, 267), who states, "Common usage tends to associate 'race' with biologically based difference between

human groups, differences typically observable in skin color, hair texture, eye shape, and other physical attributes. 'Ethnicity' tends to be associated with culture, pertaining to such factors as language, religion, and nationality."

9. According to Fishman (1977, 16), "Ethnicity is rightly understood as an aspect of a collectivity's self-recognition, as well as an aspect of its recognition in the eyes of outsiders."

10. Britt and Weldon (2015) do note, however, that early on Labov made a distinction between the Black English Vernacular and the larger system of Black English, which included "a whole range of language forms used by black people in the United States … extending from the Creole grammar of Gullah spoken in the Sea Islands of South Carolina to the most formal and accomplished literary style" (Labov 1972. xiii).

11. For a recent comprehensive reader, see Lanehart 2015.

12. See Harper (1996, 54–73) for a nuanced historical discussion of racial designations of persons of African descent in the United States.

13. Blake and Shousterman 2010; Blake, Shousterman, and Newlin-Łukowicz 2015.

14. By the beginning of the twenty-first century, NYC had one of the largest populations of West Indians outside of the Caribbean (Foner 2001, 4). The 2006 American Communities Survey reports that foreign-born people comprise nearly a third (31 percent) of NYC's Black population, with the vast majority being West Indian. According to Foner (ibid.), when the second generation is combined with the migrant population, two-fifths of NYC's Black population can trace their heritage to the West Indies. Further, if the migrants from the Anglophone Caribbean were added together, they would comprise the largest immigrant group in NYC.

15. In Trinidad and Tobago, for instance, r-lessness is the norm.

16. Black New Yorkers are not the only non-White group in New York City who have this feature, as raised BOUGHT is also found in the English spoken by New York City's Chinese Americans (Wong 2007) and Latinos (Slomanson and Newman 2004).

17. Although St. Thomas is a district of the United States Virgin Islands, it is located in the Caribbean Sea and many of its residents identify as West Indian.

18. The data were analyzed using GoldVarb X, a statistical program that measures the strength of an independent variable by providing a number between 0 and 1, which represents a weight or probability for the conditioning factor. A factor weight less than .5 shows a disfavoring effect, whereas a factor weight greater than .5 shows a favoring effect (.5 is considered neutral).

References

Alcoff, Linda Martín. 2000. Is Latina/o identity a racial identity? In *Hispanics/Latinos in the United States: Ethnicity, Race, and Rights*, ed. Jorge J. E. Garcia and Pablo de Greiff, 23–44. London: Routledge.

Alim, H. Samy. 2004. *You Know My Steez: An Ethnographic and Sociolinguistic Study of Styleshifting in a Black American Speech Community*. Durham, NC: Duke University Press.

Alim, H. Samy. 2009. "Racing Language, Languaging Race." Paper presented at the "Race and Ethnicity in Language, Interaction and Culture" Symposium. University of California, Los Angeles, February 27.

Becker, Kara. 2010. "Social Conflict and Social Practice on the Lower East Side: A Study of Regional Dialect Features in New York City English." Ph.D. dissertation, New York University.

Blake, Renée. 2014. African American and black as demographic codes. *Language and Linguistics Compass* 8(11): 548–63.

Blake, Renée, and Cara Shousterman. 2010. Second Generation West Indian Americans and English in New York City. *English Today* 26(3): 35–43.

Blake, Renée, Cara Shousterman, and Luiza Newlin-Łukowicz. 2015. African American Language variation in New York City. In *The Oxford Handbook of African American Language*, ed. Sonja Laneheart, 280–98. Oxford: Oxford University Press.

Bobo, Lawrence. 2001. Racial attitudes and relations at the close of the twentieth century. In *America Becoming: Racial Trends and Their Consequences*, vol. 1, ed. Neil J. Smelser, William Julius Wilson, and Faith Mitchell, 264–301. Washington, DC: National Academy Press.

Britt, Erica, and Tracey Weldon. 2015. Middle class African American English. In *The Oxford Handbook of African American Language*, ed. Sonja Laneheart, 800–16. Oxford: Oxford University Press.

Bucholtz, Mary, and Kira Hall. 2005. Identity and interaction: A sociocultural linguistic approach. *Discourse Studies* 7(4–5): 585–614.

Cutler, Cecelia A. 1999. Yorkville crossing: White teens, Hip Hop, and African American English. *Journal of Sociolinguistics* 3(4): 428–42.

Dodson, Howard. 2007. What's at Stake: Redefining African American, 6.3. Logos 6. http://www.logosjournal.com/issue_6.3/dodson.htm. Last accessed: June 8, 2016.

Dubois, Sylvie, and and Megan Melançon 2000. Creole is, Creole ain't: diachronic and synchronic attitudes toward Creole identity in Southern Louisiana. *Language in Society* 29: 237–58.

Eckert, Penelope. 2000. *Linguistic Variation as Social Practice: The Linguistic Construction of Identity in Beltran High*. Malden, MA: Blackwell.

Eckert, Penelope 2003. Elephants in the room. *Journal of Sociolinguistics* 7(3): 392–97.

Fishman, Joshua A. 1977. Language and ethnicity. In *Language, Ethnicity and Intergroup Relations*, ed. H. Giles, 15–58. New York: Academic Press.

Foner, Nancy, ed. 2001. *Islands in the City: West Indian Migration to New York*. Berkeley and Los Angeles: University of California Press.

Fought, Carmen. 2006. *Language and Ethnicity*. Cambridge: Cambridge University Press.

García, Ofelia, and Zeena Zakharia. 2010. Positioning language and ethnic identity. In Handbook of Language and Ethnic Identity: Disciplinary and Regional Perspectives, edited by Joshua A. Fishman and Ofelia García, 521–25. Oxford: Oxford University Press.

Greer, Christina M. 2013. *Black Ethnic: Race, Immigration, and the Pursuit of the American Dream*. Oxford: Oxford University Press.

Román, Miriam Jiménez and Juan Flores, eds. 2010. *The Afro-Latin@ Reader: History and Culture in the United States*. Durham, NC: Duke University Press.

Guy, Gregory. 2001. Variable shibboleths: The linguistic correlates of speech community identity. Presented at the 30th annual meeting, New Ways of Analyzing Variation (NWAV-30), North Carolina State University.

Harper, Phillip Brian. 1996. *Are We Not Men?* Oxford: Oxford University Press.

Irvine, Judith T., and Susan Gal. 2000. Language ideology and linguistic differentiation. In *Regimes of language*, ed. Paul Kroskrity, 35–83. Santa Fe, NM: School of American Research Press.

Johnstone, Barbara. 2000. *Qualitative Methods in Sociolinguistics*. New York: Oxford University Press.

Kasinitz, Philip, John H. Mollenkopf, Mary C. Waters, and Jennifer Holdaway. 2008. *Inheriting the City: The Children of Immigrants Come of Age*. New York: Russell Sage Foundation.

Labov, William. 1972. *Language in the Inner City: Studies in the Black English Vernacular*. Philadelphia: University of Pennsylvania Press.

Labov, William, Sharon Ash, and Charles Boberg. 2006. *The Atlas of North American English: Phonetics, Phonology, and Sound Change*. New York: Mouton de Gruyter.

Lanehart, Sonja. 2015. *The Oxford Handbook on African American Language*. Oxford: Oxford University Press.

LePage, Robert, and Andrée Tabouret-Keller. 1985. *Acts of Identity: Creole-Base Approaches to Language and Ethnicity*. Cambridge: Cambridge University Press.

Mitchell-Kernan, Claudia. 1971. *Language Behavior in a Black Urban Community*. Monographs of the Language-Behavior Research Laboratory, No. 2, University of California, Berkeley.

Morgan, Marcyliena. 1994. Theoretical and political arguments in African American English. *Annual Review of Anthropology* 23: 325–45.

Morgan, Marcyliena. 2014. *Speech Communities*. Cambridge: Cambridge University Press.

Myers, Greg. 2006. Where Are You From?: Identifying Place. *Journal of Sociolinguistics* 10: 320–43.

Nero, Shondel. 2001. *Englishes in Contact: Anglophone Caribbean Students in an Urban College*. Cresskill, NJ: Hampton Press.

Pavlenko, A., and A. Blackledge, eds. 2004. *Negotiation of Identities in Multilingual Contexts*. Clevedon, UK: Multilingual Matters.

Pennycook, Alastair. 2000. English, politics, ideology: From colonial celebration to postcolonial performativity. In *Ideology, Politics, and Language Policies: Focus on English*, ed. T. Ricento and T. Wiley, 107–19. Amsterdam: John Benjamins.

Pratt-Johnson, Yvonne. 2006. Teaching Jamaican Creole-speaking students. In *Dialects, Englishes, Creoles and Education*, ed. Shondel Nero, 119–36. Mahwah, NJ: Lawrence Erlbaum Associates.

Rickford, John R. 1985. Ethnicity as a sociolinguistic boundary. *American Speech* 60 (3): 90–125.

Rickford, John R. 1992. Grammatical variation and divergence in Vernacular Black English. In *Internal and External Factors in Syntactic Change*, ed. Marinel Gerritsen and Dieter Stein, 174–200. Berlin and New York: Mouton.

Slomanson, Peter and Michael Newman. 2004. Peer group identification and variation in New York Latino English laterals. *English World-Wide* 25(2): 199–216.

Smitherman, Geneva. 2000. *Talkin That Talk: Language, Culture and Education in African America*. London and New York: Routledge.

Spears, Arthur. 1988. Black American English. In *Anthropology for the Nineties*, ed. Johnetta Cole, 96–113. New York: Free Press.

Turner, J. Michael. 2002. The Road to Durban—and Back. *NACLA* (North American Congress on Latin America) 35: 6.

Warner, William Lloyd, and Leo Srole. 1945. *The Social Systems of American Ethnic Groups*. New Haven, CT: Yale University Press.

Waters, Mary C. 1999. *Black Identities: West Indian Immigrant Dreams and American Realities*. Cambridge, MA: Harvard University Press.

Wong, Amy. 2007. Two vernacular features in the English of four American-born Chinese. In Toni Cook and Keelan Evanini, eds., *Selected Papers from NWAV 35. University of Pennsylvania Working Papers in Linguistics* 13(2): 217–30.

Zentella, Ana Celia. 1997. *Growing Up Bilingual: Puerto Rican Children in New York*. Malden, MA: Blackwell.

Zéphir, Flore. 1996. *Haitian Immigrants in Black America: A Sociological and Sociolinguistic Portrait*. Wesport, CT: Bergin and Garvey.

Zéphir, Flore. 2001. *Trends in Ethnic Identification among Second-Generation Haitian Immigrants in New York City*. Wesport, CT: Bergin and Garvey.

9

Jews of Color

Performing Black Jewishness through the Creative Use of Two Ethnolinguistic Repertoires

SARAH BUNIN BENOR

> The conversation usually goes like this: *"Do you consider yourself (ethnicity) first or Jewish first? Are you (ethnicity) or Jewish? You seem to have identity issues. What does this matter? Aren't we all just Jewish?"* That conversation makes just as much sense as asking the color purple if it's "red" first or "blue" first. It's. Both. Likewise *we* are both.
> —MaNishtana 2012; emphasis in original

This excerpt from Black Jewish writer MaNishtana's "not-autobiography" represents the feelings of many Americans who are both Black and Jewish.[1] Others take a different approach, highlighting either their blackness or their Jewishness. Still others prefer to blend into their surroundings and highlight their blackness when interacting with other Black non-Jews and their Jewishness when interacting with other Jewish people. No matter what approach individuals take, language plays a critical role in how they represent their identity. Black Jews may make selective use of elements of the distinctive linguistic repertoires associated with African Americans and with Jewish Americans, known as African American English (AAE) and Jewish English (JE), respectively. This chapter analyzes one type of communication among Black Jews: self-conscious presentations of their combined Black-Jewish identities in videos available online.

Background on Black Jews

The majority of the six to seven million American Jews are of European descent and are generally considered White within the current American racial landscape.[2] A term often used for a majority of White Jews is *Ashkenazi*, meaning descended from Jews who lived in Germanic lands in the Middle Ages and sub-sequently throughout Central and Eastern Europe before immigrating to the United States (and elsewhere) in the nineteenth and twentieth centuries.[3] This term is often used in contrast to *Sephardi* Jews, those descended from Jews expelled from Spain in the fifteenth century; and also to *Mizrahi* (lit. "Eastern") Jews, those with roots in other communities around the Jewish Diaspora, includ-ing the Middle East and North Africa. These Jews may be seen as White or Middle Eastern, and they represent a much smaller percentage of the American Jewish population than those with Ashkenazi heritage (although these distinctions are diminishing due to intergroup marriage; see also chapter 10, this volume).

Part of and somewhat distinct from these populations are Jews of Color, including those with African American, Latino, Asian American, and Native American heritage (while Sephardi and Mizrahi Jews are sometimes considered Jews of Color, White Ashkenazi Jews are not). A nationwide study from 2000 estimated that 7 percent of American Jews, or 435,000 individuals, are Jews of Color (Tobin et al. 2005, 21), and a more recent study of Jews in the New York area found the percentage to be 10 percent and increasing (Cohen et al. 2012, 250). As for the number of people who identify as both Black and Jewish, my analysis of data from a recent nationwide study conducted by the Pew Research Center yields a rough estimate of 90,000 adults. In addition, an estimated 270,000 adults who identify as Black say they were raised Jewish or had a Jewish parent but do not consider themselves Jewish now or have a religion other than Judaism.[4]

Black Jews have diverse origins. Although we have no definitive quantita-tive data, the most common origin seems to be unions between White Jews and Black non-Jews. Their biracial children are sometimes raised as "Jews by religion," sometimes as "Jews by heritage," and sometimes with no Jewish iden-tity. Another common origin is when White Jewish parents adopt children from Africa or from African American birth parents and raise them as Jews, some-times officially converting them. In addition to these individuals who grow up Black and Jewish, many Black people adopt Judaism later in life. Some of these converts are attracted to Judaism for spiritual or theological reasons, and oth-ers for social, cultural, or communal reasons, such as having Jewish friends or partners. Smaller numbers of Black Jews immigrated to the United States from Jewish communities in Ethiopia, Uganda, Nigeria, and elsewhere in sub-Saharan Africa (Tobin et al. 2005). Finally, a small percentage of Black Jews are descendants of Black people who converted to Judaism or had children with White Jews several generations ago. In some families, Judaism goes back to the days of slavery, when Black slaves sometimes adopted the religion of their White owners, a small percentage of whom were Jewish.

Some discussions of Black Jews also include people who adhere to Messianic Judaism (practicing some elements of Jewish religion and accepting Jesus as Messiah) and communities known as Hebrew Israelites, some of whom adopted

Jewish religious beliefs and practices over the last several decades. Among Black Jews who are not Messianic Jews or Hebrew Israelites (and among Jews who are not Black), there is some controversy about whether to consider these groups Jewish, due to their rejection of the Jewishness of European-origin Jews and their adoption of Judaism without official conversion (see, e.g., MaNishtana 2012). Although Hebrew Israelites are beyond the scope of this paper, their language deserves in-depth analysis, as it represents a fascinating combination of elements of the AAE and JE repertoires, including the extensive use of Hebrew loanwords with pronunciation distinct from that of other Hebrew users in America.

In the past few decades, Black Jews have become more visible in the public sphere, due partly to press coverage of prominent individuals—especially rapper Drake and actress Rashida Jones, both of whom have Black non-Jewish fathers and White Jewish mothers; rapper Shyne, who converted to Judaism; and Rabbi Capers Funnye, a prominent Black rabbi who is related to First Lady Michelle Obama. Beyond these and other celebrities, the Jewish and general press has published a number of articles about Black Jews, including discussion of increasing connections between mainstream Jews and Hebrew Israelites. The Internet has also facilitated connection among Black Jews around the country and world, as we see in a number of blogs and forums and several new organizations geared toward Jews of Color.[5] The Jewish Channel has contributed to this growing infrastructure by producing a forum on Jews of Color, available on YouTube.[6]

Several Black Jewish writers have published memoirs, including Julius Lester in 1995 (a Black man who grew up Christian and converted to Judaism), Rebecca Walker in 2001 (daughter of Black non-Jewish writer Alice Walker and White Jewish lawyer Mel Leventhal), and MaNishtana in 2012 (pseudonym of Shais Rison, who grew up as an Orthodox Jew with two Black Jewish parents). There have also been a few academic studies of Black Jews, some as part of broader discussions of Jews of Color (e.g., Azoulay 1997; Tobin et al. 2005).

A common theme in these studies, memoirs, and forums is the reactions Black Jews have endured from Black non-Jews and White Jews, ranging from confused stares and curious questioning to insensitive comments and racist and anti-Semitic actions. Identity also features prominently in these works. Individuals talk about presenting themselves differently in different situations or in different stages of life, sometimes highlighting their blackness, sometimes their Jewishness, and sometimes the intersection between the two. As the analysis below indicates, language plays a key role in their self-presentation.

Theoretical Approach: Ethnolinguistic Repertoire

As I have argued elsewhere (Benor 2010), speaking of a bounded linguistic entity like African American English or Jewish English is problematic. It is true that many African Americans and Jews speak in ways that some would characterize as AAE and JE. But what about an African American who uses only a few features of AAE—should we consider her a speaker of AAE? What about an excerpt of speech that starts out using many features of JE and then uses few—should we consider it an excerpt of JE? The notion of "ethno-linguistic repertoire," influenced by theoretical representations of linguistic repertoire and style (e.g., Gumperz 1964; Eckert 2000), offers a solution to these and other theoretical conundrums regarding language and ethnicity. Instead of speaking about ethnolects or language varieties, this approach focuses on an ethnolinguistic repertoire, a collection of distinctive linguis-tic features associated with a group, similar to Fought's "pool of resources from which members of a speech community draw the linguistic tools they need" (2006, 21). Rather than talk about AAE, JE, Latino English, and so on as bounded linguistic entities, we can analyze individuals' speech as English with the incorporation of linguistic features from the AAE, JE, and Latino English repertoires.

Some scholars take the desire not to identify bounded ethnic dialects to the other extreme and, instead, analyze individuals as using one linguistic repertoire with many sources as they present their multifaceted identities in conversation. I find this approach lacking, as it erases the strong connections (indexical links) between linguistic forms and groups of people. For example, imagine an English conversation between a Latino man and a European American woman, during which the man used a Spanish word, a few Spanish-influenced vowels, and some distinctive grammatical features, all of which have been associated with Latinos in previous research. If we simply said that the man was using a diverse lin-guistic repertoire, we would be missing out on a key fact: many people, likely including the two speakers, associate these linguistic features with Latinos. The ethnolinguistic repertoire approach allows us to analyze his speech as English with the addition of a repertoire of linguistic features associated with Latinos, as he presents himself (perhaps consciously and with full control, or perhaps not) as Latino.

When the terms "AAE repertoire" and "JE repertoire" are used in this paper, they refer not to dialects but rather to the pools of distinctive linguistic resources that are commonly associated with African Americans and Jews. This is not to say that only African Americans and Jews can use these resources (certainly many elements of these repertoires have spread beyond these groups), and it is not to say that all African Americans and Jews use them (many do not). Even so, it is important to link these features to these groups, as they play important roles in how individuals perform and perceive complex identities.

While this approach can be applied to any group that speaks in a marked way,[7] it is particularly useful in an analysis of individuals who are part of two minority groups with distinctive language patterns. Instead of arguing about which "language variety" such individuals are speaking at a particular moment, we can say that they speak American English and then analyze their use of linguistic elements of both repertoires. As I detail below, Black Jews distinguish their English from that of other Americans through the variable use of features from two distinctive repertoires: AAE and JE.

Both of these repertoires have been described by linguists. The AAE repertoire includes multiple features at all levels of language, including phonology (e.g., postvocalic /r/ deletion or vocalization [*sister* becomes *sista*], word-final consonant cluster reduction [*last* becomes *lass*], and monophthongization of diphthongs [*my* becomes *mah*]), morphology (e.g., plural -*s* absence, third-person -*s* absence), morphosyntax (e.g., stressed *BIN*, copula absence, and habitual *be*), prosody (distinctive voice quality and intonation, including falsetto), lexicon (e.g., *ashy, saddity,* and many fleeting slang terms), and discourse (e.g., signifyin, the repetition in Black preacher style) (see Smitherman 1977; Rickford 1999; Green 2002; Alim 2004).

The JE repertoire involves the use of hundreds of loanwords from Yiddish (an Eastern European Jewish-Germanic language spoken by many of the Ashkenazi ancestors of American Jews), Israeli Hebrew (through Hebrew education and current connections between American Jews and Israel), textual Hebrew, and Aramaic (through prayer recitation and study of the Bible and rabbinic literature). In addition, many Orthodox Jews use grammatical influences from Yiddish (e.g., *staying by them,* preposition absence, and present for present perfect tense), distinctive phonological features (e.g., nonraised prenasal /æ/ [the vowel in *man* sounds like the vowel in *mad*], word-final devoicing [*goingk*], and frequent word-final /t/ release and affrication [the /t/ in *not* and *right* sounds like *t-h* or *tsss*], and distinctive prosody [fast speech rate, rise-fall intonation contours, and quasi-chanting intonation]) (see Gold 1985; Benor 2011, 2012).

While the ethnolinguistic repertoire approach focuses the analytic spotlight on individuals' use of distinctive linguistic features such as these, it does not take a position on questions of awareness, control, and indexicality. Just because a linguist can describe an individual African American's use of -*s* absence or monophthongization does not mean that the individual is aware that she is using those features and has control over them. Even if she is aware of them and has control over them, it is possible that she uses them not as a way of aligning herself with other African Americans (or distinguishing herself from non–African Americans), but rather as a way of indexing certain stances or personas (Ochs 1992). Questions like these can be answered through interviews and playback of speech samples, as can questions of audience members' interpretation of distinctive features—questions that are beyond the scope of the current chapter.

Performative Contexts of Black Jews' Language Use

This chapter focuses on a specific communicative situation: individuals explicitly presenting themselves as Black Jews through prepared performances and extemporaneous interviews. All excerpts analyzed are videos available on the Internet.

PERFORMANCES

- Aaron Samuels, "Black and Jewish," performance piece for college poetry slam (http://www.youtube.com/watch?v=WN9P0ShELok).
- Kat Graham and Kali Hawk, "Black and Jewish" music video parody of "Black and Yellow" (http://www.youtube.com/watch?v=1TXNU1nh4E4).

PRESENTATIONS

- Yavilah McCoy, speaking about Black Jewish music to several groups made up mostly of White Jews. (http://www.pbs.org/wnet/religionandethics/episodes/january-26-2007/african-american-jews/3594/; http://www.youtube.com/watch?v=UnCoOi3_6-4; http://www.youtube.com/watch?v=ZLSApjCysoU&feature=endscreen&NR=1).

INTERVIEWS

- Simone Weichselbaum, interviewed about being a Black Jew on Arise News (http://www.youtube.com/watch?v=gPILYQ3Z0Mo).
- MaNishtana, interviewed for *Be'chol Lashon* (http://www.youtube.com/watch?v=fkZ0FBcz3BA).
- Yavilah McCoy, participating in a forum about Jews of Color (see links in note 6).
- Yitz Jordan (Hip Hop artist Y-Love), participating in the same forum.

Performing Black Jewishness through Language

In almost all of the sources examined, the individuals presenting themselves to the public as Black Jews use features of both AAE and JE. Sometimes the features appear to be used rather straightforwardly throughout the presentations, but in other instances they are used in strategic ways. First, I analyze the performances.

In a spoken word performance, a young man named Aaron Samuels uses language, gesture, and mention of Black and Jewish symbols to narrate how he embraced his Jewishness and his blackness at different points in his life and how he now prefers an integrated version of Black Jewish identity. He recalls learning that he was Jewish at a Jewish Community Center preschool and learning that he was Black through racist encounters in elementary school. He found that it was "cool" to embrace blackness in middle school: "As I let my pants sag more and more, my Jewish star found its way from around my neck to my back pocket. I traded my peyos [translations below] for cornrows, yarmulkes for fitted hats, seder plates for soul food." Later, he came to embrace integration: "I'm 100% Black and 100% Jewish, and I'm about to Lift Every Voice and Sing-Hatikvah . . . I eat my seder plates with soul food, wear magen davids on my dog tags. I get hollaz for challah, and I gamble my gelt with my dollaz." And he says he is "representin" for Sammy Davis Jr., Lisa Bonet, Shyne, and several other Black Jewish celebrities.

Samuels represents his combined Black Jewish identity linguistically by using features of the JE and AAE repertoires. From the JE repertoire he uses several Hebrew and Yiddish loanwords: *peyos* (sidelocks), *yarmulke* (skullcap), *Shabbat* (Sabbath), *kosher* (acceptable), *seder* (Passover ritual) plate, *magen david* (Star of David), *Mimouna* (Moroccan post-Passover celebration), *Hatikvah* (Israel's national anthem), and *gelt* ([chocolate] money [for Hanukah]). From the AAE repertoire he uses a few phonological and prosodic features, including some postvocalic /l/ vocalization (*old* is pronounced more like *owd*), a bit of monophthongization (*my* becomes *mah*), and elongation of the [I] vowel in "kids." Some of his AAE phonological features are lexically specific, such as glottalization of /nt/ and alveolarization of *ing* (becomes "in") in "representin" and *gonna* > *a* in "I'm a represent." His /r/ following vowels is mostly present, but it is deleted in certain words: *hollaz, dollaz*. Finally, he uses *girl* as a term of address to Rebecca Walker: "I know you know how it is, girl."

It is clear that Samuels uses these features consciously and strategically. He uses a few JE features and very few AAE features when explaining how he identified as Jewish as a young boy; when he talks about embracing his Black identity in middle school he uses several AAE features and no JE features. When he narrates his current desire to integrate his Black and Jewish identities, he uses features of both repertoires in deliberate combinations (e.g., "I gamble my *gelt* with my dollaz"). This performance piece illustrates quite explicitly how some Black Jews use language (in combination with other cultural practices) to indicate their blackness, their Jewishness, and their Black Jewishness.

Not only was Samuels's use of Black and Jewish practices conscious, it was clearly exaggerated for the sake of the performance. He begins, "I traded my *peyos* for *cornrows, yarmulkes* for fitted hats." While he may at some point have worn *cornrows*, *yarmulkes*, and fitted hats, it is unlikely that he ever wore *peyos*, the curly sidelocks common among Hasidic Jews. Similarly, in his everyday life, he may use fewer elements of the JE and AAE repertoires, and when he does use them, he may reserve them for Jewish audiences and Black (or Hip Hop-oriented) audiences. His combined use of features associated with African Americans and with Jews is intended to enhance his performance; he uses language creatively to highlight his merged Black Jewish identity. This kind of performance relies on commonly held raciolinguistic ideologies: if Samuels's audience did not associate specific linguistic features with African Americans and Jews, his use of these features would not serve their intended purpose of performing Black, Jewish, and Black Jewish identities.

The second performance takes a similarly integrative approach to Black Jewish identity, but with a more exaggerated and outrageous use of stereotypical practices. In the music video "Black and Jewish," available on the comedy site *Funny or Die*, Black Jewish actresses Kali Hawk and Katerina ("Kat") Graham present a parody of Wiz Khalifa's "Black and Yellow." The video intersperses images of Black Jewish celebrities with scenes of Hawk and Graham combining stereotypical visual symbols and activities associated with Jews and with Black people: "My nose and ass—they're both big," "Had my bat mitzvah at KFC," counting money and picking an afro, wearing a large Star of David necklace, pouring hot sauce on lox and bagels, chasing people with a menorah, gambling with *dreidels* (Chanukah tops), drinking *OE* ("Olde English," a malt liquor popular in urban Black communities) at a Passover *seder*, and pouring "*Manischewitz* (a kosher brand of sweet wine) for the *homies*," to name just a few.

The actresses also demonstrate the combination of stereotypical Black and Jewish practices in their integrated use of elements of the JE and AAE repertoires: "*L'chaim* [to life/cheers], bitch," "We on the corner, shootin' *dreidels*," "On Rosh Hashana [Jewish New Year] I blow the *shofa[r]* [ram's horn], get my hair did," "*Shalom* [hello/goodbye/peace] to your muvva [mother]," and so on. They use nineteen Hebrew and Yiddish loanwords from the JE repertoire, including names of holidays (*Rosh Hashana, Shabbes, Chanukah*), items and concepts related to religious observance (*seder, shofar, Torah, bat mitzvah, menorah, dreidel, kosher*), foods (*gefilte fish, lox, latkes, challah*), and others (*l'chaim, shalom, shul* [synagogue], *shtetl* [village/hood]). And they use several morphosyntactic, phonological, and lexical features of the AAE repertoire, including copula ("to be") absence, third-person -*s* absence, multiple negation, "of" absence ("comin straight up out the *shtetl*"), th>d or v, absence of /r/ after a vowel, and several AAE words like *reppin* (representing), *crackin* (happening), and *thugged out* (appearing to be part of ghetto culture).

The humor in this video stems from its startling, outrageous combinations. Audience members associate certain practices (including linguistic ones) with

Jews and other practices with Black people. When Hawk and Graham combine them, the result is incongruous, and therefore funny. However, as with any outrageous parody, this performance has invited some controversy. As Black Jewish blogger MaNishtana says, "All that does is make JOCs [Jews of Color] look like a joke. . . . 'Parody' can only happen when something serious has been presented in the first place."[8] While such critiques are valid, humorous videos like this do raise awareness about the existence of Black Jews, and they demonstrate the importance of language and other cultural practices in individuals' self-presentation as members of both groups.

At the same time, one can read this video as a critique of commonly held ideologies of race and culture. If the video were presented in a serious tone, viewers might believe that Hawk and Graham actually utter sentences like *"L'chaim, bitch"* and "On Rosh Hashana I blow the *shofa[r], get my hair did.*" But because of the humorous, parodic frame, and because many viewers are familiar with actresses Hawk and Graham speaking unmarked English in other contexts, they most likely see this performance as outrageous. It effectively mocks essentialist understandings of language and identity, as well as ideologies of biraciality as additive (Race A + Race B = Race A + B). Even as the creators of the video express their pride in being Black Jews, they also send a message that one does not have to participate in all—or any—cultural practices associated with Black and Jewish people to be an authentic Black Jew. We see this critique offered in a more explicit way below.

The two videos analyzed so far are highly performative: the speakers perform membership in particular communities by using exaggerated versions of linguistic features that they expect audience members to associate with these groups. We see a less outrageous but still somewhat performative context in video clips of educator Yavilah McCoy speaking about Black Jewish music. McCoy grew up as a Black Orthodox Jew in Brooklyn, and she speaks to Jewish groups around the country to raise awareness about Jewish diversity and racism, partly through musical encounters. Based on the video clips available online and my attendance at such a session, it is clear that her public persona involves the use of many features of the AAE and JE repertoires, including Hebrew and Yiddish loanwords and phonological (e.g., postvocalic /r/ absence, monophthongization), prosodic, and discourse features of AAE. It is also clear that she makes creative use of these features. For example, at a concert in New York, she leads a call and response exchange with the audience: "If everybody in here has a spirit, say 'Amen!' If everybody wanna see this again, say 'Mazel tov!' If everybody in here wants to go, say 'Oy vey!' If everybody here loves the spiritual journey we've been on, say 'Mm-hmm.' All right!" Her use of call and response involving repetition (and variable third-person -s absence) relies on Black preacher style, while simultaneously incorporating select Hebrew and Yiddish phrases. In another presentation to a Jewish group, in response to a question about which *Haggadah* (Passover seder guidebook) her family uses, she says—using falsetto and a pro-sodic contour associated with African Americans: "We use the Maxwell House Haggadah like everybody else!" (see Alim 2004 on Black American falsetto). The content of this statement reminds the Jewish, mostly White audience that she is similar to them. At the same time, her prosody highlights her African American distinctiveness and conveys what seems to be a stance of mild annoyance with the question.

In an interview context, McCoy uses a similar combination of AAE features—several in phonology and prosody but very few in morphosyntax. This combina-tion might be described as Black Standard English (Taylor 1971; Rahman 2008), a way of speaking English that allows individuals to present themselves as Black while maintaining mostly "standard" English grammar. However, McCoy adds several Hebrew and Yiddish loanwords into the mix. We can analyze her speech here as English with the incorporation of several features from the AAE and JE repertoires, but only features that align with mainstream notions of standard grammar.

Like McCoy, writer MaNishtana uses similar clusters of features in a video interview: a few prosodic and phonological features of AAE, such as vowel elon-gation, /l/ vocalization, *pin-pen* merger ("when" sounds like "win"), word-final consonant cluster reduction, and a few Hebrew loanwords (*Shabbat*, *parsha* [Torah portion], *Moshe* [Moses], and his chosen pseudonym, *MaNishtana*, which he explains to be based on the Passover question: "What makes this night differ-ent from all other nights? What makes me so different from all other Jews?"). In addition, MaNishtana's language also includes several features characteris-tic of Orthodox Jews: frequent word-final /t/ release with affrication and long duration (the /t/ in *about* sounds like [tssss]), word-final devoicing (the /v/ in *of* becomes [f]), a hesitation click (which is similar to AAE *suck-teeth*—see Rickford and Rickford 1976—but its discourse context here is more common among Orthodox Jews). Through language, MaNishtana aligns himself with Orthodox Jews in ways that the other individuals profiled here do not. And by using fea-tures of the AAE repertoire, specifically those associated with Black Standard English, he also aligns himself with many middle-class African Americans.

All of the excerpts discussed so far have involved the use of elements of both the AAE and the JE repertoires. The one exception in the videos I analyzed is Simone Weichselbaum, a young Black Jewish woman with a German Jewish father and a British mother of Jamaican descent. In a televised video interview with Black (presumably non-Jewish) interviewers, she talks about her childhood in Crown Heights, Brooklyn, and her identity as a Jew of Color. In this interview she uses no AAE features and a few JE features: *yenta* (gossiping woman), *Hasidic*, *already* with semantic/pragmatic influence from Yiddish *shoyn* (already), and a few high-falling-pitch boundaries (Benor 2012) marking the end of introductory clauses ("Growing up in New York CI-ty [HIGH-falling tone]"). It is unclear whether she associates her prosody and her "already" with Jewishness, but her use of *yenta* demonstrates her awareness that her non-Jewish audience might not be familiar with this word. When one of the interviewers asks, "When you tell your friends that you're of Jewish descent, what do they say?" she responds, "It's pretty obvious. If you know, like, the way I act and talk, talk with our hands, it's a very Jewish thing. I can't hide it ... I'm more of a *yenta*, if you've heard of that."

In this interview, Weichselbaum reports being a proud Jew of Color and contrasts herself with friends who choose just one parent's culture: "being biracial is an honor ... in my family we embrace both heritages." Given this, one might expect her to combine elements of the JE and AAE repertoires. Her non-use of AAE features may be influenced by a lack of exposure to the AAE repertoire in her childhood: "Being a proud Jamaican, it's a lot different culture than African American, so actually, I didn't have African American friends or knew a lot about even our history until I went to college." It is possible that she was exposed to the AAE repertoire in college, and perhaps in other contexts she uses elements of it, but the fact that she does not do so here indicates her ideology that proudly identifying as African American does not entail using elements of the linguistic repertoire associated with African Americans (see chapter 8, this volume). At the same time, she does use language to highlight her Jewishness in this decisively non-Jewish setting, and by adding the tag, "if you've heard of that" after her use of *yenta*, she positions her interviewers as outsiders to her Jewish speech community.

Yitz Jordan (Y-Love), a black man who converted to Orthodox Judaism and became a popular Hip Hop artist, expresses a different ideology—one of merged Black and Jewish identity, expressed through the use of elements of the AAE and JE repertoires. In a forum about Jews of Color, he rejects the "idea that you're supposed to give up your Black identity and transform that into ... a Jewish identity." He says that when he uses "African American Vernacular," the reaction of other Jews implies, "That's ghetto, that's something you should give up. If you're going to speak in a broken English, speak it with Yiddish." He counters this stance by using elements of the JE and AAE repertoires, both in this interview and in his music. Most of the JE features he uses are lexical, and most of the AAE features he uses are prosodic and phonological.

Yavilah McCoy expresses a similar ideology. Speaking in the same forum, she says:

> Me bringin my full self to this experience is essential. ... But when
> I come, I'm comin on my terms. ... And when I come to the *bimáh*

[synagogue pulpit/stage], I want to be able to sing in my song, in my soul, let it be. Don't start telling me about how it's gotta sound like *My Yiddishe Mamma* [popular Yiddish song, lit. "My Jewish Mother"]. It does not have to sound like *My Yiddishe Mamma* to be Jewish, or authentically Jewish. It needs to sound like this [points to her body], because this is what *is*.

At this point, Jordan says, "Cause you're an authentic Jew." McCoy responds using AAE prosody, "Honey, and this is what it looks like" and then laughs. Through both content (what she says) and form (the use of AAE and JE features), McCoy indicates her positive attitude toward her merged Black Jewish identity. At the same time, her statement, "It does not have to sound like *My Yiddishe Mamma* to be Jewish, or authentically Jewish"—and Jordan's supportive response—serve to contest common constructions of authenticity, in which an authentic member of a group must use linguistic features commonly associated with that group. This exchange makes clear that however a Black Jew speaks should be considered authentic Black Jewish language.

Conclusion

In the early twenty-first century many Americans identify as Black Jews. Some of them use language to indicate their hybrid identities and align themselves with Black and Jewish communities. In the videos analyzed in this chapter, seven Black Jews make differential use of elements of the AAE and JE repertoires, offering multiple versions of how Black Jews speak English. All of them use some Hebrew or Yiddish loanwords common among Jews, and some also use phonological and prosodic features associated with Jews, especially Orthodox Jews. All but one use linguistic features associated with African Americans, some only phonological and prosodic features, and others morphosyntactic and lexical features as well. Individuals also use different features in different parts of the videos analyzed. This interspeaker and intraspeaker variation remind us that we should not consider African American English, Jewish English, or Black Jewish English as ethnolects that can only be used in an all-or-nothing fashion. Instead, they are used variably; Black Jews sometimes distinguish their English from that of other Americans through more or less use of linguistic elements typically understood as "Black" and/or "Jewish." As they do so, they present themselves to the world in unique ways as Black and Jewish.

These examples highlight the importance of language and language ideology in how individuals present themselves as members of racial, ethnic, and religious groups. Because many people associate a linguistic feature with a group, when an individual uses that feature, she indicates to others that she is aligning with that group. At the same time, this analysis questions common assumptions that the use of particular features maps straightforwardly onto one's ethnoracial identification. Not all Black Jews use linguistic features commonly associated with Black and Jewish people. And when they do, they sometimes do so in a humorous or parodic way, mocking the essentialized understanding of language and racial identity. As these prominent Black Jews remind us, people use language in creative ways as they present their complex identities to the world.

Notes

1. The author would like to thank H. Samy Alim and John Rickford for their close reading and valuable comments on this chapter.
2. But see Modan 2001 and Bucholtz 2011 on contested racial ideologies among Jews; see also Brodkin 1998 on how Jews came to be seen as White in the mid-twentieth century.
3. Note that some Black Jews also identify as Ashkenazi, based on their family heritage and traditions. See, e.g., http://www.notacontradiction.com/2012/08/28/deepening-dialogue-expanding-ashkenazi/#more-63.
4. Due to methodological limitations, and depending on how one defines "Jewish," this estimate could be off by tens of thousands.
5. E.g., http://www.manishtanasmusings.com/, http://www.blackandjewish.com/bajpages/bajindex.html, http://www.blackgayjewish.com/, Be'chol Lashon (In Every Tongue), Jewish Multiracial Network, Jews in All Hues, and Jews of Color United.
6. http://www.youtube.com/watch?NR=1&feature=endscreen&v=4a4s4xmcjdM, http://www.youtube.com/watch?NR=1&feature=endscreen&v=CujmiIllSVc, http://www.youtube.com/watch?NR=1&feature=endscreen&v=HbzJLINa84k.
7. As Benor (2010, 172) explains, there are ethical and analytic problems with seeing some groups' language as marked and other groups' language as the norm upon which the comparison is based. Even so, this type of analysis is better than the alternatives.
8. http://kehilamagazineofficial.wordpress.com/2012/09/21/thoughts-from-a-unicorn-an-interview-with-manishtana/.

References

Alim, H. Samy. 2004. *You Know My Steez: An Ethnographic and Sociolinguistic Study of Styleshifting in a Black American Speech Community*. Durham, NC: Duke University Press.

Azoulay, Katya Gibel. 1997. *Black, Jewish, and Interracial: It's Not the Color of Your Skin, but the Race of Your Kin, and Other Myths of Identity*. Durham, NC: Duke University Press.

Benor, Sarah Bunin. 2010. "Ethnolinguistic Repertoire: Shifting the Analytic Focus in Language and Ethnicity." *Journal of Sociolinguistics* 14/2: 159–83.

Benor, Sarah Bunin. 2011. "*Mensch, Bentsh*, and *Balagan*: Variation in the American Jewish Linguistic Repertoire." *Language and Communication* 31/2: 141–54.

Benor, Sarah Bunin. 2012. *Becoming Frum: How Newcomers Learn the Language and Culture of Orthodox Judaism*. New Brunswick, NJ: Rutgers University Press.

Brodkin, Karen. 1998. *How Jews Became White Folks and What That Says about Race in America*. Piscataway, NJ: Rutgers University Press.

Bucholtz, Mary. 2011. *White Kids: Language, Race, and Styles of Youth Identity.* Cambridge: Cambridge University Press.

Cohen, Steven M., Jack Ukeles, and Ron Miller. 2012. "Jewish Community Study of New York: 2011 Comprehensive Report." New York: UJA Federation of New York.

Eckert, Penelope. 2000. *Linguistic Variation as Social Practice.* Oxford, UK: Blackwell.

Fought, Carmen. 2006. *Language and Ethnicity.* Cambridge: Cambridge University Press.

Gold, David. 1985. "Jewish English." In *Readings in the Sociology of Jewish Languages,* ed. Leiden: Brill, 280–98.

Green, Lisa. 2002. *African American English: A Linguistic Introduction.* Cambridge: Cambridge University Press.

Gumperz, John J. 1964. "Linguistic and Social Interaction in Two Communities." *American Anthropologist* 66: 137–54.

Lester, Julius. 1995. *Lovesong: Becoming a Jew.* New York: Arcade Publishing.

MaNishtana. 2012. *Thoughts from a Unicorn: 100% Black, 100% Jewish, 0% Safe.* New York: Hyphen Publishing.

Modan, Gabriella. 2001. "White, Whole Wheat, Rye: Jews and Ethnic Categorization in Washington, DC." *Journal of Linguistic Anthropology* 11/1: 116–30.

Ochs, Elinor. 1992. "Indexing Gender." In *Rethinking Context: Language as an Interactive Phenomenon,* ed. A. Duranti and C. Goodwin. Cambridge: Cambridge University Press. 335–358.

Rahman, Jacquelyn. 2008. "Middle-Class African Americans: Reactions and Attitudes Toward African American English." *American Speech* 83: 141–76.

Rickford, John R. 1999. *African American Vernacular English: Features, Evolution, Educational Implications.* Oxford: Blackwell.

Rickford, John R., and Angela E. Rickford. 1976. "Cut-Eye and Suck-Teeth: African Words and Gestures in New World Guise." *Journal of American Folklore* 89.353: 294–309.

Smitherman, Geneva. 1977. *Talkin and Testifyin: The Language of Black America.* Detroit: Wayne State Press.

Taylor, Orlando. 1971. "Response to Local Dialects and the Field of Speech." In Roger W. Shuy, ed., *Sociolinguistics: A Crossdisciplinary Perspective.* Washington, DC: Center for Applied Linguistics, 13–20.

Tobin, Diane, Gary A. Tobin, and Scott Rubin. 2005. *In Every Tongue: The Racial and Ethnic Diversity of the Jewish People.* San Francisco: Institute for Jewish and Community Research.

Walker, Rebecca. 2001. *Black, White, and Jewish: Autobiography of a Shifting Self.* New York: Riverhead Books.

10

Pharyngeal Beauty and Depharyngealized Geek

Performing Ethnicity on Israeli Reality TV

ROEY GAFTER

A current direction in sociolinguistic variation studies focuses not only on how linguistic variables correlate with social categories but rather on the social meaning of variables (Eckert 2008).* Such research aspires to understand why and under which circumstances a speaker adopts specific variables, and how her style interacts with the construction of her identity. In this chapter, I adopt this approach to describe the social meaning of the Hebrew pharyngeal segments [ħ] (a voiceless pharyngeal fricative) and [ʕ] (a voiced pharyngeal approximant). These segments are merged with their nonpharyngeal counterparts by most current speakers of Hebrew, but they do occur in the speech of some *Mizrahis* (Israelis of Middle Eastern descent). Although they are infrequent, the pharyngeals are extremely salient in Israeli discourse about language. They are enregistered (Agha 2003) as a Mizrahi feature, and as such they are a valuable resource for indexing attributes associated with stereotypical Mizrahi personae.

In order to account for the interplay of different meanings that the pharyngeals can index, I adopt Eckert's (2008) notion of an indexical field, showing how meanings range from an old-fashioned kind of formality to social stereotypes regarding Mizrahis. I base my analysis on two types of data. I first examine the rich metalinguistic commentary offered by Hebrew speakers regarding the pronunciation of pharyngeals. I then examine data from two Israeli reality TV shows, revealing that speakers who do not consistently pharyngealize can nevertheless use them occasionally and draw upon their range of meanings in performing Mizrahi identity.

Introducing Ethnicity in Israel

When trying to understand Israeli culture and identity, ethnic divisions surface on every level. Among Israelis, Jewish ethnicity is usually understood as a dichotomy between Jews of European descent, referred to as *Ashkenazi* Jews, and Jews of Middle Eastern descent, referred to as *Mizrahi* Jews (see Swirski 1981 and Shalom Chetrit 2009, among many others). One's ethnic origin has been an important social category in Israel ever since its founding in 1948. While the Zionist movement was predominantly Ashkenazi, as were most of the first immigrants to Israel, the 1950s saw massive waves of Jewish immigration from neighboring Arab and Muslim countries. These Mizrahi immigrants were hired mostly for low-income jobs, and during the first decade of Israel's independence, inequality in earnings and in education between Ashkenazis and Mizrahis quickly became a fact. While the demographics of Israel rapidly changed to become more Mizrahi, the political establishment and cultural and economic elite remained thoroughly Ashkenazi.

Recent years have seen a shift toward greater ethnic equality, with a rise in interethnic marriages and Mizrahi Jews occupying high-profile jobs, but the inequality in education and earnings still persists. Dahan et al. (2003) found that according to the 1995 census, the percentage of high-school graduates among Mizrahi Jews is 22 percent lower than that of Ashkenazi Jews. With respect to economic status, according to the survey reported in Swirski et al. (2008), the average earnings of Ashkenazis are more than 30 percent greater than those of Mizrahis.

This social stratification is unsurprisingly coupled with persisting perceptions of Mizrahis and Ashkenazis in Israeli society. Shohat's (1989) critical survey of ethnic stereotypes in Israeli cinema draws a bleak picture. According to Shohat, Ashkenazis are described as "just Israelis," the unmarked category. Mizrahis, on the other hand, are portrayed in a stereotypically Orientalist way—they are uneducated, primitive, vulgar, sexist, and violent; they are also warm, hospitable, and have good food. A similar conclusion was reached by Swirski (1981), who conducted interviews with several Mizrahi Israelis concerning ethnic inequality. The Mizrahis were described as innocent, kind, and warm, but on the other hand irrational and quick to get angry. The Ashkenazis were described as the opposite—distant in their relationships, condescending and cunning, but on the other hand very skilled and rational. As can be expected by the stereotyping of the category "Mizrahi" in Israel, the stereotypes also extend to how Mizrahis speak, and the feature that is most associated with Mizrahi speech—their alleged use of the pharyngeal sounds—is the focus of this chapter.

Introducing the Pharyngeal Sounds

When considering sociolinguistic variation in Israel, some attention must be paid to the unique history of the language. Hebrew had not been a spoken language for generations, and was revitalized in the late nineteenth and early twentieth centuries (by the early Zionists, who were mostly Ashkenazis). In current Israel, Modern Hebrew is now the mother tongue of most speakers, and is used in all domains of life. The remarkable success of the revitalization is a point of great pride among Israelis, but it has also had an effect on prevailing language attitudes. Despite conscious attempts to reconstruct the language as it was historically spoken, the Hebrew that emerged from the revitalization is, of course, not the same as Biblical Hebrew, or any other historical form of Hebrew, and has been greatly influenced by the first languages of the early revitalizers (Zuckermann 2005). This has particular consequences for the pharyngeals and their relationship with ethnic identity.

Biblical Hebrew had two pharyngeal sounds, represented by the Hebrew letters *het* (ח) and *ayin* (ע). In the Mizrahi liturgical reading tradition, *het* was pronounced as [ħ] (a voiceless pharyngeal fricative) and *ayin* was pronounced as [ʕ] (a voiced pharyngeal approximant). Furthermore, many early Mizrahi immigrants were fluent in Arabic, a close relative of Hebrew that has these pharyngeal sounds. Although the pronunciation used by Mizrahis was considered truer to the Semitic roots of the language, most Hebrew speakers during the early years of the revival were Ashkenazis. These early Ashkenazi revitalizers of Hebrew were native speakers of European languages with no pharyngeal segments, and they could not pronounce them (or chose not to). The result was that virtually all Ashkenazi speakers, from the days of the early revival to current times, do not normally produce these segments.

Blanc (1968), the first description of the sociolinguistic situation in Israel, already includes a prominent reference to the pharyngeals and their distribution. Blanc describes two distinct varieties of Hebrew, which he named "General Israeli," the emergent standard spoken by Ashkenazis, and "Oriental Israeli," spoken by Mizrahis. He specifies three distinctions between the two varieties, all of which are in the realm of consonants. Specifically, "Oriental Israeli" has the two pharyngeal sounds that "General Israeli" has collapsed with their non-pharyngeal counterparts, and it uses a trilled apical rhotic, as opposed to the "General Israeli" uvular rhotic. In Yaeger-Dror's (1988) discussion of the same variables, she also refers to two varieties of Hebrew, but uses the terms "Modern Koiné" (MK) for what Blanc called "General Israeli" and "Mizrahi Hebrew" (MH) for "Oriental Hebrew," and I will adopt these terms here.

In all the cases in which the segment inventory of Mizrahi Hebrew and the Modern Koiné differ, Mizrahi Hebrew is considered more similar to Biblical

Hebrew. This has important consequences, since the ideological goal of the revitalization of Hebrew was to resurrect Biblical Hebrew as it was believed to have been spoken. With respect to the rhotic sounds, there is no way of knowing how the Biblical Hebrew rhotic was actually produced, but the Mizrahi apical variant is considered the original one (Yaeger-Dror 1988). In the case of the pharyngeals, however, it is not just a case of one production replacing another—Mizrahi Hebrew maintains a distinction that clearly existed in Biblical Hebrew and is always preserved in writing, but has been lost in the Koiné.

In the modern Koiné, the pronunciation of *ayin* has merged with that of the biblical glottal stop, though in current usage, both are usually not pronounced at all. As for *het*, it merged with another biblical sound, [x], represented by the letter *xaf* (כ)[1]. This is shown in Table 10.1.

As discussed earlier, Ashkenazis tend to be of higher socioeconomic status than Mizrahis, and are considered by many to be the "unmarked" Israeli. As such, the variety of Hebrew that lacks the pharyngeal sounds may be considered "standard" Hebrew, and indeed, it is the one most widely used in the media. Nevertheless, due to the unusual history of the language, prescriptive norms in Israel have taken an atypical turn. Unlike many places in which the prestige standard is the language of the elites, in Israel the model was the reconstructed "Semitic" pronunciation, which retains the biblical distinctions (Zuckermann 2005). Up until recent years, newscasters would always use the "correct" pharyngeal pronunciation. While the trend has shifted in this decade and newscasters now speak in the Modern Koiné, the "correct" pronunciation still carries prestige, and is always used (for example, by the host of Israel's annual independence day ceremonies). Thus, the pharyngeal segments occupy a special position—they are a marker of lower socioeconomic status, and at the same time they are considered the "correct" and authentic pronunciation. This ambiguous position contrasts sharply with the sociolinguistic variables in Labov's (1966) classic study of New York City English, in which socioeconomic class, style, prestige, and sound change are all neatly aligned on the same axis, with the move from more casual to more careful speech in intraspeaker variation reproducing the class differences observed in interspeaker variation. Crucially, the social evaluation also

Table 10.1 **The pharyngeals and their nonpharyngeal counterparts**

Hebrew letter	Pharyngeal?	Biblical Hebrew	Modern Koiné
aleph (א)	No	ʔ	ʔ/Ø
ayin (ע)	Yes	ʕ	
xaf (כ)	No	x	x
het (ח)	Yes	ħ	

mirrored this unified axis, in what Eckert calls "a folk connection between old and new, formal and informal, better and worse, correct and incorrect" (Eckert 1990, 249). Eckert warns that interpreting gender differences solely along such a unified axis cannot fully account for women's linguistic behavior, since women do more than simply be more or less conservative than men. This critique applies to analyses of ethnic variation as well, and strikingly so in the case of pharyngeals in Modern Hebrew, where the axes do not align even in the folk perception, in which the "old," "correct," "authentic," and "prestigious" are at odds.

This combination of features coupled with the immense importance of the Mizrahi-Ashkenazi distinction makes the pharyngeals pregnant with social meaning. Labov (1972) makes a distinction between indicators, markers, and stereotypes. While indicators distinguish social or geographic categories, but have not been noticed by speakers, markers have garnered their attention. Stereotypes, like markers, are noticed by speakers; both are likely to play a role in stylistic variation, but the difference is that speakers are consciously aware of the stereotypes, and they are thus the topic of overt social commentary. In this typology, the use of pharyngeal segments is certainly a stereotype, as it is quite often referred to in Israeli discourse, and Israelis have a term to refer to it—*ledaber be-het ve-ayin* ("to speak with *het* and *ayin*"). As I will show in the next section, this term is used quite often, showing the salience of the stereotype and its ideological link to Mizrahi-ness.

However, due to the small number of community studies conducted in Israel, it is hard to assess how many Mizrahis currently use pharyngeals in speech and to what extent. The consensus from the extant literature gives us little more than the observations that the pharyngeals are very rare in current Israel, and that if they are used at all they are used by Mizrahis (though less and less so). As mentioned before, Blanc (1968) presented the pharyngeals and the apical /r/ as the sole features distinguishing a Mizrahi pronunciation; however, he immediately proceeded to claim that they are uncommon among Mizrahis as well. Subsequent work followed that trend.[2]

Davis (1984) interviewed Mizrahis in predominantly Mizrahi towns and noted that younger speakers use them far less than adults. With pharyngeal use around only 5 percent for his group of 12-year-olds who were not bilingual in Arabic, Davis stated that "in a generation or two, the pharyngeals will have disappeared completely from Israeli Hebrew" (31). The trend reported by Davis was found by others as well, though possibly to a less extreme degree. Lefkowitz (2004) conducted sociolinguistic interviews in Haifa with ninety Israelis, and found that only a minority of Mizrahis pharyngealized to any noticeable extent, all of them over 40 years old. Zuckermann (2005, 215) anecdotally comments, regarding the Semitic pharyngeal, that "most Israelis do not pronounce them but they are used, for example, by old Yemenite Jews (though less and less by young ones)."[3] To conclude, the extant literature does not give a clear picture of the extent to which pharyngeals are currently used, but strongly suggests an advanced stage of a change in progress in which the pharyngeals are being lost.

Getting at the Social Meaning

Since the existing research suggests most Mizrahis do not use the pharynge-als, and that their disappearance from the language of all Israelis (including Mizrahis) is all but complete, the reader may wonder whether these variables are worth exploring.[4] The answer, I believe, is a resounding yes. It is important to acknowledge a crucial aspect that sets the pharyngeals apart—their great salience in the Israeli internal discourse about language and ethnicity. When we consider the extraordinary number of references in the media to a variable that, after all, not many people use, it is clear that Israelis are obsessed with the pharyngeals.

If most Mizrahis do not produce pharyngeals, they are no longer simply a marker of ethnicity (if they ever were); however, as described earlier, histori-cal and social circumstances have made the pharyngeal pronunciation pregnant with a rich and multilayered social meaning. It is important, at this point, to consider what it means for a linguistic feature to carry social meaning. In this case, we are not likely to find any one fixed social correlate (such as one simply indicating "Mizrahi"). I argue that the great importance of the pharyngeals in Israeli discourse stems from the ideological links created between their use and stereotypical aspects of a Mizrahi persona. As mentioned earlier, Ashkenazis are described as "just Israelis," the unmarked category, in mainstream Israeli discourse. Mizrahis, on the other hand, are often portrayed in stereotypically Orientalist ways, as noted above. These stereotypes are linked with the pharyn-geals, alongside the complicated history that makes them the authentically cor-rect pronunciation.

A useful concept to consider here is indexical orders (Silverstein 2003)—in this framework, membership in a certain population (such as being an Ashkenazi or Mizrahi Israeli) is a lower-order index (or "n-th order index" in Silverstein's terms). The forms used by this population are always available for reinterpre-tation, linking the social characteristics attributed to this population with the variable, and constantly construing higher-order indexical links. As we will see, the salient social meaning that keeps the pharyngeals an important part of the discourse concerns the higher-order indexicals—the associations not only with Mizrahi-ness per se, but with conceptualizations of what it means to be Mizrahi.

As a first step toward getting a grasp on what social meanings the pharyn-geals have, and the great importance ascribed to them, we can first observe what Israelis *say* about them. As mentioned before, Israelis have a term for producing the pharyngeals—*ledaber be-het ve-ayin*[5] ("to speak with *het* and *ayin*"). Searching Google for this phrase produces a vast range of comments, demonstrating its salience in Israeli discourse. The comments that I have collected demonstrate the intense love-hate relationship Israelis have with the pharyngeals, as they are ideologically linked to matters that are at the heart of Israeli identity.

Perhaps the most famous comment on the use of pharyngeal segments comes from a well-known song, "Me, Simon and Little Moiz," performed by Yosi Banay. In the song he nostalgically recounts the long-gone days of his childhood in a city that is never named but is easily recognizable as Jerusalem. For Banay, who is Mizrahi, the pharyngeal segments are a thing of beauty, reminiscent of simpler times, and specifically, of a beautiful form of Hebrew.

---

(1) be-na3aley šabat ve-kova šel baret,   "With Sabbath shoes and a beret hat

ve-be-3ivrit yafa 3im 3ayin ve-im   And in beautiful Hebrew with
7et   *ayin* and *het*

daharnu 3al 3anan 3asuy mi-kariot   We rode on a cloud made of pillows

u-ve-ekda7 pkakim hitba3nu   And with a toy gun we sank ships."[6]
oniyot.

As could be expected, many of the other examples found online link the pharyngeals with ethnicity, either tacitly or explicitly. Of course, not all opinions about the pharyngeals are positive, which is not surprising for a linguistic feature that is so strongly associated with a community that is in many ways marginalized. Consider the following remark from a blog post titled "Am I still ashamed to be Mizrahi?"

---

(2) be-yalduti hitbayašti be-horay biglal še-hem hayu mizra7im . . . avi ha-kehe, še-diber 3im 7et ve-3ayin groniyot, lo hegia3 me-3olam le-bet ha-sefer az ze dey hergia3 oti.

"When I was young I was ashamed of my parents because they were Mizrahi . . . My dark skinned father, who spoke with guttural *het* and *ayin*, never came to my school—so I felt relieved."[7]

Still less positive stereotypes associated with users of *het* and *ayin* can be seen in the following example, which refers to Margalit "Margol" Tsan'ani, a Yemenite-Israeli singer. The writer is discussing her recent addition to the cast of the Israeli TV show *Koxav Nolad* (a remake of *American Idol*) as a judge—the popular conception being that she was added as a "good cop," to balance the other three (Ashkenazi male) judges.

---

(3) naxon, lif3amim hi lo mehukca3at, medaberet be-7et ve-3ayin, hi lo mitya-
     meret lihyot mašehu še-hi lo, ve-lif3amim ze nišma kcat behemi o mešulal
     takt, aval ze 3adif pi elef 3al kol ha-lakek ve-ha-dawinim šel 3amitea
     la-bizness

     "True, sometimes she's unpolished, talks with *het* and *ayin*, she's not trying
     to be something she's not, and sometimes that may sound vulgar or tact-
     less, but it's a million times better than the sucking up and showing off for
     her (show) biz colleagues"[8]

As noted in the previous section, being vulgar and crude is often attributed to Mizrahi Israelis. The writer of this passage links the use of *ayin* and *het* with sounding vulgar and unpolished, exemplifying the higher-order indexing. Of course, there is nothing inherently vulgar-sounding about pharyngeal sounds (or any other sound, for that matter)—in Arabic, for example, they are a part of the *tajwid* register, the "perfect" recitation of the Koran, which has great pres-tige. However, in Israel they are imbued with locally significant meaning, and it is the association with certain types of speakers that creates the link with vulgarity. Nevertheless, it is important to notice that in this passage, Tsan'ani's style is at once both criticized and respected. There is a way in which vulgarity and tactlessness can be a good thing, and that is when it is opposed to being fake. Tsan'ani is described as real and authentic, yet again echoing the link with ethnic stereotypes discussed in Swirski (1981).

Negative stereotypes about Mizrahi men are strongly exemplified by the Hebrew word *ars*. This word is an ethnicized pejorative—it is typically applied to Mizrahi men, and denotes a derogatory stereotype of males displaying bad manners, vulgarity, and contempt for social norms. Unsurprisingly, the proto-typical *ars* evoked by this stereotype speaks with *het* and *ayin*, as shown in this comment from an Israeli web forum.

---

(4) ve-ze ha-3ars ha-macuy. 3im šaršeret ve-gormetim, 3im ha-dibur 3al
     elohim, 3im ha-silsulim um-kultum šik, 3im ha-dibur be-7et ve-3ayin,
     ve-be3ecem, ma la3asot, be-signon še-nora mazkir et bney-dodenu . . .

     "This is your common *ars*. With the necklace and bracelets, talking about
     god, with the Umm Kulthum style singing, speaking in *het* and *ayin*, in a
     style that, what can you do, is reminiscent of our cousins."[9]

Umm Kulthum is a famous Egyptian singer, and "our cousins" is a euphemistic term used when referring to Arabs, mostly in pejorative contexts; the writer is saying that if you use *het* and *ayin* you sound like an *ars*, and an *ars* sounds like an Arab. Of course, the pharyngeal segments do indeed occur in Arabic, but the writer is creating an ideological link—tying pharyngeal segments with traits attributed to speakers of Arabic. While surveying the stereotypes of Arabs in Israeli society is well beyond the scope of this paper, using the pharyngeals to link Arabic identity and Mizrahi identity is clearly interpreted as challenging the place Mizrahis get to occupy in Israeli society, reproducing a discourse of othering.

These metalinguistic commentaries demonstrate the wide range of indexical meanings associated with the pharyngeals. When trying to assess the plethora of related meanings invoked by the metalinguistic comments made about pharyngeals, we may make use of the semiotic process of iconization (Irvine and Gal 2000). Iconization is the process by which "linguistic differences appear to be iconic representations of the social contrasts they index—as if a linguistic feature somehow depicted or displayed a social group's inherent nature or essence" (Irvine 2001, 33). In our case, we can see how the pharyngeals come to be linked with supposed characteristics of pharyngeal users.

As I have attempted to show, the social meaning of the pharyngeals cannot be reconciled into one scale, as it has elements of hyperarticulation, clarity, and an old-fashioned kind of learnedness, on the one hand, and elements of Mizrahi-ness, warm-bloodedness, and authenticity on the other. Building upon Silverstein's order of indexicality, Eckert (2008) developed the notion of an *indexical field* of meaning for sociolinguistic variables. In this framework variables do not have a fixed value; rather, a dynamic structure is created by the constant linking of form and meaning, without the previous reconstruals disappearing. The social meaning of the Hebrew pharyngeal segments is an example of why such an approach is necessary. Following Eckert, I will try to couch these meanings within an indexical field, which includes both momentary stances and permanent qualities, as well as social types that provide the anchor for the interpretation of this variable (see Figure 10.1).

Figure 10.1 Indexical field of the pharyngeals.

Boxes = social types, black = permanent qualities, gray = stances.

Most of the qualities on this chart can be directly associated with the old-fashioned standard, the Mizrahi stereotype, or the hyperarticulated aspect of *ayin*; some of them, like "old-fashioned," relate to all three. Other features may require more explanation: "means business" has to do with their supposed Mizrahi no-nonsense, "real" attitude to getting things done.

Performative Uses on Reality TV: Two Case Studies

The previous sections showed that even though the extant research suggests that pharyngeals are all but extinct, they are extremely salient in Israeli discourse. Therefore, a question arises—if the pharyngeals are laden with such important social meaning in the Israeli view, but are in general uncommon, can they still be used as a stylistic resource by speakers who use them infrequently? In this section I use data from two Israeli reality TV shows to demonstrate that the rich indexical meanings of the pharyngeals are indeed available as a resource, even when used sparingly.

Beauty and the Geek

The first source of data is the Israeli show *Ha-yafa ve-ha-xnun*, an Israeli remake of the American show *Beauty and the Geek*. The show, as the producers put it, places "11 beautiful women and 11 nerdy men in a villa"—each "geek" is paired with a "beauty," and the couples are made to perform tasks that portray the men (that is, the "geeks") as highly intelligent but socially awkward, and the "beauties" (that is, the women) as their polar opposites—beautiful and socially adept, but not too bright. The show derives much of its alleged humor from highlighting and reiterating gender stereotypes. However, an interesting thing happened in the Israeli remake, which makes it an excellent source of data for looking into questions of ethnicity. Although the show is based on a gendered conflict, in the second season it turned out that the men and women were also differentiated ethnically—all but one of the geeks were Ashkenazi, and 7 of the 11 beauties were Mizrahi. This is not too surprising, since the misogynistic stereotypes perpetuated by the show parallel, to some extent, stereotypes about Mizrahis—both women and Mizrahis are accused of being rash and thinking with their heart instead of their head (unlike the stereotypically cold and rational Ashkenazi geeks). Since the show is a charged arena for performing ethnic identities, it is interesting to observe the use of pharyngeals therein.

Unsurprisingly, none of the geeks (who were almost all Ashkenazi) used any pharyngeals. Most of the women did not produce pharyngeals either, which is not surprising in itself, as the participants are all in their twenties, and most younger Mizrahis do not produce them. However, two of the female participants, Lital and Sivan, did use pharyngeals *some* of the time, and focusing on their variable usage is telling. First, it is important to note that although most of the female contestants were Mizrahi, Sivan and Lital made a point of singling themselves out as more authentically Mizrahi in other ways as well. For example, both of them made constant references to their Mizrahi ethnicity and their predominantly Mizrahi hometowns.[10]

In order to explore the variation more carefully, the speech of Lital and Sivan in six hours of the show was coded by two native speakers of Hebrew for potential and actual pharyngeal productions (potential productions were defined by where the orthography marks a historical pharyngeal). The results show a clear difference between the use of *het* and *ayin*: while the two women produce a pharyngeal *ayin* ([ʕ]) in about 5.5 percent of its possible occurrences (20/368 tokens), there were no instances of a pharyngeal *het* ([ħ]) in 320 potential occurrences.

Table 10.2 and Table 10.3 present the pharyngeal productions of Lital and Sivan.

A few observations can be drawn from the numbers—the first is that, contrary to the common stereotype of "speaking with *het* and *ayin*," it appears that, at least for these women, *het* and *ayin* exhibit different distributions—namely, *ayin* but not *het* is useful as a stylistic resource. Of course, even *ayin* is not used very often, but the key observation is that it is used often enough to be noticed, as we can tell from metalinguistic commentary about the show, such as this tweet[11] about Sivan (emphasis added):

Table 10.2 **Lital's use of *het* and *ayin* in the Israeli version of *Beauty and the Geek***

	Pharyngeal	Nonpharyngeal
ayin (/ʕ/—Ø)	6.7% (17/252)	93% (235/252)
het (/ħ/—/x/)	0% (0/227)	100% (227/227)

Table 10.3 **Sivan's use of *het* and *ayin* in the Israeli version of *Beauty and the Geek***

	Pharyngeal	Nonpharyngeal
ayin (/ʕ/—Ø)	2.6% (3/116)	97.4% (113/116)
het (/ħ/—/x/)	0% (0/93)	100% (93/93)

(5) yeš li kcat kraš 3al lital seleb beer ševa3it me-ha-yafa ve-ha-7nun. muzar, davka ani še-beer-ševa3 ve-fre7ot 3im 7et ve-3ayin 3osot lo b7ila bederex klal

"I have a little crush on Lital, the Beer-Sheva celebrity from Beauty and the Geek. It's funny, cause usually Beer-Sheva and *frehas* **with *het* and *ayin*** make me sick."[12]

For this writer, two key things define Lital: she speaks with *het* and *ayin* and she is a *freha*. The word *freha* is an ethnicized and gendered pejorative term that is applied to Mizrahi women (suggesting both "vulgar" and "bimbo"), and as we see here, this stereotype is also ideologically linked with the pharyngeals. Crucially, as this example shows, despite low rates of production, Lital's use of *ayin* is doing social work that does not go unnoticed. As such, *ayin* appears to be in a special class of sociolinguistic variables, where very few occurrences can still have significant social meaning. One could think of English equivalents—for example, an English speaker's single use of *ain't* can easily spell failure in a job interview, and similarly, an Israeli speaker's single use of *ayin* can carry a lot of weight.[13]

Another important observation is *when* the women on this show use a pharyngeal *ayin*. Due to the small number of tokens, a quantitative analysis would not be very useful, but a qualitative approach is revealing. When examining the occurrences of the pharyngeal *ayin*, we can see that they are not arbitrary. Lital and Sivan use the pharyngeal *ayin* to index the stereotypical Mizrahi traits discussed in the previous section, and to construct a "down to Earth" or "don't mess with me" persona. This is apparent since *ayin* occurs primarily when they are distancing themselves from their (Ashkenazi) geek counterparts, as can be seen in examples (6) and (7). In (6), Sivan is arguing with her partner, and in (7), Lital is telling the audience how she was flustered by her partner and what she had told him—and in both cases a strongly pharyngealized *ayin* is produced. (In these examples, and all the following ones, *ayin* that was actually produced as a pharyngeal [ʕ] is represented in bold as ʕ, while orthographic *ayin*, which is not pronounced as such, will still be marked as 3.)

(6)	takšiv,	pa3am	a7rona	še-	ata	mitʕarev	li	ba-	7ayim
	listen	time	last	that	you	interfere	to.me	in.the	life

"Listen, this is the last time you interfere in my life."

(7)	ani	karega3	te3una	miday-	bišvil	laʕazor	lexa
	I	now	charged	too	to	help	to.you

"I'm too annoyed now to help you."

To conclude, a few strategically placed *ayin*s are useful for Sivan and Lital in creating a persona they are very much invested in—one that is associated with the stereotypical Mizrahi. As the next section shows, this type of usage is not unique to them.

Koxav Nolad

The second set of data comes from the reality show *Koxav nolad* ("A Star Is Born"), an Israeli adaptation of the American television show *American Idol*. I focus on the host of the show, Tsvika Hadar, who is a popular Israeli comedian television personality. Hadar, born in 1966, is of Romanian descent and was raised in Be'er-Sheva, a small city in southern Israel (also the hometown of Lital from *Beauty and the Geek*). In considering the more performative uses of the pharyngeals, Hadar provides an interesting case study, since he is not technically Mizrahi, but nevertheless sometimes uses pharyngeals. It is possible that by virtue of his coming from a lower-middle-class background, and from Israel's peripheral south, he is not considered a prototypical Ashkenazi. Thus, his life story and his immense popularity within all echelons of Israeli society allow him to perform Mizrahi-ness without it being perceived as ridicule.

In order to explore Hadar's use of pharyngeals, his speech in the fourth season of the show was coded by two native speakers of Hebrew for potential and actual pharyngeal productions. The results show that his frequency of use is quite similar to that of Lital and Sivan from *Beauty and the Geek*—in the course of four hours, he produced a noticeably pharyngeal *ayin* only 9 times out 379 potential occurrences (2.3%), and during these four hours, he did not produce a single pharyngeal *het*.

As with *Beauty and the Geek*, Hadar's use of the pharyngeal segment is by no means frequent, and yet it does not go unnoticed. For example, consider the following commentary on his hosting skills from the Israel website "Stage Magazine" (emphasis added):[14]

---

(8) nisyono šel Hadar lehitkarev le-paštut, le-3amamiyut, garar gam oto
     lesagel le-3acmo et ha-7et ve-3ayin ha-mizdamnot, ve-ilu et ha-3ivrit ha-
     nexona hu kore mi-kartisiyot, bišvil še-lo yexašev le-7axam miday

     "Hadar's attempt to come close to simplicity and folksiness, made him
     adopt a *het* and *ayin* every so often, whereas he reads correct Hebrew
     from cards, so that no one would think he's too smart."

Crucially, as in the case of Lital and Sivan, the instances in which Hadar uses *ayin* are not arbitrary. In all but one case, it appears to index a departure from the serious host persona, performing a friendlier, warmer, more down-to-earth character. In addition, he seems to use *ayin* primarily when addressing Mizrahi speakers. Most of the occurrences of *ayin* are when addressing Margalit Tsan'ani, one of the judges on the show. Tsan'ani, as has already been mentioned, is a Yemenite-Israeli, and he does use *ayin* frequently, although not always. In one case, after saying that she had given a certain contestant an evil review, Hadar jokes and says:

(9)	at	yexola	lihyot	raʕa	marjales?	at	yexola	lihyot	raʕa?
	you	can	be	evil	marjales?	you	can	be	evil?

"Can you be evil, Marjales? Can you be evil?"

His friendly tone is obvious from his calling Tsan'ani by the nickname Marjales, but also from his very pronounced *ayin*, conjuring a less serious persona than he usually maintains in the show. It is noteworthy that when Tsan'ani referred to herself as evil, she did not pronounce the word *ra3a* ("evil") with a pharyngeal *ayin*. However, the fact that she does often use *ayin*, and is Mizrahi, is likely to have facilitated Tsvika Hadar's choice to use it when addressing her.

There is only one example in which Hadar uses the pharyngeal *ayin* when speaking to an Ashkenazi speaker. In one of the episodes, Yehudit Ravits, a well-known Israeli singer who is Ashkenazi, appeared as a guest star. Hadar gushed and said that he had to confess that when he was growing up in Be'er-Sheva, he was a big fan of hers. In this sentence he pronounces a pharyngeal *ayin* in the name *beer-ševa3* ("Be'er-Sheva"). In this case the stance he is making may be to highlight his own humble upbringings, and the link *ayin* has with noncentral Be'er-Sheva.

Why *Ayin* and Not *Het*?

These two case studies show that speakers who do not consistently use the pharyngeals can still use *ayin* as a stylistic resource to index aspects of a stereotypical Mizrahi persona. The pharyngeals are so laden with social meaning, and so salient, that even a single use may carry a lot of weight and be noticed and commented on.

One remaining question is why can *ayin* be used in this way, at least by the speakers in my data, but not *het*? First, it is interesting to note that a preference for *ayin* over *het* in some uses had been mentioned by Blanc in his original 1968 paper. He discusses Ashkenazis who sometimes use *ayin* as "a sort of decorative device" and he claims: "the effect it is intended to produce is hard to pinpoint . . . . this does not apply to *het*."

A possible explanation for the difference between *het* and *ayin* may lie in the fact that although they are both pharyngeal, the competing "standard" pronunciation in each case is different. Recall that for most speakers of the Modern Koiné, *ayin* is not pronounced at all, whereas *het* is pronounced as a dorsal fricative. Thus while pharyngeal *ayin* is clearly a hyperarticulation, pharyngeal *het* is not. As the nonpharyngeal *het* is audibly noticeable, replacing it with the pharyngeal does not achieve the same emphatic effect as replacing a zero with a very salient segment. When discussing the issue of /t/ release in English, Eckert (2008) ties its indexical meanings with a broader ideological association—linking hyperarticulation with care, and hypoarticulation with laziness. She proceeds to compare /t/ release with /th/ stopping, and claims that while /th/ stopping is a fortition, it is not likely to have the same indexical values associated with clarity that the hyperarticulated released /t/ does. The case of the Hebrew pharyngeals may provide an interesting parallel. Both *het* and *ayin* can be considered as more strictly adhering to the older "newscaster" standard, as well as to the orthography (which always distinguishes these segments). However, it may be that only in the case of *ayin*, which is clearly emphatic, can the whole array of indexical meanings—ranging from the old-school style of Hebrew to the warm-blooded Mizrahi stereotype—be readily used by the speaker (or understood by the interlocutor).

Conclusion

The Hebrew pharyngeals are commonly associated with Mizrahi speech, but most Mizrahis do not use them. Therefore, when they do play a role in sociolinguistic variation, they are not simply a marker of ethnicity. By examining metalinguistic commentary and data from an Israeli TV show, we see that the pharyngeals do not have a fixed social meaning, but rather a wide spectrum of interrelated ones. I argue that only when we consider the special history of the segments, as well as the locally significant stereotypes, can we begin to understand their rich, multilayered meaning. In the case of *ayin*, I have shown that it is used in stylistic variation associated with the higher-order indexical values—that is, not indexing simply being Mizrahi, but rather the attributes associated with Mizrahi-ness.

Quantitative sociolinguistics usually focuses on percentages and ratios, but *ayin* seems to be a different kind of variable: even when it appears infrequently, it has a large impact. Why the speakers in these TV shows seem to use only *ayin* and not *het* in this way could benefit from further exploration. But it is clear that the great social salience of the pharyngeal makes them useful as a linguistic resource, even if they are no longer very common in everyday discourse.

Notes

* I would like to thank the Stanford Center for Comparative Studies in Race and Ethnicity and the Israel Institute for fellowships that facilitated the research reported in this paper.

1. Blanc states that the Modern Koiné merged *het* and *xaf* into a velar fricative (as does Yaeger-Dror 1988 and other writers), whereas Zuckermann (2005) states that it is a *uvular* fricative. To my knowledge, these claims are all based on auditory perception. I will refer to the merged phoneme here as /x/, while remaining agnostic on the actual phonetic realization. See Gafter (2014) for further discussion.

2. The trilled /r/, which Blanc (1968) defines as the third shibboleth of Mizrahi Hebrew, has also given way to the Koiné uvular pronunciation, perhaps to a greater extent than the pharyngeals (see Yaeger-Dror 1988 for details). However, it is not as salient a stereotype in the Israeli speech community, and will not be examined in this paper.

3. An important exception is Bentolila (1983), who examines the pharyngeals among Mizrahi speakers from a small isolated rural community, settled primarily by immigrants from the same small town in Morocco. To my knowledge, his is the only study that shows high levels of pharyngealization, for both adults and children, and in fact, higher rates for the children, approaching 100% for some.

4. See Gafter (2014) for evidence that while the pharyngeals are by no means the norm, in specific communities they are alive and well, with some younger speakers exhibiting robust pharyngealization.

5. When transliterating Hebrew into English letters, most writers adopt a broadly phonetic representation of "standard" Hebrew, which means that *ayin* is not transcribed at all, and *het* is rendered as *x* (making it indistinguishable from the letter *xaf*, which is indeed the case for most speakers). However, in this chapter such an approach would be very confusing. On the other hand, consistently using the International Phonetic Alphabet symbols ʕ and ħ would give the impression that they are always pronounced as such, which is not true either. The approach I chose was to base my transliteration on Hebrew *orthography* (in which the pharyngeal sounds have dedicated letters), without making claims with respect to the pronunciation. I adopt a common convention for spelling Arabic in English letters, and therefore use 3 for *ayin* and 7 for *het*.

6. The metalinguistic commentary consistently refers to "speaking with *het* and *ayin*," in that order. In these lyrics, the order is reversed ("*ayin* and *het*"), which is unusual. This was likely done only for poetic reasons, so that *het* would rhyme with the previous line.

7. https://yaelisrael.wordpress.com/2007/01/27/סאה-ינא-עדּיו-מתבשייתּ-במרזחרויתי/. Last accessed: June 8, 2016.

8. zone.walla.co.il/?w=/2726/1110227. Last accessed: June 8, 2016.

9. www.tapuz.co.il/blog/ViewEntry.asp?EntryId=470082. Last accessed: June 8, 2016.

10. Be'er-Sheva and Ashdod, respectively.

11. A *tweet* is a message on the social networking site Twitter.

12. http://twitter.com/#!/noyalooshemusic/status/7377013870432256. Last accessed: June 8, 2016.

13. It is also interesting to note that the use of *ayin* alone is enough to invoke the *het* and *ayin* stereotype.

14. http://stagemag.co.il/Articles/375. Last accessed: June 8, 2016.

References

Agha, Asif. 2003. The social life of cultural value. *Language and Communication* 23: 231–73.

Bentolila, Yaakov. 1983. "The sociophonology of Hebrew as spoken in a rural settlement of Moroccan Jews in the Negev." PhD thesis, Hebrew University.

Blanc, Haim. 1968. The Israeli Koine as an emergent national standard. In *Language Problems of Developing Nations*, ed. Joshua A. Fishman, Charles A. Ferguson, and Jyotirindra Das Gupta, 237–25. New York: John Wiley.

Dahan, Momi, Natalie Mironichev, Eyal Dvir, and Shmuel Shye. 2003. Have the Gaps In Education Narrowed? On Factors Determining Eligibility for the Israeli Matriculation Certificate. *Israeli Economic Review* 2: 37–69.

Davis, Lawrence M. 1984. The pharyngeals in Hebrew: Linguistic change in apparent time. *Folia Linguistica Historica* 5: 25–32.

Eckert, Penelope. 1990. The Whole Woman: Sex and Gender Differences in Variation. *Language Variation and Change* 1: 245–67.

Eckert, Penelope. 2008. Variation and the indexical field. *Journal of Sociolinguistics* 12: 453–76.

Gafter, Roey J. 2014. "'The Most Beautiful and Correct Hebrew': Authenticity, Ethnic Identity and Linguistic Variation in the Greater Tel Aviv Area." PhD thesis, Stanford University.

Irvine, Judith. 2001. Style as distinctiveness: The culture and ideology of linguistic differentiation. In *Style and Sociolinguistic Variation*, ed. Penelope Eckert and John R. Rickford, 21–43. Cambridge: Cambridge University Press.

Irvine, Judith T., and Susan Gal. 2000. Language ideology and linguistic differentiation. In *Regimes of Language: Ideologies, Polities, and Identities*, ed. Paul V. Kroskrity, 35–83. New Mexico: School of American Research Press.

Labov, William. 1966. *The Social Stratification of English in New York City*. Washington, DC: Center for Applied Linguistics.

Labov, William. 1972. *Sociolinguistic Patterns*. Philadelphia: University of Pennsylvania Press.

Lefkowitz, Daniel. 2004. *Words and Stones: The Politics of Language and Identity in Israel*. Oxford: Oxford University Press.

Shalom Chertit, Sami. 2009. *Intra-Jewish Conflict in Israel: White Jews, Black Jews*. London and New York: Routledge.

Shohat, Ella. 1989. *Israeli Cinema: East/West and the Politics of Representation*. Austin: University of Texas Press.

Silverstein, Michael. 2003. Indexical order and the dialectics of sociolinguistic life. *Language and Communication* 23: 193–229.

Swirski, Shlomo. 1981. *Not disadvantaged but disenfranchized—Mizrahis and Ashkenazis in Israel*. (Hebrew: "lo nexšalim ela menuxšalim—mizraxim ve-aškenazim be-israel: nitux sociologi ve-sixot im peilim ve-peilot.") Haifa: maxbarot le-mexkar ve-bikoret.

Swirski, Shlomo, Eti Connor-Atias, and Hala Abu-Hala. 2008. *Israel: A Social Report 1998–2007*. (Hebrew: "tmunat macav xevratit 1998-2007.") N.p.: Adva Center.

Yaeger-Dror, Malcah. 1988. The influence of changing group vitality on convergence toward a dominant norm. *Language and Communication* 8: 235–305.

Zuckermann, Ghil'ad. 2005. Abba, Why Was Professor Higgins Trying to Teach Eliza to Speak Like Our Cleaning Lady?: Mizrahim, Ashkenazim, Prescriptivism and the Real Sounds of the Israeli Language. *Australian Journal of Jewish Studies* 19: 210–31.

11

Stance as a Window into the Language-Race Connection

Evidence from African American and White Speakers

in Washington, DC

ROBERT J. PODESVA

The role that language plays in constructing race and ethnicity cannot be overstated. Speakers draw on a variety of linguistic resources—including pronunciation, grammar, and vocabulary, to say nothing of heritage languages and code-switching (Fought 2006; 21–23)—not only to communicate a linguistic message but also to position themselves socially. But what positions are speakers taking up? Some of these positions may correspond directly to identity categories (e.g., a speaker could use elements of African American English to mark themselves as African American). But importantly, I argue that scholars of language and race must attend to the ways that speakers employ linguistic features to take stances on issues that implicate race. Stance-based analyses of language enable a rich perspective on the raciolinguistic dynamics of communities in which such stances are taken.

Stance can be understood as "a public act by a social actor, achieved dialogically through overt communicative means (language, gesture, and other symbolic forms), through which social actors simultaneously evaluate objects, position subjects (themselves and others), and align with other subjects, with respect to any salient dimensions of the sociocultural field" (Du Bois 2007, 163). While speakers can take stances independently of variation in their production of sounds, words, and sentences (i.e., through discursive practices), and indeed while most research on stance focuses on the level of discourse (e.g., Kärkkäinen 2006; Englebretson 2007; Jaffe 2009), recent studies have shown that linguistic variables also serve as resources for stancetaking (e.g., Kiesling 2009). In the context of the present volume, it may prove fruitful to consider how stancetaking might be enacted by the use of linguistic features associated with racial or ethnic varieties. While one outcome of identity construction is the establishment and maintenance of identity categories, Bucholtz and Hall (2005, 592) caution that "temporary and interactionally specific stances and participant roles" are an equally important dimension of identity. To think about racial identity categories without reflecting on stance is to miss out on a great deal of why speakers choose (whether above or below the level of consciousness) to use one linguistic feature over another in interactional contexts, and how race factors into that decision.

Consider the excerpt in (1), taken from a conversation with Marsha, a 40-year-old African American resident of Washington, DC. Marsha had been talking at length about gentrification, one of the most salient socioeconomic issues in the city (Modan 2007; Grieser 2013), and has just been asked whether she viewed gentrification as a deliberate process. Her response, which reflects her ambivalence on the issue, also features two elements of African American English (AAE). The first of these features is (-t/d) deletion, whereby the sounds /t/ and /d/ can be omitted in same-voice consonant clusters at the ends of words. In the excerpt, omitted (-t/d) is marked with (ø), while retained (-t/d) is marked with (ʰ). The second feature is falsetto, a voice quality produced with uncommonly high pitch, indicated in boldface. Pauses are indicated with periods.

Excerpt (1): Marsha (40-year-old African American woman)

The property taxes are going up, and people are on their fixed(ʰ) incomes, and(ø) you can't(ø) **afford**(ʰ) to repair your house and(ø) pay your taxes. And(ø) so you just(ø) kind(ø) of have to **choose**. which one. So, I **think it's** happening, but I **don't**(ø) **think it's** happening all of the time on purpose. I think in some of the communities, I **think it does** happen on purpose.

When considering the relation between language and race, one question we might ask is whether Marsha is speaking AAE in the excerpt. Although Marsha's speech categorically lacks grammatical features of AAE, she produces falsetto and (-t/d) deletion at rather high rates, so one might reasonably conclude that her phonology is consistent with that of an AAE speaker, or perhaps that her phonology may serve as a resource for constructing African American identity. However, treating features like (-t/d) deletion and falsetto as unproblematic markers of AAE may prevent us from considering a more illuminating question: What do features of AAE enable Marsha to accomplish in this interaction? In other words, what kinds of stances is Marsha taking, and how do those stances participate in the construction of her racial identity? In the remainder of this chapter, I examine the use of (-t/d) dele-tion and falsetto in Washington, DC, at both the community level, where the analysis focuses on quantitative trends across groups, and the individual level, where stancetaking practices are the analytical focus. While cross-com-munity patterns generally show higher rates of (-t/d) deletion and falsetto among African Americans, the analyses of stancetaking provide insight into why these gross tendencies emerge and shed light on the politics of race in Washington, DC.

(-t/d) Deletion

Numerous studies have cited (-t/d) deletion, and more generally consonant clus-ter simplification, as a feature of African American English (e.g., Labov et al. 1968; Fasold 1972; Thomas 2007). It is noteworthy that one of the earliest studies on the phenomenon (Fasold 1972) was based on data collected in Washington, DC, the community under investigation here. In spite of Fasold's foundational work, which uncovered considerable diversity among African Americans with respect to the variable, no studies have revisited (-t/d) deletion in Washington, DC, in the decades since. This represents a significant gap, given the dramatic demo-graphic changes that have seen the district shift from a predominantly African American to a multiracial city. This shift is the result of a massive influx of new immigrants (Guatemalans, Salvadorans, Chinese, Koreans, and Vietnamese), as well as African American migration to the suburbs neighboring the district proper following the Fair Housing Act of 1968 (Manning 1998). That the Latino/a population in Washington, DC, has risen in recent decades further complicates the connection between (-t/d) deletion and racial identity, given that the feature has been identified as a component of Chicano English (Santa Ana 1996; Fought 2006, 81).

The data considered here are twenty-four audiorecorded sociolinguistic inter-views with lifelong residents of Washington, DC. The interviewees fall into four racial categories, according to speaker self-identification: African American, Asian American, Latina/o, and White. Each racial affiliation is represented by six speakers, half women and half men. Topics discussed in the interviews vary from one interview to the next, but all interviewees were encouraged to provide their views on the community, as well as distinctive patterns of language use. A total of 2,400 (-t/d) tokens, 100 from each speaker, were coded for the realiza-tion of the variable, a number of linguistic factors affecting the realization of the variable, and the social factors of race and sex (age was not considered given the stability of the feature). While previous studies on consonant cluster simplifica-tion differ in whether they exclude function words or clusters of the form /nt/,

I do none of the above for the purposes of this paper, as the presence of (-t/d) is variable in all cases in the data under consideration. Previous studies also differ in whether they treat /r/ as a consonant, vowel, or class unto itself. For the purposes of this paper, /r/ is treated as a consonant, as it exhibits different patterns from vowels.[1] A logistic regression was conducted with GoldVarb to determine which factors significantly influenced the realization (-t/d).

The statistical model reveals that, while taking into account the effect of linguistic and social constraints on the realization of (-t/d), speaker race emerges as a significant predictor of deletion rates. The race effects are summarized in Figure 11.1, which plots factor weights as a function of racial group. Factor weights higher than 0.5 indicate factors that favor deletion, while those lower than 0.5 indicate factors that inhibit deletion. The distance from 0.5 corresponds to the strength of the effect. As Figure 11.1 shows, African American interviewees strongly favor deletion and Latino/a interviewees slightly favor deletion, while White and Asian American interviewees disfavored deletion.

On the one hand, the finding that African Americans exhibited the highest rate of (-t/d) deletion is unsurprising. But the fact that (-t/d) deletion is a feature of AAE is not in itself an explanation for why African Americans in the study use it the most. To better understand speakers' motivation for producing the pattern, it is necessary to ask what race means in the context of Washington, DC, and in particular in the context of sociolinguistic interviews that focus on talk about the local community. In the data under analysis here, as well as the larger corpus from which they are taken, the topic under discussion in the great majority of cases in which race is mentioned is gentrification.

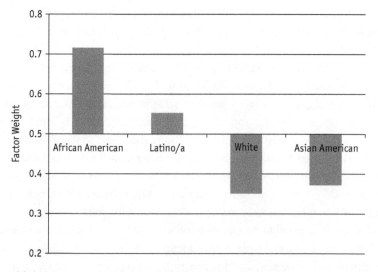

Figure 11.1 Factor weights for (-t/d) deletion, according to race.

In order to explore the potential connection between (-t/d) deletion and gentrification, I examined the variation patterns of two speakers who talk about gentrification in the greatest depth: Phil and Carla. That these speakers talk about gentrification at length facilitates a quantitative comparison of their deletion rates when talking about this versus other topics. Each word-final (-t/d) token in both interviews was coded for whether (-t/d) was omitted. Interviews were divided into a series of temporally ordered topics, and the rate of deletion was calculated for each topic; each topic consisted of 32–140 tokens of (-t/d). Previous work by Rickford and McNair-Knox (1994), Schilling-Estes (2004), and Rickford and Price (2013) has shown that the distribution of sociolinguistic features can vary systematically according to topic, and that topic-based variation can be used to construct ethnicity by aligning or disaligning with interlocutors.

Despite their shared penchant for discussing gentrification, Phil and Carla differ in a number of respects, including their racial identities and stances toward gentrification. Carla is a 31-year-old African American woman who grew up and currently lives in the Northeast quandrant, while Phil is a 41-year-old White man living in a rapidly gentrifying neighborhood in the Northwest quadrant. It is worth noting that both speakers were interviewed by White men in their mid-twenties, so Carla and Phil are orienting to interactants who share a common ethnicity (even if the speakers diverge in their orientations). The results for the two speakers appear in Figure 11.2. The figure illustrates that although Carla has slightly higher deletion rates overall, the rates for both speakers are highly variable according to topic. Phil produces high deletion rates (at 56%) when discussing leisure activities, as opposed to some of the more serious topics like his career, political views, and gentrification. In the case of Carla, on the other hand, deletion rates reach their peak (at 66%) when she discusses gentrification in her neighborhood, a significant difference, χ^2 (df = 6, N = 943) = 13.497, p < 0.036.[2]

I suggest that Carla deletes (-t/d) frequently not just because she is African American, nor because she is a speaker of AAE (though she may be in some circumstances), but instead because there is something at stake in the talk. During the interview, Carla unsurprisingly characterizes gentrification as a negative force, for which White people are responsible ("White people want this town and they are going to take it") and which she herself must resist. As she states, "[O]ne of the main reasons I worked at [the satellite radio company] is because I felt like, oh, this big ass company's going to move in my neighborhood, I'm getting a piece of it. I mean, I don't know, it's just I feel a very strong ownership." Carla deletes (-t/d) at high rates, particularly when talking about gentrification in her community, as a consequence of her high involvement in her talk. Deletion is a component of a phonological style that facilitates the discursive move of taking an invested stance.

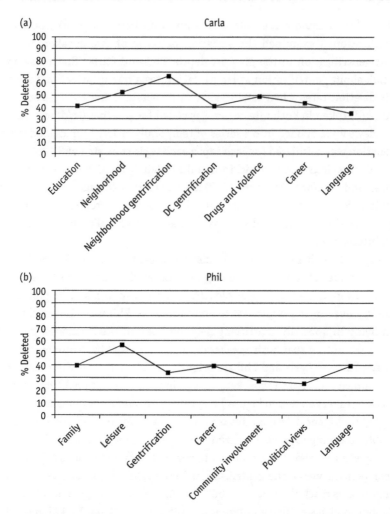

Figure 11.2 Rates of (-t/d) deletion according to topic for (a) Carla and (b) Phil.

The same level of investment is not evident in Phil's talk about gentrification, excerpted in (2). Phil recognizes that gentrification is a perceived problem in his community, but unlike Carla who takes on an agentive role in response to gentrification, Phil actively denies his own participation by constructing what might be termed a bystander stance. As Du Bois (2007) argues, every stance is constructed in opposition to other stances, and the subject of every stance is contrasted against another stancetaking subject. In this excerpt, Phil contrasts his own stance as an uninvolved bystander against an accusatory stance of the people being driven out of his neighborhood. Although he does not explicitly describe the subject of this accusatory stance in great detail, referring only to people being forced out and "people who may be getting state assistance," it can be inferred from the system of contrasts ("Black, White, Hispanic, uh, poor, wealthy") that this subject is also a person of color.

Excerpt (2) Phil (41-year-old White man)

I would say that my neighborhood is pretty much on the leading edge of—
of what has become known these days um unfortunately it's become a bad
term, uh, gentrified. Uh, which I hate that term because that, you know,
the implication is that I'm, people like me are forcing people out. You know,
that's not really, you know, it's not my intention to force and make anybody
move. Uh there's—D.C. is only so large and when you have a demand for
people to come in and live there, uh prices go up. That's just purely econom-
ics, it's got nothing, I don't care if someone in my neighborhood is Black,
White, Hispanic, uh, poor, wealthy. It doesn't matter to me really at all uh,
the only thing that matters is that this is where I would like to live. And so
unfortunately people who may be getting state assistance . . . you know,
some places they can't afford it any longer. That's unfortunate, but you
know it's not my fault. I didn't do it. (laughs) But I hate that word because
it really does, they make it seem like we did, like there is some sort of purpose behind it, like I sought out to drive them out.

The uninvolved nature of the bystander stance is evident in the degree of reso-
nance across Phil's explicit statements concerning his own role in gentrification,
diagraphed (Du Bois 2007) in (3). The expletive subject *it* depersonalizes the
act of gentrification. Further, the recurrence of the negative particle illustrates
that the bystander stance is a defensive one defined in opposition to prevalent
discourses associating gentrification with, as Phil states, "people like me." This is
also evidenced by Phil's use of first-person pronouns in predicate versus subject
position, which works to portray Phil as patient rather than agent.

Excerpt (3) Diagraph of Phil's statements about his role in gentrification

---

It	's	not	my intention	to force and make anybody move
it	does	n't	matter to me	really at all
it	's	not	my fault	

Taking stock thus far, we have seen two different scenarios of how (-t/d) deletion
participates (or does not participate) in the construction of race. Carla uses relatively high rates of (-t/d) deletion. While it is reasonable to think that this pattern
could play some role in the construction of an African American identity, the
intraspeaker patterns in Figure 11.2 show that Carla employs the feature most

often when talking about gentrification in her own neighborhood—a socioeconomic issue that is tightly imbricated with race. (-t/d) deletion enables Carla to take a stance on a racially charged issue, suggesting that when it comes to features of ethnolinguistic repertoires (Benor 2010), what matters is not just who uses them, but what kinds of race work they are used to do. Standing in contrast to Carla is Phil, who uses relatively low rates of (-t/d) deletion, deletes most often when talking about topics that have little to do with race, and independently of his (-t/d) deletion patterns downplays his own role, as well as the relevance of race, in the gentrification process. His use of high deletion rates when he talks about leisure activities is compatible with the commonly held view that a speaker's most vernacular forms are used in the most informal contexts (though, importantly, Carla's pattern casts doubt on the universality of this trend).

While the foregoing analysis of (-t/d) deletion patterns offers a window into the connection between language and race, (-t/d) deletion is just one of many features that participate in the construction of African American identity, and it is not a very salient feature at that. In the next section, I consider the use of falsetto in the same community. This relatively salient feature of speech (where salience is assessed on the basis of both phonetic and social characteristics, as described below) exhibits some patterns that resemble those for (-t/d) deletion, but it also differs in a couple key respects.

Falsetto

Falsetto is a mode of phonation (i.e., vocal fold vibration) wherein the vocal folds are stretched thin and tightly adducted, resulting in a relatively high pitch. Falsetto's characteristically high pitch endows the feature with significant stylistic potential, enabling it to be used a resource for constructing sexuality and a variety of gendered personas (Podesva 2007), as well as African American identity. In one of the earliest studies linking falsetto to African American identity, Tarone (1973) describes African American adolescents' use of falsetto as a form of protest when playing games. Subsequent research has argued that falsetto functions similarly in a variety of other contexts, such as when speakers are taking an oppositional stance. For example, Alim (2004, 67–73) discusses Black Northern California youths' and his own use of falsetto when engaged in the discursive practice of *battlin*, an important mode of interaction both in Sunnyside, California, and in Black speech communities more broadly. He argues that falsetto can be used in the context of *battlin* as a means of emphasizing a point or challenging one's interlocutor. Similarly, Nielsen (2010) uses the methods of quantitative discourse analysis to show that an African American adolescent uses more acoustically extreme falsetto when responding to (and disagreeing with) the way an interactant character-izes him. He concludes that falsetto represents a means of taking a stance of indignation. What these previous studies have in common is their treatment of falsetto not merely as a marker of African American identity, but as a dis-tinctively African American way of taking an oppositional stance. In this sec-tion, I will draw on a quantitative study of falsetto use in Washington, DC to ask who uses falsetto; whether they do so to take an oppositional stance, as has been claimed in previous literature; and crucially, if so, what kinds of things speakers are opposing.

For this section of the chapter, I examine interview data for African American and White speakers only. Recordings for thirty-two speakers were analyzed, half male and half female, with members of both groups evenly distributed according to age. Whereas the data for (-t/d) deletion spanned various topics, we considered only talk about the local community. The phonation type (e.g., modal, falsetto, creaky) of each syllable was coded and double-checked by a second researcher. Over 55,000 syllables were examined, in nearly 10,000 intonational phrases. The percent of syllables uttered in falsetto was calculated for each phrase, and a mixed-effects linear regression model including both linguistic and social factors was constructed. (See Podesva 2013 for additional details about the study and its findings.)

The statistical analysis reveals that, while taking linguistic factors like phrase position and discourse context into account, gender significantly affects the use of falsetto such that women use falsetto more than men ($p < 0.0297$). However, as is evident in Figure 11.3, this effect is driven entirely by the African American

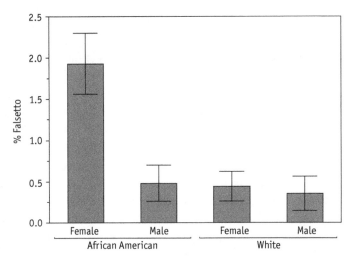

Figure 11.3 Mean percentage of phrase realized in falsetto, according to gender and race.

women, who use falsetto to the greatest extent (error bars represent 95% confidence intervals). This effect is confirmed by a significant interaction between gender and race ($p < 0.0201$).

Although the pattern in Figure 11.3 poses problems for viewing falsetto as a distinctively African American feature, given that African American men use falsetto at the same rate as White men and women, I do not mean to suggest that falsetto is not a feature of AAE. The extract in (4) includes a dialect performance of AAE by Zadie, a 21-year-old African American woman. As Zadie shifts into the performance frame, she uses habitual *be* ("I be talking"), and continues with suck-teeth (a discursive feature of African American English and African/Caribbean expression more generally, as discussed by Rickford and Rickford 1976 and Alim 2004), and falsetto. Crucially, the segment of speech in falsetto is incomprehensible; the words are of lesser significance than the voice quality, which is what more saliently represents African American identity in the performance.

Excerpt (4) Zadie (21-year-old African American woman)

You know, like slavery and oppression has like messed us up, [but] we have never lost our culture. Like it's—it's different, but it's still there. Like the way we practice religion, the way we talk to our friends, even—even in the way we talk. Like I was telling my mom how she used to always get on me for how I talked, cos I talk like this when I'm at home, and I be talking to my dad like—see, "I be talking"—I be talking to my dad like, "<suck-teeth> I mean, da:d **<incomprehensible>** I don't understand," you know.

The ideological association between falsetto and African American identity notwithstanding, the falsetto practices summarized in Figure 11.3, specifically why African American women use this feature in particular, require explanation. To address this issue, we have to consider how the production of falsetto is situated. The instances of falsetto under discussion are situated in talk about the local community in sociolinguistic interviews; recall that we limited our analysis to talk about the local community. The speech activity of the interview and the topic of conversation provide interviewees with opportunities to articulate their ideologies about issues significant to the community. Falsetto is also situated in particular discourse contexts, in moments of interaction, as interactants shift in their alignments toward one another and their stances toward objects of discussion. Examining how falsetto is used at these moments may shed valuable light on why African American women use falsetto four times more than others.

To pursue an analysis of stancetaking in utterances produced with falsetto, I focus on the most highly falsetto segments of talk in the corpus: turns of talk where multiple phrases contain three or more falsetto syllables per phrase.

Using these rather strict criteria, 17 turns were identified for deeper analysis. For each of these turns, the speaker (i.e., the stancetaker in the highly falsetto turn), the nature of the stance taken (i.e., positive or negative evaluation), and the stance object were recorded.

A number of stance-related patterns emerged for these 17 utterances. Bear in mind that these patterns pertain to highly falsetto stretches of talk; other, less phonetically extreme realizations of falsetto could in principle yield different results. Nevertheless, with respect to the issue of who produces these turns containing strong falsetto, 13 of the 17 turns were produced by African Americans, and of these, 10 were produced by women. Thus, even though these highly falsetto turns represent a small subset of the entire dataset, they show essentially the same pattern as that observed in the larger dataset: that African American women use falsetto the most.

Perhaps more strikingly, all 17 highly falsetto turns were instances of negative evaluation of the stance object. It is important to note that even though this pattern is consistent with the previous research on falsetto discussed above, falsetto need not be used for negative evaluation, as Podesva (2007) exemplifies in a handful of cases where falsetto is used for positive evaluation. Under the assumption that falsetto utterances are indicative of moments when speakers are emotionally invested in their talk, in the context of talk about DC, speakers were more invested in aspects of their community that they viewed in negative terms.

The aspects of the community toward which (mostly) African American women took negative stances were racism and gentrification, issues of great social concern in the community. Although gentrification might be viewed as a socioeconomic issue on the surface, it is of course a racial issue as well, frequently described by our interviewees as a phenomenon whereby Whites are driving African Americans out of traditionally Black neighborhoods into more affordable housing in the suburbs, as characterized by Phil in (2). Modan (2007) discusses the racial underpinnings of gentrification in Washington, DC, at length, and similar patterns are evident in other U.S. urban environments, such as the Latina/o community of El Barrio, East Austin, Texas (Flores Bayer in preparation) and Northern California's formerly predominantly Black community of Sunnyside (Alim 2004 considers gentrification at length). It is worth noting that the data under analysis cover a number of other topics apart from racism and gentrification, but it is these topics that inspire speakers—African American women, in particular—to use falsetto speech.

To better understand how falsetto functions in these data, consider once again the example in (1). The excerpt is reproduced in (5), with two modifications: the maximum pitch levels for stretches of talk in falsetto have been indicated in parentheses, and Marsha's realization of (-t/d) has been omitted, given the current focus on falsetto. Before considering falsetto's role in stancetaking, it is important to take stock of the linguistic environments in which falsetto occurs. As Podesva (2013) reports, falsetto is more likely to appear in phrase-initial position, as well as in constructed dialogue or reported speech. Given that this extract lacks reported speech and that the first two examples actually occur phrase-*finally*, falsetto cannot be attributed solely to linguistic factors and is motivated in part by its social functions. Chief among these social functions is taking a stance against gentrification. Marsha first asserts the position that gentrifiers are not intentionally driving out longstanding inhabitants of the community, but later shifts her stance to emphasize that in some cases, gentrifiers may be taking a more active role in the process, making gentrification "happen on purpose." She employs falsetto when enacting this shift. Importantly, falsetto reaches its highest pitch level—at 543 Hz—at this point, in spite of a general tendency for pitch levels to decline over phrases and larger units of discourse.

Excerpt (5) Marsha (40-year-old African American woman)

The property taxes are going up, and people are on their fixed incomes, and you can't af**ford** (502 Hz) to repair your house and pay your taxes. And so you just kind of have to **choose** (407 Hz). which one. So, I **think it's** (470 Hz) happening, but I **don't think it's** (392 Hz) happening all of the time on purpose. I think in some of the communities, I **think it does** (543 Hz) happen on purpose.

We have thus far seen that falsetto is commonly used to negatively evaluate social issues like gentrification and racism, but why do African American women in particular exercise this practice more than African American men and White men and women? I can only speculate about why this pattern surfaces, but it is likely due to intersectionality. The legal scholar Kimberlé Crenshaw (1989) stresses that intersecting dimensions of identity do not simply amount to the sum of the component identities. That is, African American women's experiences cannot be viewed as the intersection of women's and African Americans' experiences. Taking such a view fails to take into consideration the fact that African Americans experience womanhood, and women experience being African American, in unique ways.

The four most vociferous falsetto users in these data, all African American women, are all strongly tied to their communities, and none of their traditionally African American neighborhoods are immune from the gentrification that puts their socioeconomic vitality as risk. Zadie, for example, is a student at Howard University, a historically Black university in the district. Howard is located in the Shaw neighborhood, which borders on the U Street corridor, the epicenter of gentrification in the district where thousands of luxury condos have been built in the last ten years. Carla works as an audio technician at a radio station just blocks away from her home in Northeast DC. Recall from the previous section that Carla took her job in response to the encroachment of the radio station. Marsha works for a local nonprofit organization, and Olivia is the president of her neighborhood association. None of these women explicitly comment on the gender inequalities they experience. But their use of falsetto, I would argue, is motivated not so much by their gender identities, but rather by the locally oriented positions they occupy. That these women talk about gentrification and racism more often when they talk about their local communities, communities in which they are particularly invested, and that they use falsetto when doing so, is no coincidence. For them, falsetto is a linguistic act of resistance to the sometimes hostile or unwelcoming environment in which they live and work.

Discussion

In this section, I briefly contrast the findings for falsetto and (-t/d) deletion. These features show remarkable similarity in their broad distributional patterns, as both predominate in the speech of African American speakers. Furthermore, there is evidence that both features are used to take stances about salient racial issues in the community: an African American woman uses her highest rates of (-t/d) deletion when talking about gentrification, as opposed to other topics, and African American women generally use falsetto to negatively evaluate gentrification and racism.

In spite of these similarities, there are key differences to note as well. Falsetto offers a more transparent window into how linguistic features are used in stancetaking. Stancetaking was apparent in all cases of strong falsetto, suggesting that the use of the feature might be viewed as a stancetaking act in itself. This could be attributed in part to falsetto's phonetic and social salience, or to the likely role that falsetto plays in the realization of high intonational tones, which themselves convey semantic and pragmatic information. Each instance of (-t/d) deletion, by contrast, is unlikely to constitute an act of stancetaking in itself. Accordingly, the analysis did not focus on the stancetaking moves in each utterance containing an ommited (-t/d), but rather sought to identify trends in the rate at which (-t/d) was deleted across topics.

While analyses of these features can be conducted in isolation, both falsetto and (-t/d) deletion are better understood as components of linguistic styles. Even though isolated uses of particular features, like Zadie's use of falsetto in the dialect performance in (4), can be performed or understood as indexes of race in stylized moments in discourse, they more commonly take on meaning through their co-occurrence with other features. For example, one might have concluded that African Americans' high rates of (-t/d) deletion were merely indicative of an informal style, but the fact is that—at least in the speech of African American women—deletion occurred alongside falsetto (a feature whose social meaning cannot be fully captured in terms of formality) in talk about gentrification. In a similar vein, Nylund (2013) reports that African Americans vocalize /l/ more than White speakers in Washington, DC do, and that African American women in particular do so at their highest rates when talking about DC. It appears, then, that features like /l/-vocalization are packaged, along with features like (-t/d) deletion and falsetto, into a linguistic style of resistance. Conclusions like these are only possible under a stylistic analysis (see also Grieser 2013).

Conclusion

The analyses of (-t/d) deletion and falsetto above illustrate how these features can be viewed as components of African American ways of speaking, but also highlight the importance of viewing them as resources for taking stances about race and racially charged issues. To better understand the social meaning of elements of language linked to race, we have to consider not only who uses them, but what they are using them to do. To be clear, the argument is not that features previously identified as features of AAE do not index African American identity, but rather that they are also powerful resources for carrying out many other kinds of identity work. This identity work may have everything to do with race and how language-users position themselves with respect to race.

I will conclude by reflecting briefly on the growing field of raciolinguistics and consider the ways in which it has been fruitful to *race language* and to *language race* (Alim 2009). Beginning with racing language, it is imperative that linguistic analyses be guided by ethnographic and theoretical understandings of race. The knowledge that gentrification, which most speakers conceptualize as a racial issue in Washington, DC, emerged as such a salient issue across the corpus of interviews, influenced the decision to examine how (-t/d) deletion might vary depending on whether speakers are talking about gentrification. Similarly, the concept of intersectionality reminds us not to expect African Americans to pattern together uniformly, given that gender may not play out in the same ways in the African American community as it does in other cultural contexts. Thinking of race and gender in intersectional terms brought to light a pattern (that African American women use falsetto the most) that might not have otherwise emerged.

At the same time, linguistic analysis can provide insights that enrich the study of race and ethnicity (i.e., languaging race). For example, knowledge of a linguistic feature's broad distributional patterns enables the analyst to better tease apart language-internal effects from those motivated by social factors, including race, insofar as they are separable. For example, falsetto's meaning potential may be weaker when it is produced in favored linguistic environments (e.g,. phrase-initially in reported speech) than in disfavored contexts where linguistic factors would not predict its occurrence. On a related note, different linguistic features carry different levels of salience. Not all features from which racial identities are constructed do the same ideological work. While past studies have shown that grammatical and phonological features may differently contribute to the construction of ethnic identities (e.g., Rickford 1985; Sharma 2005), we have seen here that even phonological features (i.e., falsetto vs. (-t/d) deletion) differ in their relative salience. This difference may lead features with varying levels of salience to exhibit distinct distributional patterns or perhaps necessitate the different analytical methods to investigate stancetaking practices (as discussed in the previous section). Finally, linguistic patterning can reveal important components of racial dynamics. While the theoretical concept of intersectionality might have inspired the practice of analyzing African American women separately from African American men, it is the difference in falsetto patterns for these two groups that motivated the need to think more deeply about why African American women (or at least the African American women in this study) might experience race differently from African American men.

In sum, I have in this chapter provided two examples of how to bring stance into the study of the linguistic construction of racial identity. It is hoped that future work will continue moving in this direction, thus refining our understanding of the relation between language and race.

Notes

1. Like Labov et al. (1968) and most previous sociolinguists, Guy (1980, 8) excludes clusters with a preceding *r* from the rule deleting *t* and *d* in syllable final consonant clusters in American English: "As cases of deletion after /r/ were rare or nonexistent, we decided to consider postvocalic /r/ as being essentially a vowel for purposes of this rule." However, Guy and Boberg (1997, 155), in a more general examination of the role of preceding segments in *t,d* ("coronal stop") deletion in a corpus of Philadelphia English, found that while preceding /r/ did produce the lowest percentage of deletion among preceding consonants (7%, factor weight 0.13), it was just below the noncoronal nasals /m/ and /ŋ/ (11%, factor weight 0.33), and distinguishable from preceding vowels, which were reported to show "nearly categorical retention, i.e. ≈0."

2. Chi square was computed on Carla's rate on this topic vs. her rate over the other topics.

References

Alim, H. Samy. 2004. *You Know My Steez: An Ethnographic and Sociolinguistic Study of Styleshifting in a Black American Speech Community.* Durham, NC: Duke University Press.

Alim, H. Samy. 2009. "Racing Language, Languaging Race." Paper presented at the Race and Ethnicity in Language, Interaction and Culture Symposium, University of California, Los Angeles, February 27.

Benor, Sarah Bunin. 2010. Ethnolinguistic repertoire: Shifting the analytic focus in language and ethnicity. *Journal of Sociolinguistics* 14: 159–83.

Bucholtz, Mary, and Kira Hall. 2005. Identity and interaction: A sociocultural approach. *Discourse Studies* 7: 585–614.

Crenshaw, Kimberlé. 1989. Demarginalizing the intersection of race and sex: A black feminist critique of antidiscrimination doctrine, feminist theory, and anti- racist politics. *Chicago Legal Forum* 1989: 139–67.

Du Bois, J. W. 2007. The stance triangle. In Robert Englebretson, ed., *Stancetaking in Discourse: Subjectivity, Evaluation, Interaction.* Amsterdam: Benjamins, 137–82.

Englebretson, Robert, ed. 2007. *Stancetaking in Discourse: Subjectivity, Evaluation, Interaction.* Amsterdam: John Benjamins.

Fasold, Ralph. 1972. *Tense Marking in Black English.* Arlington, VA: Center for Applied Linguistics.

Flores Bayer, Isla. In preparation. The Social and Attitudinal Internal Boundaries of Chicano English in "El Barrio," Austin, Texas. Ph.D. dissertation, Stanford University.

Fought, Carmen. 2006. *Language and Ethnicity.* Cambridge: Cambridge University Press.

Grieser, Jessica. 2013. Locating style: Style-shifting to characterize community at the border of Washington, DC. *University of Pennsylvania Working Papers in Linguistics* 19.2: 80–89.

Guy, Gregory R. 1980. Variation in the group and the individual: The case of final stop deletion. In William Labov, ed., *Locating Language in Time and Space*, 1–36. New York: Academic Press.

Guy, Gregory R., and Charles Boberg. 1997. Inherent variability and the obligatory contour principle. *Language Variation and Change* 9: 149–64.

Jaffe, Alexandra, ed. 2009. *Stance: Sociolinguistic Perspectives.* Oxford: Oxford University Press.

Kärkkäinen, Elise. 2006. Stancetaking in conversation: From subjectivity to intersubjectivity. *Text & Talk* 26.6: 699–731.

Kiesling, Scott. 2009. Style as stance: Stance as the explanation for patterns of sociolinguistic variation. In Alexandra Jaffe, ed., *Stance: Sociolinguistic Perspectives.* Oxford: Oxford University Press, 171–94.

Labov, William, Paul Cohen, Clarence Robins, and John Lewis. 1968. A study of the non-standard English of Negro and Puerto Rican speakers in New York City. Report on cooperative research project 3288. New York: Columbia University Press.

Manning, Robert D. 1998. Multicultural Washington, D.C.: The changing social and economic landscape of a post-industrial metropolis. *Ethnic and Racial Studies* 21: 328–55.

Modan, Gabriella. 2007. *Turf Wars: Discourse, Diversity, and the Politics of Place.* Malden, MA: Blackwell.

Nielsen, Rasmus. 2010. "I ain't never been charged with nothing!": The use of falsetto speech as a linguistic strategy of indignation. *University of Pennsylvania Working Papers in Linguistics* 15.2: 111–21.

Nylund, Anastasia. 2013. Phonological Variation at the Intersection of Ethnoracial Identity, Place, and Style in Washington, DC. Ph.D. dissertation, Georgetown University.

Podesva, Robert J. 2007. Phonation type as a stylistic variable: The use of falsetto in constructing a persona. *Journal of Sociolinguistics* 11: 478–504.

Podesva, Robert J. 2013. Gender and the social meaning of non-modal phonation types. *Proceedings of the Annual Meeting of the Berkeley Linguistics Society* 37.1: 427–48.

Rickford, John R. 1985. Ethnicity as a sociolinguistic boundary. *American Speech* 60.2: 99–125.

Rickford, John R., and Angela E. Rickford. 1976. Cut-eye and suck-teeth: African words and gestures in New World guise. *Journal of American Folklore* 89: 194–309.

Rickford, John R., and Faye McNair-Knox. 1994. Addressee- and topic-influenced style shift: A quantitative sociolinguistic study. In Douglas Biber and Edward Finegan, eds., *Sociolinguistic Perspectives on Register*. Oxford: Oxford University Press, 235–76.

Rickford, John R., and McKenzie Price. 2013. Girlz II women: Age-grading, language change and stylistic variation. *Journal of Sociolinguistics* 17: 143–79.

Santa Ana, Otto. 1996. Sonority and syllable structure in Chicano English. *Language Variation and Change* 8: 63–89.

Schilling-Estes, Natalie. 2004. Constructing ethnicity in interaction. *Journal of Sociolinguistics* 8: 163–95.

Sharma, Devyani. 2005. Dialect stabilization and speaker awareness in non-native varieties of English. *Journal of Sociolinguistics* 9: 194–224.

Tarone, Elaine. 1973. Aspects of intonation in Black English. *American Speech* 48: 29–36.

Thomas, Erik. 2007. Phonological and phonetic characteristics of African American Vernacular English. *Language and Linguistics Compass* 1: 450–75.

12

Changing Ethnicities

The Evolving Speech Styles of Punjabi Londoners

DEVYANI SHARMA

South Asians are the largest ethnic minority group in the United Kingdom. They have been present in the United Kingdom since the earliest British colonial encounters with the Indian subcontinent 400 years ago, but have migrated in substantial numbers since the mid-twentieth century. Although the position of this minority group has changed markedly in the last fifty years, it is still common, as with many racial minority groups, to define the community primarily by race or ethnicity and to overlook internal heterogeneity arising out of historical change and internal social diversity.

In this chapter, I take a recent historical perspective on the community, describing its development not only in terms of migration generations (e.g., first and second generations) but also in terms of finer degrees of historical change that give rise to major differences within the second generation. Looking at natural conversational speech used in a Punjabi community in London, we find subtle changes in styles of English use. From these, we can build a deeper understanding of how large-scale social structures in the community and fine-grained individual identities have changed over time. Crucially, we will see that these evolving uses and meanings of ethnic speech features can only be understood if factors such as gender, history, and class are taken into account. Indeed, as H. Samy Alim argues in the introduction to this volume, race and ethnicity are ultimately found to be inseparable from these other dimensions of social life.

Ethnic Speech Styles in Cities

In recent years, major studies of language use in urban ethnic minorities have been initiated in such regions as the United States, Canada, the United Kingdom,

Denmark, Sweden, Norway, Germany, Netherlands, France (e.g., Boberg 2004; Svendsen and Røyneland 2008; Quist 2008; Wiese 2009; Hoffman and Walker 2010; Fagyal and Stewart 2011; Cheshire et al. 2011; Nagy and Kochetov 2013). A common initial interpretation of speech forms used by a given ethnoracial minority group is, quite naturally, simply one of ethnic meaning. These styles are often described as "vehicles of ethnic identities" (Hinskens 2011, 125). However, particularly in the case of "visible minorities"—those who are phenotypically distinctive from the majority group—ethnoracial distinctiveness can be distractingly salient to an observer, leading not just the general public but also researchers to potentially overascribe ethnic meaning to all linguistic behaviors associated with the group, and to overlook other effects.

In fact, resources "that appear to be specifically ethnic can index far more than ethnicity" (Eckert 2008; see also Benor 2010; and chapters 10 and 11, this volume). Recent research has shown the emergence of strong gendering in the use and meanings of ethnolectal forms, as well as emergent distinctions based on peer group subcultures (Alim 2004; Eckert 2008; Quist 2008; Alam and Stuart-Smith 2014). Other studies have shown the emergence of local class meanings out of originally migrant ethnic meanings. Johnstone (2011) describes how original markers of Polishness, even names such as "Kachowski," came over time to index working-class meanings in Pittsburgh. Labov (2001) similarly describes originally Italian and Irish markers becoming associated with local working-class meanings in Philadelphia. And Multicultural London English (Cheshire et al. 2011) has emerged from the interaction of multiple ethnoracial minorities to signal a primarily working-class, multiethnic London identity. A simple focus on ethnicity as the primary function of distinctive speech forms in these communities may therefore involve "erasure" of important internal differences (Irvine and Gal 2000), including competing or changing meanings.

Examining three generations of Punjabi Londoners, this study asks: Have the social meanings conveyed by community accent features changed over time? Do we see systematic links between ethnic and other social meanings? Are these interactions idiosyncratic at the individual level or systematic in the community? Since my analysis explores change over time, a brief history of the community is in order.

History of the Community

In the 2011 U.K. Census, South Asians represented 7.5 percent of the total population, with 35.9 percent of British South Asians living in London. The relationship between South Asia and the United Kingdom dates back to the early British colonial presence in South Asia, starting from 1600. The Indian subcontinent and other British colonies achieved independence incrementally, beginning shortly after World War II. At the time, the United Kingdom faced severe postwar labor shortages and encouraged labor migration from former colonies through the British Nationality Act of 1948, which initially permitted unrestricted entry to the United Kingdom from the Commonwealth. The Asian population in the United Kingdom grew substantially until 1971, before a series of immigration acts began to limit numbers, but migration has continued to the present day.

The data for this study were collected in Southall, a suburb within the West London borough of Ealing. Since the mid-twentieth century, Southall has attracted Punjabi speakers from India and Pakistan, as well as Indian communities evicted from East Africa in the 1960s. Southall is considered the historic heart of the British Punjabi community, encompassing large numbers of Sikh, Hindu, and Muslim Punjabis. Demographic estimates vary. The 2011 Census found that, of a total population of 98,000 in Southall, 69.5 percent were classified as nonwhite, and 51 percent as Asian. Some neighborhoods in the borough have very high concentrations of Asians, even by official census figures (e.g., 80.7 percent in the ward of Southall Broadway). Other sources (DMAG 2006; Ealing JSNA 2010) offer higher estimates of minority ethnicities and Asians in Southall. Taking into account undocumented residents, it is reasonable to estimate that the Asian population exceeds 60 percent and the overall ethnic minority population may exceed 80 percent.

The population of Southall includes both India-born (first generation, or "Gen. 1") and British-born (second generation, "Gen. 2"; and third generation, "Gen. 3") residents. Members of the Gen. 1 group were born in South Asia and migrated to the United Kingdom in adulthood; this group is continually renewed through ongoing migration. Due to their continuous arrival, the Gen. 2 group—born in London to migrant parents—has a very diverse age range. The earliest British-born are now in their fifties, even sixties, but children being born now to recent India-born migrants are also technically Gen. 2 individuals. As we will see, the recent history of Southall is crucial to understanding ethnicity and language variation in the area. In particular, the history points to two broad phases, which led to starkly different life experiences for Gen. 2 individuals of different ages.

The first phase (late 1940s–late 1980s) was characterized by the migration of a visible minority of Asians, accompanied by infamous episodes of racial conflict in Southall and similar neighborhoods around Britain. By the late 1970s, 30 percent of the population of Southall was Asian—still a minority but a large and highly visible one. The economic climate and British public opinion had shifted, and Southall became a lightning rod for racial tension (CARF 1981, 43; Oates 2002, 107). Far-right, anti-immigration parties held rallies in the town, leading to violent riots and racially motivated deaths. These experiences, in schools and on the streets, were formative for older Gen. 2 participants, all of whom repeatedly alluded to them in their interviews.

In the second phase (late 1980s–present), although racial tension persisted through the 1990s, Southall saw a striking reduction of overt hostilities. It is no coincidence that this change in race relations corresponded to a shift in Southall demographics, such that the Commonwealth heritage population, mostly South Asians, became the majority, and the white community the minority (Oates 2002, 107). Southall schools became far more multiracial, with the proportion of minority ethnic origin students in Ealing schools now ranging from 40 percent to 99 percent (Ealing JSNA 2010, 18). Today, many public signs in Southall are in English and Punjabi (even at the local pub), and the town's lively Punjabi atmosphere is popular and well known in London.[1] Younger Gen. 2 residents raised during this phase grew up in a climate in which wider British society accepted an increasingly visible, legitimated, and even celebrated middle-class British Asian culture (Herbert 2009). These participants rarely volunteer narratives of racial tension. In contrast to older Gen. 2 individuals, they also described a subtle decline in the degree to which they experienced traditional practices such as men being expected to go into their father's business and women having arranged marriages at a young age.

The remainder of this chapter will show how deeply these historical transformations have impacted the development of British Asian accents, and implicitly the identities associated with those styles of speaking. In particular, I will suggest that there are no simple "ethnic identities" that are not also gendered, classed, and historically situated identities.

Ethnicity and Gender

In the present study, "ethnic" speech features are broadly limited to accent or grammatical features in the English of British Asians that derive originally from Indian language influence (bearing in mind that not all markers in such communities necessarily derive from ancestral languages). How can we start to understand and explain the use of such forms in the community?

One common approach is simply to tally how often an individual uses such forms, and assume that frequency of use directly reflects strength of ethnic identity. Much work in sociolinguistics has argued, however, that a more precise understanding can be gained not from a simple tally of speech from one interview, but rather by looking closely at whether and how a person *shifts* their style of speaking as they move from one situation to another, or from one audience to another (e.g., Bell 1984; Rickford and McNair-Knox 1994; Alim 2004; and others).

One way to do this is to collect recordings of an individual in many settings—usually achieved by asking individuals to record themselves as they go about their daily life—and then to track their use of different accent features. In the Southall community, Sharma (2011) looked at the resulting style repertoires of older and younger second-generation British Asians. Given that all the participants studied had strong ties within the same community, one possible prediction might have been that they would all show similar use of ethnic features, perhaps favoring them more with close Asian friends or relatives and less in other settings. However, the analysis in fact found major differences in ethnolinguistic repertoire variation, which related more specifically to gender and time than to ethnicity alone.

Figure 12.1 summarizes the patterns of situational variation found for four representative individuals. All are second-generation British Asians. Sharma (2011) provided results for four other "parallel" individuals to indicate the consistency of the patterns found. Figure 12.1 shows that, although all four individuals make common use of Asian phonetic variants (the grey bars), the most *separated or differentiated* use of these forms is found in older men and younger women. It is these two groups who opt to dramatically "turn on" or "turn off" their use of Asian or British forms, depending on situation, whereas the other two groups, though variable, had a more *fused* style, deploying both Asian and British forms within a single situation type.

A comment is needed on the reliability of comparing the repertoires in Figure 12.1. All interviews were conducted by two female speakers of standard Indian English, who were unknown personally to interviewees and were similar in age; interview contexts are therefore comparable across individuals. Similarly, "friend" contexts for both younger groups involve British Asians. However, due to the vagaries of relying on individuals to self-record, other aspects of the sample are not strictly comparable. For instance, some of the younger men had such little contact with white British people that they did not provide recordings of their style in such settings. Nevertheless, Sharma (2011, 481) offers several arguments to support the overall description of repertoires.

First, the self-recorded data collection always gathered data from *two* individuals per demographic group. Sharma (2011, 492) shows that the four individuals paired to those in Figure 12.1 have strikingly parallel repertoire types. A second type of support comes from ethnographic observation with 75 participants over 9 months, which persuaded both researchers independently that younger men broadly maintain their "fused" style across their interactions, with younger men and women even commenting on this. By contrast, many older men and younger women in the sample were routinely observed to be switching "on" and "off" their Asian styles. Thus, despite the difficulty—perhaps even impossibility—of

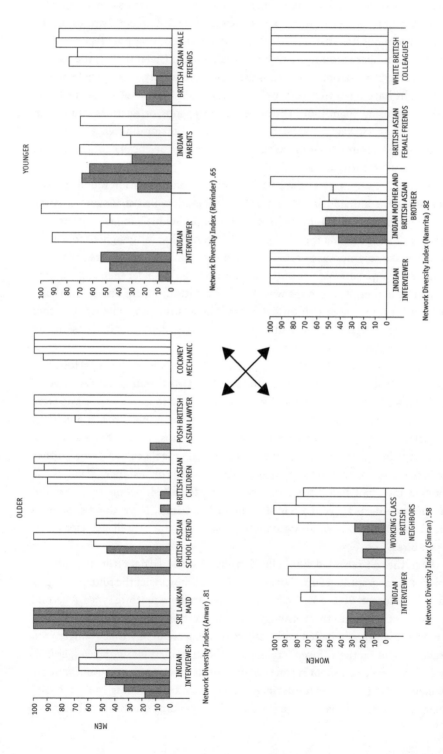

Figure 12.1 Use of ethnolectal features by gender and age. Grey bars: Asian variants [ʈ], [e], [ɭ], [l]. White bars: British variants [t], [eɪ], [əʊ], [ɫ]. (taken from Figs. 3–6 in Sharma 2011.)

collecting a strictly comparable set of repertoire recordings, a triangulation of methods offers some support for the broad differences described.

Returning to Figure 12.1, how do we account for the apparent gender reversal in repertoire types? The Network Diversity Index indicated below each repertoire profile indicates how diverse each individual's personal social network was, that is, how many unrelated groups of individuals the person interacted with on a regular basis. In this community, the diversity of a person's network correlates closely with whether they vary dramatically across their repertoire. The surprising gender reversal in repertoire type can therefore be traced to a gendered reversal in network diversity.

Why did this change in networks occur? In the older generation, even though all individuals grew up in the United Kingdom, they were the first group to do so, and their parents continued fairly traditional Punjabi practices of early marriage and frequent involvement in family businesses, particularly with boys expected to take over their father's businesses. The men in particular often had close dealings with India or Pakistan as a result, but were also the first British Asian political activists, claiming their rights as British and carving out their local space against hostile right-wing politics. They effectively developed and continued a role as "brokers" between the two cultures, operating much more at the interface of the community than women, who were somewhat more inside the community. This traditional gender arrangement appears to have been replaced by a typical working- and lower-middle-class British gender arrangement in the younger group. In direct contrast to the older group, younger women were slightly more educated, more widely employed outside the community, and thus interfaced *more* with non-Asians than their male counterparts. The younger men tended to have more social and work activities within the community and expressed less ambivalence toward traditional cultural practices. This gender pattern and associated speech effects are very reminiscent of similar class groups in Ireland (Milroy 1987), Hungary (Gal 1978), and South Carolina (Nichols 1979). Although in the present case the younger women do not quite abandon community speech styles, they compartmentalize them more.

In short, the analysis of accent repertoires shows that, over two generations, British-born Asians have moved from retaining a traditional Punjabi social arrangement of gender roles toward a typically British urban arrangement. This contradicts common perceptions of such groups as uniformly insular, unintegrated, and primarily oriented to their ethnic identity.

The analysis also shows that British Asians do not share the same use of ethnic accent features simply by virtue of being ethnically Asian. Usage differs substantially from one subgroup to the next. Naturally, the kind of speech repertoire each person develops does convey some ethnically specific information, but this alone cannot account for the complex and changing pattern we see.

The pattern is based not in ethnicity alone but in the gendered historical trajectory of this group (which appears to be a common trajectory in some other European immigrant groups, e.g. Keim 2007 on gender differences over time among Turkish Germans).

Ethnicity and Class

Let us turn from gender to class, and explore, once again, whether class is as deeply implicated in the use of "ethnic" language features in this community. In order to examine this, it is helpful to sketch out an approximate field of potential sociolinguistic reference points. A classic representation of class-based hierarchy in British dialect variation (Trudgill 2002, 173, citing Ward 1929) takes the form of a triangular arrangement, with Standard English at the apex and regional vernaculars at the base. The apex represents a relatively narrow and regionally nonspecific standard and the base represents a range of regional and nonstandard class-based varieties.

Rather than seeing the introduction of ethnic variants through migration as unrelated to this space, we can model contact between Indian and British cultures in London as contact between *two* such triangles. This is shown in Figure 12.2. Recall that English is a well-established language within South Asia, and so the added Asian triangle itself comprises a range of more and less standard forms, corresponding to more and less proficient varieties of Indian English.

Figure 12.2 models two (of many) dimensions of ideological space: a vertical or "up-down" class binary and a horizontal or "we-they" ethnic group dimension. In this formulation, it is impossible for ethnicity not to also correspond to some class-linked location. In other words, positions of ethnicity intrinsically

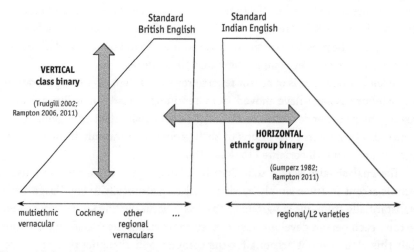

Figure 12.2 Modeling the sociolinguistic space of contact.

have (i.e., include some elements of) class and vice versa. Nevertheless, how a speaker navigates this space may vary considerably, perhaps focusing heavily on the "up-down" class dimension, the "inside-outside" ethnic dimension, or both.

In order to explore how members of the present community move through this space, and whether they do so in comparable ways, let us look at how two phonetic forms are used by different subgroups. One is a typical Asian ethnic form: postalveolar articulation of /t/, that is, pronouncing /t/ further back than in British English, a common feature of Indic languages and Indian English. Another is a typical British class form: glottal replacement of /t/, which sounds like a brief pause rather than a /t/.

One expectation might be that the ethnic and class meanings of each of these two forms are fairly stable across the entire social space. Postalveolar /t/ would be expected to signal ethnic meanings and glottal replacement of /t/ would be expected to signal class meanings. In fact, what we find is that first-generation immigrants (those who grew up in India and migrated to the United Kingdom as adults) often invoke the ethnic dimension in their use of *both* variants. The oldest second-generation British Asians show complex orientation to both dimensions. And the younger second-generation British Asians frequently orient to the British class dimension in their use of *both* variants.

In other words, rather than the maintenance of static meanings over time, we see incremental movement from the periphery to the centre of the British class dynamic. Ethnic meanings come to intersect increasingly with class for individuals as we move through the social history of the community from Gen. 1 to the most recent Gen. 2 groups, much as in studies of long-term American migrant contexts cited earlier (Labov 2001; Johnstone 2011).

Given space limitations, I sketch support for this shift using a few selected examples, first quantitative and then qualitative. A long-standing proposal in sociolinguistics (from Labov 1972 onward) has been that people's varying styles of speaking according to formality indirectly encode awareness of class-based variation in their social group. Dividing segments of an interview recording into formal and informal speech segments, we can evaluate whether an individual's speech shows this sensitivity to class or prestige, particularly predicted for the use of the "class" feature.

Tables 12.1 and 12.2 present a simple formality analysis for each core demographic group in the Southall community for the "class" and "ethnic" variable in question.

The raw percentages are not dramatically different, but statistical tests suggest that both variables move toward greater class or prestige sensitivity over time. Gen. 1 appears not to orient primarily to British prestige associations for *either* form. By contrast, by the time we reach the youngest Gen. 2 group, we see significant correlations with formality for *both* the "class" and "ethnic" variables, correlations that are typically interpreted as prestige sensitivity in the vertical dimension in Figure 12.2.

Table 12.1 **Glottal replacement of /t/**

Group	Formal segments	Informal segments	Total tokens	chi-square	
Gen. 1	6.8%	8.6%	2,492	**not significant**	$c^2(1) = 2.95$, p =.0858
Gen. 2 older	29.4%	33.6%	1,585	**not significant**	$c^2(1) = 3.15$, p =.0757
Gen. 2 younger	56.7%	62.4%	2,130	**significant**	$c^2(1) = 7.39$, p =.0006

Table 12.2 **Postalveolar articulation of /t/**

Group	Formal segments	Informal segments	Total tokens	Regression
Gen. 1	30.6%	39.1%	3,810	**not significant**
Gen. 2 older	12%	19.8%	2,330	**significant**
Gen. 2 younger	7.2%	9.7%	3,210	**significant**

In the case of glottal replacement, this may be pure class-based sensitivity; in the case of postalveolar /t/, this may be a case of registering that the community form bears less overt prestige. In other words, the ethnic association of the form is not absent from the developing formality usage in Table 12.2, but rather is being assigned a place in a hierarchy of prestige in the British scene. A few selected examples may help illustrate the lack of correlation with formality in the usage of Gen. 1 individuals and the strong correspondence among younger Gen. 2 individuals.

In example (1), we see Gen. 1 speakers, who have very little use of glottal replacement overall, favoring it early in their interview in their most formal speech formal segments, which is quite atypical of British usage:

(1) a. Mala: no no, no? a? the moment yeah i've go? indian passport.

   b. Priya: i've go? british passport now.

   c. Priya: no my husband eh went to punjab and then we go? married there and then i came. He- yeah he's born and brough? up here.

Unlike individuals who grew up in Britain, Gen. 1 individuals did not seem to turn down their use of the form in formal speech. Clustered with a set of other quite British forms, the resulting effect was strongly one of signalling *Britishness*, not specifically formality. These uses might serve to signal legitimacy, belonging, and local competence to an interviewer affiliated with a British institution. Even though glottal stops are so strongly associated with the vertical dimension for British speakers, these migrants were using it to move along the horizontal dimension, to present themselves as a part of British social space. Kerswill (1994) notes a similar use of informal urban features by rural migrants in Norway to signal urbanness (again, a kind of "inside-outside" contrast), rather than formality.

In the case of their use of postalveolar /t/, the lack of a formality effect for some speakers derived simply from their overwhelming use of this form as a default in their dialect, in contrast to Gen. 2 speakers, in whose British-accented speech the form takes on a more marked status. A few Gen. 1 individuals showed slight shifts in their use of the Asian form to mark *non-Britishness*, such as Indian affiliation, "villageness," or outsider status—once again, shifts that move along the horizontal "ethnic" dimension.

In their interviews, Gen. 1 individuals were overwhelmingly preoccupied with recent experiences of immigration and of "fitting in," finding their place within a new community. It may not be surprising that their shifts show this repeated orientation to "us-them" contrasts. This is not to suggest that Gen. 1 is unconcerned with class. Rampton (2013) describes a particular Gen. 1 individual from this dataset who shows incipient class sensitivity in his variation, which may arise from greater interaction with British contacts. Others may have more limited access (to use a term from Le Page and Tabouret-Keller 1985, 182) to British English, which limits their ability to acquire "accurate" local class meanings for forms. In addition, English may simply not be the place to look for class in Gen. 1: fine-grained class differences were continually indicated in their Punjabi interactions. Finally, signaling class may be fundamentally complicated for this group, as they generally experienced a type of "class clash," in that they tended to have relatively high status in their villages and towns of origin (being among the few with sufficient resources and contacts to migrate) but were immediately associated with a lower status once in the United Kingdom. This mismatch between their own and others' perception of their status makes it less clear what class positions they would even aim to signal in English.

Moving to the other end of the three generational groups, recall that Tables 12.1 and 12.2 showed significant formality sensitivity in the younger Gen. 2 group for *both* variables, unlike Gen. 1, who showed neither. In example (2), we see that Namrita shows the classic British formality pattern in her use of glottal forms in informal speech and alveolar /t/ forms in formal speech. This use of glottaling to down-shift toward a vernacular voice in informal contexts is typical of the vertical prestige dimension in Figure 12.2.

---

(2) Namrita (younger Gen. 2 woman)

a. (formal)	ahm, you get to meet a lot of people in the community
b. (informal)	you can? say well i'm going to a club tonigh? because i wanna go and mee? some people!
c. (informal)	see i never wear my whi?e skir?! i've only worn i? like three times!

Interestingly, we see Namrita doing the same shift in her use of postalveolar variants when she moves from interview speech, where she uses no such forms, to much more informal speech at home. This shift is clearly related to prestige much like her use of glottaling, as she eliminates the form entirely from her recording with the researcher but uses them regularly with her mother and brother at home.

In sum, the static view of glottal /t/ as a "class" variable and postalveolar /t/ as an "ethnic" variable fails to capture the rich range of uses and changing functions for these forms in this ethnic minority community. Both forms tend to be recruited to the most salient concerns of a particular subgroup, depending on migration stage, exposure, and social position. In line with previous work (e.g., Labov 2001; Johnstone 2011), we seem to see a shift in the meanings of speech forms over time from a heightened focus on ethnic boundaries to a focus on local class positions.

Variation in Discourse

The discussion of ethnicity so far has shown (a) that it is inseparable from gender and class; and (b) that, in both cases, deep and regular transformations take place over the early generations of a migrant community, influencing the use of community speech styles. A final question that arises is this: When we hear these ethnically identifiable pronunciations, are speakers *actively* designing their style? Are they always aiming to achieve particular effects, identity-related or otherwise? Or are these simply a routine feature of their speech, more or less beyond their control or even awareness?

In this final section, I comment briefly on how speech varies *within* single individuals ("intra-individual variation"). This more microlevel focus—on what individuals do rather than groups—allows us to examine whether individuals actively exploit ethnic and other speech forms to reinscribe or reshape ideological reference points in the community. Once again, we find that the historical phase at which an individual happens to be located deeply affects their type of language use.

To look at intra-individual variation, we cannot rely on overall frequencies of use of ethnic features. For instance, in the present community, older and younger men had very similar overall average rates of use of ethnic features (e.g., approximately 15% postalveolar articulation of /t/). We might conclude that older and younger men are very similar in how they signal Asian identity, and little has changed over forty years. But in fact, a close examination of discourse variation reveals stark differences in how "activated" their use of these forms is.

In order to show this, we need to look closely at how a specific individual varies their speech during interactions or narratives. Sharma and Rampton (2015) propose one way of tracking degrees of shifting in the use of ethnic and class speech features. We devise a quantitative measure of how much a speaker is moving toward three different dialect styles: Indian English, Standard British English, and Vernacular British English. (In terms of Figure 12.2, the first of these contrasts with the latter two along the horizontal "ethnic" dimension, and the contrast between the latter two broadly corresponds to the vertical "class" dimension.)

Starting with a long segment of interaction or narrative, we first break it down into chunks based on clausal boundaries and footing shifts, and then, for each chunk, calculate the percentage of use of the three dialect styles. The calculation is based on coding only those accent features that contrast for the three dialect styles. For instance, word-final /t/ would be pronounced in different ways in each of the three dialect styles. The analysis generates a graph of how much the speaker fluctuates in their use of dialect styles in real time during discourse, a process we term "Lectal Focusing in Interaction," or LFI. (See Sharma and Rampton 2015 for full details.)

Figures 12.3a and 12.3b show a notable contrast in LFI for two individuals. Figure 12.3a shows that Anwar (seen earlier in Figure 12.1) exhibits dramatic fluctuation in his use of all three ethnic and class styles; although details are not provided here, these fluctuations are very closely tied to such interactional work as footing, stance, voicing, and topic. By contrast, Ravinder (also seen earlier in Figure 12.1), in Figure 12.3b, consistently shows relatively "flat" distributions, particularly for variable use of ethnolinguistic features (compare the solid line in each graph), that is, he shows much less evidence of fine-tuned links to interactional moments.

In Sharma and Rampton (2015), we note that these patterns are not specific to these individuals, but are characteristic of men in each age group. We suggest that the older men are continually reinscribing ethno-political stances in their

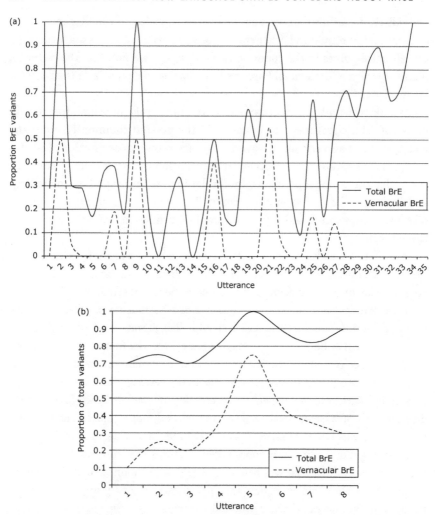

Figure 12.3 a. Higher lectal focusing in a narrative told by Anwar, an older Gen. 2 man (from Sharma and Rampton, 2015). b. Lower lectal focusing in a narrative told by Ravinder, a younger Gen. 2 man (from Sharma and Rampton, 2015).

speech, orienting to all four corners of Figure 12.2 in different interactions, a practice that arises out of their particular early life experiences. The younger men, by contrast, have developed a much less fine-grained set of social meanings for the same linguistic forms, perhaps due to their experience of a much less conflicted and marginalized status, growing up during a later stage of the community. These younger men still use ethnic pronunciations as an integral part of their British Asian accent, but hardly signal anything beyond community membership. Indeed, one volunteered the view that "it happens unintentionally . . . I'll speak an English word but it'll come out with an Indian accent."

Interestingly, this younger set of men does not show the same flat distribution for their variation between standard and vernacular British English. This can be seen in the wider range of fluctuation in the broken line in Figure 12.3b, as compared to the solid line in that figure. They systematically exploit British standard-vernacular contrasts throughout their interactions for a range of interactional functions, much as their non-Asian peers do. Although they retain regular overall use of ethnic forms, close analysis of their variation shows that they have to some extent left behind the early tensions of the older Gen. 2, and resemble their non-Asian peers more closely in many respects.

Conclusions

This case study of the Punjabi London community has pointed to fundamental complexities in ethnic styles of speaking. Far from finding stable, shared uses of ethnic speech features in the community, we see that these forms are inherently gendered and classed and, furthermore, that their use changes as the community moves through phases of migration and settlement in the United Kingdom. In terms of social change, gendered uses of ethnic forms pointed to a gradual development of more British-like gender roles in the community. Similarly, the influence of class on the use of accent features was shown to increase over time, with the youngest group once again showing the greatest resemblance to their British counterparts. The examination of variation within discourse also showed the youngest group to be the group least engaged in sustained ethno-political signaling in routine interactions. It is crucial to bear in mind, however, that in both cases—intersections with gender and with class—this gradual social shift toward British cultural practices does not mean that the youngest group does not use ethnic forms at all. In fact they show quite robust and widely noticed use of such forms. It is their *way* of using the forms that is distinctive from earlier stages, with new, local meanings.

These observations about how language use changes over time, and by extension how the community itself has changed over time, were only possible through a triangulation of many different kinds of analysis, including looking at details of changing social history and local politics, overall frequencies of use of features, accent repertoires, and style fluctuation within individual conversations. Only this combined analysis allows us to see both where an individual is situated in terms of sociohistory and habitus (Bourdieu 1990) and their degree of agency and ideological engagement with these social positions in the community. Ultimately, this type of analysis can help highlight how and why ethnicity, gender, and class come to vary in their salience over time in different communities and for different individuals.

Note

1. Several participants even suggested that the peak of Southall's Punjabi culture has now passed, with an upwardly mobile movement of South Asians out of the area and new, more working-class, non-Asian migrants coming in.

References

Alam, Farhana, and Jane Stuart-Smith. 2014. Identity, ethnicity and fine phonetic detail: An acoustic phonetic analysis of syllable-initial /t/ in Glaswegian girls of Pakistani heritage. In Marianne Hundt and Devyani Sharma, eds., *English in the Indian Diaspora*, 29–53. Amsterdam/Philadelphia: John Benjamins.

Alim, H. Samy. 2004. *You Know My Steez: An Ethnographic and Sociolinguistic Study of Styleshifting in a Black American Speech Community*. Durham, NC: Duke University Press.

Benor, Sarah Bunin. 2010. Ethnolinguistic repertoire: Shifting the analytic focus in language and ethnicity. *Journal of Sociolinguistics* 14(2): 159–83.

Bell, Allan. 1984. Language style as audience design. *Language in Society* 13: 145–204.

Boberg, Charles. 2004. Ethnic Patterns in the Phonetics of Montreal English. *Journal of. Sociolinguistics* 8/4: 538–68.

Bourdieu, Pierre. 1990. *The Logic of Practice*. Stanford, CA: Stanford University Press.

CARF (Campaign against Racism and Fascism). 1981. *Southall: The Birth of a Black Community*. London: Institute of Race Relations.

Cheshire, Jenny, Paul Kerswill, Sue Fox, and Eivind Torgersen. 2011. Contact, the feature pool and the speech community: The emergence of Multicultural London English. *Journal of Sociolinguistics* 15(2): 151–96.

DMAG (Data Management and Analysis Group, Greater London Authority) Briefing. 2006. Accessed on 3 November 2010 from www.london.gov.uk.

Ealing JSNA (Joint Strategic Needs Assessment) report. 2010. Accessed on 3 November 2010 from: http://www.ealingpct.nhs.uk/Publications/needs-assessment.asp

Eckert, Penelope. (2008). Where do ethnolects stop? *International Journal of Bilingualism* 12(1): 25–42.

Fagyal, Zsuzsanna, and Christopher Stewart. 2011. Prosodic style-shifting in preadolescent peer-group interactions in a working-class suburb of Paris. In Friederike Kern and Margret Selting, eds., *Ethnic Styles of Speaking in European Metropolitan Areas*. Amsterdam/ Philadelphia: John Benjamins, 75–99.

Gal, Susan. 1978. Peasant men can't get wives: language change and sex roles in a bilingual community. *Language in Society* 7: 1–16.

Herbert, Joanna. 2009. Oral histories of the Ugandan Asians in Britain: gendered identities in the diaspora. *Contemporary South Asia* 17(1): 21–32.

Hinskens, Frans. 2011. "Emerging Moroccan and Turkish varieties of Dutch: ethnolects or ethnic styles?" In F. Kern and M. Selting, eds., *Ethnic Styles of Speaking in European Metropolitan Areas*. Amsterdam/Philadelphia: John Benjamins, 103–31.

Hoffman, Michol, and James Walker. 2010. Ethnolects and the city: Ethnic orientation and linguistic variation in Toronto English. *Language Variation and Change* 22: 37–67.

Irvine, Judith, and Susan Gal. 2000. Language ideology and linguistic differentiation. In P. Kroskrity, ed., *Regimes of Language: Ideologies, Polities, and Identities*. Santa Fe, NM: School of American Research Press, 35–84.

Johnstone, Barbara. 2011. Presentation on panel on "Ethnicity and English in Four North American Cities." NWAV 40 conference, Georgetown, USA.

Keim, Inken. 2007. Socio-cultural identity, communicative style, and their change over time: A case study of a group of German-Turkish girls in Mannheim/Germany. In Peter

Auer, ed., *Style and Social Identities: Alternative Approaches to Linguistic Heterogeneity*, 155–86. Berlin/New York: Mouton de Gruyter.

Kerswill, Paul. 1994. *Dialects Converging: Rural Speech in Urban Norway*. Oxford: Clarendon Press.

Labov, William. 1972. *Sociolinguistic Patterns*. Philadelphia: University of Pennsylvania Press.

Labov, William. 2001. *Principles of Linguistic change*. Vol. 2, *Social Factors*. Oxford: Blackwell.

Le Page, Robert, and Andrée Tabouret-Keller. 1985. *Acts of Identity: Creole-based Approaches to Language and Ethnicity*. Cambridge: Cambridge University Press.

Milroy, Lesley. 1987. *Language and Social Networks*. 2nd ed. Oxford: Wiley-Blackwell.

Nagy, N., and A. Kochetov. 2013. Voice Onset Time across the generations: A cross-linguistic study of contact-induced change. In *Multilingualism and Language Contact in Urban Areas: Acquisition—Development—Teaching—Communication*, ed. P. Siemund, I. Gogolin, M. Schulz, and J. Davydova. Amsterdam: John Benjamins, 19–38.

Nichols, Patricia. 1979. Black women in the rural South: conservative and innovative. In Betty Lou Dubois and Isabel Crouch, eds., *The Sociology of the Languages of American Women*. San Antonio: Trinity University.

Oates, Jonathan. 2002. *Southall and Hanwell*. London: History Press.

Quist, Pia. 2008. Sociolinguistic approaches to multiethnolect: Language variety and stylistic practice. *International Journal of Bilingualism* 12(1): 43–61.

Rampton, Ben. 2013. Styling in a language learned later in life. *Modern Language Journal* 97(2): 360–82.

Rickford, John R., and F. McNair-Knox. 1994. Addressee- and topic-influenced style shift: A quantitative sociolinguistic study. In D. Biber and E. Finegan, eds., *Sociolinguistic Perspectives on Register*. New York, Oxford University Press, 235–76.

Sharma, Devyani. 2011. Style repertoire and social change in British Asian English. *Journal of Sociolinguistics* 15(4): 464–92.

Sharma, Devyani, and Ben Rampton. 2015. Lectal focusing in interaction: A new methodology for the study of style variation. *Journal of English Linguistics* 43(1): 3–35.

Svendsen, Bente Ailin, and Unn Røyneland. 2008. Multiethnolectal facts and functions in Oslo, Norway. *International Journal of Bilingualism* 12(1–2): 63–84.

Trudgill, Peter. 2002. *Sociolinguistic Variation and Change*. Edinburgh: Edinburgh University Press.

Wiese, Heike. 2009. Grammatical innovation in multiethnic urban Europe: New linguistic practices among adolescents. *Lingua* 119: 782–806.

Part III

LANGUAGE, RACE, AND EDUCATION
IN CHANGING COMMUNITIES

13

"It Was a Black City"

African American Language in California's Changing Urban Schools and Communities

DJANGO PARIS

Miles[1] and I were deep in an interview about his community as we sat in the empty high school gym waiting out an early winter rainstorm. Miles was one of several youth I conducted social language research with during the 2006–2007 school year at South Vista High, a public charter high school in urban California. As we talked, Miles, an African American young man who grew up in South Vista, mapped out how his school and community were changing.

> Miles: We have very little Black people, it's mostly Hispanic people. . . .
> So it's really not diverse; it's really Hispanic, very Hispanic, and if you
> don't like Hispanic people, don't come to this school. Because I think
> that there's a lot of Hispanic people moving in, and everybody else is
> kinda moving out, like a lot of Black people have moved from South
> Vista to the Central Valley cities and all that.

As Miles saw it, his school was not really racially and ethnically diverse; it was primarily made up of Latino/a students, a result of large numbers of Latinos/as moving into the city of South Vista and some African Americans moving out to the smaller, less expensive cities of California's Central Valley.

Carlos, a Mexican American young man, was one of Miles's peers at South Vista High. He had moved to South Vista from Mexico with his mother and siblings in 1999. Like Miles, Carlos was part of this changing community. As we sat on a bench near the school's athletic field one day in early spring, Carlos related his perspective on these changes in South Vista.

Carlos: It used to be all Black people. It was a Black city ... like, '91, '92, '94 it was all Black people. .... There was some Latinos, but over time, I guess, they started moving away and then more Latinos started moving in. Like our family—at first it was only my uncle. And then he brought his family over from Mexico. .... And then he told my dad that there was jobs over here, and so my dad came over here, and then he brought us.

I would learn a similar story from Ela, a Samoan young woman who also attended South Vista. Ela's aunt had emigrated from the Samoan Islands with her children to join relatives already living in South Vista. Ela, her grandparents, and other family members followed. Carlos, Ela, Miles, and their families were part of a major demographic shift in South Vista. This city, nestled in a major metropolitan area of California, had been shifting since the 1980s from a predominantly African American city to a predominantly Latino/a city. A growing population of Pacific Islanders had also been part of this shift. During the year of my research, 17 percent of the students at South Vista High were African American, 10 percent were Pacific Islander, and 73 percent were Latino/a—mainly Mexican or Mexican American.

The changes lived by these youth are part of a larger story of changing urban schools and communities sweeping California. Coupled with the continued residential and educational segregation of communities of color, one major effect of these shifts has been that many of California's urban communities that were once predominantly African American are now predominantly Latino/a, with significant populations of Pacific Islanders, Southeast Asians, and other immigrant communities of color. From Oakland to Long Beach, from South Central Los Angeles to South San Francisco, schools and communities are changing in just the way Miles, Ela, and Carlos experienced in South Vista (see chapter 5 in this volume for a set of different but related shifts).

These changing urban populations have brought Black and Brown students together in classrooms and communities in complex new ways. What are the linguistic outcomes of such dramatic shifts? How has the linguistic landscape of urban schools and communities been altered by these changes? And, most important, how can schools respond to the linguistic realities of young people as they grow up in such changing multilingual and multiethnic contexts? These questions are important to me as a former English Language Arts teacher, as a scholar of language and literacy, and as a Black/biracial man (with an immigrant Black Jamaican father and a White American mother) who was born and attended public schools in California. But these are also questions of vital importance to all interested in language and educational equity in California and across the United States. In addition to neighborhood, school, and city demographic

shifts like those in South Vista, it also true that the broader U.S. population continues major demographic shifts toward a multilingual, multicultural majority
of people of color (with Latinos/as being the largest group and Asians/Asian
Americans being the fastest-growing group). The experiences of youth in South
Vista, then, are quickly becoming the norm in schools and communities across
the nation.

African American Language among African American Youth

One major linguistic outcome of these changes, particularly in urban schools
and communities like South Vista, is that immigrant students like Carlos and Ela
often learn English within longstanding African American Language–speaking
communities. African American Language (AAL) is a systematic English spoken
as at least one of the languages of most African Americans in California and
across the nation. African American Language has a history that is intimately
connected with oppression and resistance as well as with the rich linguistic, spiritual, and literary achievements of African Americans. Like any language, AAL is
learned and used in social interaction, so only people who participate over time
within a community of AAL speakers will have reason to learn and use AAL.
Historically, this learning and use has been a part of the linguistic socialization
of many African Americans for reasons of segregation and solidarity, although
as I will discuss in this chapter, many Latinos/as, Pacific Islanders, and other
communities of color also participate in AAL in changing urban communities.
Although I focus in this chapter on face-to-face interactions in one urban community, it is also important to note that in an evolving globalized and digitally
mediated world, such participation, community, and linguistic socialization may
occur in embodied (face-to-face) and digital (e.g., Facebook, Twitter, Tumblr)
space and through media and popular cultures (e.g., film, music, Hip Hop).

Many decades of linguistic research has shown that AAL has a set of grammatical features, a pronunciation system, a vocabulary, and rhetorical traditions
that differ significantly from the Dominant American English or DAE (commonly
called "standard" English) demanded for access in schools and many workplaces
(Smitherman 1977; Rickford and Rickford 2000). This research is based in a historical understanding that AAL is the linguistic legacy of American slavery and
its aftermath—a creole language forged from the languages and cultural traditions of Africans forced into slavery and the languages (mainly Englishes) of
White slave owners, masters, and servants. Given these decades of linguistic and
historical research, it is not surprising that all of the African American students
I knew at South Vista were speakers of AAL, nor is it surprising that the majority

of African American students in California's schools speak AAL as at least one of their Englishes (I use the term *Englishes* to denote the understanding that there are many distinct language varieties called *English*).

Any person familiar with the grammar, pronunciation system, vocabulary, and rhetorical traditions of AAL would easily recognize it in the everyday talk of African American students inside and outside of urban schools. South Vista High and the city of South Vista are no different from other AAL-speaking communities across the nation. In interviews, everyday conversations, and interactions within and beyond classrooms, I witnessed frequent examples of all of the major features of AAL in the oral-language use of the African American students I came to know. I focus here on just four prominent grammatical features that help to illuminate how AAL is distinct from DAE. As I draw these linguistic distinctions, it is important to keep in mind that grammatical differences between AAL and DAE are often at the heart of educational and social concerns about the language and literacy learning of AAL speakers. It is also important to note that each of these linguistic features is optional for speakers of AAL and are dependent on both social context (e.g., with whom, where, and about what a speaker is communicating) and linguistic context (e.g., what precedes and follows the feature in an utterance). Therefore, in AAL as with all language varieties, speakers vary in how much of the variety they use depending on sociolinguistic factors. It is also important to mention that some features of AAL are shared with other languages and with other varieties of English (like Chicano English or some varieties of Southern White English), though they are generally marked as AAL in contexts like South Vista, where AAL is a primary language of interaction. A caution on the language examples that follow: Although I isolate these examples to show distinctions in grammar, they should be seen in the context of these youth living their lives across school, home, and community and within the centuries-old struggle for social equality.

I begin with an example from early in my year of research as I was preparing to practice with the boys' basketball team. I asked Miles if the team was practicing later that day. "We practicing today," he told me. In his response Miles chose the AAL option of not using the copula or "linking" verb *to be*, saying, "We practicing" instead of the DAE "We *are* practicing" or "We*'re* practicing." The option of not using the copula *to be* is a major feature of AAL grammar, available to speakers when other English varieties would insert *is* or *are*.

Rochelle, an African American young woman who was raised in South Vista, was another youth I worked with. After many months of school visits and a developing friendship, I spent some time visiting Rochelle and her mother in their home. One afternoon as Rochelle was telling me about her block and giving me a tour of her house, I asked her about the nearby park and she responded, "I don't *be* over there." Later, Rochelle described the multiple posters on her walls by saying, "I *be* putting hella posters up." In these examples Rochelle used a hallmark feature of AAL grammar that linguists refer to as the *habitual be*. "I don't be over there" is used for a rough DAE translation of "I'm usually not/ never over there" and "I be putting hella posters up" for the approximate DAE "I usually/always put a lot of posters up." As part of AAL's complex tense-aspect system, which marks when and how an action occurs, habitual *be* denotes an action that is regularly or habitually performed.

Another common and optional feature in AAL grammar is use of the *third-person singular* –s. This was a feature Rochelle employed when she was telling me about her science class. "You just listen to what the teacher *say*," she explained. In this example, Rochelle did not use the *s* in the AAL "the teacher *say*," in contrast to the DAE version "the teacher *says*."

Let me provide just one more example of African American youth at South Vista using systematic features of AAL grammar. One day after school I was standing with a few of the school's basketball players, both boys and girls, near a mural in a hallway. I remarked on a detail of the mural that I had just noticed, and Sharon replied, "We *BIN* noticing that." In her response, Sharon, an African American young woman raised in South Vista, used the *remote verbal marker stressed BIN* to denote the fact that she and her peers had noticed the details of the mural for some time and were still noticing them at the present moment. As another part of the complex tense-aspect system of AAL, the stressed pronunciation of *been* changes the form's grammatical function; this is one of many features that highlight how AAL can differ significantly from DAE.

The above examples are but a few select features of the many components of AAL that African American youth used daily at South Vista as they lived their linguistic, cultural, and academic lives. This participation in the AAL-speaking community shows these young people forging their identities as African Americans through sharing in AAL just as generations before them had done in South Vista and in African American communities across California and the United States. Miles and Rochelle often spoke of AAL as "our" language and recognized a distinct way of speaking among African Americans. And yet they also understood that the changes in South Vista meant that AAL was not theirs alone anymore. In fact, many of Miles and Rochelle's Latino/a and Pacific Islander peers used the very same features of AAL grammar that have been used by African Americans for centuries.

African American Language among Latino/a and Pacific Islander Youth

As I stated earlier, one major linguistic outcome of the dramatic demographic shifts in urban California and urban U.S. contexts from predominantly African American populations to predominantly Latino/a populations with significant populations of other groups of color is that youth like Carlos and Ela learn English in longstanding AAL-speaking communities. For Carlos, Ela, and many of their Latino/a and Pacific Islander peers, this meant that they learned and used the same elements of AAL employed by their African American peers. My interviews, conversations, and interactions with these youth, then, were also brimming with AAL. For comparative purposes, I will provide examples of the same grammatical features I showed being used above among African American youth at South Vista.

The AAL feature of optional copula, for instance, was common among Latino/a and Pacific Islander youth. During one conversation I had with Carlos, he told me which teacher he wanted to judge his academic exhibition. "I want Mr. Johnson, he cool," Carlos said. In his comment, Carlos did not use the copula in the AAL "he cool" for the DAE "he *is* cool" or "he's cool." Ela, a Samoan American young woman, also often varied her use of the copula. When I first met Ela, she commented on my height by saying, "Damn, you tall!" (instead of the DAE "you *are* tall!" or "you're tall!")

That hallmark, unique feature of AAL, the habitual *be*, was also used by Carlos, Ela, and their peers. For her part, Ela deployed the habitual *be* in every possible social context in which I observed her—from the classroom to her Samoan church to the basketball court. One day during some downtime in her biology class, for example, we were looking through pictures of food from my father's native Jamaica and her native Samoa. We came to a picture of breadfruit, a staple of Jamaican fare. Ela remarked that this food was also popular in Samoa with her comment, "Everybody *be* eating that, but I don't like it" (DAE: "Everybody habitually/always eats that"). Another example of the habitual *be* comes from an interview about Ela's use of Samoan language, when she told me, "Yeah, I *be* speaking [Samoan] at school."

Latino/a youth used the habitual *be* as well. Gloria, a Mexican American young woman who was born in South Vista and had spent a significant number of her childhood years in Mexico, reported during an interview that another Latina was spreading rumors about her. "Patricia *be* talking on me," she said (DAE: "Patricia is always talking badly about me"). It's also worth noting that Gloria's use here of "on" in "talking on me" is another feature associated with AAL rather than with DAE. These uses of the habitual *be* by Latino/a and Pacific Islander youth show a deep participation in the complex tense-aspect system of AAL that goes far beyond simply "sounding like" a speaker of AAL. These youth had taken on a way of expressing how actions occur that is intimately tied with the past and present of AAL.

Ela and her Latino/a and Pacific Islander peers also employed third-person singular –*s* variability. In the same interview when we were talking about Samoa and Samoan language, Ela explained, "Well, my grandpa *say* we only go back to Samoa after we graduate." Finally, Ela also used stressed *BIN* when she responded to an African American peer's question with "Sharon *BIN* left" (DAE: "Sharon left some time ago and she's still gone").

These are only some of the many ways that Latino/a and Pacific Islander youth used AAL in their school, homes, and other community spaces. Although the amount of AAL used by these youth varied, they all employed it across various social and academic contexts. In addition to employing the full range of AAL structures, words, and sounds, many Latino/a and Pacific Islander youth also joined their African American peers as consumers and producers of Hip Hop music, Hip Hop language, Hip Hop clothing styles, and other urban cultural practices born in African and Caribbean American youth communities. Within this broader participation in African American and Hip Hop culture, the distinct features of AAL grammar in the everyday language of South Vista's Latino/a and Pacific Islander youth show that AAL is being learned and used across ethnicities in this changing California community. Carlos, Ela, Gloria, and many of their Latino/a and Pacific Islander peers shared social space, cultural practices, and relationships with their African American peers, and so they shared in their ways with language as well. Although Spanish, Samoan, and other heritage languages were also a crucial part of the cultural and linguistic landscape, AAL had become a common language used within and across ethnicities—a sort of lingua franca set against the backdrop of the DAE demanded of all these young people for access and opportunity in school and the broader society (see Ibrahim 2003 for examples of such AAL and Hip Hop participations in the Canadian context). Understanding how this AAL learning and use happened has major implications for changing urban schools and communities in California, the broader United States, and beyond.

Language Socialization in a Changing Multilingual Community

Carlos and Miles both knew that their community was undergoing major demographic shifts. They were growing up in the changing urban landscapes of California and the nation. Both of these young men also showed an understanding of what this meant for the Englishes used in their city. For his part, Carlos had arrived in South Vista from Michoacán, México in 1999. He had come as a Spanish monolingual and had immediately enrolled in a South Vista public middle school. Carlos recounted his early journey of learning English during an interview one day on a bench near the school.

> Carlos: What happens is, like, when kids are coming—like English learners, since they're around Black people sometimes, they learn the slang instead of, like, the English-English. Like, what is it, formal

English? . . . But that's what happened with me, because when I was in middle school, most of the kids were African Americans.

Carlos and many of his immigrant peers arrived in South Vista from Mexico, Central America, and the Pacific Islands to schools and peer communities with large African American and AAL-speaking populations. This meant that in addition to the DAE taught in their classrooms and the various languages used in their homes (e.g., Spanish, Samoan, Fijian, Tongan), many of these young people became proficient in AAL as part of their linguistic socialization into American Englishes. This socialization into AAL was true not only of immigrant youth in South Vista but also of the many Latino/a and Pacific Islander youth who were born and raised in the city. As Miles told me in an interview when I asked him about the AAL use of his Latino/a peers, "They're just being themselves because they were born here and raised here." Miles's view was that such language use by his peers across ethnic boundaries was a natural part of *language socialization*.[2] If you were born and raised in a community where AAL was a prominent English, of course you would learn to use it. Coupled with Carlos's point about the English-language learning of immigrant young people, Miles's ideas about language socialization show how Latino/a, Pacific Islander, and other youth in California's urban centers can come to speak AAL with their African American peers.

Through the process of sharing their language with Latino/a and Pacific Islander peers, South Vista's African American young people were ensuring that AAL would continue to be an important part of the linguistic landscape of their changing community. Yet even as AAL is shared across ethnic groups by many youth in changing urban communities, it is important to recognize that AAL is intimately connected with the oppression, resistance, and achievements of African Americans. This recognition has become increasingly important as African Americans in California and across the nation experience a shrinking urban presence, with Latinos/as now the largest community of color in neighborhoods and schools that were once predominantly African American. Coupled with the continued failure of schools to serve the needs of African American students and the fact that African American young people continue to lead dropout and incarceration rates, these shrinking numbers are yet another reason to focus on positive educational programs to support African American students—and AAL must remain a major resource in such programs. The fact that AAL is used by both African Americans and many of their peers from other ethnic groups should be seen as an opportunity to bolster African American students' pride in AAL as well as to foster all students' knowledge about the past, present, and future of AAL and African American culture in changing urban communities. Such a focus has the potential to support students in learning much about language, race, and ethnicity in ways that could build alliances between students who share neighborhoods, schools, and experiences of marginalization.

In addition, the deep linguistic sharing in AAL at South Vista offers us knowledge about both traditional and evolving ways that young people in our changing communities, schools, and nation enact race and ethnicity through language. Too often research and popular assumptions about relationships between language, race, and ethnicity imagine a one-to-one mapping of, for instance, Spanish use only among Latinos/as or AAL use only among African Americans. Recent linguistic, educational, and cultural scholarship has pushed against the tendency to assume unidirectional correspondence between race, ethnicity, language, and cultural practice (e.g., Paris 2011; Paris and Alim 2014); and, in the tradition of this chapter, has shown that such relationships must be understood as dynamic and varied rather than as fixed and monolithic.

To gain a full appreciation of the scope of U.S. (and global) demographic change and language sharing for evolving understandings of race, ethnicity, and cultural practice, we must consider all the languages present in our changing urban schools and communities. Although this chapter is focused on AAL sharing across ethnicity at South Vista, it is crucial to point out that there was also small but important sharing in Spanish words and phrases by African American and Pacific Islander youth and that youth in both groups expressed desire to learn Spanish as a necessary language in their city, state, and nation. Due to a complex set of factors, including the linguistic intelligibility distance between Spanish and English (versus DAE and AAL) and also the fact that DAE was the dominant language of school and society, Spanish was not learned and shared in as deep and sustained a way as AAL. Pacific Islander languages (Samoan, Fijian, Tongan), used by many Pacific Islander students with elders and in-group peers, were not shared by African American and Latina/o youth due mainly to the small number of speakers of those languages and the lack of prestige and reasons for use in the school. Yet the desire and use of Spanish and the fact that Pacific Islander languages were used by many Pacific Islanders throughout the community shows the ways both traditional notions of race and ethnicity tied to heritage and changing contemporary notions are enacted through language as ethnic groups share social and cultural spaces and institutions.

Educational Implications for Learners of American Englishes

Demographic change and shifting enactments of race and ethnicity through language have major implications for education. Returning to my focus in this chapter on AAL as a crucial and prevalent example, we must understand that beyond linguistic and historic knowledge, ethnic pride, and interethnic respect, AAL can be a powerful educational resource in learning the DAE language and literacy skills demanded in schools. The fact is that students from all three of

South Vista's largest ethnic communities are among those faring most poorly in the nation's urban schools. This continued general failure of schools to successfully meet the needs of poor communities of color, in conjunction with the AAL use of many urban youth of color, makes AAL a crucial resource for designing classroom learning experiences that simultaneously honor and explore AAL while extending the language and literacy repertoires of AAL speakers. Fortunately, over the past few decades many classroom teachers and researchers have found effective ways to critically compare and contrast the grammar, vocabulary, pronunciation system, and rhetorical traditions of AAL with DAE in writing and reading curriculum (Rickford et al. 2013). Such generative contrastive analysis, done with respect for AAL and other Englishes and languages used in the community, and in conjunction with critical discussions about race, ethnicity, and equality, can help students identify the distinctions between these different Englishes so they can learn to fluidly use each variety effectively with multiple audiences and for multiple purposes.

In addition to supporting students in comparing and utilizing their everyday languages and the language demanded in most school settings, research has also shown that there are many rich resources for learning about the past, present, and future of AAL while simultaneously studying DAE. African American literature—from Zora Neale Hurston, to Toni Morrison, to Alice Walker—is laden with AAL in the voices of character and narrators. Hip Hop culture, a core culture of many American urban (and suburban) youth and youth globally, is also teeming with AAL. Guiding students to explore AAL, African American culture, and the continuing struggle for cultural equity in these sources while simultaneously reading and writing in DAE has yielded many positive educational outcomes in classrooms across the Unites States (Alim 2007; Hill 2009).

The linguistic reality of South Vista as a microcosm of America's changing urban landscape shows that researchers' and educators' vast knowledge of how to use AAL as an asset in classroom learning must be applied to the teaching not only of African American speakers of AAL but also to their peers from other ethnic groups who are speakers of AAL. Providing access to DAE remains one critical goal of public education; welcoming AAL as a level partner in the process of achieving this goal will continue to be important. Fostering an understanding of the equality of all people and their languages and cultures also remains a critical goal of public education; as such, the study of AAL will continue to be crucial in the changing urban schools of the United States.

In addition to the considerable practical implications of Latinos/as, Pacific Islanders and other urban youth sharing in AAL with their African American peers, teachers, researchers, and policymakers must consider both *how* languages are learned and *which* languages are learned in changing urban landscapes. The nation's increasingly multiethnic and multilingual population and the continual flow of immigrants have long made the education of English Language Learners (ELLs) a priority. And yet the term ELLs does not always accurately describe the urban immigrant students of California and across the United States. As Carlos recounted above, he was learning at least two Englishes—AAL and DAE—in his early years in the United States. Urban immigrant young people, then, are often Learners of American Englishes (LAEs) rather than simply learners of some monolithic language called "English." Indeed, they are learning American Englishes in their peer communities and classrooms in the way people always learn language—by using it with others for real purposes. The conception of LAEs would allow educators to serve Carlos and Ela while accounting for all of the language communities they participate in. Of course, Miles, Rochelle, and their U.S.-born Latino/a and Pacific Islander peers could also benefit from a broadened dialogue about American Englishes. Although their journeys to DAE proficiency are very different from those of recent immigrant students who are learning DAE and AAL as newcomers, it remains crucial to consider the negotiations of U.S.-born students with American Englishes as well.

To take these educational implications beyond my focus in this chapter on AAL and DAE, we must also consider what it would mean to support African American and Pacific Islander students in learning the Spanish language they desired and, in small ways, shared. Additionally, it is true that many Pacific Islander young people in South Vista were also losing proficiency in Pacific Islander languages as they sought to meet the DAE demands of school and the AAL demands of popular youth cultures. Indeed schools must continue to play a key role in language sharing, language maintenance, and broadened notions of the dynamic and varied ways race and ethnicity are enacted and will be enacted. Current scholarship has shown us that with U.S. demographic shifts toward a majority multilingual, multicultural society of people of color embedded in an ever more globalized world, cultural and linguistic flexibility in multiple languages and varieties of language are increasingly needed for access to power in society (Alim and Paris, 2015; Alim and Smitherman 2012). Schools must join these demographic, linguistic, and social changes to equip students of all backgrounds with the abilities to navigate a multilingual present and future.

Unfortunately, U.S. schools by and large remain driven by monolingual and monocultural ("Standard") English policies and practices that fly in the face of changing demographics and the social, linguistic, and cultural changes they engender. To offer teachers and researchers a way to support the linguistic and cultural pluralism needed in contemporary society and enacted by young people like those is South Vista, I have offered the term, stance, and practice of *culturally sustaining pedagogy* (Paris 2012; Paris and Alim 2014; Paris and Alim 2017). Building from many decades of crucial asset pedagogy work, which repositioned the languages, literacies, and cultures of youth of color as an asset rather than a deficit to classroom learning (e.g., Ladson-Billings 1994; Lee 2007), culturally sustaining pedagogy seeks to perpetuate and foster—*to sustain*—linguistic and cultural pluralism as part of the democratic project of schooling and as a needed response to demographic and social change.

While students like Carlos and Miles know firsthand that their cities and schools are changing, school curricula and general societal perspectives are slow to embrace the evolving ethnic, linguistic, and cultural landscapes of the United States. One important step in embracing, utilizing, and sustaining the extraordinary linguistic and cultural plurality of urban America is for schools to take up the rich and complex ways language is used across the shifting cultural geography of the nation. Toward that end, culturally sustaining pedagogy joins the long tradition of research and practice in the asset pedagogy tradition to support the equality of all people and languages through public schooling. As I have detailed in this chapter, a major player in this shifting cultural and linguistic geography is AAL as it is employed across ethnic borders and social spaces in urban communities. "It was a Black city," said Carlos. "There's a lot of Hispanic people moving in," said Miles. This is the new urban California—in many ways this is the new urban United States. And understanding and sustaining the ways African American Language is learned and shared in this new urban United States will continue to be a vital factor in the futures of our cities and schools and the lives of young people.[3]

Notes

1. All names of people and places from the research are pseudonyms.
2. *Language socialization* refers to the process of learning a language and the expected ways of thinking and acting in a culture through prolonged participation in social interactions in that language.
3. My thanks to the youth represented in this chapter, to the editors of this volume H. Samy Alim, John Rickford, and Arnetha Ball, and also to Mary Bucholtz for her comments on an earlier version of this chapter.

References

Alim, H. S. 2007. "The Whig Party don't exist in my hood": Knowledge, reality, and education in the Hip Hop Nation. In H. S. Alim and J. Baugh (Eds.), *Talkin Black Talk: Language, Education, and Social Change*, 15–29. New York: Teachers College Press.

Alim, H. S., and D. Paris. 2015. "Whose Language Gap?: Critical and Culturally Sustaining Pedagogies as Necessary Challenges to Racializing Hegemony." *Journal of Linguistic Anthropology*, 25(1), Invited forum, "Bridging 'the Language Gap'", pp. 66–86.

Alim, H. S., and G. Smitherman, G. 2012. *Articulate while Black: Barack Obama, Language, and Race in the U.S.* New York: Oxford University Press.

Hill, M. L. 2009. *Beats, Rhymes and Classroom Life: Hip-Hop Pedagogy and the Politics of Identity.* New York: Teachers College Press.

Ibrahim, A. 2003. "Whassup homeboy?" Joining the African diaspora: Black English as a symbolic site of identification and language learning. In S. Makoni, G. Smitherman and A. Spears (Eds.), *Black Linguistics: Language, Society, and Politics in Africa and the Americas.* London: Routledge, pp. 169–85.

Ladson-Billings, G. 1994. *The Dreamkeepers: Successful Teachers of African American Children.* San Francisco: Jossey-Bass.

Lee, C. D. 2007. *Culture, Literacy, and Learning: Taking Bloom in the Midst of the Whirlwind.* New York: Teachers College Press.

Paris, D. 2012. Culturally sustaining pedagogy: A needed change in stance, terminology, and practice. *Educational Researcher* 41(3): 93–97.

Paris, D. 2011. *Language across Difference: Ethnicity, Communication, and Youth Identities in Changing Urban Schools.* Cambridge, UK: Cambridge University Press.

Paris, D., and H. S. Alim. 2014. What are we seeking to sustain through culturally sustaining pedagogy?: A loving critique forward. *Harvard Educational Review* 84(1): 85–100.

Paris, D., and H. S. Alim, eds. 2017. *Culturally Sustaining Pedagogies.* New York: Teachers College Press.

Rickford, J., J. Sweetland, A. Rickford, and T. Grano. 2013. *African American, Creole, and Other Vernacular Englishes in Education: A Bibliographic Resource.* New York: Routledge.

Rickford, J., and R. Rickford. 2000. *Spoken Soul: The Story of Black English.* New York: John Wiley and Sons.

Smitherman, G. 1977. *Talkin and Testifyin.* Detroit: Wayne State University Press.

14

Zapotec, Mixtec, and Purepecha Youth

Multilingualism and the Marginalization of Indigenous
Immigrants in the United States

WILLIAM PEREZ, RAFAEL VASQUEZ, AND RAYMOND BURIEL

In recent decades, the number of Mexican immigrants who identify as both "Hispanic" and "Native American" according to U.S. Census categories has increased, marked most significantly by an influx of indigenous immigrants from southern Mexico and Guatemala (Huizar, Murillo, and Cerda 2004). Starting in 2000, researchers began to identify these indigenous immigrants who had previously been absent from processes of international immigration to the United States. Currently, Mixtec, Nahuas, Purepechas, Triques, and Otomi communities are among the largest indigenous groups migrating to the United States (Rivera-Salgado 2005). Overall, it is estimated that at least one million indigenous immigrants have settled throughout the United States (Holmes 2006). Figure 14.1 shows that Latino indigenous immigrants can be found in all but a handful of states, with the largest concentrations residing in Arizona, California, Colorado, Illinois, New York, and Texas. Indigenous Latinos in California numbered around 200,000 in 2010 (Fox 2013). Table 14.1 indicates that indigenous Latinos in California are dispersed around the state across twenty different counties. Although the largest concentration is found in Los Angeles County, numbering almost 54,000 in 2010, other counties experienced significant population increases between 2000 and 2010, including Monterey County (70% increase) and Kern County (65% increase).

As their numbers, long-term settlement, and geographic concentration increase, indigenous immigrants, particularly Mixtecs and Zapotecs, have begun to establish transnational communities by recreating elements of their hometowns in the United States (Besserer 2002; Kearney 2000). This has resulted in the emergence of distinctive forms of social organization and cultural expression, ranging from civic-political organizations such as binational newspapers,

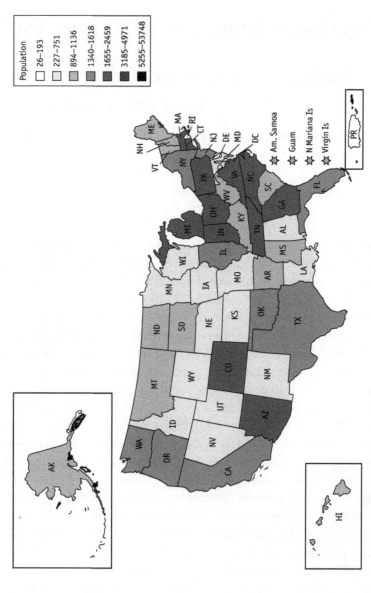

Population
- 26–193
- 227–751
- 894–1136
- 1340–1618
- 1655–2459
- 3185–4971
- 5255–53748

☆ Am. Samoa
☆ Guam
☆ N Mariana Is
☆ Virgin Is

Figure 14.1 Distribution of Latino indigenous immigrants in the U.S. in 2010.

Table 14.1 Latinos of Indigenous Origin, Top 20 California Counties

	2000	*2010*	*Growth 2000–2010*
California	154,362	200,551	29.9%
1. Los Angeles County	51,379	53,942	5%
2. Orange County	11,492	11,916	3.6%
3. San Bernardino County	10,111	14,166	40.1%
4. San Diego County	9,084	12,242	34.7%
5. Riverside County	8,033	12,779	59%
6. Fresno County	6,567	9,670	47.3%
7. Santa Clara County	6,080	8,918	46.7%
8. Sacramento County	4,289	6,433	50.0%
9. Kern County	4,114	6,783	64.9%
10. Ventura County	3,929	5,679	44.5%
11. Alameda County	3,840	5,610	46%
12. San Joaquin County	2,846	4,017	41.1%
13. Tulare County	2,726	3,670	34.6%
14. Santa Barbara County	2,649	3,642	37.5%
15. Monterey County	2,420	4,103	69.5%
16. Stanislaus County	2,193	3,032	38.3%
17. Contra Costa County	2,182	3,138	43.8%
18. Sonoma County	1,912	2,905	51.9%
19. San Mateo County	1,594	2,184	37.0%
20. Madera County	1,518	2,346	55%

Source: U.S. Census Bureau, Census 2000 Summary File 1; Census 2010 Summary File 1.

indigenous radio programs, and indigenous language translation and preservation as well as public celebration of religious holidays, Catholic Mass celebrations of patron saints from hometowns of origin, and traditional Oaxacan music and dance festivals such as the Guelaguetza (Rivera-Salgado 2005). Currently, at least sixteen Guelaguetzas are celebrated annually throughout the United States—mainly in California cities such as Los Angeles, San Diego, Fresno, Oxnard, San Jose, Bakersfield, San Marcos, Santa Rosa, Santa Maria, and Santa Cruz, but also increasingly in cities in other states such as Seattle, Washington, Poughkeepsie, New York, Salem, Oregon, Odessa, Texas, and Atlantic City, New Jersey (Fox 2013). These large-scale public cultural events serve as an indicator of the broad geographic distribution of indigenous communities in the United States.

Despite their Mexican origins, indigenous immigrants possess numerous characteristics that set them apart from their nonindigenous counterparts. They speak one or more of the sixty-eight identified indigenous languages spoken in Mexico, most of which do not have written forms. Many speak little or no Spanish, have low levels of literacy and education, and are often poorer than their nonindigenous counterparts (Poole 2004). For example, Figure 14.2 shows that the poverty rate for Mexican immigrants is almost three times as high as that for Whites (29% vs. 11%) but among indigenous Mexicans, 9 in 10 live in poverty. Significant barriers also include fears associated with immigration status, limited professional interpretation services, and limited access to transportation, particularly in more rural and isolated communities (Mines, Nichols, and Runsten 2010). Since they have also faced centuries of social and political marginalization in Mexico, the racial hierarchy that permeates Mexico and allocates indigenous peoples to the lowest levels of the racial stratification system is reproduced within communities of Mexican immigrants in the United States, and is further overlaid with U.S.-based racial categories (Stephen 2007).

The findings presented here are based on a two-year study of the educational and linguistic experiences of Zapotec, Mixtec, and Purepecha high school students. These youths reside in three different communities in Southern California where large numbers of indigenous Mexican immigrants have settled: Coachella, Oxnard, and Los Angeles. In the course of collecting survey and interview data from 150 participants, we also conducted field observations and informal interviews with teachers and members of indigenous community-based and student organizations to gather multiple perspectives and develop a deeper understanding of the numerous challenges faced by indigenous youth. Despite the fact that

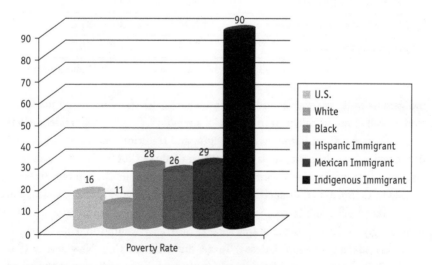

Figure 14.2 High poverty rates of indigenous immigrants.

indigenous youth are a significant and growing population in school districts across the United States, they remain virtually invisible because most school administrators straightforwardly consider them "Mexican" or "Hispanic" and often incorrectly classify them as Spanish heritage speakers. For example, we heard numerous stories like the following account of a Mixtec young man about his experience when he first enrolled in a U.S. school:

> When they talked to me I didn't respond because even though I understood a little Spanish I couldn't speak it. When I didn't respond they thought I was mute and that I didn't know anything. Eventually they realized I didn't speak Spanish when they asked me and I said, "No, only Mixteco." Then they asked, "Mixteco, what is that?" I didn't know what to say.

The rich linguistic experiences of indigenous immigrant youth are often complicated by an ignorance and discrimination that constructs their emerging trilingualism as a deficit rather than an asset.

Raciolinguistic Discrimination

In the United States, indigenous youth continue to experience the historically oppressive rhetoric of Mexico's ethnic and racial classifications. Anti-indigenous beliefs, sentiments, and old prejudices migrate to the United States along with immigrants. Within the broader Mexican immigrant community, nonindigenous Mexicans hold stereotypes that construct indigenous Mexicans as stubborn, lazy, backward, primitive, and intellectually inferior. Because of the colorism that permeates all sectors of Mexican society, indigenous youth are often marginalized due to their "darker" skin color and "*indio*" features (Barrillas-Chón 2010; Gálvez-Hard 2006). Many end up feeling ashamed, develop a "secret" identity, and even stop speaking their native language, choosing only to speak Spanish and English to disassociate with being indigenous and escape teasing and discrimination (Kovats 2010). As one Purepecha young man expressed, "Sometimes I feel embarrassed talking in front of the class in my own language with my friends because they start calling us names or curse at us. When they do that I'd rather just not talk or tell them I'm from another place." Rather than identify as indigenous, many youth use the more general term of "Mexican" as a way to disguise their indigenous background (Stephen 2007).

In fact, indigenous Mexican immigrant youth face complex forms of racism, classism, and xenophobia. They are often treated as "illegals" in an increasingly hostile American political and legal climate, as "Mexicans" or "Latinos" by those who don't know enough to distinguish their indigenous background, and as "inferior" by nonindigenous Mexicans because of their cultural, linguistic, and geographic roots as indigenous peoples. For indigenous youth, all these influences result in gradual language loss that produces new forms of alienation—this time, by other indigenous Mexicans. Many indigenous youth feel acute embarrassment over limited indigenous-language competencies (Lee 2013). Such insecurities lead to a preference to speak Spanish or English and influence whether youth use their existing indigenous language competencies with others. As one young woman whose primary language was *mixteco* as a child relayed to us, "Before I did not know Spanish just *mixteco* and now I forgot the *mixteco* . . . that's the bad thing . . . I do understand it but I cannot speak it. I tried speaking it but then they made fun of me so I said, 'I am no longer going to speak it again!'" Her attitude is similar to that of Navajo youth in previous studies who expressed frustration and chose not to speak their language if they felt scolded or teased by their relatives or peers for mispronunciation or grammatical errors (Lee 2007). The youth in our study often experienced multiple, and multidirectional, forms for discrimination—stigmatized by broader society and nonindigenous Mexicans for speaking their indigenous language in public, while at the same time, stigmatized by indigenous adults for not speaking it properly. When youth feel embarrassed about their mixed language practices, they are likely to shift further toward dominant languages (Garcia 2009).

As a result of widespread social marginalization in both the United States and Mexico due to language, some indigenous parents decide not to pass their language on to their children, hoping this will decrease their experiences of racism and linguistic discrimination (Pérez Báez 2013; Perry 2009). Their reasoning seems to be that the further removed one is from indigeneity, the more economic and professional opportunities one has (Menchaca Bishop and Kelley, 2013). As one young Mixteca woman in our study explained:

> As a child my grandmother was taught that *mixteco* was lower [less valued] than Spanish and that we had to learn Spanish and not *mixteco*. So that's why my grandma and my mom only spoke Spanish to us. When my grandma and my mother went out to large cities, they only knew *mixteco* and could not speak Spanish. That is a reason why they thought that *mixteco* is not something good to speak, because they thought it meant less opportunities.

Linguistic assimilation for the sake of economic prosperity does not emerge in the United States, but rather, has roots in Latin America. According to Messing (2013), Spanish-speakers in Mexico and Latin America tap into the hegemonic discourse of *salir adelante* (to forge ahead and create a better socioeconomic future). She posits that *salir adelante* is a broadly circulating metadiscourse of modernity that is used in indigenous and nonindigenous settings to justify linguistic assimilation and/or denigration of indigenous languages when people talk about creating a better economic and professional future for their families.

Despite accounts of indigenous language loss and consistent marginalization, we found great variability in indigenous language proficiency. Some youth receive various forms of support and encouragement from parents and other family members. A young Zapotec woman proudly shared:

> We have some family who ... try not to speak *zapoteco* in public. My mom says, "No, that's what we speak." On the bus we're always being asked, "Oh that's not Spanish, what language is that you're speaking?" We tell them we speak *zapoteco*. ... My mom tells me "Don't be ashamed of who you are."

The young woman's remarks echo recent studies that suggest some Mexican indigenous immigrant parents in the United States use fluid multicultural identities as camouflage to protect themselves from marginalization, xenophobia, and anti-indigenous sentiments as well as to preserve indigenous language and culture (Machado-Casas 2006; Sanchez 2007). Machado-Casas (2012) argues that pedagogies of survival are passed on from parents through child-rearing practices. As a Purepecha student described, "Wherever we go he [father] always speaks it [Purepecha], so we could never forget our language and be proud of who we are ... and not be ashamed of it because what other people say and just don't listen to them." These narratives of linguistic pride and empowerment notwithstanding, indigenous parents face a variety of challenges becoming involved in their children's education. They may only speak their indigenous language, with little facility in English and Spanish, and schools do not provide Spanish or indigenous language interpreters consistently or at all. Ironically, mainstream American society's general English monolingualism, combined with their parents' monolingualism and their Mexican peers' bilingualism (English-Spanish), has created a generation of indigenous youth who function as trilingual language brokers. Despite widespread linguistic stigmatization, indigenous youth—supported by their parents and peers—have learned to navigate social life in the United States through an impressive display of language learning that is not often recognized by the school system.

Multilingual Abilities and Linguistic Assets

Since children of immigrants are usually the first members of their families to learn English and acquire knowledge of U.S. culture, they are often called upon to translate, interpret, and mediate linguistic and cultural information for their parents and other non-English-speaking members of their communities in a process called "language brokering" (Buriel et al. 1998). Language brokers act as liaisons between the home linguistic/cultural environment and the larger dominant society. As emerging trilinguals, indigenous youth engage in language brokering across three different languages as described by a young Zapotec woman in our study:

> I've translated a lot for my mom, like the forms she gets, mail, my dad's insurance forms ... when I translate for them it's usually from English to *zapoteco*. For my cousin who arrived from Oaxaca, I took her to get enrolled in high school and I just explained the whole process in *zapoteco*. ... At my little brothers' open house and back to school nights the teachers present in either Spanish or English and I just tell my mom what they said in *zapoteco*.

As this chapter is the first scholarly account of language brokering among indigenous immigrant youth, we are just beginning to understand the complex process of how trilingual indigenous youth codeswitch between and translate multiple languages on a daily basis. Among indigenous youth in our study that spoke an indigenous language, 92 percent indicated that they translated for their parents in English and Spanish and 73 percent reported translating between English and their indigenous language (Zapotec, Mixtec, or Purepecha). Indigenous youth raised in bi-/multilingual households and environments develop complex communicative repertoires that include linguistic expertise (receptive, spoken, written) in diverse varieties of one or more indigenous languages, English, and Spanish (McCarty et al. 2009).

They are able to draw upon multiple semiotic systems for different purposes in specific contexts. For example, a Zapotec young woman explained how she can translate most things from English to Spanish but some things she can only translate from English to Zapotec: "In school sometimes when the teacher talks to a person in English, and I don't know how to say it in Spanish, I usually say it in *zapoteco* to my friend that knows [*zapoteco*]. ... Sometimes I just don't know how to explain it in Spanish but I do know how to explain it in *zapoteco*." Ruiz and Barajas (2012) found that relative to other English learners, Mixtec students seemed to acquire English faster. The observed differences may be related to higher linguistic aptitude on the part of the trilingual indigenous students, which is certainly plausible given the exposure to multiple and disparate languages (e.g., Mixtec is a tonal language while Spanish is not), or from the immense pressure to learn English rapidly, stemming from severe discrimination. Valdez (2003) argues that like other children who demonstrate above-average mental talent, children who language broker should be considered "gifted" due to their extraordinary use of languages and interpersonal skills in sometimes challenging situations.

Despite the impressive linguistic sophistication of trilingual language brokers, many educators working with indigenous multilingual children see indigenous languages as an impediment. Since youth are the objects of regulation and development in school, and are symbols of the future and of what is at stake in contests over cultural identity, it is important to study how their school context affects them and how young people themselves experience, understand, resist, or challenge the cultural politics that inform their daily lives (Stephens 1995). According to Skutnabb-Kangas (2000), educational systems maintain and reproduce unequal power relations by using deficiency-based models that invalidate the linguistic and cultural heritage of minority children and their parents. Multilingual indigenous students entering U.S. public schools are typically characterized as being "Limited English Proficient." This labeling elevates the value of the English language while rendering the student's home language invisible, positioning the latter as an impediment to academic and intellectual proficiency. Skutnabb-Kangas (2000) adds that this type of rhetoric seeks to veil the dominant group's efforts to subjugate minority groups by framing these efforts as "helping" them. In the case of indigenous students, a recent study reported that a parent was scolded by a teacher who insisted that her child was doing poorly because of the use of the indigenous language and that if she did not want to be the reason for his academic failure, she needed to stop using the indigenous language with her child (Machado-Casas and Flores 2011). Another study included the following comment by a teacher about an indigenous Mexican mother: "That lady is not teaching her kids anything; she is only confusing them and making our lives more difficult. . . . He will be confused by all those phrases that she calls languages" (Machado-Casas 2009, 205).

Not surprisingly, the term *dialecto* continues to be widely used to refer to indigenous languages—both in Mexico and in the United States—with the implication that they are not legitimate languages. Some indigenous people themselves, including many youth in our study, use the term *dialecto* to refer to their own languages, rather than the term *lengua* (language) used by indigenous language activists (Call 2011). In this context, it is not surprising that while some parents may continue to promote indigenous linguistic pride, others become concerned that promoting trilingualism will pose an undue burden on their children.

Indigenous Language and Ethnic Identity

Indigenous immigrant youth who attend schools that socially integrate different types of Latino students and explicitly promote cultural pride seem to do best in embracing at least some aspects of their indigenous ethnic identity (Stephen 2007). Avenues of cultural expression that explicitly call on indigenous forms of dance, music, art, sports, writing, and language seem to be one of the most successful vehicles for indigenous immigrant youth to achieve some level of civic integration in their schools and communities. One young woman from our research shared, "I'm in a Oaxacan dance group where we learn all the Oaxacan dances. . . . Most of us are Mixtecos from Oaxaca . . . I wanted to learn more about Oaxacan culture and represent it." Such avenues of cultural expression were highlighted in a recent study that described a popular Oaxacan dance troupe called Se'e Savi (Song of the Rain) in Madera, California, which has a multigenerational membership of children, adolescents, and adults (Equipo de Cronistas Oaxaquenos 2013). For the youth, their participation is often a transformative experience that allows them to "come out" publicly as indigenous in the most celebratory, dignified, and supportive way.

When indigenous immigrant youth begin to educate themselves about their cultural roots and push for the integration of indigenous forms of cultural expression in venues defined as "Mexican," they are more likely to feel validated and experience positive interactions based on their indigenous heritage rather than just racial insults (Stephen 2007). In addition to self-education and activism, we learned about various other outlets of cultural expression that encouraged indigenous language maintenance and renewal. A Zapotec young woman described her participation in a high school club that promoted Oaxacan culture:

> A tradition in the club was to have a graduation ceremony where we celebrated all the high school Oaxacans who graduated. . . . During Cesar Chavez day . . . we gave a speech in English, Spanish, and Zapoteco about the oppression of Oaxacan individuals and about how even after many years of oppression we're not going to give up, we're going to fight for what we believe and fight for our rights.

Increasingly, young adults are creating their own terms of engagement with their indigenous communities. For example, a recent study describes the effforts of a group called Autónomos founded by Oaxacan indigenous youth in Fresno, California, to provide a space to reclaim their indigenous identity (Equipo de Cronistas Oaxaquenos 2013). Their inaugural event in 2011 was called *NA'A INTANTOSO YOO NEE IKI'XIO*, which in Mixteco means, "Let's not forget where we come from." The gathering included a first-time performance by a new Oaxacan Hip Hop artist called Bolígrafo, who performed a Mixtec-Spanish-English trilingual song titled "UNA ISU" (Mixteco is a language). Through his lyrics Bolígrafo proclaims his indigenous Mixtec language and trilingualism and encourages indigenous youth to rescue their culture and language in the face of societal pressure to assimilate. Using art and Hip Hop, members of Autónomos aspire to promote a different way of learning and preserving their Oaxacan culture that complicates notions of cultural and linguistic expression. These efforts of linguistic and cultural preservation are similar to those used by other indigenous youth language activists who have taken efforts to include elements that resonate with indigenous youth (Kroupa 2013; Tulloch 2013).

Indigenous language loss complicates indigenous identification for youth (Smith 1995). Many scholars argue that because language is so integral to identity, losing a language can seriously jeopardize a person's sense of self and group membership (Crystal 2000; Garcia 2009). Norton and Toohey (2001) argue that the language choices available to children and their parents, as well as the discursive practices that are encouraged and supported in school, have an important impact on children's identity and their possibilities of developing agency or resisting. When we asked youth in our study if they identified as indigenous during the in-depth interviews, indigenous language proficiency often determined whether they identified or not. For example, a student that did not identify stated, "not really cuz I don't even know the language [Mixteco]," while another stated that he did identify as Mixteco: "Because I speak Mixteco and my family also speaks Mixteco." Despite widespread language shame and ambivalence, we found that many indigenous youth are finding ways, both formal and informal, to maintain fluency in all three languages. As more youth express pride in their indigenous language, they serve as role models for others to claim their indigenous language heritage. Youth are providing models of peer-to-peer language learning that requires our further attention.

Indigenous youth often express their indigenous identity through English or Spanish due to indigenous language loss. In particular, youth in our study whose community of origin in Mexico had already experienced a significant linguistic shift to Spanish were more likely to describe efforts to preserve indigenous culture that did not include language. The following example from a Zapotec student in our study illustrates this point:

> Even though we're in Los Angeles we try to do the best we can to still maintain the culture with the Guelaguetza and the foods. . . . I grew up with my *tíos* [uncles] and *tías* [aunts] and my mom, they still maintain the pride of being Oaxacan, but usually it's Spanish here [in the United States]. They never really had time to teach me the Zapoteco. . . . In Tlacolula almost everyone speaks Spanish. . . . There are some elders who speak Zapoteco but there aren't that many.

Native American poet and author Simon Ortiz expressed a similar sentiment in a public lecture in which he stated, "I may not be fluent in my indigenous language, but I am fluent in my indigenous consciousness" (as cited in Lee 2013, 146). Defining an indigenous identity for youth is not a simple, uncomplicated process as it may encompass multiple levels of cultural access, participation, and knowledge with or even without the indigenous language. Much like Bolígrafo from Autónomos, some youth adopt what Wyman (2013) calls *linguistic survivance*— the use of communicative practices to connect to community knowledge and express indigeneity using multiple languages and symbolic practices—as well as translanguaging, the moving across or intermixing of languages and language varieties (Garcia 2009).

Higher-education institutions and indigenous transnational organizations play an important role in supporting indigenous youth to reclaim their indigenous culture and language. A Zapotec young woman who began college during our study expressed the following regret:

> I didn't know there's a negative aspect to being indigenous or having indigenous roots . . . I had a lot of friends who were from Mexico City, Jalisco, Guerrero, but we were all raised in the U.S., we were just proud of being Mexicans in general . . . I didn't know about the stereotypes until I got to college in my Chicano class.

A recent study found a similar pattern among Zapotec students in California who rejected their indigenous identity due to discrimination, but became politically conscious after taking college courses where they learned about their history and contemporary indigenous issues (Nicolas 2012). In college, these youth appropriated their "dark skin" and "short height" as a proud symbol of their Oaxacan indigeneity. In another study, Mixtec youth also report embracing an indigenous identity and relearning the Mixtec language after taking college courses that discussed Mexican indigenous cultures and languages (Kovats 2010). After rediscovering her indigenous roots in college, the young woman from our study has become dedicated to cultural preservation efforts. "I'm proud of being a oaxaqueña . . . I know we have so much culture, from the way we dress to the way we speak to the way we live. It still has strong indigenous roots." Unlike the subtractive schooling practices during K–12, the cultural aspects that set indigenous youth apart from their nonindigenous peers was affirmed and valued by college professors and classmates, which led to positive self-identification. This shift in perspectives is promising because it illustrates that cultural change is not always unidirectional (Messing 2013). Ambivalence is at the center of youth language ideologies, which can change over time. Further attention needs to be paid to youth's language socialization practices and the role of shifting individual language ideologies in this process. If ideological orientations can change over time, then young adults may reactivate their passive linguistic knowledge (Messing 2013).

Conclusion

While students of Mexican origin face similar cultural, linguistic, and structural challenges in U.S. schools, the Mexican-origin population is multiethnic and multilingual. Schools and policymakers often fail to recognize the significant diversity within this population that has increased over the past two decades as a result of the growth of indigenous immigrants. When indigenous Mexican students enter public schools, educators are not aware of their indigenous backgrounds or that they are emerging trilinguals who may speak one of many pre-Columbian languages (Galvez-Hard 2006). Outside the classroom, indigenous youth endure discrimination from both their U.S.-born and Mexican nonindigenous peers. Due to a legacy of linguistic discrimination, indigenous youth often cloak or uncloak language competencies as they engage with, contest, and co-construct language ideologies and language learning opportunities (Mendoza-Denton 2008). Indigenous families must often negotiate tensions related to heritage language loss in order maintain unique funds of knowledge and foster strong intergenerational relationships (Gonzalez et al. 2005).

Despite ambivalence about their indigenous language and culture, youth are shaping language practices that are much more dynamic than those of adults while maintaining claims to indigeneity (McCarty and Wyman 2009). Through innovative practices and the creation of new physical and virtual spaces for indigenous languages that contain cultural traditions and ceremonies, they have been able to develop an emotional commitment to indigenous ideals (Kroupa 2013). Furthermore, youths' ease with technology and pop culture gives them greater flexibility in ways of using language. Language practices in the twenty-first century are increasingly multimodal, and linguistic modes of meaning are intricately bound up with other visual, audio, gestural, and spatial semiotic systems (Kress 2003). This integrated discourse is also reflected in indigenous youth linguistic practices, as meaning and semiotic systems of both the majority and minority cultures and languages become integrated. However, as McCarty and Wyman (2009) warn, youth require a larger nexus of authorizing agents to nurture their possibilities, and cannot be expected to act alone.

Recent studies suggest some progress in school efforts to support indigenous students. Individual educators are taking it upon themselves to learn the history, culture, and specific challenges that their indigenous students face in school and to make appropriate pedagogical adaptations (Velasco 2010). Instead of framing students' linguistic assets as deficits, some teachers encourage indigenous Mexican parents to use their languages with their children, invite them to indigenous-focused events, and provide them with children's books in indigenous languages (Menchaca Bishop and Kelley 2013). Some teachers have traveled to Mexico to gather information about their indigenous students' language and culture and incorporated their findings to create lessons based on the students' prior knowledge and cultural and linguistic references, resulting in higher levels of school engagement (Pick et al. 2011; Swanson, Ballash, and Cost 2006). One school used videotaped interviews of indigenous families to learn about their experiences and histories in more detail. In doing so, they identified their students' educational needs and secured resources to support indigenous language and cultural preservation for both students and parents (Galvez-Hard 2006). Another school formed partnerships with indigenous-led community-based organizations to include parents in their children's education (Flynn 2005). Large-scale efforts like these could make a significant positive impact both socially and academically on students of immigrant indigenous backgrounds. In addition, indigenous youth multilingualism might serve as a model for monolingual American students and help encourage a linguistic pluralism to counter backward-looking "English Only" ideologies.

The school is a cultural institution that can support, ignore, or denigrate its students' heritages and sociocultural backgrounds (Lee 2013). Teachers of Mexican indigenous students face a great challenge. Even bilingual teachers who speak Spanish are often not familiar with the funds of knowledge and languages of indigenous Latino immigrants (Gonzalez et al. 2005; Machado-Casas 2009). Based on our research findings, we suggest that schools need to consider how the lives of indigenous students have been shaped by their ability to speak multiple languages and take into account the emotional ties they have with each language and how that can be harmed by not including any of those languages in the formal school setting. Schools should also directly address discriminatory practices toward indigenous students and provide instructional information about the histories of indigenous groups in Mexico (Barillas-Chon 2010).

More broadly, these issues need to be addressed in school curricula, teacher education programs, and ongoing teacher trainings within school districts. Being knowledgeable about students' cultural and linguistic backgrounds could allow a teacher to recognize and prevent the type of teasing endured by many indigenous students. Ability to foster academic success can be enhanced by awareness of the needs and challenges of parents who speak indigenous languages, such as the desire to transmit the indigenous language and culture to their children. As the indigenous immigrant population from Latin America continues to grow and increase our cultural and linguistic diversity, we will need more research to understand how and why indigenous languages spoken by immigrant populations continue to be stigmatized and the possible implications for indigenous heritage maintenance and positive development for indigenous youth.

References

Barillas-Chón, D. W. 2010. Oaxaqueño/a students' (un)welcoming high school experiences. *Journal of Latinos and Education* 9(4): 303–20.

Besserer, F. 2002. Politica cuantica: el uso de la radio por comunidades transnacionales. *Nueva Antopología* 25(57): 11–21.

Buriel, R., W. Perez, T. L. DeMent, D. V. Chavez, and V. R. Moran. 1998. The relationship of language brokering to academic performance, biculturalism, and self-efficacy among Latino adolescents. *Hispanic Journal of Behavioral Sciences* 20: 283–96.

Call, W. 2011. *No Word for Welcome: The Mexican Village Faces the Global Economy.* Lincoln: University of Nebraska Press.

Crystal, David. 2000. *Language Death.* Cambridge: Cambridge University Press.

Equipo de Cronistas Oaxaquenos (ECO), ed. 2013. *Voices of Indigenous Oaxacan Youth in the Central Valley: Creating our Sense of Belonging in the California.* Santa Cruz, CA: Center for Collaborative Research for an Equitable California.

Flynn, E. 2005. "Accessing opportunity? A study of Oaxacan civic participation and parental involvement in education in Central California." Unpublished monograph, School of Education, Stanford University, Palo Alto, CA.

Fox, J. 2013. Introduction: Indigenous Oaxacan Immigrants and Youth-led Organizing in California. In Equipo de Cronistas Oaxaquenos, ed., *Voices of Indigenous Oaxacan Youth in the Central Valley: Creating our Sense of Belonging in the California,* 8–26. Santa Cruz, CA: Center for Collaborative Research for an Equitable California.

Gálvez-Hard, E. 2006. "Building positive identity for Mexican indigenous students in California schools: A participatory research study." Doctoral dissertation. Retrieved from ProQuest Dissertations and Theses database. (UMI No. 3238245).

Garcia, O. 2009. *Bilingual Education in the 21st Century: A Global Perspective.* Malden, MA: Wiley-Blackwell.

Gonzalez, N., L. C. Moll, and C. Amanti, eds. 2005. *Funds of Knowledge: Theorizing Practices in Households, Communities, and Classrooms.* Mahwah, NJ: Erlbaum.

Huizar Murillo, J., and I. Cerda. 2004. Indigenous Mexican migrants in the 2000 U.S. Census: "Hispanic American Indians." In J. Fox and G. Rivera-Salgado, eds., *Indigenous Mexican Migrants in the United States,* 311–33. La Jolla: University of California, San Diego.

Holmes, S. M. 2006. An ethnographic study of the social context of migrant health in the United States. *PLoS Medicine* 3(10): 1776–93.

Kearney, M. 2000. Transnational Oaxacan indigenous identity: The case of Mixtecs and Zapotecs. *Identities* 7(2): 173–95.

Kovats, A. G. 2010. "Invisible Students and Marginalized Identities: The Articulation of Identity among Mixteco Youth in San Diego, California." San Diego State University, Latin American Studies, Masters' thesis.

Kress, G. 2003. *Literacy in the New Media Age.* London and New York: Routledge.

Kroupa, K. T. 2013. Efforts of the Ree-volution: Revitalizing Arikara Language in an Endangered Language Context. In L. T. Wyman, T. L. McMarty, and S. E. Nicholas, eds., *Indigenous Youth and Multilingualism: Language Identity, Ideology, and Dynamic Cultural Worlds,* 168–86. New York: Routledge.

Lee, T. S. 2007. "If they want Navajo to be learned, then they should require it in all schools"—Navajo teenagers' experiences, choices, and demands regarding Navajo language. *Wicazo Sa Review* (Spring): 7–33.

Lee, T. S. 2013. Critical Language Awareness among Native Youth in New Mexico. In L. T. Wyman, T. L. McMarty, and S. E. Nicholas, eds., *Indigenous Youth and Multilingualism: Language Identity, Ideology, and Dynamic Cultural Worlds,* 130–48. New York: Routledge.

Machado-Casas, M. 2006. "Narrating Education of New Indigenous/Latino Transnational Communities in the South." Unpublished dissertation, University of North Carolina at Chapel Hill.

Machado-Casas, M. 2009. The politics of organic phylogeny: The art of parenting and surviving as transnational multilingual Latino indigenous immigrants in the U.S. *High School Journal* 92(4): 82–99.

Machado-Casas, M. 2012. Pedagogías del camaleón/Pedagogies of the chameleon: Identity and strategies of survival for transnational indigenous Latino immigrants in the US South. *Urban Review* 44(5): 534–50.

Machado-Casas, M., B. Flores. 2011. Trabajando y Comunicando con Nuestras Comunidades Indigenas Inmigrantes. In Bustos Flores, B., Hernandez Sheets, R., Riojas Clark, E. (Eds.). *Teacher Preparation for Bilingual Student Populations: Educar para Transformar* (pp. 205–216). New York, NY: Routledge.

McCarty, T. L., M. E. Romero-Little, L. Warhol, and O. Zepeda. 2009. Indigenous youth as language policy makers. *Journal of Language, Identity, and Education* 8(5): 291–306.

McCarty, T. L., and L. T. Wyman. 2009. Indigenous youth and bilingualism—Theory, research, praxis. *Journal of Language, Identity, and Education* 8(5): 291–306.

Menchaca Bishop, L., and P. Kelley. 2013. Indigenous Mexican Languages and the Politics of Language Shift in the United States. *Language Issues in Contemporary Education* 1(1): 97–113.

Mendoza-Denton, N. 2008. *Homegirls: Language and Cultural Practice among Latina Youth*. Malden, MA: Blackwell.

Messing, J. 2013. "I Didn't Know You Knew Mexicano!": Shifting Ideologies, Identities, and Ambivalence among Former Youth in Tlaxcala, Mexico. In L. T. Wyman, T. L. McMarty, and S. E. Nicholas, eds., *Indigenous Youth and Multilingualism: Language Identity, Ideology, and Dynamic Cultural Worlds*, 111–29. New York,: Routledge.

Mines, R., S. Nichols, and D. Runsten. 2010. California's indigenous farmworkers (Final Report of the IFS). Retrieved from Indigenous Farmworker Study website: http://indigenous-farmworkers.org/IFS%20Full%20Report%20_Jan2010.pdf. Last accessed: June 8, 2016.

Nicolás, B. 2012. "Reclamando lo que es nuestro: Identity Formation among Zapoteco Youth in Oaxaca and Los Angeles." University of California, San Diego, Master's thesis.

Norton, B., and K. Toohey. 2001. Changing perspectives on good language learners. *TESOL Quarterly* 35(2): 307–22.

Pérez Báez, G. 2013. Family Language Policy, Transnationalism, and the Diaspora Community of San Lucas Quiavini of Oaxaca, Mexico. *Language Policy* 12(1): 27–45.

Perry, E. 2009. *The Declining Use of the Mixtec Language among Oaxacan Migrants and Stay-at-Homes: The Persistence of Memory, Discrimination, and Social Hierarchies of Power*. Working Paper No. 180, Center for Comparative Immigration Studies, University of California, San Diego.

Pick, H., W. Wolfram, and J. López. 2011. Indigenous language students from Spanish-speaking countries: Educational approaches. Heritage Briefs Collection. Washington, DC: Center for Applied Linguistics.

Poole, S. 2004. *The changing face of Mexican migrants in California: Oaxacan Mixtecs and Zapotecs in perspective* (TBI Border Brief). Retrieved from University of San Diego, Trans Border Institute website: http://catcher.sandiego.edu/items/peacestudies/Brief_Poole.pdf. Last accessed June 8, 2016.

Rivera-Salgado, G. 2005. "Equal in dignity and rights: The struggle of indigenous peoples of the Americas in an age of migration." Inaugural address, Prince Claus Chair in Development and Equity, University of Utrecht, Netherlands.

Ruiz, N. T., and M. Barajas. 2012. "Multiple Perspectives on the Schooling of Mexican Indigenous Students in the United States." Paper presented at the American Educational Research Association Conference, Vancouver.

Sánchez, P. 2007. Cultural authenticity and transnational Latina youth: Constructing a meta-narrative across borders. *Linguistics and Education* 18(3–4): 258–82.

Skutnabb-Kangas, T. 2000. *Linguistic Genocide in Education—Or Worldwide Diversity and Human Rights?* Mahwah, NJ: Erlbaum.

Smith, N. J. 1995. Linguistic genocide and the struggle for cultural and linguistic survival: A participatory research study with a Zapotec community in California (Doctoral dissertation). Retrieved from ProQuest Dissertations and Theses database. (UMI No. 9611509).

Stephen, L. 2007. *Transborder Lives: Indigenous Oaxacans in Mexico, California, and Oregon.* Durham: Duke University Press.

Stephens, S. 1995. Introduction: Children and the Politics of Culture in "Late Capitalism." In S. Stephens, ed., *Children and the Politics of Culture*, 3–48. Princeton: Princeton University Press.

Swanson, B., K. Ballash, and M. Kost. 2006. No culture left behind: Reaching the Purepecha indigenous people. *ORTESOL Journal* 11(1): 1–14.

Tulloch, S. R. 2013. Igniting a Youth Language Movement: Inuit Youth as Agents of Circumpolar Language Planning. In L. T. Wyman, T. L. McMarty, and S. E. Nicholas, eds., *Indigenous Youth and Multilingualism: Language Identity, Ideology, and Dynamic Cultural Worlds*, 149–67. New York: Routledge.

Valdez, G. 2003. *Expanding the Definition of Giftedness: The Case of Young Interpreters from Immigrant Communities.* Mahwah, NJ: Lawrence Erlbaum.

Velasco, P. 2010. Indigenous students in bilingual Spanish-English classrooms in New York: A teacher's mediation strategies. *International Journal of the Sociology of Language* 206: 255–71.

Wyman, L. T. 2013. Youth Linguistic Survivance in Transforming Settings: A Yup'ik Example. In L.T. Wyman, T. L. McMarty, and S. E. Nicholas, eds., *Indigenous Youth and Multilingualism: Language Identity, Ideology, and Dynamic Cultural Worlds*, 90–110. New York: Routledge.

15

On Being Called Out of One's Name

Indexical Bleaching as a Technique of Deracialization

MARY BUCHOLTZ

In a skit from the Comedy Central show *Key and Peele*, Keegan-Michael Key, a comedian of African American and European American heritage, plays Mr. Garvey, a black substitute teacher from the inner city, taking roll in a suburban high school classroom.[1] As Mr. Garvey calls the name of each of the white students in the room, however, it becomes clear that what is at issue is more than a matter of simply taking attendance. After insisting on the pronunciation of *Jacqueline* as [ˌdʒejˈkwɛlə̃n] and *Blake* as [bəˈlɑˌkej], he goes on to a third student:[2]

---

(1) Mr. Garvey: Denise. <[ˈdiˌnajs]>

   Mr. Garvey: Is there a Denise? <[ˈdiˌnajs]>

   Mr. Garvey: <shaking head> If one of y'all, says some *silly-ass* name, this
                whole cla:ss is gon. Feel. My. Wrath. Now. Denise. <[ˈdiˌnajs]>

   Denise: <raises hand slightly> Do you mean Denise? <[dəˈnis]>

   Mr. Garvey: Son of a bitch! <breaks clipboard in two across his knee>

   Mr. Garvey: <points to Denise> You say your name right. Right no:w.

   Denise: Denise?= <[dəˈnis]>

   Mr. Garvey: <rapidly> =Say it right.=

   Denise: =Denise.= <[dəˈnis]>

   Mr. Garvey: =Corr↓ectly.=

   Denise: =Denise.= <[dəˈnis]>

| Mr. Garvey: | =Right.= |
| Denise: | =Denise.= |

               <[dəˈnis]>

Mr. Garvey: =Right.

Denise: <tightens lips, shakes head> Denise. <[ˌdiˈnajs]>

Mr. Garvey: <extends arms> That's better.

<Denise sighs>

Mr. Garvey: Thank you.

<Denise rolls eyes, shakes head>

Mr. Garvey: Now. <looks at paper> Aaron! <[ˌʔejˈʔejˌrãn]>

This skit brilliantly parodies an all-too-common practice in American classrooms: the renaming, denaming, and misnaming of students from linguistically marginalized and ethnoracially minoritized backgrounds. In the skit's neat reversal, it is majority students, those with "simple," "normal," "American" names, who are forced to undergo this process of public shaming and renaming. And although as comedy Key's performance remains safely in the domain of farce rather than tragedy, it calls pointed attention to an experience of identity theft that for many American schoolchildren can be both traumatizing and dehumanizing. Judith Butler calls such politicized uses of language that have the potential to harm others "injurious speech." As she states, "To be injured by speech is to suffer a loss of context, that is, not to know where you are. . . . one can be 'put in one's place' by such speech, but such a place may be no place" (1997, 4). Likewise, loss of context and social displacement are central to the African American expression from which I take my title, *to call someone out of their name*, which means to defame or insult, particularly through name calling (cf. Smitherman 1994, 75).

Scholars of language and culture have long recognized that names involve interwined issues of personhood and power (e.g., Rymes 2001; Vom Bruck and Bodenhorn 2006). Given the power of naming as a performative act of interpellation that renders the bearer culturally recognizable as a social subject (Butler 1997), such research abundantly demonstrates that names are not merely referential forms that pick out specific individuals, as has often been discussed in the philosophy of language. Rather, they are also, and more importantly, indexical forms, with social meanings that are intimately tied to the contexts of their use. Hence a particular name may simultaneously index such sociocultural positionalities as gender, generation, ethnicity, religion, region, class, kinship, and more.

Because indexical meanings are contextual, they are constantly subject to change. Sociocultural linguists have begun to investigate the processes that lead indexical forms to acquire new levels and ranges of social meaning over time (Eckert 2008; Johnstone et al. 2006; Silverstein 2003). However, the converse phenomenon, whereby an index sheds part of its social meaning, is less well understood. Lauren Squires (2012) has proposed the concept of *indexical bleaching*—on analogy with the linguistic concept of semantic bleaching—to characterize this process in the circulation of a media catchphrase. In this chapter, I argue that indexical bleaching may also be used as a technique of deracialization, or the stripping of contextually marked ethnoracial meaning from an indexical form. The deracializing potential of indexical bleaching enables white teenagers to appropriate black youth slang without claiming an affiliation with black youth culture (Bucholtz 2011). And this same technique allows the literal reshaping of ethnoracially marked names—phonologically, orthographically, and even lexically—in ways that reduce their ethnoracial specificity. As the *Key and Peele* parody that opens this chapter demonstrates, the indexical bleaching of a marked name is often imposed by a cultural outsider. At other times, however, renaming may be a more or less agentive choice on the part of the name's bearer; as Butler argues, despite the capacity of language to harm, language is itself vulnerable to challenge and redefinition, so its power is not total.

This chapter examines the interplay of structural power and individual agency as Latina youth in California confront the politics of renaming in their lives. Focusing on the everyday, institutional, and political responses of bilingual Chicana teenagers whose names have been subject to indexical bleaching, the analysis demonstrates the agentive capacity of sociolinguistically subordinated young people to critically reflect on and challenge the hegemonic language ideology that denies them the right to their own names.

"Names That Make Us Strangers to Ourselves"

It is particularly at the borders where ethnoracialized groups come into contact that names become sites of negotiation and struggle over cultural difference, linguistic autonomy, and the right to self-definition. It is perhaps unsurprising, then, that racialized processes of renaming have received a great deal of attention among professionals concerned with teaching English to immigrants and international students, where this issue arises daily (Edwards 2006; Taylor-Mendes 2003). To be sure, individuals may take the opportunity to assert their complex cultural identities by selecting a new and often highly creative or personally meaningful name (Heffernan 2010; Kim 2007; McPherron 2009). But as can be seen in governmental renaming projects around the world, within institutional contexts individuals' names must be "legible" to the state and are therefore subject to its authority (Scott et al. 2002). In the context of U.S. schooling, institutional legibility typically requires that a personal name be recognizable, or at least pronounceable or adaptable to a form more familiar to institutional representatives.

The phenomenon of being positioned by educational institutions as having a "funny name" is so widespread in the United States that it is a common trope in the now-substantial literary genre of immigrant memoirs. Such narratives are replete with accounts of the mispronunciation or displacement of a given name that is "too hard" or "too foreign." For a handful of immigrants, the acceptance of an "Americanized" name may be experienced as an opportunity to seize the American dream: Chicano author Richard Rodriguez, for example, declares in his pro-assimilationist autobiography *Hunger of Memory*, "The social and political advantages I enjoy as a man result from the day that I came to believe that my name, indeed, is *Rich-heard Road-ree-guess*" (1982, 27). Nevertheless, the vast majority of authors recount feelings of personal loss, not gain, associated with the indexical bleaching of their names; as Eva Hoffman, a Jewish immigrant from Poland to Canada, writes, these imposed renamings are "names that make us strangers to ourselves" (1989, 105). For Rodriguez and Hoffman, renaming was largely a matter of anglicization, but more ethnoracially marked names may be subject to extreme linguistic violence in the form of phonological mutilation or wholesale erasure. Thus Iranian American author Firoozeh Dumas (2003, 66–67) recalls being addressed as "Fritzi Dumbass" at the doctor's office as an adult, and as a child being dismissively referred to by a friend's mother as merely "the F-word." Little wonder that Dumas elected to be known as Julie until her college years.

Debates over naming rights have even entered the public sphere, as when President Barack Obama, himself no stranger to the complex racial politics of names, nominated federal judge Sonia Sotomayor to the Supreme Court.[3] In response, conservative commentator Mark Krikorian (2009) asserted that Americans should not be expected to try to pronounce her name correctly, as [sotoma'jor]:

> Deferring to people's own pronunciation of their names should obviously be our first inclination, but there ought to be limits. Putting the emphasis on the final syllable of Sotomayor is unnatural in English. . . . [O]ne of the areas where conformity is appropriate is how your new countrymen say your name, since that's not something the rest of us can just ignore, unlike what church you go to or what you eat for lunch. And there are basically two options—the newcomer adapts to us, or we adapt to him. And multiculturalism means there's a lot more of the latter going on than there should be.

Never mind the fact that Sotomayor is by no means a "newcomer" to the United States, having been born and raised in the Bronx; for observers like Krikorian, the pronunciation of her name marks her as permanently different from "the rest of us" and hence must be replaced with a deracialized version.

Such views, however, have not gone unchallenged. In a 2005 decision, the U.S. Ninth Circuit Court of Appeals ruled in favor of Mamdouh El-Hakem's claim of racial discrimination in the workplace, on the basis of the fact that his employer insisted on calling him "Manny" over his repeated objections. In its ruling, the court noted, "Defendants argue that they could not be held liable for intentionally discriminating on the basis of race . . ., because the name 'Manny' is not a racial epithet. We disagree with Defendants' premise. . . . A group's ethnic characteristics encompass more than its members' skin color and physical traits. Names are often a proxy for race and ethnicity" (*El-Hakem v. BJY, Inc.* 2005).

The exertion of hegemonic power upon one's name is an experience by no means unique to immigrants and their descendants. African Americans and Native Americans were forcibly stripped of their names as part of historical processes of racial subjugation (Benson 2006; Stuckey and Murphy 2001). Under colonialism, both groups were literally christened with European names, and even well into the twentieth century European Americans retained what Maya Angelou calls the "racist habit" (1969, 43) of renaming African Americans, as illustrated by her white employer's insistence on calling her "Mary." African Americans from Sojourner Truth and Frederick Douglass to Malcolm X and Muhammad Ali have pushed back against this form of political subordination, rejecting names imposed through a history of slavery and adopting new names— or symbolically marking a lost African name with the Nation of Islam X (Lincoln 1994)—as a form of public self-definition. Meanwhile, Native Americans may use anglicized personal and/or surnames in institutional settings while preserving the names given to them by their families for ingroup cultural contexts (e.g., Kroskrity 1993).

But if naming is a political issue, is it truly a racial issue? After all, the practice of adapting new lexical items, including names, to native phonology has long been recognized as a general cross-linguistic phenomenon (Weinreich [1953] 1970). In the context of the white West, however, this process is also closely bound up with race. Jane Hill (1993) notes that the hyperanglicized pronunciation of words seen as other-than-English is a fundamental strategy of white racial dominance through language, as she demonstrates with respect to Mock Spanish, a jocular Anglo version of Spanish. Anticipating part of Hill's argument nearly two decades earlier, John Lipski (1976) suggests that the hyperanglicized pronunciation not only of ethnoracially marked names but also of ethnic and national labels, such as *Italian* as [ˌajˈtʰæljən], *Arab* as [ˈejˌræb], and *Vietnam* as [ˌvijəʔˈnæm], is peculiar to outgroup members with negative attitudes toward the groups in question (see also Hall-Lew et al. 2010). Despite white speakers' protestations that their use of Mock Spanish is not racist but simply fun-loving, Hill persuasively argues that pronunciation strategies that trivialize nondominant languages indexically reproduce racial hegemony. Indeed, simply uttering a name may invoke boundaries of ingroup and outgroup, with mispronunciation signaling nonmembership in an ethnic category, and correction of such mispronunciations displaying ethnic membership (Markaki et al. 2010, 1529).

To be sure, many white people also have "funny names." I have a notoriously unpronounceable name of my own, which led me to propose as a freshman in high school that my entire family change its name to "Beechwood"—a German speaker had informed me that this was the most likely translation of my questionably spelled surname. But while my German and Polish immigrant ancestors no doubt faced confusion and even mockery for their names, their ethnic otherness quickly abated as they were incorporated into the racial structures of working-class whiteness. Meanwhile, for members of groups that continue to be ethnicized and racialized, naming remains a focal point for indexical bleaching, whereby acts of linguistic racism and violence are perpetrated on a daily basis, often without redress or consequence.

Notwithstanding analyses that frame the primary issue as the linguistic "problem" or "difficulty" facing the native speaker who is forced to deal with a "foreign" name (Rosenhouse 2000), it is clear that it is the bearer of a name who carries the heaviest responsibility for the "public management of name pronunciation" (Wolf et al. 1996, 415). Those with linguistically problematized names must develop a set of strategies for dealing with this situation, from clarifying their name through spelling or rhyming terms to altering the pronunciation toward the hegemonic phonological system to selecting a different name altogether, yielding what Riki Thompson (2006) terms a "binominal identity." Regardless of an individual's solution to the problem of misnaming, however, none of these strategies should be seen as either simple linguistic accommodation or coerced cultural assimilation. Rather, all such strategies are acts of ethnoracial agency that claim the right to name oneself as one sees fit in a given context.

In the remainder of this chapter I illustrate this point by examining the issue of Anglo mispronunciation of Spanish-heritage names, drawing on data from a multisited program fostering community engagement and social, linguistic, and educational justice. Based on students' own discussions of names and naming, I argue that personal names are critical sites for reproducing, managing, and undoing the ethnoracial regimes enforced by indexical bleaching.

"That's Not My Name": Youth Negotiations of Naming Rights

The data analyzed below are taken from a research and academic outreach program created in 2009 by faculty, graduate students, and undergraduates at the University of California, Santa Barbara, in collaboration with students, faculty, and other personnel at public high schools in Santa Barbara County, which serve majority working-class Latina/o students. The program, known as SKILLS (School Kids Investigating Language in Life and Society), guides high school students to conduct original research on language use in their friendship groups, families, and local communities and to raise their own and others' awareness of both linguistic diversity and linguistic racism. Because SKILLS is founded on a commitment to sociolinguistic justice (Bucholtz et al. 2014), the student researchers receive mentoring and academic preparation toward college as well as ample opportunities to critically examine and evaluate the politics of language in everyday life. Throughout the program, the question of names has repeatedly emerged as an important issue for the student participants, not simply as an academic topic but as a deeply felt personal matter. The following analysis examines three different instances at two different school sites in which SKILLS students, unprompted by adult researchers and instructors, engaged with the politics of names and naming in their lives.

The following examples illustrate the different positionalities and actions that students may take toward the issue of renaming, from recognition to critique to social activism. The first example is taken from audio data of youth interaction collected in 2011 by two SKILLS student researchers, Edith Reyes and Melinda Sánchez, for their study of slang use at Carpinteria High School, a small, rural high school. The recording involves a schoolyard conversation among a group of junior girls, including Edith, Melinda, their friend Liliana, and a fourth girl who preferred not to have her data included in this study; her speech has been omitted from the transcript, but these gaps do not substantively affect the analysis. In addition, Liliana's name has been changed in the transcript, but the student researchers' names have not, in order to recognize their scholarly contribution. The example opens immediately after Edith jokingly uses an insult term in both English and Spanish phonology, apparently prompting her to reflect on the differences between the two languages.

(2) Carpinteria High School, schoolyard interaction (January 19, 2011)

1 Edith: You know what's funny?
2   Like when you call-
3   Like when you-
4   You know how we ha-
5   when we have a substitute?
6   (0.5)

7		They like,

7   They like,
8   *want,*
9   they like,
10   ta:king ro:ll,
11   and they say your na:me,
12   and they pronounce it,
13   i:n,
14   a different way?
15   (1.4)
16 <3.4 sec. omitted in accordance with human subjects agreement.>
17 Liliana: They always do that to me.
18   They always pronounce my name wr*o*ng.
19   (0.8)
20 Melinda: They ↑d*o:*?
21 Edith: I don't get what's the difference of English and Spanish though.
22   Like for my name?
23 <4.4 sec. omitted in accordance with human subjects agreement; girls try out
   English and Spanish pronunciations of omitted participant's name>
24 Melinda: Sounds the ↑*same* somehow.
25 Liliana: Edith <[ˈidɪθ]>,
26   [and E]dith <[ˌeˈd̠it̠]>.
27 Edith: [Edith.] <[ˌeˈd̠it̠]>.
28 Liliana: Okay,
29   th*a*t's different.
30 Melinda: Edith <[ˌeˈd̠it̠]>.
31   Edith <[ˈidɪθ]>.
32 Liliana: Liliana <[ˌlɪɬijˈæn̪ə]>.
33   Liliana <[l̪i̪l̪ iˈan̪a]>.
34   Liliana <[ˌlɪɬijˈæn̪ə]>.=
35 Edith: =Liliana <[ˌl̪i̪l̪ iˈan̪a]>. =
36 Melinda: =@Liliana <[ˌlɪɬijˈæn̪ə]> #
37 (6.5; sounds of disposing of trash, zipping up backpacks)
38 Edith: ↑Pretty much the s*a*me.
39   It's just,
40   different i:n,
41   some sort of way.

Edith, who raises the topic of substitute teachers' pronunciation of students' names, takes up a stance of curiosity toward the phenomenon, assessing it as "funny" (line 1), and Liliana implicitly aligns with her (lines 17–18). Liliana, however, takes an upgraded stance: where Edith characterized substitute teachers' pronunciations as merely "different" (line 14), Liliana frames these acts as linguistically injurious to her (line 17: *They always do that to me*) and flatly states that variant pronunciations are "wrong" (line 18). The stance differential that emerges between the two girls is not pursued for the remainder of the exchange, however, as the group begins to try out different pronunciations of their own and one another's names. In this example, Edith adopts the linguistic sensibility fostered by SKILLS by framing the difference between Spanish and English pronunciations as a matter of phonological variation (only Edith and Melinda are participants in the program). Liliana, moreover, goes even further, displaying her own critical language awareness (Alim 2005) as she evaluates some pronunciations of her name as correct and others as incorrect.

In example (2) above, the focus is on others' pronunciation of students' names; in the following example, the converse situation is addressed: how students must adjust the pronunciation of their names in order to be understood by outgroup members. The example is taken from classroom interaction recorded in the 2012 SKILLS program at Santa Barbara High School, a large urban school. Led by two graduate teaching fellows, Eva Wheeler and Meghan Corella Morales, who are both bilingual in Spanish and English, the group has been discussing several feature film clips illustrating the same speaker's use of different accents in different settings. The issue of names only comes up when it is proposed as an example by one of the students in response to a question from Eva. It is clear that this suggestion is unexpected given Eva's surprised response.

---

(3) Santa Barbara High School, classroom interaction (April 5, 2012)

1 Eva: <off camera> Do *you* ever:,

2   do you ever find yourself,

3   changing your accent [when you're]=

4 Estefania: [@@ I do.   ]= <nods>

5 Eva: = speaking with someone?

6 <Raquel nods>

7 ?:   Yeah.

8 <Reyna nods>

9 Eva: To be understoo:d,

10   or for other reasons?

11   W-

12		H*ow* do you do that?
13	Reyna:	What do you mean,
14		how do you *do* it?
15	Eva:	Yea::h.
16		Like if somebody—
17		Ill-
18		In-
19		Do you have an example of like something that you s:*ay*:,
20	<Estefania raises her hand>	
21	Eva:	that you have to:,
22	Raquel:	[Your name?]
23	Eva:	[change your accent] for?
24		Oh-
25		Your ↑n*a*me?
26	Raquel:	<smiling> Yeah.=
27	Girl:	<off camera> =Oh [yeah.]
28	Estefania:	<lowers hand> [like] my l*a*st [name?]
29	Reyna:	[*Oh*] yeah.
30	Estefania:	They like,
31		won't understand it unless [####]
32	Meghan:	<off camera> [Who won't?] Who won't under[stand it?]
33	Estefania:	<turning toward Meghan> [Like,]
34		in the *o*ffice or something?=
35	Eva:	=[A:h!]
36	Estefania:	=[(Or the)] teachers?=
37	Eva:	=At schoo:l.
38	Estefania:	I have to say,
39		Gutierrez <[gutiˈjɛɹɛz]>,
40		but,=
41	Eva:	=Guti[errez] <[gutiˈjɛɹɛz]>?
42	Estefania:	<touches chest> [Iː] say Gutierrez <[guˈtjeres]>,
43		because that's how it's supposed to be?
44		But then they won't understand it so I have to change it.
45	Eva:	Guti[errez] <[gutiˈjɛɹɛs]>?
46	(Meghan:	[O:h,
47		wow.])

48 Raquel:	<nods> [It's like the same thing] with me.
49 Mirián?:	<off camera> Your last na:me,
50	[##]
51 Eva:	[Last name?]
52 <Raquel nods>	
53 Eva:	Last name?
54 <Reyna nods; Raquel continues to nod>	
55 Reyna:	Yeah.
56 Eva:	And is it the same for you?
57 Reyna:	Yeah.
58 Eva:	Reyna?
59 <Reyna nods>	
60 Eva:	A:h!

When Eva asks the students whether they have varied their accent based on their interlocutor, several students immediately respond in the affirmative (lines 4–8). When she asks for an example, before she has even finished her question Estefania raises her hand (line 20) and Raquel proposes, "Your name?" (line 22). Eva displays surprise at this response, but other students immediately align with Raquel, and Estefania goes on to offer an elaboration, followed by further alignment from Raquel and Reyna. Here young people are forced to claim for themselves names that are not their own; in order to be quite literally "culturally intelligible" in Butler's (1990, 167) sense, they must do linguistic violence to their own names.

Although at this point the instructors returned the discussion to the broader topic of accent and setting, they took note of this issue, and several weeks later, when the students were developing project ideas for their public awareness campaign, they encouraged Estefania, Raquel, and two other students, Diana and Melissa, to pursue the topic of name pronunciation. The video produced by these four student researchers was sparked by the initial discussion in example 3 several weeks earlier.

In the video, as each girl displays a card with the orthographic spelling of her name, she pronounces it in American English phonology; this sequence is then repeated with alternative and increasingly incorrect English pronunciations. When the fourth girl, Estefania, displays her name card for the second time (Figure 15.1a), she simply says dismissively, "I can't pronounce it" in an unmistakable "Valley Girl" accent, which is often ideologically racialized as white in the California context. Estefania's embodied performance exemplifies what

(a)

(b)

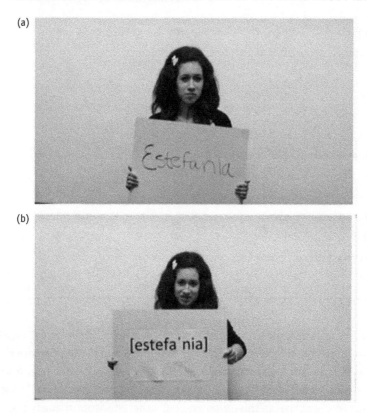

Figure 15.1 a. Estefania mispronounces her name in "la voz gringa." b. Estefania displays the correct pronunciation of her name, transcribed in the International Phonetic Alphabet.

Lauren Mason Carris (2011) calls "la voz gringa," a counterform of mock language that she argues serves to "disrupt the dominant sociolinguistic order and elevated status of white Mainstream English with respect to Latina/o language practices; and ... challenge racial/ethnic power dynamics between whites and Latina/os" (2011, 476). A further reversal of the relative political positionality of English and Spanish phonology is evident in the third sequence of the video, as the four girls flip their name cards to reveal the correct Spanish pronunciation of their names in the International Phonetic Alphabet, authoritatively invoking a technical notation system in order to reject hegemonic anglicized pronunciations (Figure 15.1b).

Besides its impact on the student researcher-activists and their classmates, the video has reached an audience well beyond the students' classroom: It was played for UC Santa Barbara faculty and students as well as local community members at a formal academic conference where students presented the results of their work at the end of the SKILLS program, and it is also permanently available via the SKILLS website (http://www.skills.ucsb.edu). Thus, not only did the videomakers succeed in publicly challenging indexical bleaching by voicing their own pronunciations of their names, but they did so using the academic resources of an educational system that has all too often worked to erase their names and identities.

In these examples, Latina youth engaged with their peers in various forms of sociopolitical critique of the hegemonic language ideologies of their schools and societies. In yielding mangled and unfamiliar versions of their names through the deracializing technique of indexical bleaching, these ideologies strike youth at the very heart of their identities. While the process of phonologically whitening names viewed by the dominant culture as racially and culturally Other continues to be commonplace within the United States, these young people's linguistic acts of self-naming negotiate, interrogate, and at times quite literally overturn this process.

Conclusion: Taking Names

This chapter has taken as its starting point a simple historical fact: As members of politically and linguistically subordinated groups—including indigenous peoples, immigrants, and enslaved Africans and their descendants—have entered into the U.S. ethnoracial system, they have frequently endured the degrading experience of being renamed against their will, whether through processes of mispronunciation, deliberate anglicization, or the outright imposition of a new name. This process indexically bleaches the original name of its ethnoracial specificity and renders it safely deracialized and normative. At the same time, however, many groups and individuals have claimed the right to name themselves, whether by developing ethnoracially distinctive naming practices, maintaining multiple pronunciations and spellings of their name, rejecting an old name or choosing a new name as a political statement, or establishing situationally specific names. Thus the institutional power that imposes a deracialized version of a name is met and at times overmatched by the sociolinguistic agency of those whose names are vulnerable to indexical bleaching. As Butler notes, "The terms by which we are hailed are rarely the ones we choose (and even when we try to impose protocols on how we are to be named, they usually fail); but these terms we never really choose are the occasion for something we might still call agency, the repetition of an originary subordination for another purpose, one whose future is partially open" (1997, 38). Indeed, given the evidence presented in this chapter, we might state the situation even more hopefully: Being called out of one's name creates the opportunity to publicly re-call one's own name, to reassert one's identity in the face of its potential erasure.

The foregoing analysis has demonstrated that often what is at stake in naming rights is a political contest between competing lexical, orthographic, and especially phonological systems. The phonological inventory of a language is intimately tied to the body and hence to the self. It has been widely noted that acquiring a new phonology is the most difficult aspect of second language learning, both because of our embodied habits of language use (Bourdieu 1977) and because of the deep connection of speech sounds to one's sense of self. Thus it may seem that I am unfairly demanding that all speakers must master an entire set of unfamiliar phonemes from the world's languages. On the contrary: As a university professor (of linguistics!) who often stumbles over my students' names, I understand all too well the difficulties facing speakers who are unable to produce or even approximate the acoustic and articulatory shapes of other languages.

The fundamental issue, however, is not a speaker's language abilities but her or his language ideologies. In light of the ethnoracial hierarchy that continues to govern linguistic practice in the United States, ethnoracial misnaming cannot be dismissed as a simple linguistic process of phonological nativization or an inevitable social process of cultural assimilation. Rather, it must be recognized and challenged as a deracializing and often dehumanizing act of indexical bleaching. And although I have focused primarily on how misnaming is wielded by whites against other racialized groups, this act can be perpetrated by anyone who benefits from structural power on the basis of race, class, language, and/or citizenship—that is, members of most groups at one point or another. The responsibility of those in such situations is therefore not to master all possible names but to avoid symbolically dominating others through misnaming.

To conclude, then, I offer a few tips on how to avoid "calling people out of their names." Though aimed at anyone who struggles with names they view as unfamiliar, in the U.S. context these suggestions are especially important for those of us who are white, affluent, English-dominant, and U.S.-born and who therefore have the least to lose in the raciolinguistic politics of misnaming—and who therefore have the greatest responsibility not to misname others. The recommendations below are especially relevant when speaking with new or distant acquaintances, but it is wise to exercise caution even when talking with friends about their names, since names are an intimate part of selfhood.

(1) Don't remark on the unusualness of a name or its spelling. Don't ask about the origin of a name (or worse, blurt, "What is *that*?"). Avoid treating some names as normative and others as nonnormative.

(2) Ask people how they prefer that you address them, and always address them that way. Don't object if the name they prefer that you use toward them is different from that used by others (e.g., family members, close friends). Never use a nickname or otherwise adapt or change someone's name without their explicit indication that this new name is welcome.

(3) Make the effort to correct your ignorance; don't expect the bearer of the name to do the work for you. It can be useful to ask other acquaintances how to pronounce someone's name, but don't assume that what they tell you is correct. The Internet is also a helpful resource for this purpose, but keep in mind that people may not pronounce their names in line with prescriptive guidelines.

(4) Finally, if you remain in doubt about what to call someone or about how to spell or pronounce their name, simply ask—politely and apologetically. Never blame someone for their name.

(And for the record, it's [ˈbʌkˌholts].)

Notes

1. Acknowledgments. I gratefully acknowledge the work of all the SKILLS team members, and especially student researchers Edith Reyes and Melinda Sánchez, graduate teaching fellow Audrey Lopez, and master teacher Gene Bisson at Carpinteria High School; and student researchers Melissa Campuzano, Diana Escobar, Raquel García, and Estefania Gutierrez, graduate teaching fellows Meghan Corella Morales, Sebastian Ferrada, and Eva Wheeler, and research assistants Kris Horowitz and Stefani Guzmán at Santa Barbara High School. Special thanks to audiences at the American Anthropological Association and at the University of California, San Diego, to my graduate and undergraduate students, and to Samy Alim, Inés Casillas, Elaine Chun, Sara Hinojos, Alastair Pennycook, and Angie Reyes for invaluable suggestions and encouragement.
   Key and Peele, "Substitute Teacher," October 17, 2012, Comedy Central, http://www.youtube.com/watch?v=Dd7FixvoKBw. Accessed June 28, 2013.
2. Transcription conventions follow Bucholtz (2011), xiii
3. During the run-up to the 2008 election, President Obama was known among some African American voters as "the brotha with the funny name" (Alim and Smitherman 2012, 3). Contrasting with this affectionate characterization is the disturbing tendency for journalists and politicians to confuse the names of Barack Obama and terrorist Osama bin Laden. The most widely discussed of such "gaffes" was made in 2007 by Presidential candidate Mitt Romney during the Republican primary (Silverstein 2011).

References

Alim, H. Samy. 2005. Critical language awareness in the United States: Revisiting issues and revisiting pedagogies in a resegregated society. *Educational Researcher* 34: 24–31.

Alim, H. S., and G. Smitherman. 2012. *Articulate While Black: Barack Obama, Language, and Race in the U.S.* New York: Oxford University Press.

Angelou, Maya. 1969. *I Know Why the Caged Bird Sings*. New York: Random House.

Benson, Susan. 2006. Injurious names: Naming, disavowal, and recuperation in contexts of slavery and emancipation. In Gabrielle Vom Bruck and Barbara Bodenhorn, eds., *The Anthropology of Names and Naming*. Cambridge: Cambridge University Press, 177–99.

Bucholtz, Mary. 2011. *White Kids: Language, Race, and Styles of Youth Identity*. Cambridge: Cambridge University Press.

Bucholtz, Mary, Audrey Lopez, Allina Mojarro, Elena Skapoulli, Christopher VanderStouwe, and Shawn Warner-Garcia. 2014. Sociolinguistic justice in the schools: Student researchers as linguistic experts. *Language and Linguistic Compass* 8(4): 144–57.

Butler, Judith. 1990. *Gender Trouble: Feminism and the Subversion of Identity*. New York: Routledge.

Butler, Judith. 1997. *Excitable Speech: A Politics of the Performative*. New York: Routledge.

Dumas, Firoozeh. 2003. *Funny in Farsi: A Memoir of Growing up Iranian in America*. New York: Random House.

Eckert, Penelope. 2008. Variation and the indexical field. *Journal of Sociolinguistics* 12(4): 453–76.

Edwards, Rachel. 2006. What's in a name?: Chinese learners and the practice of adopting "English" names. *Language, Culture, and Curriculum* 19(1): 90–103.

El-Hakem v. BJY, Inc., 415 F.3d 1068 (9th Cir. 2005). http://caselaw.findlaw.com/us-9th-circuit/ 1150161.html. Accessed December 18, 2012.

Hall-Lew, Lauren, Elizabeth Coppock, and Rebecca L. Starr. 2010. Indexing political persuasion: Variation in the *Iraq* vowel. *American Speech* 85(1): 91–102.

Heffernan, Kevin. 2010. English name use by East Asians in Canada: Linguistic pragmatics or cultural identity? *Names* 58(1): 24–36.

Hill, Jane H. 1993. Hasta la vista, baby: Anglo Spanish in the American Southwest. *Critique of Anthropology* 13(2): 145–76.

Hoffman, Eva. 1989. *Lost in Translation: A Life in a New Language*. New York: Penguin.

Johnstone, Barbara, Jennifer Andrus, and Andrew E. Danielson. (2006. Mobility, indexicality, and the enregisterment of "Pittsburghese." *Journal of English Linguistics* 34(2): 77–104.

Kim, Tae-Young. 2007. The dynamics of ethnic name maintenance and change: Cases of Korean ESL immigrants in Toronto. *Journal of Multilingual and Multicultural Development* 28(2):117–133.

Krikorian, Mark 2009. It sticks in my craw. National Review Online, May 29. http://www. nationalreview.com/corner/182354/it-sticks-my-craw-mark-krikorian. Accessed June 1, 2016.

Kroskrity, Paul V. 1993. *Language, History, and Identity: Ethnolinguistic Studies of the Arizona Tewa*. Tucson: University of Arizona Press.

Lincoln, C. Eric. 1994. *The Black Muslims in America*. 3rd ed. Trenton, NJ: Africa World Press.

Lipski, John M. 1976. Prejudice and pronunciation. *American Speech* 51(1/2): 109–18.

Markaki, Vassiliki, Sara Merlino, Lorenza Mondada, and Florence Oloff. 2010. Laughter in professional meetings: The organization of an emergent ethnic joke. *Journal of Pragmatics* 42: 1526–42.

Mason Carris, Lauren. 2011. La voz gringa: Latino stylization of linguistic (in)authenticity as social critique. *Discourse and Society* 22(4): 474–90.

McPherron, Paul. 2009. "My name is Money": Name choices and global identifications at a South-Chinese university. *Asia Pacific Journal of Education* 29(4): 521–36.

Rodriguez, Richard. 1982. *Hunger of Memory: The Education of Richard Rodriguez*. New York: Bantam.

Rosenhouse, Judith. 2000. Native speakers' pronunciation of foreign names: The case of names of French origin in (American) English. *Babel* 46(3): 245–57.

Rymes, Betsy. 2001. Names. In Alessandro Duranti, ed., *Key Terms in Language and Culture*. Malden, MA: Blackwell, 158–61.

Scott, James C., John Tehranian and Jeremey Mathias. 2002. The production of legal identities proper to states: The case of the permanent family surname. *Comparative Studies in Society and History* 44(1): 4–44.

Silverstein, Michael. 2003. Indexical order and the dialectics of sociolinguistic life. *Language and Communication* 23(3–4): 193–229.

Silverstein, Michael. 2011. Presidential ethno-blooperology: Performance misfires in the business of "message"-ing. *Anthropological Quarterly* 84(1): 165–86.

Smitherman, Geneva. 1994. *Black Talk: Words and Phrases from the Hood to the Amen Corner*. Boston: Houghton Mifflin.

Squires, Lauren. 2012. The lady pond beyond "the lady pond": Variation in circulation, from TV to Twitter. Paper presented at the 41st Conference on New Ways of Analyzing Variation, Bloomington, IN, October. http://prezi.com/ykwflvcbqenv/nwav-2012/.

Stuckey, Mary E., and John M. Murphy. 2001. By any other name: Rhetorical colonialism in North America. *American Indian Culture and Research Journal* 25(4): 73–98.

Taylor-Mendes, Cosette. 2003. Our names. *TESL Canada Journal* 21(1): 97–101.

Thompson, Riki. 2006. Bilingual, bicultural, and binominal identities: Personal name investment and the imagination in the lives of Korean Americans. *Journal of Language, Identity, and Education* 5(3): 179–208.

Vom Bruck, Gabrielle, and Barbara Bodenhorn, eds. 2006. *The Anthropology of Names and Naming.* Cambridge: Cambridge University Press.

Weinreich, Uriel. [1953] 1970. *Languages in Contact: Findings and Problems.* The Hague: Mouton.

Wolf, George, Michèle Bocquillon, Debbie de la Houssaye, Phyllis Krzyzek, Clifton Meynard, and Lisbeth Philip. 1996. Pronouncing French names in New Orleans. *Language in Society* 25: 407–26.

16

Multiculturalism and Its Discontents

Essentializing Ethnic Moroccan and Roma Identities in Classroom Discourse in Spain

INMACULADA M. GARCÍA-SÁNCHEZ

Education in Spain has historically been a crucial site through which issues of national identity and linguistic diversity have been both contested and reproduced (Pujolar 2007). Even before transnational migrants changed the demographic composition of many Spanish schools during the last few decades, education has been at the center of criss-crossing tensions between ideologies of diversity and homogeneity. Given that schools are among the first institutions involved in the settlement processes of immigrant families, it is perhaps not surprising that schools have also become one of the major battlegrounds in heated debates about immigration and the new politics of societal inclusion (García Castaño and Carrasco Pons 2011).

Much of the recent language policy scholarship in contemporary Spain has been devoted to documenting schools' management of increasing multilingualism and cultural diversity (e.g., Martín Rojo 2010). Still, little is known about classroom practices and interactions in the growing number of multiethnic schools across the country. Generating this knowledge, however, is critical to understanding the relationship between educational discourses about multiculturalism and diversity and what the practice of multicultural education looks like on the ground (Dietz and Mateo Cortés 2011). Towards that end, I analyze discourses about multicultural education in relation to how Moroccan immigrant and Spanish Roma minority children's ethnic identities are constructed through the discursive production of classroom narratives.

In this chapter, I show how teachers engage in *distinction, authentication,* and *authorization* practices (Bucholtz and Hall 2004) by drawing on essentialist notions of immigrant and minority children's identities and reproducing homogeneous and static notions of culture. *Distinction* refers to the mechanisms by which salient difference is produced. *Authentication* involves the social production of identities that are considered (non-)genuine. Authentication usually plays on essentialist notions of identities and the language practices associated with them. Finally, *authorization* involves legitimating an identity through hegemonic or institutional authority. I also consider the extent to which Moroccan immigrant and Roma minority children reject these essentialist formulations of cultural identity, and how everyday school experiences may impact these students' sense of belonging (See also García-Sánchez 2013).

Some Notes on the Larger Study, Methodology, and Analysis

This analysis is part of a larger linguistic ethnography of the lives of Moroccan immigrant children (eight- to eleven-years-old) in a small town in South-Central Western Spain.[1] I observed and videotaped children's interactions at the local elementary school, where I followed a class of fourth graders in a range of activities in and outside of the classroom. The total number of students at the school was 678, out of which 251 (37%) were children of Moroccan immigrant families. The large percentage of Moroccan immigrant students at this school is explained by the fact that this rural community has been a major settlement area for Moroccan immigrants since the early 1990s.[2] In the fourth grade class I observed, the total number of students was twenty-four, out of which seven were Moroccan immigrant children and two were Spanish students of Roma descent.

Using linguistic anthropology and classroom discourse analysis methods (see also chapter 17, this volume), the analysis in this chapter focuses on teacher-student interactions and discussions during social studies and language arts classes. In previous work (García-Sánchez 2013), I examined five interactional and literacy strategies as part of a repertoire of communicative resources that educators draw on to construct students' identities:

1. Speaker selection and forms of class participation;
2. Explicit membership categorization devices:[3] appellation and labeling;
3. Implicit membership categorization devices: constrastive deixis;
4. IRE (Initiation-Response-Evaluation) sequences; and
5. Storytelling and elicitation of narratives.

These strategies are particularly important to illuminate the on-the-ground dynamics of multiculturalism and diversity in the classroom because these are interactional elements that build a classroom's intellectual life, allowing or hindering a variety of perspectives from being voiced.

These five interactional resources serve one of two larger functions: they either served to mark individual students as representatives of ethnolinguistic groups; or alternatively (and sometimes concomitantly), they constructed unitary and discrete identities for students. Therefore, I categorized these resources into two practices that mutually constitute each other, *tokenization* and *membership by ethno-prototype*:

(A) **Tokenization** (Wortham 2001): A metonymic practice through which a particular student becomes a representative of an entire national, cultural, or ethnic group.

(B) **Membership by Ethno-Prototype**: An extreme formulation of ideal membership to a national, cultural, or ethnic group which precludes multiple allegiances and erases hybridity of belonging to multiple groups.

By examining specifically how students' narratives are elicited, I analyze how, by playing on essentialist notions of ethnicity, teachers are involved (often inadvertently) in reproducing monolithic and artificial, yet authoritative, versions of ethnic *authenticity* for immigrant and minority students. Importantly, I also consider how children counter the essentialist claims underlying these practices.

Culture Comes to School

My particular school site provides a privileged vantage point to investigate the everyday dynamics of multicultural inclusion efforts. Not only does the school have a high concentration of Moroccan immigrant and Spanish ethnic minority children, such as Roma students, but it also has an explicit commitment to diversity. The school administration's dedication to provide quality education for all students had indeed earned this school two prominent awards, one by a prestigious human rights organization, for its investment in inclusive pedagogical models.

The inclusive nature of the institution was made highly visible through well-orchestrated public displays on the school walls and in its stated curricular goals and principles. In the year 2000, the school launched an overhaul of its curricular programs, systematizing the practices that they have been developing since the mid-1990s when the number of Moroccan immigrant students increased exponentially. The issue of the *new diversity* of the school took central stage in the curriculum revision. The school curriculum's main tenets focused on creating a strong sense of community and a spirit of tolerance for the cultural and linguistic heterogeneity of the student body.

From my earliest observations, however, I noticed that, in spite of the many efforts of the school professionals, the ways these tenets were realized in practice often had the unintended consequence of marking immigrant and minority children as the ethnic *Other*. For instance, special schoolwide celebrations were taken as opportunities to celebrate diversity. These celebrations ranged from traditional Spanish national holidays and school festivities, such as the end-of-the-year Festival, to more specific events, such as the International Day of Human Rights. Although these celebrations were different in nature, they all routinely incorporated diversity as the essentialization of folkloristic manifestations of ethnic traditions. Moreover, they reified static notions of "culture" as the property of only those students different from the majority group.

Interculturality Day, for instance, is a prime example of how *culture* was usually regarded to be embodied in the *Other*. In spite of the prefix inter- (in Interculturality Day), this celebration featured unilateral activities, consisting of demonstrations of body decoration with henna or sampling of traditional Moroccan dishes. Another example is the way in which diversity was made part of traditional Spanish holidays, such as Christmas or Carnival. The school went about these celebrations as usual, for instance, with the traditional Christmas Carol Festival or the Costume Parade. After the regular program of events was over, a traditional Moroccan dance was usually performed by a group of Moroccan girls in the higher grades almost as an add-on but not as part of the *mainstream* culture of the school. Thus, these schoolwide activities also unwittingly identified minority children as culturally different and exotic.

Essentializing Ethnic Identities in Classroom Discourse

Beyond festivals and special events, it is important to understand how ethnic differences are (re)produced in everyday classroom interactions between teachers and students. In this section, I present an in-depth analysis of an extended piece of classroom discourse, comprising almost a whole social studies class session. To illustrate the point under discussion, the teacher elicited wedding narratives from several students in the class. The technique of asking for stories from students was a common pedagogical strategy used by the fourth grade classroom teacher to make abstract academic concepts more familiar to students. The specific examples I offer here are representative of how this type of class discussion usually unfolded (See also García-Sánchez 2013).

SPEAKER SELECTION AND ELICITATION OF NARRATIVES

In this classroom, teachers often allocated the floor according to the ethnic distribution of the student body. Thus, teachers selected as next speakers a non-Roma Spanish student, a Moroccan immigrant student, and a Spanish student of Roma descent. In line with these practices, the elicitation of wedding narratives in the example below also follows this pervasive trend of floor allocation. An important point to be made, in this regard, is that the tokenizing pattern described here, however, was exclusively observed in social studies and language arts class discussions. The very same teacher did not follow this sort of next-speaker selection strategy in other content areas. Therefore, this marked difference in speaker-selection cannot be attributed to different styles by different teachers. The fact that this pattern was particularly marked in specific classes is relevant because this could make it more salient to the immigrant and minority children when they were being tokenized, or singled out according to their ethnicity.

In this first example (EXAMPLE 1—"Lower Your Hands"), the teacher is selecting the student-speakers to offer their wedding stories. Turn-taking organization in the classroom is ordinarily constructed so that the teacher has maximized participation rights and the students have minimized participation rights. This differential, however, is very commonly managed in classrooms, particularly during class discussions of this kind, by the teacher inviting students to self-select (by raising their hands, for example) and then teacher choosing among those who have self-selected (Cazden 2001). In this data excerpt, however, the teacher opens a class discussion in a more unusual way, directing speakership to three particular speakers, whom she selects by name, while telling the rest of students to stop self-selecting, or to lower their hands.

Example 1 **SPEAKER SELECTION AND ELICITATION OF NARRATIVES—"Lower Your Hands"**

01 **Teacher:** Vosotros (.)
You-2nd Person Plural (.)

habeis ido alguna vez en vuestra vida a alguna boda,verdad?
have gone some time in your life to a wedding, right?

02 **Students:** Yo, yo//Sí//Sí//Yo sí
Me, me//Yes//Yes, I have ((As they raise their hands frantically))

03 **Teacher:** Bajad la mano (.) Bajad la mano
Lower your hands (.) Lower your hands

Y las bodas Sí QUE SON diferentes dependiendo del sitio
And weddings really ARE different depending on the place

04 **Teacher:** Aquí yo se que vosotros me vais a contar=
Here I know that you are going to tell me=

=tres tipos de boda diferente
=three different types of wedding

> 05 **Teacher:** Yo sé que por ejemplo Juan me va a contar una boda=
> **I know that for instance Juan is going to tell me a wedding=**
>
> =totalmente diferente de la boda que Mimon nos va a contar=
> **=totally different from the wedding that Mimon is going to tell us=**
>
> =y de la boda que Daniela nos va a contar.
> **=and to the wedding that Daniela is going to tell us.**
>
> 06 **Teacher:** BAJAD LA MANO
> **LOWER YOUR HANDS**
>
> 07 **Teacher:** Entonces, por ejemplo, Juan nos va a explicar=
> **Then, for instance Juan is going to explain to us=**
>
> =cómo son las bodas a las que él va
> **=how the weddings he goes to are**

The teacher selects as the next three speakers: Juan (a non-Roma Spanish student), Mimon (a Moroccan immigrant student), and Daniela (a Spanish student of Roma descent). Next-speaker selection, then, becomes a means for tokenization (Wortham 2001). Moreover, this ethnic-based mechanism of floor allocation was underscored by a strict regimentation of the topics that the chosen next-speakers were assigned to talk about. This regimentation of topics goes beyond the expected moderating role played by teachers to make sure that the students stay focused on the themes of the lesson, by insisting instead that each speaker elaborates on the theme under discussion from their supposed ethnic, cultural, or national affiliation. These classroom management practices, which are instances of tokenization, also serve the dual purpose of *authentication* and *distinction* by creating a field of social difference through which only certain students are *authenticated* as genuine to speak precisely because they have been tokenized.

Thus, each child is chosen as a representative of their ethnicity so that they can each give three different accounts of how a wedding is: the unmarked Spanish wedding, the Moroccan wedding, and the Gypsy wedding. Difference is discursively underscored by the extreme case formulation (Pomerantz 1986) "**totalmente** diferente" (**totally** different—line 5). The teacher's use of this extreme case formulation is congruent with findings in nonclassroom discourse contexts, in which extreme case formulations have been found to be one of the most common linguistic devices to mark immigrant and minorities as the exotic, often deviant, cultural *Other* (e.g., Augoustinos and Every 2007). As the examples that follow will show, these three wedding stories will be constructed respectively as the default, *normal*, wedding; the foreign exotic wedding; and the colorful Spanish ethnic wedding.

THREE TOTALLY DIFFERENT WEDDING STORIES

Following the teacher's injunction to Juan to explain "how the weddings he goes to are" (Example 1, line 7), Juan proceeds to tell the first wedding story (Example 2, below). In response to the teacher's elicitation of a wedding narrative, Juan initiates the telling with the recounting of a prank that was played on the bride and the groom. Developing stories around a problematic or an unexpected event is common in the narrative structure of stories of personal experience (Ochs and Capps 2001). The student's orientation is, therefore, appropriate from a discursive and sociolinguistic point of view. The teacher, however, evaluates this response negatively in line 2; she dismisses it as the "anecdotes," indirectly implying that Juan is focusing on unimportant aspects.

Example 2 **The Spanish Wedding or The Default**

01 **Juan:**   Cuando pasaron por el pasillo=
          When they went through the hallway

          =par- para entrar en "El Refugio" ya=
          =to- to go already into "The Shelter"=

          =le tenían una (xxx) arriba y tenía to' lleno de sal=
          =they had for them a (xxx) above and everything was full of salt

          =y les cayó encima   [porque ya (xxx)
          =and it fell on top of them [because already (xxx)

02 **Teacher:**   [A ver.
                    [Let's see.

          Tú~me~estás~contando~las~anécdotas~Juan=
          You are telling me the anecdotes Juan=

          =pero esa no es la pregunta=
          =but that's not the question

03 **Teacher:** Yo te estoy preguntando que me expliques cómo es una boda.
          I'm telling you to explain to me how a wedding is

04 **Juan:**   Ah=

05 **Teacher:**   Tú- a la boda que fuiste de tu tío-
You- Your uncle's wedding you went to-

vamos a ver dónde se casaron?
let's see where did they get married?

06 **Juan:**   En la iglesia=
In the church=

07 **Teacher:**   =En la iglesia de ahí, verdad?
=In the church over there, right?

08 **Teacher:**   Y cuéntame quién llegó
primero?
**And tell me who
arrived first?**

09 **Juan:**   El novio
The groom

10 **Teacher:**   Llegó el novio (.) con
quién?
**The groom arrived
(.) with whom?**

INITIATION

RESPONSE

EVALUATION
+
INITIATION

11 **Juan:**   Con (.) su hermana=
With (.) his sister=

12 **Teacher:**   =Llega con una señora que puede ser su madre=
He arrives with a lady who can be his mother=

=su hermana o quien le=
=his sister or whoever

=parezca que se llama? [madrina
he wants who is called?

13 **Students:**   [La madrina
                                   [The godmother

14 **Teacher:**   Vale?   (.) Y esperan a quién?
Okay?   (.) And they wait for whom

15 **Juan:**   A la novia
The Bride

16 **Teacher:**	Que viene acompañada de?	
	Who is accompanied by?	
17 **Juan:**	Su:::: padrino	
	Her godfather	
18 **Teacher:**	El padrino. Vale	
	The godfather. Okay	

The teacher, then, proceeds to regiment the student's telling. This regimentation (starting in line 5 until the end) is accomplished with "Known-answer" Initiation-Response-Evaluation (IRE) sequences (Rymes 2009) that prompt the rote regurgitation of information known to both teacher and students—as compared to open-ended types of IRE sequences (Heath 1983) that may encourage more critical thinking of the part students. This strict regimentation is accompanied by reformulations of the student's answers to erase any kind of personal specificity in the telling. For example, in line 11, when Juan responds that the groom arrived "With (.) his sister," the teacher reformulates his answer as "He arrives with a lady who can be his mother, his sister or whoever he wants who is called?" In response to the reformulation, the rest of the students start providing choral or group responses to the teachers' questions (as in when they respond "the godmother" in line 13), effectively acknowledging that this is not really the narrative of a specific wedding, but rather a prototypical version of a Spanish wedding. This is the version that the teacher evaluates positively in line 18 with her "vale" (okay).

Furthermore, this version is also rendered to be the *normal* wedding story. Central to the discursive construction of the Spanish wedding as the default is the teachers' shift in tense and aspect from past perfect to present tense in line 12. While the occurrence of the historical present, or the use of the present to refer to past events, has been documented in narrative analysis as a discourse strategy to imbue the narration with vividness (e.g., Silva-Corvalán 1983), the use of the present tense in this wedding narrative is markedly different from those examples of the historical present. Rather, in this narrative, the present tense that prevails from line 12 until the end is used to convey habitual events and statements that are considered general knowledge. The naturalization of the Spanish narrative as the mainstream type of wedding amounts to a form of *authentication* of what constitutes a *genuine* cultural wedding narrative. Because these practices are embedded in an institutional formation, like the classroom, where the teacher has an authoritative position, this type of prototypical cultural narrative also becomes a powerful form of *authorization*. It is meant to serve as a model for the kind of *authentic* narrative that is expected from the other two selected student-speakers.

The beginning of Mimon's story (Example 3, below) is preceded by a coda to Juan's story that underscores the Spanish wedding story as the default. In line 1, the teacher produces an epistemic metacommentary of Juan's story—"we all know that type of wedding"—that again discursively positions the Spanish wedding as the familiar, the mainstream. This epistemic stance, along with the extreme case formulation **"Todos—We all,"** construct the prototypical Spanish wedding as the "normal" against which the other narratives will be evaluated. This is even more visible in the transcript below, when just a few turns later the teacher produces an epistemic metacommentary about Mimon's story that stands in stark contrast with the one she produced earlier about Juan's story ("We all know that type of wedding," line 2 vs. "We don't know that wedding," line 7). This metacommentary marks Mimon's wedding story as different and foreign.

Example 3 **The Moroccan Wedding or The Foreign Exotic**

01 **Teacher:**   Este tipo de boda las conocemos todos, verdad?
We all know that type of wedding, right?

02 **Teacher:**   Ahora nos va- nos va a contar Mimon una boda
Now Mimon is- is going to tell us a wedding

(...)[4]

03 **Teacher:**   A ver explicanos
Let's see explain to us

04 **Mimon:**   Que- Vinio primero la novia y luego vinio el novio
That- The bride arrived first and then arrived the groom

05 **Teacher:**   Ah ↑sí::?
Oh ↑rea::lly?

06 **Mimon:**   Sí primero
Yes first

07 **Teacher:**   Primero la novia y la novia como va vestida?=
First the bride and the bride- what's she wearing?=

=Explicanos porque esa boda no la concemos
=Explain to us because we don't know that wedding

08 **Mimon:**   Y tiene por aquí así- de blanco-
And she has over here like this- in white-

ella ve pero- está- y tiene así u:::n
she can see but- she's- and she has a::: ((Trails Off))

---

09 **Students:**   °Velo
                   °Veil

10 **Teacher:**   Ella ve pero tú a ella no le ves la cara, no?
                   She can see but you can't see her face, right

11 **Mimon:**   [No, se le ve
                   [No, it can be seen

12 **Teacher:**   [O sea la cara tapada
                   [So her face is covered

13 **Mimon:**   Sí=
                   Yes

14 **Teacher:**   Sólo se le ven los ojos=
                   Only her eyes are visible=

15 **Teacher:**   =Y que tiene por aquí collares?
                   =And what does she have necklaces over here?

                   Tú lo que tienes que hacer es explicar porque-=
                   What you have to do is to explain it to us because-

                   =a ver es interesante
                   =let's see, it's interesting

16 **Mimon:**   No, tiene como eso que se hace en las bodas=
                   No, she has like that that is done at weddings=

                   =que se(tiene) así
                   =that is worn like this

17 **Students:**   =un velo
                   =a veil

In addition to theses contrasting metacommentaries, semiotic processes of *distinction* are also accomplished through phonological features, such as marked rising intonation to express surprise, "Ah ↑sí::?" (Oh ↑rea::lly?—line 5), which the teacher produces in response to Mimon's statement that the bride arrives before the groom. The teacher's affective stance and rising intonation marks this event as extraordinary. The teacher, then, proceeds to regiment Mimon's telling and asks him to describe the bride's garments. In trying to describe the bridal outfit, Mimon launches a word-search sequence that seems to indicate that what he means is "veil." Word searches usually elicit candidate words from other participants (Goodwin and Goodwin 1986), and indeed some of Mimon's classmates actually propose the word "velo" (veil) in line 9. The teacher, however, does not propose any candidate words. Instead, in line 10, she initiates a multiturn description of how she imagines the bride to be dressed: "So her face is covered"; "Only her eyes are visible"; "Does she have necklaces over here?" (lines 10 through 15). The teacher's description of the imagined bride's garments resembles orientalist versions of the exotic Arabic bride. Her misrecognition of the type of dress Mimon was trying to describe (in fact, Mimon was attempting to describe a fairly unmarked white bridal gown with a veil), and her affective stance of fascination ("Let's see. It's interesting"—line 15), resembles Western fantasies of the veiled women of the Orient. In spite of the teacher's claim that "we don't know that wedding," it turns out that she held many ideological assumptions about it. In this light, her contrasting epistemic metacommentaries, "we all know that type of wedding" (in line 2, referring to Juan's) versus "we don't know that wedding" (in line 7, referring to Mimon's) can also be analyzed as reminiscent of what Said (1978) called the "us" and "them" of Orientalist discourse.

Critical in this example is that Mimon counters this Orientalist characterization of the bridal outfit twice. His first counterattempt in line 11 receives no uptake, as it is produced in overlap with part of the teacher's description. In line 16, Mimon makes a second countermove and resumes his word search with more overt gestures to represent a veil: he starts with his hands outstretched behind his head, moves them over the top of his head, and ends by bringing them in front of his face (see framegrabs above). Finally, one of his classmates produces the word Mimon was looking for, "a veil" (line 17), loudly enough to register in the official space of the classroom, giving Mimon the opportunity to finish the telling.

Finally, the last data excerpt features the wedding narrative of Daniela, a Spanish Roma student in the class (Example 4, below). Just like Mimon's story, Daniela's wedding story is used to construct her as the colorful Spanish ethnic, as the teacher again exoticizes her descriptions of the wedding. In this case, semiotic processes of distinction are accomplished through emphatic repetition of several of Daniela's responses. The first of these repetitions can be found in line 8, below, "everything, everything, everything." These repetitions mark the countryside as an unusual place to hold a wedding. Similarly, toward the end of the narrative, in line 25, we find another example of this emphatic repetition, "Her hair down? (.) down, down, down?" marking the way the bride had styled her hair as extraordinary. This second example of repetition is important because the teacher's surprise is tied to her stereotypes about what ethnic Roma brides wear—namely big, impossible-to-miss tiaras, and veils with long trains. As with Mimon's narrative above, the teacher's questions make her ideological assumptions visible. After Daniela produces a fairly unmarked description of what the bride was wearing (white bridal gown and curled-up hairdo), the teacher asks: "And the woman wears a big tiara like this and all that?" and "and a- a veil?" (see lines 21 through 25).

A significant dimension of these data is that, as in the case of Mimon, Daniela takes advantage of open-ended IRE sequences to reject the teacher's rigid formulations of her ethnic and cultural identity (see lines 22 and 24).

Example 4 **The Gypsy Wedding or The Spanish Ethnic**

01 **Teacher:**　Ahora Daniela nos va a contar una boda que ella ha ido
Now Daniela is going to tell us a wedding that she's gone to?

(...)

02 **Teacher:**　Dónde se casó tu hermano?
Where did your brother get married?

03 **Daniela:**　En- Fuimos a- a arreglar el- el campo
In- we went to- to fix the- the countryside

(...)

04 **Teacher:**　O sea que la boda fue en tu campo=
So then the wedding was in the countryside=

05 **Daniela:**　=El campo
=The countryside

06 **Teacher:**　Pero allí fue todo? (.) La ceremonia? ((Daniela nods))
But everything was there? (.) The ceremony

07 **Students:**　La celebración?
The celebration?

08 **Teacher:**   Todo, todo, todo? ((Daniela nods))
Everything, everything, everything?

09 **Teacher:**   Yo te quiero preguntar que cómo era- que có- que cómo es-
I want to ask you that how it was- that how-that how it is-

que cómo se casan? (.) cómo es eso?
that how do they get married? (.) how is that?

10 **Daniela:**   Los montamos aquí las mujeres a ella y a él los hombres=
We carry them here- women carry her and men carry him=

11 **Teacher:**   =Sí
=Yes

12 **Daniela:**   Y tiramos
almendras
**And we throw
almonds**

13 **Students:**   (xxx) almendras
(xxx) almonds ((laughing))

14 **Daniela:**   =Y bailamos y hacemos una juerga
=And we dance and we throw a "noisy party"

15 **Teacher:**   Sí. Vale, muy bien
Yes. Okay, very well

16 **Teacher:**   Y como iba vestida la novia?
And what was the bride wearing?

17 **Daniela:**   De blanco
In white

18 **Teacher:**	De blanco
	In white
19 **Daniela:**	Todo rizao el pelo y suelto
	Her hair all curled up and down
20 **Teacher:**	Sí
	Yes
(...)	
21 **Teacher:**	Y la mujer lleva asi una tiara grande y eso?
	And the woman wears a big tiara like this and all that?
22 **Daniela:**	No=
	No=
23 **Teacher:**	=No (.) y un- un velo?
	=No (.) and a- a veil?
24 **Daniela:**	No
	No
25 **Teacher:**	No (.) El pelo suelto? (.) suelto, suelto, suelto?
	No (.) Her hair down? (.) down, down, down?

Another similarity between the discursive structure of Daniela's story and the previous two narratives is that the teacher regiments the telling through questions, at least initially. A remarkable aspect of Daniela's story, however, is that Daniela, having had the benefit of listening to Juan and Mimon's stories, displays an acute awareness of the kind of story she has to produce to obtain a positive evaluation from the teacher. Therefore, with fewer prompting questions, Daniela produces a prototypical version of a *gypsy* wedding. As part of this prototypical narrative, she offers dramatic and vivid details of those aspects of a Roma wedding that are markedly different and, therefore, more likely to be positively evaluated as *authentic*. Through a combination of discourse and gesture (see framegrabs above), she shares how the bride and the groom are lifted up and carried by family members and wedding guests, and the tradition of throwing almonds at the bride.

Critically, it can be argued that the details that Daniela foregrounds in her narrative are not only culturally prototypical, but more similar to the narrative that a non-Roma Spanish person would produce if asked about a gypsy wedding. Daniela's narrative could be analyzed as produced from a sense of *double consciousness*, as defined by W. E. B. Du Bois (1903) as: "the sense of looking at one's self through the eyes of others; of measuring's one soul by the tape of a world that looks on in amused contempt." It is important to note that, in spite of the teacher's several injunctions to be quiet and to listen respectfully, Daniela's classmates punctuate her narrative by laughing in a derogatory manner (see line 13). Moreover, central to this double-consciousness is the multivalenced indexicality of the word "juerga" (noisy party), with which Daniela describes the wedding celebration party. The use of this term captures both "negative" (or racialization) and "positive" (or ethnicization)[5] stereotypes about the Roma ethnic minority in Spain, such as their supposed laziness and lack of interest in holding jobs, but also as the source of their exquisite flamenco artistry. *Juergas* can be seen as boisterous celebrations involving spirited dancing, singing, and drinking, but also as morally suspect, involving hedonism and excess. *Juerga* can also be understood to function as a racialized *ethno-index*, not only as something that Gypsies do during wedding celebrations but also, from the perspective of non-Roma, as something that Gypsies do all the time.

Conclusion

In examining processes of *distinction, authentication*, and *authorization* through classroom literacy events, I have shown how forms of multiculturalism meant to promote inclusion and participation may have unintended, paradoxical consequences. In this case, these well-intentioned practices further marked Moroccan immigrant and Roma minority children's identities as different and as *outsiders*. I have analyzed how authentication and authorization are accomplished through next-speaker selection and regimentation of tellings. I have also described how distinction is accomplished through marked phonology, emphatic repetitions, epistemic and affective metacommentaries of the narratives, and evaluations of students' responses as (in)appropriate. Furthermore, because of the teacher's role as agent of the institution, and because of her privileged position as a member of the dominant Spanish non-Roma majority, these practices of authentification and distinction become the authoritative version of immigrant and minority children's ethnic and cultural identities.

This is problematic because, in classroom discourse, minorities and immigrants cannot represent themselves, or as Said (1978, 283) more eloquently put it with regards to *orientalism*: "The Orient has a kind of extrareal, phenomenologically reduced status that puts them out of reach of everyone except the Western expert." In this case, it is the educational expert. However, I have also paid attention to children's attempts to resist these forms of misrecognition. One of the most interesting aspects of these data is that children often take advantage of open-ended interactional sequences to contest essentialist cultural characterizations and to assert more realistic perspective of themselves and their communities.

Are these unintended, yet exclusionary, consequences an integral part of multiculturalist discourse and practice, in general, or are they just an outcome of how one teacher implemented it? As I have recently argued (García-Sánchez 2013), the answer is neither. Attributing such exclusion to multicultural pedagogies, in general, would be reckless. The entire field of critical multiculturalism, for example, pays explicit attention to how multicultural discourses reproduce the hierarchical systems that they were designed to dismantle. Further, seeing these discursive practices as merely the property of individual schools or teachers would fail to recognize one of the most important implications of the analysis: in many liberal nation-states, like Spain, social actors, including teachers and students, are working within a structural-ideological field that belies our attempts to promote equity, diversity, and justice. In particular, the analysis in this chapter provides further insight into the ideology of "homogeneism" (Blommaert and Verschueren 1998). The normative beliefs that a homogenous society is the unmarked, and diversity is both suspect and problematic, continue to plague much of contemporary Europe. I have shown how these normative beliefs are (re)created in everyday classroom interaction, belying curricular goals of inclusion and interculturality. In highlighting differences and suppressing similarities, multicultural practices, when enacted within a structural-ideological field characterized by *homegeneism*, will continue to uphold normative assumptions about so-called homogenous societies. Because these normative assumptions mask the dynamics of cultural change and syncretism, achieving a sense of belonging for immigrant and minority children may continue to be fraught with a sense of exclusion and alienation. As I have shown, these normative assumptions about multiculturalism and diversity can make their way even into the best-intentioned multicultural education plans. Until we disrupt ideologies that frame diversity as suspect and problematic, those who genuinely struggle to address racial and ethnic inequalities will most likely continue to reproduce them.

Notes

1. During 2005–2007, I conducted fieldwork in a rural Spanish town, approximately 125 miles southwest of Madrid's urban area, with a total population of 10,815. The immigrant population makes up 38% of the total population of the town, with the bulk of this percentage being overwhelmingly of Moroccan origin.
2. This percentage is much higher than the national average. According to the national average, Moroccans make up 15.5% to 18.5% of the total number of immigrant students. All national data have been obtained directly from the Ministerio de Educación, Cultura y Deporte del Gobierno de España [http://www.educacion.gob.es/portada.html]. Last accessed: June 7, 2016.
3. For more on the notion of Membership Categorization Devices, please see, e.g., H. Sacks (1989) and Schegloff (2007).
4. (...) represents the omission of a small fragment of discourse. These omitted fragments interrupt the progressivity of the prior line of talk, and are not directly related to this line of talk. I omitted these sequences for reasons of space and relevance.
5. Following the distinction originally made by Urciuoli (1996).

References

Augoustinos, M., and D. Every. 2007. The Language of "Race" and Prejudice: A Discourse of Denial, Reason, and Liberal-Practical Politics. *Journal of Language and Social Psychology* 23: 123–41.

Blommaert, J., and J. Verschueren. 1998. *Debating Diversity: Analysing the Discourse of Tolerance*. London and New York: Routledge.

Bucholtz, M., and K. Hall. 2004. Language and Identity. In A. Duranti, ed., *A Companion to Linguistic Anthropology*. Malden, MA: Blackwell, 369–94.

Cazden, C. B. 2001. *Classroom Discourse: The Language of Teaching and Learning*. Portsmouth, NH: Heinemann.

Du Bois, W. E. B. 1903. *The Souls of Black Folk*. Project Gutenberg E-book.

Dietz, G., and L. S. Mateo Cortés. 2011. Multiculturalism and Intercultural Education Facing the Anthropology of Education. In B. A. U. Levinson and M. Pollock, eds., *A Companion to the Anthropology of Education*. Malden, MA: Wiley-Blackwell, 495–516.

García Castaño, F., and S. Carrasco Pons, eds. 2011. *Población Inmigrante y Escuela: Conocimientos y Saberes de Investigación*. Madrid: Ministerio de Educación, Secretaría General Técnica.

García-Sánchez, I. M. 2013. The everyday politics of "cultural citizenship" among North African immigrant school children in Spain. *Language and Communication* 33: 481–99.

Goodwin, M. H., and C. Goodwin. 1986. Gesture and Coparticipation in the Activity of Searching for a Word. *Semiotica* 62(1/2): 51–75.

Heath, S. B. 1983. *Ways with Words*. New York: Cambridge University Press.

Martín Rojo, L. 2010. *Constructing Inequality in Multilingual Classrooms*. Berlin: De Gruyter Mouton.

Ochs, E., and L. Capps. 2001. *Living Narrative: Creating Lives in Everyday Storytelling*. Cambridge, MA: Harvard University Press.

Pomerantz, A. 1986. Extreme case formulations: A way of legitimizing claims. *Human Studies* 9: 219–29.

Pujolar, J. 2007. Bilingualism and the nation-state in the post-national era. In M. Heller, ed., *Bilingualism: A Social Approach*. New York: Palgrave Macmillan, 71–95.

Rymes, B. R. 2009. *Classroom Discourse Analysis: A Tool for Critical Reflection*. Cresskill, NJ: Hampton Press.

Sacks, H. 1989. Lecture six: The M.I.R. membership categorization device. *Human Studies* 12(3/4): 271–81.

Said, E. 1978. *Orientalism*. London: Routledge & Kegan Paul.

Schegloff, E. 2007. A tutorial on membership categorization. *Journal of Pragmatics* 39(3): 462–82.

Silva-Corvalán, C. 1983. Tense and aspect in oral Spanish narrative: Context and meaning. *Language* 59(4): 770–80.

Urciuoli, B. 1996. *Exposing Prejudice*. Boulder, CO: Westview Press.

Wortham, S. 2001. Education and policy in the new Latino diaspora. In S. Wortham, E. Murillo, and E. Hamann, eds., *Education in the New Latino Diaspora: Policy and the Politics of Identity*, 1–16. Westport, CT: Ablex.

17

The Voicing of Asian American Figures

Korean Linguistic Styles at an Asian American Cram School

ANGELA REYES*

Allow me to begin with an *Angry Little Girls* cartoon by Lela Lee (see Figure 17.1, see also http://www.angrylittlegirls.com). This cartoon features Kim, also known as "angry little Asian girl," and her friend/enemy Deborah. Kim is a feisty, short-tempered character, and Deborah is a rich, princessy type.

DEBORAH: Wow! You speak English so well!
KIM: I was born here you dumbass!

In this cartoon, a compliment is greeted with an insult: "Wow! You speak English so well!" with "I was born here you dumbass!" Kim's snappy retort attempts to expose an assumption in Deborah's compliment. The assumption is that Kim was not born in the United States. We know this assumption because Kim presupposes it by saying: "I was born here." In the end, the explicit phrase, "you speak English so well"—a linguistic assessment, to be sure—is identified as containing the implicit assumption, "you were not born here."

What is going on here? Deborah—whether unwittingly or not—is understood as assuming that Kim was not born here. Is this assumption about Kim as an individual? Is this assumption about a group of people to which Kim has been recruited as a member? What kinds of circulating ideas about people presumably like Kim come to bear upon this interactional event? How do these ideas lead listeners like Deborah to imagine certain things about Kim? We will explore some of these questions in the following pages.

I open with this cartoon because it illustrates two central arguments of this chapter. The first is that to understand language is to understand how it gets linked to people. The second is that linking language to people involves how images of people, or "figures of personhood" (Agha 2005), are "voiced" (Bakhtin 1981), or given recognizable qualities. I argue that we need to conceptualize the

Figure 17.1 Angry Little Girls cartoon.

link between language and race as one that interrogates *the voicing of figures*. After unpacking some of the theory behind these arguments, I will illustrate these ideas by drawing on ethnographic and discourse data of Korean American youth in an Asian American supplementary school. I will examine how the social meanings of linguistic practices are mediated by circulating figures of racial personae. The analysis will illustrate how these figures are mobilized to do interactional and ideological work in the classroom. Specifically, I will illustrate how drawing on recognizable figures of Koreanness allows youth to: sort out the available ways to be identifiably Korean; locate themselves in this complex milieu; accomplish specific kinds of interactional work; and contribute to circulating racial ideologies. I end by arguing that if we are to understand issues of language and race, we must consider the central role of social interaction.

Stereotypes, Racialization, and Imagination

Let us first consider the concept of stereotypes. A stereotype is a widespread typification that links attributes to entities (Reyes 2007). In the United States, for example, widely circulating stereotypes often frame Asian Americans as "forever foreigners" or "model minorities." The "forever foreigner" stereotype produces the image of Asian Americans as permanently alien to the United States, so that even Asian Americans who have been in the United States for four or more generations are often viewed as never wholly American (Tuan 1998). The "model minority" stereotype produces the image of Asian Americans as academic high-achievers and exemplars of the American ideology of meritocracy (Lee 1996). Asian Americans might experience the foreigner stereotype when people ask them, "where are you from?" And Asian Americans might experience the model minority stereotype when people assume that they are good at math. Yet these stereotypes are not mutually exclusive: Asian American success is often attributed to the supposed "cultural values" that have been brought over from Asia. In other words, Asian Americans are a "model" of success because of their essentially "foreign" values.

There are linguistic components to these stereotypes. That is, these stereotypes can be involved in how people imagine the ways in which Asian Americans speak. The model minority stereotype might expect Asian Americans to linguistically assimilate to speech norms considered mainstream or "white." And the forever foreigner stereotype might expect Asian Americans to speak a foreign language or nonnative English. For Deborah discussed above, it seems she assumes the latter. Deborah expects poor English skills from Kim and is surprised that Kim speaks English "so well." Similar assumptions about unexpected good English extend to other racialized groups as well, namely those who get read as "articulate while black" (Alim and Smitherman 2012). Yet Alim and Smitherman (2012, 47) also discuss a self-identified "half-Korean and half mixed white" research participant who expresses her thoughts about being called "articulate":

> Asian-American speech doesn't get stereotyped as inarticulate like black and Latino speech does, but it does sometimes get stereotyped as accented. Maybe the person was trying to give me a compliment, but Asian immigration to the U.S. is not new, the U.S. as a multiracial society is not new, and multiracial people aren't new. I would feel Othered and out of place, even though this is my place.

This research participant's perspective eerily echoes Kim's fictional experience: comments about how well they speak feel less like a compliment and more like being positioned as foreign.

Some stereotypes, like the "forever foreigner" and "model minority," circulate through processes of racialization. Racialization can refer to how people get recruited into systems of racial categorization and stratification. Bonnie Urciuoli (1996) emphasizes that racialization is fundamentally about the nation, whereby a group seen as harmful to the nation is called a race, and a group seen as beneficial to the nation is called an ethnicity. In fact, Urciuoli argues that every group considered an ethnicity was once considered a race. An oft-cited example of this is the Irish in the United States (Ignatiev 1995). In the early twentieth century, the Irish were understood as a race when they were seen as a threat to the nation. But within the span of a few decades, the Irish became understood as an ethnic group as their relationship to the nation shifted.

Thus, in one respect, racialization is about categorizing groups with respect to their perceived relationship to the nation. In another respect, it is about categorizing individuals into those groups. In terms of the cartoon, we can ask if Deborah is racializing Kim—that is, recruiting Kim into the racial category of Asian. And we can also ask what relationship that Asian racial category is seen as having to the nation. Considering that Deborah's compliment is understood as containing the implicit assumption that Kim was not "born here," we might conclude that the relationship between Asians and the United States is one of not belonging—that is, of being foreign to the nation.

Many scholars have noted the fundamental role of imagination in the construction of seemingly stable concepts, such as race (Omi and Winant 1986), nation (Anderson 1983), and language (Makoni and Pennycook 2005). For example, race is about socially constructed difference that often masquerades as "real" difference, and stereotypes are not "truths" but ideas that circulate as truths. Indeed, imagination is central to perceptions of people. Yet my use of "imagination," here, is not to suggest that there are "real" things and there are "imagined" things and that we must distinguish between the two. Instead, the idea I would like to foreground is that when we encounter an individual, the signs that that individual is understood as displaying (be it linguistic or other behavioral signs) are not directly experienced by us. Instead, these signs are mediated by stereotypes about groups that come to recruit those individuals as members. Deborah, for example, does not directly encounter Kim. She can't; none of us can. Instead, Deborah relies on stereotypes to instruct her how to interpret signs. A stereotype is so potent that it can create infinite realities: it can compel us to hear signs that are not there, translate visual signs into audible signs, or ignore or erase signs that do not cooperate with its logic (Gal and Irvine 1995).

Figures and Voicing

This discussion, I hope, has led to this central idea: that to understand language is to understand how it gets linked to people. And I'm not talking about *real* people, but *ideas about* people—what I have been referring to as stereotypes, or what Asif Agha (2005) calls "figures of personhood" (compare Goffman 1974). Figures, as I will call them, may have very little to do with the flesh-and-blood individuals they purport to represent. Figures are recognizable social personae that circulate among some set of individuals. And this circulation can be traced along identifiable trajectories across space and time. Since to speak of figures is not to speak of "real people" (or "real language" for that matter), researchers must attend to discursive processes that propel images of people into circulation and thus into realms of social life where such figures can be recognized, emulated, parodied, admired, criticized, and so on.

The Bakhtinian (1981) concept of "voicing" becomes useful here. Voicing recognizes that to speak is to always invoke the types of people who are linked to that speech. Although the concepts of voice and figure are actually quite equivalent in that they both refer to a socially recognizable position, I will mainly use "voicing" to describe the process of assigning identifiable qualities to figures, and "figures" to name the actual types of personhood that are being voiced. To voice a figure, then, is to make that figure identifiable to others because it is a socially recognized type of some named or unnamed sort: for example, "young Latina/o professional" (chapter 3, this volume), "secretive, deceptive Asian" (chapter 5, this volume), "nervous white liberal" (Reyes 2011), and so on. Consider when Deborah says, "Wow! You speak English so well!" What types of people might be linked to this utterance? We get our answer from Kim. When Kim says, "I was born here you dumbass!," she potentially identifies a figure: someone who believes that Asians are foreigners. This figure is assigned to Deborah. Allow me to provisionally call this the "racist" figure (compare Hill 2008; Reyes 2011). In fact, "you speak English so well" are words that get understood by Kim as what the "racist" figure says to another figure brought into play: the "Asian foreigner" figure. And Kim potentially brings another identifiable figure into the interaction—the "angry person of color" figure (Reyes 2011)—by taking offense to a seemingly benign compliment. Thus, there are potentially three figures invoked—the racist, the Asian foreigner, and the angry person of color—and such figures can be reinforced as they circulate through these types of repeated instances of voicing.

Importantly, voicing requires *voicing contrasts* and *speaker alignments* (Agha 2005). Voicing contrasts render a voice recognizable by situating it relative to other voices from which it can be differentiated. For example, the figure of the young Latina/o professional only becomes recognizable by contrasting it from other kinds of competing figures, such as the figure of the "illegal immigrant" in U.S. popular imagination. Speaker alignments occur when participants in an interaction are inevitably positioned relative to the voices they encounter. For example, if the figure of the secretive, deceptive Asian is invoked, participants can display identifiable orientations toward that figure: fear, disgust, sympathy, resemblance, and so on. Considering the three potential figures in the cartoon, it seems Deborah's utterance potentially positions Kim as the Asian foreigner figure until Kim's utterance positions Deborah as the racist figure and Kim as the angry person of color figure. Moreover, since Kim and Deborah are merely "animating" words of which Lela Lee is the "author" (Goffman 1974), we can also ask what kinds of positions Lela Lee is taking by voicing these characters this way.

In sum, when voicing is accomplished, a recognizable figure has been invoked in a social encounter; it has been contrasted from other identifiable figures; and participants have displayed recognizable alignments, or "footings" (Goffman 1974), relative to those figures.

Authenticity and Agency

With this focus on *the voicing of figures*, I want to further push against notions of the *authentic speaker* and *speaker agency*. Research that attempts to capture authentic speech by authentic speakers often understands such speech to be unselfconscious ordinary language that is normally spoken. But Bucholtz (2003) and others have questioned whether authentic is something that speech and speakers can, in fact, be. Instead of looking for authenticity, Bucholtz and Hall (2005) look for "authentication": the processes through which speech gets *understood* as real or natural. This shifts the focus from authenticity as something that is already "there", to authenticity as produced. When a figure is voiced, then, the question is not how authentic it is, but how mechanisms of authentication construct that figure as real.

In many ways, this means that researchers should be careful not to overestimate speaker agency. Even though we might think that speakers are in control of the signs they choose to display and the meanings they wish to convey, there are two factors that often emerge with more significance: *textual organization*; and *listener uptake*. That is, speech can be organized (with or without speaker awareness) to reflexively act upon itself in a way that invites a particular interpretation. But whether that interpretation is taken up or not is crucial. Let's consider the cartoon again. Deborah's utterance, "Wow! You speak English so well!" may have had the sweetest intentions behind it. But the structure of the utterance contains an assumption that Kim is not expected to speak English well. This structure may invite this interpretation, but it does not determine that it will. We must look to uptake. It turns out that the utterance was, indeed, interpreted as containing this assumption. We know this because Kim replied, "I was born here you dumbass!" It could have gone a different way—Kim could have said "thanks" or any number of things. Saying "thanks" might produce a different meaning for this interaction (e.g., Kim accepted a compliment; Kim was duped, etc.). Saying "thanks" could also change the potential figures in play. Gone might be the racist figure and the angry person of color figure. Moreover, since we are privy to only two utterances in this encounter, we cannot know what other kinds of meanings may have emerged later if, for example, Deborah went on to protest or Kim took back her insult.

Indeed, the idea of listener uptake points to how "listening subjects" (Inoue 2006) are capable not only of intercepting signs that speakers may have intended for different purposes but also of entirely inventing signs—as well as inventing speakers—through the authorization of structures of inequality. This point is brilliantly illustrated by Miyako Inoue's (2006) research on the emergence of so-called schoolgirl speech (*jogakusei kotoba*) in late-nineteenth-century Japan. Inoue argues that Japanese male intellectuals purportedly "overheard" schoolgirl speech not because schoolgirls necessarily spoke this way, but because male listening subjects were wrestling with their own anxieties about modernity at the turn of the century. Her insights implore researchers to pay more attention to how listening subjects *report* the speech of others, whether that speech has actually been performed by speakers or not.

We can also explore how issues of authenticity and agency are problematized by the cartoon. Whether Kim sees herself as an authentic native English speaker or not matters very little, since she—like many Asian Americans—needs to be repeatedly authenticated as a native English speaker under the weight of the Asian foreigner stereotype. No matter how many times Kim says, "I was born here you dumbass!," her agency, as it were, can never guarantee that she will be expected to be a native English speaker in social encounters. Her being seen as American is often—if not almost always—in question.

Thus, when researchers analyze meaning in interactional events, they must pay attention to both textual organization and listener uptake. Speaker agency and intention do not determine what utterances mean; rather, meaning relies on how speech is understood.

An Asian American Supplementary School

I will now present some of my own research that exemplifies how *the voicing of figures* is central to raciolinguistics. The data was taken from a yearlong ethnographic and discourse analytic study at a supplementary school run by a Korean immigrant in New York City. The study centered on video-recorded classroom interaction in a fifth grade English language arts class that met on Fridays after school during the 2006–2007 academic year. The school is located in a middle-class Queens neighborhood of which Asian Americans—primarily Korean Americans and Chinese Americans—reportedly comprise about a quarter of the population.

The research participants were a teacher, who identified as white, and eleven students, who identified as Korean, Korean American, or Asian. The students were either second-generation (born in the United States to Korean-born parents) or 1.5-generation (born in Korea and immigrated to the United States as children). All of the students reported that they spoke both Korean and English, and they all rated their English as better than their Korean. Most described speaking Korean or "Konglish" (a mix of Korean and English) at home, but primarily English elsewhere.

Although English was the medium of instruction in the classroom, I noticed that students spoke Korean quite often during class. When I asked students about this, they gave remarkably similar replies. They explained that Korean was a "secret language" that teachers could not understand, used especially for "bad words," "curse words," and "insults." Yet while Korean was certainly used to carve out an unofficial student space that teachers could not access, Korean use was often less about teachers and more about harnessing the various ways to be recognizably Korean for purposes that seemed primarily meaningful to the students themselves.

Voicing Figures of Koreanness

The following excerpts focus on how various linguistic performances were involved in the voicing of four figures of recognizable Koreanness: the "pleading Korean child," "authoritative Korean adult," "Korean immigrant fob," and "ideal Korean American." I do not suggest that these figures represent authentic speakers that exist naturally in the world. I understand them less as "real people," and more as figures that circulate through voicing routines that get mutually recognized by participants.

Korean language was often used when voicing the child and adult figures. These figures were invoked when making pleas or issuing commands, respectively. As I will demonstrate, the pleas were recognized as revealing emotions linked to intimate subordinates seeking benevolence. Voicing the pleading Korean child figure created a "participation framework" (Goffman 1981) that characterized the one spoken to as close to yet above the speaker. The commands, on the other hand, were recognized as revealing emotions linked to dominating elders who required obedience. Voicing the authoritative Korean adult figure created a participation framework that positioned the one spoken to as lower than the speaker. Although both figures were performed in Korean, the child figure was often voiced through nasality and rising-falling intonation, whereas the adult figure was often voiced through low pitch and increased volume.

Forms of speech understood as "nonnative" were used when voicing the Korean immigrant and Korean American figures. First, "Korean-accented

English" was often used when voicing the immigrant figure. Students referred to this figure as "fob" (acronym for "fresh off the boat"), a derogatory label for recently arrived immigrants (Kang and Lo 2005). Work on language crossing and mocking finds that the fob figure can be read in a range of ways, from the strict traditionalist to the bumbling incompetent (Chun 2009; Rampton 1995; Reyes 2007). There are several linguistic features that get associated with this figure, including syllable-timed rhythm (i.e., giving each syllable the same length) and epenthetic schwa (i.e., adding a vowel to the end of a word that ends in a consonant). "American-accented Korean," on the other hand, was often used when voicing the Korean American figure. This figure was seen as "ideal" because students aligned with this figure, whereas they did not align with the fob figure.

In the following sections, I will present just four interactions among many that illustrate how drawing on these four recognizable figures of Koreanness allowed youth to: sort out the available ways to be identifiably Korean; locate themselves in this complex milieu; accomplish specific kinds of interactional work; and contribute to circulating racial ideologies. In these interactions, I am not suggesting that students are *being* Korean. Rather, I trace how they voice a world of figures that get recognized as Korean, and they mobilize this world to position themselves in meaningful ways.

Pleading Korean Child Figure

This first example illustrates how the recognizability of the pleading Korean child figure gets established. In this interaction, many boys in the class are asking the girls to help them with their worksheet. In the excerpt below, Mark is asking Joo-eun if she will help him.

Example 1. **[05/25/07; 05:24:55]**[1]

30	Mark:	can you help me
31	Joo-eun:	No
32	Mark:	**towa cwe:** ((wriggles worksheet))
		help me
33		((Lucy laughs))
34	Pete:	girls are a lot smarter
35	Mark:	((purses lips, pulls chin back, wriggles head
36		and shoulders))
37	Chul:	No

38	Mark:	**towa cwe:::** ((purses lips, wriggles head,
39		shoulders, and worksheet))
40	Chul:	they're smarter but they're uglier.
41		((Mark stands, leans forward to look at
42		Joo-eun's worksheet; Joo-eun hits Mark
43		on head with folder; Mark grabs head, whimpers))
44	Chul:	Mark, **yeca hantey tulekaci malko naykke khapi hay**
		don't go to the girls (for help), copy mine
45	Pete:	oh okay
46	Mark:	Okay

Mark first asks Joo-eun for help in English. When she refuses, he asks again but in Korean. He elongates the phrase with a rising-falling intonational contour and he begins to wriggle the worksheet in his hand. Lucy laughs. Mark then purses his lips, pulls his chin back, and wriggles his head and shoulders before he repeats "help me" in Korean. The phrase is further elongated with a more elaborate intonational contour and he continues to purse his lips and wriggle his head, shoulders, and worksheet. Yet Joo-eun still does not offer help. Then, Mark gets out of his seat to look at her worksheet. Grinning, Joo-eun lightly hits him on the head with her folder and Mark grabs his head and whimpers. Chul then offers his assistance in Korean, which provides benevolence in the language in which it is sought.

As Mark codeswitches from English to Korean, he enacts a vocal and bodily transformation that gets read as a voicing contrast. Listeners mutually recognize and orient to this figure by how they respond: from scolding a child, as Joo-eun does, to placating a child, as Chul does. Voicing the pleading Korean child figure allows Mark to accomplish interactional work: although he fails to get assistance from Joo-eun, he succeeds in getting it from Chul. His recognized display of childlike whiny and wriggly Koreanness is identified by listeners as a recognizable figure of weakness or helplessness that can be chastised or appeased.

Authoritative Korean Adult Figure

In this next interaction, which occurs during break time, Bill has Mark by the shirt and challenges him to break free. Here, the pleading Korean child figure meets the authoritative Korean adult figure.

Example 2. [06/08/07; 05:44:12]

50	Bill:	try to break out. try to break out
51		((Mark attempts to lick Bill's thumb))
52	Bill:	you're gonna lick me? you're gonna lick me?((slaps Mark))
53		((Mark points to camera and Bill; Mark uses hand to
54		loosen Bill's grip))
55	Mark:	come on. **hacima::**

                   stop it

56		((Joo-eun and Luke laugh))
57	Mark:	**hacima:: hacima- a::phe aphe** ((increased volume))

                   it hurts

58		((Bill lets Mark go))
59	Luke:	**mweya i nom** ((increased volume, low pitch, mumbled, looking at Mark))

                   hey you, what the hell's going on over there?!

60	Mark:	what'd you say?
61		((laughter))
62	Chul:	**mweya i nom. mweya i nom** ((mumbled))
63	Ike:	I think he said **mweya i nom- i nom**

Initially, Mark makes nonverbal attempts to break free from Bill's grip: first by trying to lick Bill's hand (which invites a slap), then by pointing out Bill to the imagined viewer of the video recording. As Mark is using his hand to loosen Bill's grip, he repeatedly says "stop it" and "it hurts" in Korean with increased elongation, increased volume, and rising-falling intonation. His performance attracts laughter and attention from his classmates including Bill, after which Bill lets Mark go. Then Luke, who is also laughing, looks at Mark and shouts in low-pitched Korean (though muffled because he is eating), "hey you, what the hell's going on over there?!," after which there is a brief silence before Mark asks, "what did you say?," which is greeted by laughter and repetitions of the muffled Korean phrase.

As in the last example, the pleading Korean child figure is enacted and recognized as a voicing contrast. But here, the child figure gets scolded by what comes to be identified as another recognizable figure: the authoritative Korean adult. This adult figure is enacted in response to the child figure: claiming both its relative age distinction by using language that is associated with an adult male relative scolding a child, as well as its moral authority by characterizing as problematic the whiny and cowardly behavior that has been assigned to the child figure. As the pleading Korean child figure is scolded by the authoritative Korean adult figure, both figures come to mutually identify one another.

As the analysis reveals, the Korean child and adult figures are coupled with different displays of emotion and action: childlike whining when making pleas or adultlike anger when issuing commands. By assigning different emotions and actions to different figures, these youth divide Korean ethnic types based on what these types can express and do, while demonstrating how these figures can be relied upon to do specific kinds of interactional work. By doing this, speaker alignments are achieved as youth identify these figures as the ones responsible for (or more effective at) performing specific kinds of emotions and actions. But it is not just speakers who are positioned relative to figures; figures (i.e., child and adult) are positioned relative to one another. As Korean American group membership is achieved by way of mutual recognition and evaluation of these figures, youth recirculate racial ideologies about ways to be recognizably Korean, highlighting specific versions of Koreanness—that is, a pleading Korean child and an authoritative Korean adult—as salient figures to this group.

Korean Immigrant Fob Figure

This next example illustrates explicit discourses about the term "fob" (and its derivative "Fabio"), as well as the emergence of a recognizable fob figure. In this interaction, the teacher is confirming three answers to a task on their worksheets before moving on to the next page. "Hijack" is one of the answers, and Luke jokingly says "hi, Jack."

Example 3. **[05/18/07; 06:07:21]**

90	MT:	hijack fog and blend. anybody with questions about wh-page two
91	Luke:	hi. Jack
92	Mark:	Fob
93	Luke:	you're such a fob
94	Joo-eun:	[you're a fob
95	?:	[oo::::::::::
96	Bill:	Fabio
97	Luke:	who said I am

98	MT:	does everyone understand what we're doing on page-
99	Luke:	you are
100	?:	oo::::::::::
101	Joo-eun:	(shut up) do you know what a fob is?
102	Luke:	someone who's like-
103	Mark:	someone who can't speak [American and from Korea
104	Luke:	[American and
105	MT:	English
106	Pete:	Mrs. Turner [you know?
107	Lucy:	[fresh off the boat
108	Ike:	I can talk English. see I'm talking English ((slow, syllable-timed, sudden rising
109		and falling intonation))
110	Dan:	I talk English (("Englishu" [iŋglɪːʃə]))
111	Chul:	no you- you talk- um
112	Bill:	I can talk English. me too. ((falsetto, syllable-timed))
113	Chul:	you're a Fabio
114	Bill:	I can speak English ((falsetto, syllable-timed))

Hearing "hi, Jack" inspires Mark to say "fob." Being labeled a fob gets socially recognized as an insult through various instances of listener uptake: from the long "oohs" after people are categorized as fob (i.e., "you're such a fob," "you're a fob," "Fabio," "you are") to the verbal challenges after being categorized as fob (i.e., "who said I am?," "[shut up] do you know what a fob is?"). Luke and Mark define a fob in terms of linguistic and national orientation: "can't speak American" and "from Korea," and Lucy provides the phrase upon which the term is based: "fresh off the boat." Ike, Dan, and Bill start enacting a wide range of voices: from slow, syllable-timed speech with sudden rising and falling intonation; to falsetto, syllable-timed speech; to a nonnative English pronunciation of the word "English" ("Englishu" [iŋglɪːʃə]), which conforms to ideologies about Asian-accented English (Chun 2009).

Unlike the last two examples, the fob figure is voiced not only through enactments but also through descriptions. Describing the fob figure and enacting nonnative English emerge as identifiable ways to characterize the figure of the Korean immigrant and divide Korean ethnic types based on generation and linguistic proficiency. While students position the fob figure as the linguistically incompetent first generation, they position themselves as the linguistically competent 1.5 or second generation. Listeners recognize nonnative English performances as the voice of the fob figure through two main mechanisms: the successive unfolding of four phrases within a discussion of how to define a fob ("I can talk English. see I'm talking English"; "I talk English"; "I can talk English. me too"; "I can speak English"); and the explicit labeling of these phrases as "Fabio." Youth establish speaker alignments by explicitly describing the fob figure as unable to "speak American," by demonstrating this inability with phrases recognized as nonnative, by orienting to this figure as comical, and by setting this figure in a voicing contrast from the speech that precedes and surrounds the figure.

Voicing the fob figure reproduces racial ideologies that question Asian American national belonging and that understand languages in nation-state terms (i.e., "speak American"). These ideologies are not unrelated to the forever foreigner stereotype introduced at the start of this chapter. The fob figure and foreigner stereotype are, indeed, similar: a recognizable Asianness that conforms to ideas that those understood as Asian are also expected to be foreign and nonnative English-speaking. This interaction illustrates how the large-scale foreigner stereotype is reproduced through small-scale voicing routines of the fob figure.

Ideal Korean American Figure

This last example illustrates how the figure of the ideal Korean American emerges. Here, Mark claims an inability to pronounce Joo-eun's name. He calls her: "Joo-own."

Example 4. **[03/23/07; 04:50:48]**

120	Mark:	teacher? [I mean Ms. Turner
121	MT:	[yes
122	Mark:	um when- whenever someone talks
123		like they have something to share why do you close your eyes
124	Bill:	she's imagining (it)
125	Dan:	no she's bored
126	MT:	What
127	Mark:	like last week I remember the girl
128	MT:	which girl, what girl
129	Mark:	Her

130	MT:	who is she. who are you talking about
131	Mark:	I don't know. what's her name Joo-eun? (("Joo-own" [dʒuː.oʊːn]))
132		((laughter))
133	Chul:	Joo-eun (("Joo-own"))
134	Dan:	Joo-eun
135	Mark:	Yeah, so you know what I mean
136	Bill:	Joo-eun (("Joo-own"))
137	Dan:	Joo-eun
138	Mark:	Joo- yeah you know I don't have the Korean accent so yeah
139	MT:	I don't either
140	Pete:	yeah he's Chinese
141	MT:	that's nice
142	Joo-eun:	no he's Japanese
143	Chul:	Japanese
144	Mark:	ching chow

Claiming that he does not know or cannot pronounce Joo-eun's name, Mark performs an Anglicized rendition of it: "Joo-own." Laughter follows and students repeat her name in both its Anglicized form (i.e., [dʒuː.oʊːn]) and Korean form (i.e., [dʒuʊn]). Mark explicitly claims that he does not have "the Korean accent" and the students then declare fictive ethnicities for him, which he plays along with by performing the quintessential Mock Chinese phrase: "ching chow" (see Chun, this volume). By producing nonnative renditions of sounds linked to Asian languages— "Chinese" (e.g., "ching chow") and "Korean" (e.g., "Joo-own")—Mark positions himself not as a speaker of these languages but as a native English speaker authorized to comment on Asian languages and speakers to humorous effect.

These last two excerpts illustrate how the figures of the ideal Korean American and Korean immigrant fob emerge in a voicing contrast to which speakers can align. This last example, in particular, illustrates a more explicit way in which the ideal Korean American figure is produced: through mispronouncing a Korean name and mocking Chinese language (see chapter 15, this volume, for the raciolinguistic politics of (mis)naming). Whereas the fob figure also has trouble pronouncing words, it is seen as the wrong kind of mispronouncing. Anglicized Korean and Mock Chinese, on the other hand, emerge as proud emblems of the ideal Korean American figure. This figure—under the constant threat of being seen as foreign, to be sure—desires, instead, to be seen as native English-speaking through comedic performances of "Asian" languages.

Conclusion

By examining the interactions in an *Angry Little Girls* cartoon and in an Asian American supplementary school, I hope to have demonstrated that the relationship between language and race must be recast as *the voicing of figures*. Authentic speech and authentic speakers do not exist naturally in the world. Rather, what we have come to understand as authentic must have already undergone processes of authentication that emerge from interaction and circulate within social domains. That is to say, authentication is accomplished through voicing routines, which rely on voicing contrasts and speaker alignments, as well as the textual organization of signs, and the uptake of those signs in interaction.

In my data, the voicing of figures involves youth identifying, evaluating, and harnessing the various ways to be recognizably Korean. What meanings and effects do these practices achieve? For one, these voicing routines create a Korean American group membership through the mutual identification and evaluation of figures. Also, these voicing routines divide Korean ethnic types based on small-scale interactional distinctions and large-scale categorical distinctions: that is, small-scale contrasts of emotion and action (e.g., whiney pleas of the child figure, angry commands of the adult figure), and large-scale contrasts of linguistic proficiency and generation (e.g., nonnative English–speaking first-generation fob figure, native English–speaking 1.5- or second-generation Korean American figure). In addition, these voicing routines produce interactional effects, such as enabling speakers to receive kindness (child figure), and scold others (adult figure). Moreover, these voicing routines reproduce racial ideologies, such as identifying who is the "right" kind of Asian American (Korean American figure), and who is the "wrong" kind (immigrant fob figure).

Educational settings, such as this Asian American supplementary school, prove to be productive sites in which interactional and ideological work around race takes place. In my data, the use of nonnative "accents" and the use of Korean as a "secret language" helped establish recognizable figures to which students could position themselves in educational sites. These routines helped carve out unofficial classroom spaces in which students mobilized these figures for interactional work: from getting help with school work to assigning different kinds of linguistic performances to different kinds of Asian Americans. Research on classroom discourse that more fully considers talk outside of "official" teacher-student interaction can gain better insight on the classroom practices that emerge as meaningful to students. In addition, research on how ideas about race are produced through humorous frames in educational settings reveals the ways in which potentially thorny issues like race get reworked across interactional routines (Reyes 2007, 2011).

I will end by emphasizing the absolute centrality of social interaction in the study of language and race. Both the *Angry Little Girls* cartoon and my data at the Asian American supplementary school illustrate how large-scale racial ideologies are locatable in small-scale interactional routines: whether it is Kim responding to a "compliment," or it is fifth graders defining and performing the fob figure. Yet more than being a mere site of ideology, interaction is the very site of ideological reproduction: the maintenance of racial ideologies necessarily relies on the voicing of figures in and across such interactional routines.

Notes

* Earlier versions of this chapter were presented at the Annual Meeting of the American Anthropological Association in New Orleans, Louisiana in November 2010; at the Racing Language, Languaging Race Conference at the Center for Race, Ethnicity, and Language at Stanford University in May 2012; and at the Language and Linguistics Speaker Series at Temple University in February 2013. My warmest gratitude to H. Samy Alim, Arnetha Ball, and John Rickford for inviting me to give this talk at Stanford, and for their ongoing encouragement and support of my work. I am particularly indebted to the following individuals for their generous insights and guidance on earlier versions of this chapter: Arnetha Ball, Paul Garrett, Misty Jaffe, Yasuko Kanno, Jonathan Rosa, Stanton Wortham, and especially H. Samy Alim, Elaine Chun, and Adrienne Lo. For their invaluable research assistance, I thank Eun Kyoung Lee, Ji Hyun Lee, and Samuel Lee. Finally, I thank Gayle Isa for introducing me to the *Little Angry Girls* cartoon that opened this chapter. All remaining weaknesses are, of course, my own.

1. Transcription conventions:

bold	Korean utterance in Yale romanization
italics	English translation
(( ))	transcriber comment
:::	elongated sound
-	abrupt stop
?	rising intonation
.	falling intonation

References

Agha, Asif. 2005. Voicing, footing, enregisterment. *Journal of Linguistic Anthropology* 15(1): 38–59.

Alim, H. Samy, and Geneva Smitherman. 2012. *Articulate While Black: Barack Obama, Language, and Race in the U.S.* New York: Oxford University Press.

Anderson, Benedict. 1983. *Imagined Communities: Reflections on the Origin and Spread of Nationalism.* New York: Verso.

Bakhtin, Mikhail. 1981 [1935]. *The Dialogic Imagination.* Austin: University of Texas Press.

Bucholtz, Mary. 2003. Sociolinguistic nostalgia and the authentication of identity. *Journal of Sociolinguistics* 7(3): 398–416.

Bucholtz, Mary, and Kira Hall. 2005. Identity and interaction: A sociocultural linguistic approach. *Discourse Studies* 7(4–5): 585–614.

Chun, Elaine. 2009. Ideologies of legitimate mockery: Margaret Cho's revoicings of Mock Asian. In Angela Reyes and Adrienne Lo, eds., *Beyond Yellow English: Toward a linguistic anthropology of Asian Pacific America*, 261–87. New York: Oxford University Press.

Gal, Susan, and Judith T. Irvine. 1995. The boundaries of languages and disciplines: How ideologies construct difference. *Social Research* 62: 967–1001.

Goffman, Erving. 1974 *Frame Analysis: An Essay on the Organization of Experience.* New York: Harper & Row.

Goffman, Erving. 1981. *Forms of Talk.* Philadelphia: University of Pennsylvania Press.

Hill, Jane H. 2008. *The Everyday Language of White Racism.* Malden, MA: Wiley-Blackwell.

Ignatiev, Noel. 1995. *How the Irish Became White.* New York: Routledge.

Inoue, Miyako. 2006. *Vicarious Language: Gender and Linguistic Modernity in Japan.* Berkeley: University of California Press.

Kang, M. Agnes, and Adrienne Lo. 2005. Two ways of articulating heterogeneity in Korean American narratives of ethnic identity. *Journal of Asian American Studies* 7(2): 93–116.

Lee, Stacey. 1996. *Unraveling the "Model Minority" Stereotype: Listening to Asian American Youth.* New York: Teachers College Press.

Makoni, Sinfree, and Alastair Pennycook. 2005. Disinventing and (Re)constituting Languages. *Critical Inquiry in Language Studies* 2(3): 137–56.

Omi, Michael, and Howard Winant. 1986. *Racial Formation in the United States: From the 1960s to the 1980s.* New York: Routledge.

Rampton, Ben. 1995. *Crossing: Language and Ethnicity among Adolescents.* London: Longman.

Reyes, Angela. 2007. *Language, Identity, and Stereotype among Southeast Asian American Youth: The Other Asian.* Mahwah, NJ: Lawrence Erlbaum.

Reyes, Angela. 2011. "Racist!": Metapragmatic regimentation of racist discourse by Asian American youth. *Discourse & Society* 22(4): 458–73.

Tuan, Mia. 1998. *Forever Foreigners or Honorary Whites? The Asian Ethnic Experience Today.* New Brunswick, NJ: Rutgers University Press.

Urciuoli, B. 1996. *Exposing Prejudice: Puerto Rican Experiences of Language, Race, and Class.* Boulder, CO: Westview Press.

18

"Socials," "Poch@s," "Normals" *y los demás*

School Networks and Linguistic Capital of High School Students on the Tijuana–San Diego Border

ANA CELIA ZENTELLA

Many thousands of students who live near the 2,000-mile border that separates Mexico from its former territories—California, Arizona, New Mexico, and Texas—interact on a regular basis with North Americans and Mexicans in English and Spanish, in both Mexico and the United States. Whether they were born in Mexico or in the United States of Mexican immigrant parents, most *fronterizo* (border) students cross national as well as linguistic and cultural borders frequently. Their fluent bilingual skills and extensive bicultural experiences distinguish them from first-generation Mexican immigrants who have not attended high school as well as from their second-generation counterparts in schools removed from the border. Educators, social service personnel, health professionals, and other gatekeepers are often unaware of the significant differences among these groups or of intragroup distinctions, a fact that hampers their work and hinders students' success.

Amid rising Hispanophobia in the United States (see chapter 3, this volume), the nation is polarized by arguments on behalf of and against immigrants—Mexicans in particular—without the information required to enact policies and programs that can ensure a successful future for the children of immigrants. The bilingual and bicultural talents of *fronterizos*—and the unfulfilled promise of their potential contribution to their families, the region, and the nation—make the situation especially deplorable.

Observations of student networks at Border High (a pseudonym; hereafter referred to as BH) on the U.S.-Mexico border in San Diego revealed a wealth of linguistic diversity and skills that often go unnoticed and are sometimes disparaged, even by the students. Most significant is the impact of the racial-ization processes that stigmatize Mexicans as nonwhite; imagine them, their region, and their schools as violent and out of order; and view the varieties of English and Spanish that they speak as incorrect and/or impure. As Bonnie Urciuoli (2001) has explained, while the purported postracial society of the early twenty-first century may regard public comments about skin color, noses, hair, and bodies as politically incorrect and deserving of sanctions, disparaging remarks about the way racialized groups speak are commonplace and acceptable. In this way, race has been remapped from biology onto language. But unlike race, critics believe that speakers can and should either change their ways of speaking or be held accountable. Young people—attuned to social currents—reflect these attitudes and unwittingly participate in reinforcing them in the ways they speak and how they speak about speaking.

This summary of a sociolinguistic ethnography carried out in 2007–2009 focuses on the language behaviors and attitudes of English-Spanish bilinguals, specifically students of Mexican origin at a public high school located two miles from the world's busiest land border crossing, which divides Tijuana and San Diego; it is the first such study of a border high school in California. The results reveal a range of social networks and identities at BH that confound popular "we versus they," "English versus Spanish," and "American versus Mexican" dichot-omies, as adolescents grapple with overlapping and contradictory definitions, views, and practices. The implications for teacher training, educational assess-ments, language curriculum, and student counseling deserve further study.

What Do We Need to Know?

Our principal queries are: How do Mexican-origin students in distinct high school networks envision the role that bilingualism will play in their future careers and families? What kind of bilingualism do they espouse, and what kind do they practice? Do some view their bilingualism as a part of their cultural capi-tal, accumulated like money or a personal commodity for individual advance-ment? Do students display a repertoire of views, depending on the immediate setting, interlocutors, and objective? Do members of particular networks set themselves apart from other students? How are their linguistic practices and attitudes linked to their academic success? Ultimately, we seek to document the distinct ways in which "doing being bilingual" (Auer 1984) occurs in varied high school networks of Mexican-origin students.

At the microlevel, features of the varieties of Spanish and English distinguish specific networks at BH, along with their use of language mixing or code switch-ing. In keeping with my call for an anthro-political linguistics, these data help illuminate "a stigmatized group's attempts to construct a positive self within an economic and political context that relegates its members to static and disparaged ethnic, racial and class identities, and that identifies them with static and disparaged language codes and practices" (Zentella 1997, 13). National, statewide, and local policies negatively affect the education, language, and/or immigration of students of Mexican origin, as does the intensified anti-immigrant fervor stirred by vigilante groups who pursue the undocumented. At the same time, there is increased national and international recognition that bilingual and bicultural world citizens are required for a global economy. Are some students and networks more encouraged or discouraged by these realities than others? What role, if any, do they believe bilingualism can play as they confront them?

Educators in the San Diego border region have called for a new "border pedagogy" (Venegas-García and Romo 2005). In our view, this pedagogy must be built on empirical research, including a language focus that is ethnographically rooted. Discovering the major school networks, their gathering spots, and the language behaviors and attitudes of their members required months of observations of the campus and classes, as well as tape-recorded interviews with students, teachers, and administrators after securing permissions from the district, the school, students, and parents. Bilingual student research assistants from the University of California, San Diego (UCSD) were trained in the theories and methods of ethnography relevant to educational settings, network analysis, sociolinguistic interviews, and transcription conventions.[1] But a sociolinguistic ethnography of school networks must build upon an understanding of the larger community—its socioeconomic and political context.

Border High at the Crossroads: The U.S.-Mexico Border in California

The students who attend BH live in the southernmost part of San Diego County, California, close to the international border that divides San Diego, California, from Tijuana, México, in a community we refer to as "Border Town." Situated at the busiest international crossroads of the world—sixty million people cross each year to enter the United States—Border Town is not as wealthy as the rest of San Diego, but it is not as poor as Tijuana (Kada and Kiy 2004); the income per capita in Border Town is $10,372, and household income is $31,241. The area has been hard-hit by the economic recession that began in 2008; homes have depreciated by 27 to 40 percent.[2] More than 95 percent of the student body at BH were working-class. To attend school they were bused to and from the isolated, sprawling, and attractive new 52-acre campus that opened in 2002.

The great majority of BH's 2,194 students were "Hispanic" (92.8%)—all Mexicans. A much smaller group of African Americans (2.4%) occupied second place. A few whites (1.1%) and Asians (1.1%), most of Filipino background, and an even smaller number of Pacific Islanders (.1%), completed the student body. In terms of economic and linguistic background, BH students had low incomes and low English monolingual rates, variables often linked to academic failure and social problems. More than three-fourths came from families who lived below the poverty level, and 60 percent lived at 200 percent below that line (WASC/CDE Self Study 2007–2008). Consequently, 80 percent of the student body qualified for free or reduced meals. Almost all (90%) spoke Spanish at home, and three-fourths were classified as English Language Learners. The majority of the 43 students (20 males and 23 females) we interviewed, like the others of Mexican background, were born in the United States (n = 27), and most of those born in Mexico (n = 14) had moved to the United States before the age of ten; all visited relatives in Mexico frequently.[3]

Misconceptions about Border High

Many members of the public assume that a high school for predominantly working-class Mexican students, especially near the Tijuana border, is dirty, dilapidated, unsafe, and violent. BH students know that they are often stereotyped unfairly, and many have experienced this personally. They speak of being amused/dismayed by people who are shocked to learn that they attend BH: "Oh my God, don't go there, you're gonna get shot!" Rocker (R)[4] was surprised by this reaction in Logan Heights, another predominantly Mexican neighborhood, close to downtown San Diego. In response, Zero (P) chimed in:

> "I have a friend that lives in Chula Vista in the high school over there, so she asked me, 'Where you live?' or 'Where you go to school?' 'I'm in Border High School.' And she said, 'Oh that's a lot of *cholos* [supposed gang members] over there,' so."

But Rocker challenges the misconception: "A lot of wanna be!"

The negative stereotypes are immediately dispelled with one visit to the spacious campus. The grounds are very clean (during lunch, the popular and well-respected principal and assistant principals walk around urging students to pick up trash), and quiet and empty during class hours. Students are expected to get to class on time, and classroom doors are locked to ensure that only those with passes can gain late entry. BH is the only high school in the district that requires uniforms (white shirt and dark pants/skirts, closed shoes), which contributes to a sense of unity and uniformity, although students' hairstyles, jackets, makeup, scarves, bags, and jewelry allow for individual statements linked to their social identities (see below). Whether they are streaming out of buses in the morning or boarding them at 4 p.m., or eating lunch at benches on the campus from 1:20 to 1:55, most seem orderly, calm, and respectful; in two years I did not see any fights or disturbances and heard little raucous screaming or yelling. The weather and year-round schedule makes it possible for students to eat outside almost every day, gathering with friends at the specific locales that constitute their network's "territory."

Student Networks, Territories, Languages

The first thing you notice upon entering BH is the frequency with which both English and Spanish are spoken, but a closer look reveals that specific networks are linked to specific languages. Certain locales, like the Senior Lawn and the benches that formed an "L J" where the Asian, African American, and other English monolinguals gathered along with fluent advanced placement (AP) bilinguals, have been the territories of their counterparts in previous years. Figure 18.1, an elaborated version of the view from Google Earth, maps out the

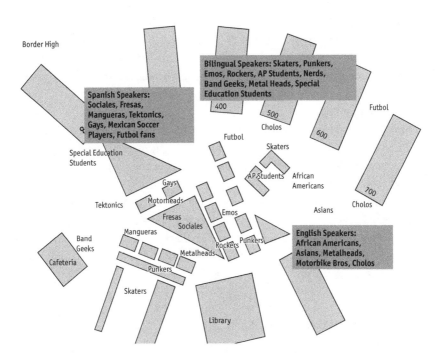

Figure 18.1 Territories occupied by Border High students and their networks.

territories occupied by the students we interviewed and their networks, as well as many others, totaling nineteen networks.

Although most students claimed they were "normals," or *normales* (N), and most of the ninth graders had not yet become linked with a labeled group, specific networks occupied a particular bench or spot and identified with one or both languages. The descriptions below, based on our ethnographic observations and hour-long interviews in both English and Spanish, reveal how students saw themselves and how others saw them. They include representative quotes of widely held views, and vocabulary items that are part of a group's argot.

Leading Spanish-Dominant Networks

Socials/*sociales* seem to be the northern Mexico and U.S.-based version of central Mexico's despised *fresas* (lit., "strawberrries," see below); nobody who is not a "social" had anything good to say about them. They are described as well dressed, sporting the same name brands and hairstyles as *fresas*. However, they are sometimes criticized as poorer wannabe versions of *fresas* who buy at discount stores. Females dress "girly," and are viewed as "very delicate" and "show offs."

Fresas are economically well-off students, usually born and raised in Mexico, well coiffed, who wear brand-name clothes, bags, and shoes (e.g., Hollister, Aeropostale, Abercrombie, Coach). They carry Nextel international cell phones, display good jewelry, and are the object of scorn: [they are] "the people who think a lot of themselves and they're always trying to impress people." Their Spanish is rapid-fire: "Oh yeah like, they talk really fast!" The most overtly stereotyped markers of *fresa* and "social" speech are the discourse marker *o sea* (see below) and an unmistakably whiny sing-song intonation that almost everyone can and does imitate.

Mangueras are wealthy males, usually born and raised in Mexico, considered *wannabe narcos*, who have pretentious tough-guy manners, and *players*, who attract women: "They just think that they are hot but they're not . . . there's girls around them all the time."

Tektonics are male "socials" who follow a French dance craze and wear Mohawk hairstyles, tight black pants, and brand-name clothes.

Electros/Cosmics like electronic music. "Electros that are here they mainly speak Spanish and they always, yeah 'cause they spend most of their time going to TJ (Tijuana), going to clubs over there."

Leading English-Dominant Groups

Monolingual African Americans and Anglos; Asians (Filipinos and Chinese) were often bilingual in Tagalog or one or more Chinese languages.

MEXICAN AMERICANS, NONE MONOLINGUAL:

Cholitos/cholitas[5] were usually second-generation Mexican Americans who tended to have tattoos; they wore high socks, baggy pants, and Ecko sneakers with a Rhino logo. Girls sported hoop earrings, dyed black hair, shaved eyebrows penciled in by "sharpies," pierced lips, short tight blouses exposing the navel, and tomboyish-style clothes. Chol@s assumed a tough attitude but *"nomás se quieren vestir así y quieren ser algo que no son y se creen mucho, pero no son realmente"* ("they just want to dress that way and they want to be something they're not and they think a lot of themselves, but they aren't really"). Their English lexicon was well known ("They got a different slang"); it was influenced by African American English (homes/homie, bro) but more so by Pachuco *caló* (*vato* = dude; *ése* [term of address]; *jaina* = girlfriend, honey; *leiva* = male), as well as Mexican slang (*¿Qué onda, güey?* = Wha's up, dude?). Sometimes they mixed influences, for example, *¿Qué onda*, homie? Chol@s were reputedly *bien groseras* [re the girls] *y bien corrientes* ("very vulgar and very common/street"); they cursed a lot, e.g., *No mames* (Don't fuck/mess around).

Nerds were few, and usually loners: *"Con sus lentes y así en la esquina . . . . en serio la mayoría usa lentes"* ("with their glasses and like that on the corner . . . seriously most wear glasses").

Bros/bro-hos were passionate about motorbikes, motor cross, quads; males wore shorts with long socks, sunglasses, spiky hair. They disdained "followers," like Tektonics.

Bilingual Networks

Skaters included first- and second-generation Mexicans. They wore Vans shoes and tight jeans, had varied hairstyles including spiky (short or long), and ear plugs.[6] Skater lexicon described the tricks they performed: heel flip, kick flip, a three sixty flip, a trade flip, a fifty fifty, grinding, board slide, down slide. They were known for their frequent use of "dude," "Dude, I couldn't bust any trick"; sometimes they mixed both languages: *"Caí un* kick flip" ("I landed a kick flip").

AP/Honor students included first- and second-generation Mexicans with conventional dress and hairstyles. To distinguish themselves from nerds, they did not play Yu-gui-oh cards, or wear "nerd-like" glasses, and were proud of their bilingual fluency.

Punkers punks/*puncos* (P) favored punk rock; they wore patches on their clothes, Mohawk hairstyles, brightly colored hair, chains on clothes, spike bracelets, and piercings.

Rockers (R) were mainly second-generation Mexicans noticeable for their many bracelets, tight sweaters and jeans, spiky hair, and t-shirts with rock bands' names.

EMOS (reportedly fewer than 10), or "emotionals," had long hair with bangs that covered one eye and half their face. They were loners, acted depressed, and refused to participate in the study.

To summarize, some networks of Mexican-origin students leaned toward Spanish and others toward English, depending on length of time in the United States and birthplace, as well as on their school activities, sports, music, and academics. But all were bilingual to greater or lesser degrees. Style determined groupings more than language, as Hermana explained: "They put them in groups because of how they look and not because, I don't think, because of how they speak." Students at both ends of the network-language spectrum (i.e., wealthier Spanish-dominant *fresas* and socials) and working-class English-dominant *cholitos/cholitas* were the most often criticized and stereotyped linguistically. Yet some students switched networks with little problem.

At the Border of Two Worlds: Language Choices and Patterns

For the vast majority of students at BH, English and Spanish were co-equal lingua francas. Both languages were so interchangeable among Mexican-origin students that it was impossible to tell, even after two years, who might address whom in English or Spanish, even if they were known to be part of a particular group. Language address patterns at school were often a reversal of patterns at home. The respect norms that require Spanish with parents but allow adolescents to speak English to a sibling were inverted at BH, where the language of respect for authority was English, and Spanish was relegated to workers with low status and fellow students. All classes (except the Spanish courses) and school business were conducted in English, and all the administrative staff and teachers insisted on addressing the students in English only. Thus, the symbolic power of English was maintained via the status of the speakers who favored one language or the other, and English was the most visible in powerful roles (e.g., notices on bulletin boards, PA announcements, the language of the classroom, and parent meetings).[7] The English-only policy was part of a schoolwide effort to promote English proficiency, in order to help students pass the California High School Exit Exam (CAHSEE), and to prepare them for future studies and careers (see "The CAHSEE Hurdle," below). Every student acknowledged the importance of learning to speak, read, and write "standard" English. It was also drilled into them by teachers, school policies, and the English part of the do-or-die CAHSEE.[8]

Nevertheless, all students also recognized the importance of Spanish in their families and in the broader community, and its link to their Mexican identity. No matter what their network or dominant language, BH students seemed uneasy with hard and fast categories and preferred a complex negotiation of languages, birth-place, legal citizenship, residence, race, and national allegiances. What many in both Mexico and the United States might consider simple distinctions, such as between Mexican and Mexican American, were challenged by students. All interviewees had at least one Mexican-born parent and were themselves citizens or legal residents of the United States, so all could legitimately claim to be Mexican American, but official designations were often trumped by personal feelings and experiences.

At least two students insisted that no students at BH ever referred to themselves as Mexican Americans ("You don't hear that"), although, in fact, eighteen did claim that identity. One of the students who said he'd never heard anyone identify as Mexican American, Voltaire (AP), explained his own identity in what amounts to a circumlocution of Mexican American: "I'm um American. That has ancestry that—with ancestry from Mexico is what I would say." Rocker, on the other hand, avoided the hyphenated label and claimed "Hispanic or Latino." Two Honor/AP students, in contrast, insisted on identifying as Mexican and rejected Mexican American because, "Mexican American people think like 'Ohhh, she thinks she's like, white or whatever.' Or that your parents have lived here, and that your grandparents have lived here and that you're not really connected with the border." But other students who did not feel disconnected from the border or Mexico chose both Mexican *and* Mexican American because they saw little difference between them, as Guadalupe ("normal") explains:

> INT: *¿No hay diferencia entre un mexicano y un méxico-americano?*
> [There's no difference between a Mexican and a Mexican American?]
> G: *Me han dicho que no soy mexicana porque no nací en México pero yo me siento mexicana porque mis papás son de México, mi familia son [sic] de México, y tengo raíces mexicanas, pero para mí no hay diferencia.*
> [I've been told that I'm not Mexican because I wasn't born in Mexico but I feel Mexican because my parents are from Mexico, my family are [sic] from Mexico, and I have Mexican roots, but to me there's no difference.]

Guadalupe had never lived or studied in Mexico, yet she always identified as closely with the country where her parents were raised as with the country where she was born and raised, as did many BH students. For others, not having lived in Mexico pushed them to identify as Mexican American, as Celia ("social") explains: "I'm not full Mexican 'cause I've never actually lived in TJ and I think it's really different how they live and how we live." And some students have switched identities; for instance, Atleta ("normal") began identifying as Mexican American when she moved to the United States after having lived in Mexico, where she identified as Mexican, although she was born in the United States.

Birthplace or residence alone was rarely enough to determine a student's preferred identity; language skills and preferences played a key role. Spanish-dominant speakers were expected to identify as Mexican and English-dominant speakers were expected to identify as Mexican-American, but race/color was sometimes mentioned in the ascription of language dominance, and it was also mentioned in decisions about national identities. It was clear that students—even the very light-skinned—believed Mexican was equivalent to non-White. Hermana ("nerd"), who had light skin and long curly black hair and brown eyes, explained her identification with the Mexican part of Mexican American based on "the physicals" as well as the language. The majority of students were conflicted about choosing a label that excluded the other part of their identity, recognizing their allegiance to two nations, languages, and cultures. Hermana provided a dramatic example of the conflict, and of ambivalent feelings:

> I think of it as like an army (laughs), like if you were in the Mexican army would you fight for Mexico or would you fight for USA [INT: *Aha.*] and I wouldn't know which to choose because I like both countries.

Perhaps Hermana and others will change their identity claims as a result of exposure to non-*fronterizo* norms and ideologies after graduation, on their college campuses, or at work. For some university student *transfronterizos*, contact with outsiders led to hurtful experiences with stereotypes that racialized Mexico, Mexicans, Spanish speakers, and the border (Zentella 2009).

Poch@s and Spanglish: Opening or Closing Doors to Both Languages?

Pocho/a was one ethnic label that almost no students used but most had no difficulty defining; it was clearly identified with the second generation and its language practices. In addition to *descolorido* (faded) and *putrefacción/podrido* (rotting/rotten) as leading definitions of *pocho*, the Larousse dictionary (2003, 810) specifies the linguistic component of the identity label, and also includes the noun that refers specifically to the mixture of Spanish and English:

> s. Mex. *Persona de origen mexicano que vive en EUA y que ha adoptado las costumbres estadounidenses y habla el español con anglicismos.* (Person of Mexican origin who lives in the USA and who has adopted U.S. customs and speaks Spanish with anglicisms.)
>   2. Mex. *Mezcla de español con inglés.* (Mixture of Spanish and English.)

The translations that BH students offered for *poch@* were similar in some respects, but confusing in others. For example, four friends who had only been in the United States for one to five years agreed that birthplace was key to the definition of *pocho/a*: "*Tú eres de aquí, tus papás de México*" ("You're from here, your parents are from Mexico"). They expanded this to include linguistic aspects, for example, making mistakes ("pos" instead of "pues"—a working-class feature), talking "cut off," and talking Spanish with an English accent. Additionally, Media, a "normal," got to the heart of the "mixed language" aspect of the definition with a criticism that made everyone laugh: "*Pochos* are people who speak Spanish and English together *y no deben hablar así* ('and they shouldn't talk that way')." Her sentence reflects the mixture that characterized the speech of most networks at BH. The low status of *poch@s* and their mixed speech also came up when Rocker and Voltaire tried to define *pocho*:

INT: Um what about *pocho*.

ROCKER: I don't know what it [xxx] My mom has told me it's someone that really never really wants to get an education or doesn't— like he speaks but he mixes too much. He doesn't really stick to one type of language. Or somebody who's um—

VOLTAIRE: Uneducated.

ROCKER: Uneducated.

VOLTAIRE: And I've heard it's someone who moves from place to place. They go to Mexico and then they go to the U.S. and then they go back to Mexico and they come back to the U.S.

In addition to linking *pocho* with "uneducated," Voltaire metaphorically extends the notion of going back and forth between languages to going back and forth between countries. In fact, switching between Spanish and English, sometimes referred to as Spanglish or *pocho*, is a verbal display of students' dual national identities, that is, it's an audible reminder of their connection to both Mexico and the United States. The fact that languages were frequently mixed at BH was widely recognized as normal and natural, as Arquea (AP) remarked:

ACZ: Do you think here it's cooler to speak only English at Border High? Or it's cooler to speak only Spanish?

ARQUEA: I—well I think it's like cooler I guess both? Like, *pochos* I guess, like.

It may be cooler at BH to "speak both," but many students have been told by relatives and teachers to avoid mixing, to avoid being identified as a *poch@*.

Yet many speak both because they *are* both. For example, Flor, a "social" who hoped to work for the FBI and reported that her mother called her a *pocha* when she mixed languages, said, "When they ask me, either I'm Mexican or I'm American." Most students know they are supposed to reject Spanglish, but few do, and some point out its benefits, including enhanced comprehension; as Princesa (normal/social) explained, "*Pues yo pienso que está bien—mezclarlo, así-[xxx] entender las cosas mejor, como son.*" (Well I think it's alright—to mix them, like that [xxx] to understand things better, how they are.) In another conversation, Pharma (social) echoed Princesa's view of Spanglish as helpful: "It's opening um, opening doors to both languages." But other students thought that Spanglish closed doors instead of opening them, because of its limited marketability, and/or they found it confusing. Yet frequency of switching is less important than knowing when, where, and with whom it was appropriate to speak Spanglish. BH's Honor students, all of whom were heading to a university, were the most fluent bilinguals and frequent Spanglish speakers, but they were also the most aware of the need to be able to keep the languages separate when necessary (*tenemos que saber cómo separarlos bien* ["we have to know how to separate them well"]).

BH students differed in terms of network affiliation, birthplace, years of residence in Mexico and/or San Diego, and language dominance, yet the overwhelming presence of *fronterizos*, who were constantly negotiating Spanish and English outside of school, led students from every network—when they commented on others—to focus on styles they did not like, not a specific language or the mixing of languages. There were, however, three discourse features that were widely stigmatized and linked to the most stigmatized networks, although they were often used by others.

Stigmatized Discourse Markers: *o sea, güey,* like

The use of *o sea* ("I mean" or "in other words") occasioned the most passionate criticism; "annoying" was a common descriptor, and it was usually linked to "socials/*fresas*," particularly females. The stereotype was so strong that nobody admitted to saying *o sea*, including "socials," and it was believed that members of other networks did not say it. Overall, the low number of *o seas* (86) in our corpus of over 42,000 Spanish words was in such stark contrast to the frequency with which it was mentioned as a descriptor of "socials/*fresas*" that it suggests the interview situation constrained its use. Nevertheless, revealing differences confirmed students' views. Whereas 46 percent of the males never said *o sea*, and it constituted only .10 percent of the males' Spanish words, the one who said it the most (n = 9) was a Tektonic leader, a "social." And although

Table 18.1 **O Sea and Like Averages for Social Networks (Rank in Parentheses)**

	O sea %	Like %
Sociales n = 10	0.31 (1)	3.71 (4)
Nerds/AP n = 9	0.18 (2)	3.86 (3)
Normals n = 14	0.14 (3)	4.22 (2)
Rockers/Skaters/Outsiders n = 8	0.03 (4)	4.23 (1)
Total n =	86	2,330

an almost identical proportion of the females (45%) never said *o sea* either, *o seas* amounted to .19 percent of their Spanish words, almost double that of males. More revealing was the fact that the girl who produced one-third of the total of all the females' *o seas* was a social. In fact, the networks were clearly ranked in expected ways in their use of both *o sea* and "like," as Table 18.1 indicates.

In contrast to the absence of *o sea*, all the students used "like" in innovative ways (3.9% of the English corpus), including as a quotative complementizer (e.g., "He's like, 'You're crazy'"); as a clause initial preposition linked to the previous topic (e.g., "Like my uncle's sister married this guy"); or as a discourse particle that signals epistemic stance/attitude (e.g., "She's like really smart") (D'Arcy 2006, 32). The females said "like" more frequently, averaging 4.7 percent, in contrast to 3 percent for the males. But a male who was an "outsider/ bro" was the leading user of "like" (8.9%), indicating that the link between network membership and "like" was stronger than gender, which is borne out by the ranking in Table 18.1. "Normals" had rates similar to the Outsiders, whereas "socials," who led in *o sea,* were the least likely to say "like." Europa, a "normal" and the second-highest user of "like" (7.2%), seemed unaware of the extent to which "like" was a habit for her:

ACZ: Do you say "like" a lot?
EUR: I do say it. But not to like, a point where it gets annoying.

"Outsiders" and "normals" like Europa thought *o sea* was annoyingly omnipresent in social females' speech, but they ignored the repeated "likes" in their own speech. Along with the whiny intonation they imitated, they identified *o sea* with a saccharine femininity that was a silly attempt at cool. They also criticized the same girls for using a predominantly male term of address, *güey,* from the word for "ox" (*buey*), which is the Mexican equivalent of "dude" (note "like *o sea* like"):

> Hermanita (AP): I think socials like—socialize—they think like—all cool, that's why girls talk like that uhm the way they talk you can easily notice like *o sea* like, just girly, like for me it's annoying and they start saying *güey* in between girls, they start saying *güey* a lot and it's like annoying.

Bucholtz (2009) has identified the important stances, including status and solidarity, that *güey* performs as an in-group marker among Mexican immigrant male students in a Southern California high school. The spread of *güey/huey* (the written form varies) among women at BH was related to some of the same stances, but because it was usually linked to males and informality, it was disparaged by most, especially those who disliked socials, like Hermanita and Europa. They may have avoided *güey* and *o sea,* but even in their critiques of socials' style and content they were poster girls for repetitive "like":

> EUROPA: Like, they talk about like—*como* like they talk about nonsense.
>   (All laugh.)

Note that Europa was an innovator in mixing Spanish *como* ("like") with English "like" to produce "*como* like." I first noted this incipient grammaticalization of "*como* like" in the speech of one working-class male college student *transfronterizo* (Zentella 2006). At BH, however, true to sociolinguistic findings about the leading role of middle-class women in innovative change, Europa and Arquea, proficient bilinguals, produced the most compelling examples of "*como* like."

In Europa's case her *como* in "*como* like" is the only insertion of Spanish enmeshed in a string of "likes" that is a critique of Spanish-dominant girls who speak endlessly about boring topics and repeat a discourse crutch, *o sea.* At the same time that she is dismissing them, she is proclaiming her bilingual identity by inserting "*como* like." Despite disclaimers, Europa and others at BH were constructing an identity that included the stereotyped markers of Spanish-dominant preppy girls (*o sea*) with those that have become stereotypical of Southern California Valley girls ("like")—both middle-class markers that reveal their class identification and/or goals. The predominance of "like" (2,330), which swamps the occurrences of *o sea* (62), is another indicator of the greater power and status of English in their lives.

The CAHSEE Hurdle

Ever since the CAHSEE math and English exams were instituted in 2006, a debate has raged about the educational benefits of using one high-stakes measure (albeit allowing eight attempts) to determine whether students can graduate with a high school diploma. The English Language Arts (ELA) section includes 82 multiple choice questions and 2 essays based on standards from six language arts strands (# of questions in parens): Word Analysis (10), Reading Comprehension (24), Literary Response and Analysis (24), Writing Strategies (11), Writing Conventions (13), and Writing Applications (2 essays); Reading Comprehension and Literary Response and Analysis account for more than 50 percent of the questions.

At BH, the schoolwide ELA results for 2009, which included Special Ed students and English learners, indicated that 65 percent passed (= 350 out of 450 possible points), and 33 percent of that group were "proficient" (i.e., they scored 380 or above). The lowest scores were earned by those students who were in Special Ed and ELD (English Language Development) courses, only 15 percent of whom passed, and none at the proficient level. The ELD students in some upper courses fared a little better: 20.2 percent passed, with 4.2 percent proficient. The best scores were earned by the students who were in the advanced English 10 courses, which included English-only speakers, mainstreamed Special Ed

Table 18.2 **Border High School Students: Social Network, CAHSEE Score, and Oral English Rating**

	Age/Yrs in US	*Birthplace*	*CAHSEE*	*OE*	*Network*
1	17/17	US	1/Pr/418	G	AP
2	17/17	US	1/Pr/413	G	AP/Nerd
3	16/13	MX	1/Pr/412	G	Social/Fresas
4	18/13	MX	1/Pr/409	G	AP
5	18/13	US*	1/Pr/409	G	AP/Nerd
6	17/17	US	1/Pr/391	G	Social
7	16/14	US*	1/Pr/385	F	Normal/Social
8	17/17	US	1/Pr/381	G	Normal
9	16/16	US	1/P/377	G	Bros
10	18/14	MX	3/P/374	F	Skaters
11	17/17	US	1/P/373	G	Social
12	18/18	US	1/P/373	G	Normal/Social
13	17/9	MX	1/P/368	G	AP
14	17/17	US	1/P/366	G	Normal
15	17/17	US	1/P/365	G	Rockers
16	17/4	US*	2/P/365	P	Outsider/Metal

(continued)

Table 18.2 **Continued**

	Age/Yrs in US	Birthplace	CAHSEE	OE	Network
17	16/12	MX	2/P/362	G	AP/Emo
18	17/2	MX	5/P/362	P	Trolo/Social
19	18/18	US	1/P/361	G	Normal
20	15/2	MX	1/P/360	P	Tek/Social
21	19/15	US+	1/P/359	F	Normal
22	15/15	US	1/P/355	F	Normal
23	18/8	MX	2/P/354	F	Normal
24	18/17	MX	1/P/351	G	Skaters
25	17/1	US+	3/P/350	P	Social
26	18/4	MX	4/P/350	F	Electronic/Punker
27	17/3	US+	5/F/333	G	Normal
28	18/5	US+	5/F/333	P	Normal

Key:

YRS in USA: Number of years lived in US

US: United States

MX: Mexico

US*: Born in US but spent years in Mexico and studied there.

US+: Lived in Mexico but did not study there; crossed border to attend US schools.

CAHSEE: # Times taken/Result (P = PASS, >350; Pr = PROFICIENT, >380; F = FAILURE, <350)/ SCORE

OE: Oral English rated by interviewers

E-Excellent

G-Good

F-Fair

P-Poor

Network: Social Network, self-assigned/assigned by other.

students, and English learners who had been reclassified: 84.8 percent passed, and 50.96 were proficient. While failing the CAHSEE can end a student's hope of graduating, passing may give them the false impression that their English skills are equal to their Spanish skills. Chubaka, an 18-year-old "skater" who was born in Mexico and came to the United States when he started BH at age 14, took the CAHSEE three times before passing it with a 374, but he believed that his oral English and Spanish were on a par, *los dos igual* ("both equal"). We found this an unrealistic assessment, since his oral English was judged only

FAIR by the student researchers and me. Not all who passed the ELA were fluent English speakers, and not all fluent English speakers passed it. Table 18.2 lists the CAHSEE scores of those who took the test, along with our evaluation of their oral English.

Overall, 15 of the 43 students had not yet taken the exam because they were ninth graders; 19 others passed it on the first try and 8 of those had proficient scores above 380. Several others took the exam up to five times before they were able to pass. Because the CAHSEE is a written exam, our evaluation of students' oral proficiency does not always correlate with CAHSEE scores. In fact, one female who planned to be a nurse and whose oral English was GOOD, in our estimation, failed the CAHSEE despite five tries and could not graduate (#27), while three students whom we deemed very weak or POOR English speakers were able to pass the exam (# 20, #16, and #18). Student #20 passed the ELA section with a score of 360 on his first try, #16 took it twice and scored 365 the second time, and #18 took it five times before passing with a score of 362. This last student was a 17-year-old who was born in Mexico and lived there until he started at BH when he was 15. During his two years at BH, he returned to Tijuana on the weekends, spoke Spanish at home and in his school networks, had limited exposure to oral and written standard English in formal settings, and reported that in his English courses at BH students were not encouraged to speak.[9] His English responses were so halting and incomplete that I was surprised to learn he had passed the CAHSEE and earned a higher score than a friend who spoke fluent English. But it took five tries before he finally passed it in February 2009, in time for graduation; the CAHSEE was a source of great tension throughout his high school career.

The valedictorian at BH was only partially correct in her assessment of the English of the students who did not pass the CAHSEE: "They don't have like the academic words; they also don't have the experiences, class backgrounds, and literary analysis techniques that will help them answer questions about a reading passage like 'On Becoming a Falconer,' or the type of 'literary device' that 'frowning forest' represents" (CAHSEE Study Guide n.d.). It is no wonder that BH designed elaborate courses for its English learners, and stressed English in all teacher-student interactions. In response to the widespread dismal CAHSEE results, "a key committee of state legislators, including longtime critics of the test, voted to eliminate the exam as a graduation requirement, saying it was unfair to require students to pass it given the massive budget cuts proposed for education"; that committee effort failed (Tucker 2009). As one of the foremost scholars on second language acquisition noted, "studies have shown that state high school exit exams in general do not result in improved academic achievement" and "do not lead to more college completion, higher employment, or higher earnings by graduates" (Krashen 2009). Fortunately, the misguided and unfair CAHSEE has been suspended as of 2016.

What Have We Learned? BH as the New Frontier of Bilingualism

Thanks to the caring and hardworking administrators, counselors, teachers, and staff at BH, its students enjoyed a safe, welcoming, and academically encouraging atmosphere. This was confirmed by the majority of positive responses by seniors in the Western Association of Schools and Colleges Self Study Report (WASC report), and by our many visits. The most important of our findings, however, is not in the WASC report (i.e., BH students were skilled bilinguals who nevertheless recognized the need to improve both their oral and written Spanish and English, for instrumental and affective reasons). They taught us important lessons that all educators in the region should learn. In contrast to university *transfronterizos* (Zentella 2009), BH bilinguals did not view their linguistic and cultural border-crossing skills primarily as a commodity pursued to reap the benefits of capitalist markets, one that made them superior to monolinguals on either side of the border. And they rejected the view of bilingualism as two monolinguals joined at the tongue, despite the fact that they were well aware of elite notions of the "ideal bilingual" who never switched languages "in unchanged speech situations, and certainly not within a single sentence" (Weinreich 1953, 73). Given that their lives at the border require constant switching from English to Spanish and back again, they speak both because they are both, and honor both.

From an anthro-political linguistic perspective, BH students contested the reproduction of linguistic and educational inequality that elevates the capital of English at the expense of Spanish, by adopting flexible identities and linguistic attitudes and practices. The reality of the shared national borders that defines their community is transferred to their school, where linguistic borders are fluid and crossable. They defy the patrolling of linguistic borders, just as they reject the stereotype that stigmatizes them as members of a violent group amid the heightened violence of the U.S. border patrol. Despite their marked differences in tastes in clothes, hairstyles, and music, they all value bilingualism and bilingual practices, such as mixing languages that blur the boundaries between students with weak English skills and those with weak Spanish skills. Most, except perhaps for members of the English-dominant networks, are likely to raise bilingual children, especially if they remain on the border and close to their parents. All understand the power of English, and the need to become proficient, but they recognize that languages, and ways of speaking them, depend on the immediate setting, interlocutors, and objectives.

The most proficient bilinguals among them are also the ones most determined and prepared to go to college. All students were nonchalant about the omnipresence of Spanish and English on the campus, and the lack of superior attitudes toward one language or the other. However, they realized that their experiences as *fronterizos* might not be duplicated elsewhere. Rey (AP), on his way to a university out of town, expected that his Spanish might suffer there "because here we're more close to the border and I donno it's like we let people speak Spanish." Suggestions for preparing Rey and other students for the next stage in their lives would include strengthening BH's supportive atmosphere by emphasizing and encouraging their bilingual talents. The specific bilingual skills required for different careers might be stressed in Spanish and English courses alike, since many students seemed at a loss about future careers. ELD classes could incorporate group discussions and intensive writing.

BH's great strength is its bilingual student body, which could be amplified by committing the entire school to advanced bilingual proficiency, building on all students' native languages—including those who are English monolinguals. The district and all of Southern California would benefit from creating flagship public high schools where Spanish and English proficiency are developed equally, but we must all advocate for an educational system that embraces bilingualism nationally.

Notes

1. We spoke to more than 100 students, and finalized the paperwork for more than half that number; 43 students completed all the interviews. The UCSD Academic Senate and the University of California (UC) Linguistic Minorities Research Institute supported the research. We are grateful to the students and their parents, and to the Principal, Mr. E.; the Asst Principals; and Ms. H., a counselor, for their support throughout the two-year project. UCSD student researchers, especially Jeanette Cobian, a BH graduate, proved invaluable.
2. http://www.bestplaces.net/zip-code/San_Ysidro-California-92173.aspx. Last accessed June 8, 2016.
3. The data for two interviewees are incomplete.
4. All student names are pseudonyms, followed by (network).
5. Students used the diminutive to indicate that the BH *cholit@s* were not hard-core gang members. Due to the lack of males in our research team we were unable to convince all male groups like Emos or Cholos to participate, although it is not clear that they would have cooperated with a male college student.
6. Ear plugs are male earrings—small circular disks with a hole that can be small or large in the center, inserted into the earlobe.
7. I witnessed a (bilingual) teacher's refusal to answer a parent's question in Spanish at a "Welcome" event.
8. The CAHSEE graduation requirement was suspended effective January 1, 2016 (http://www.cde.ca.gov/ta/tg/hs/). Last accessed June 8, 2016.
9. Limited student participation was corroborated in four visits to ELD English classes, where the focus was on filling in worksheets.

References

Auer, Peter. 1984. *Bilingual conversation*. Amsterdam: J. Benjamins.

Bucholtz, Mary. 2009. From stance to style: Gender, interaction, and indexicality in Mexican immigrant youth slang. In *Stance: Sociolinguistic Perspectives*, ed. Alexandra Jaffe, 146–70. New York: Oxford University Press.

CAHSEE Study Guide. n.d. http://www.studyguidezone.com/cahsee_english.htm Accessed January 31, 2014.

D'Arcy, Alexandra. 2006. Lexical Replacement and the Like(s). *American Speech* 81(4) (Winter): 339–57.

Kada, Naoko and Richard Kiy. 2004. Blurred borders: Trans-boundary impacts and solutions in the San Diego-Tijuana border region. International Community Foundation (March). www.borderheatlh.org/files/res_874.pdf. Last accessed June 8, 2016.

Krashen, Stephen. 2009. Unpublished letter submitted to *Time* magazine. http://www.susano-hanian.org/show_letter.php?id=1042. Last accessed June 8, 2016.

Larousse. 2003. *El pequeno Larousse ilustrado*. Barcelona: SPES.

Tucker, Jill. 2009. High school exit exam gets boost. http://www.sfgate.com/education/article/High-school-exit-exam-gets-boost-as-more-pass-3225866.php. Last accessed June 8, 2016.

Urciuoli, Bonnie. 2001. The complex diversity of language in the U.S. In *Cultural Diversity in the United States: A Critical Reader*, ed. Ida Susser and Thomas Carl Patterson, 190–205. Malden, MA: Blackwell.

Venegas-García, M., and J. Romo. 2005. Working Paper for Border Pedagogy Conference, University of San Diego, October.

WASC/CDE Self Study. 2007–2008. Focus on Learning. [BH] High School.

Weinreich, Uriel. 1953. *Languages in Contact, Findings and Problems*. New York: Linguistic Circle of New York.

Zentella, A. C. 1997. *Growing Up Bilingual: Puerto Rican Children in New York*. Malden, MA: Blackwell.

Zentella, A. C. 2006. Transfronterizo Talk: Remapping the Linguistic and Cultural Borders in Tijuana–San Diego. Southwest Linguistic Association Keynote Speaker, Texas A&M International University, Laredo, Texas. October 12.

Zentella, A. C. 2009. Conflicting Constructions of Bilingualism among U.S.-Mexico Border Crossing College Students. Lecture. Center for Latino Policy Research. University of California, Berkeley, May 8.

Index